MACMILLAN HISTORY OF LITERATURE

General Editor: A. NORMAN JEFFARES

Series Standing Order

If you would like to receive future titles in this series as they
are published, you can make use of our standing order
facility. To place a standing order please contact your
bookseller or, in case of difficulty, write to us at the address
below with your name and address and the name of the
series. Please state with which title you wish to begin your
standing order. (If you live outside the UK we may not have
the rights for your area, in which case we will forward your
order to the publisher concerned.)

Standing Order Service, Macmillan Distribution Ltd,
Houndmills, Basingstoke, Hampshire, RG21 2XS, England.

MACMILLAN HISTORY OF LITERATURE

General Editor: A. Norman Jeffares

Published

OLD ENGLISH LITERATURE
Michael Alexander

A HISTORY OF LITERARY CRITICISM
Harry Blamires

TWENTIETH-CENTURY ENGLISH LITERATURE
Harry Blamires

ENGLISH GOTHIC LITERATURE
Derek Brewer

A HISTORY OF AUSTRALIAN LITERATURE
Ken Goodwin

ANGLO-IRISH LITERATURE
A. Norman Jeffares

A HISTORY OF CANADIAN LITERATURE
William H. New

THE LITERATURE OF THE UNITED STATES
Marshall Walker

THE LITERATURE OF SCOTLAND
Roderick Watson

SIXTEENTH-CENTURY ENGLISH LITERATURE
Murray Roston

SEVENTEENTH-CENTURY ENGLISH LITERATURE
Bruce King

EIGHTEENTH-CENTURY ENGLISH LITERATURE
Maximillian Novak

NINETEENTH-CENTURY ENGLISH LITERATURE
Margaret Stonyk

Forthcoming

A HISTORY OF LITERATURE IN THE IRISH LANGUAGE
Declan Kiberd

MACMILLAN HISTORY OF LITERATURE

A HISTORY
OF LITERARY
CRITICISM

Harry Blamires

MACMILLAN

First published 1991

Published by
MACMILLAN EDUCATION LTD
Houndmills, Basingstoke, Hampshire RG21 2XS
and London
Companies and representatives
throughout the world

Edited and typeset by Povey/Edmondson
Okehampton and Rochdale, England

Printed in Hong Kong

British Library Cataloguing in Publication Data
Blamires, Harry
A history of literary criticism. — (Macmillan history of
literature)
1. Literature. Criticism, history
801.9509
ISBN 0–333–51734–2 (hardcover)
ISBN 0–333–51735–0 (paperback)

Contents

Introductory Note

This survey traces the development of English literary criticism from its roots in classical and mediaeval theory to the controversies of the present day. The standpoints of major critics are examined in their respective historical contexts, and crucial foreign influences are noted. Proportionate space is also given to many lesser writers who contributed to the liveliness of contemporary debate or provided stimulating commentaries on current literature. In this way the significant critical attitudes of succeeding ages are clearly defined.

In the case of the less easily accessible critics, I have to acknowledge gratefully that my survey is often dependent on the work of the scholars who have selected and edited representative material from succeeding centuries: R. A. Russell and M. Winterbottom (*Ancient Literary Criticism*), Allen H. Gilbert (*Literary Criticism, Plato to Dryden*), C. Gregory Smith (*Elizabethan Critical Essays*), J. E. Spingarn (*Critical Essays of the Seventeenth Century*), Scott Elledge (*Eighteenth-Century Critical Essays*), David Lodge (*Twentieth-Century Literary Criticism*), and K. M. Newton (*Twentieth-Century Literary Theory*). Another indebtedness, for which gratitude is due, is to the 'Critical Heritage' series in which nineteenth-century journalists and reviewers are represented in action. See the section *Further Reading*, for full citation of these and other sources.

Editor's Preface

THE study of literature requires knowledge of contexts as well as of texts. What kind of person wrote the poem, the play, the novel, the essay? What forces acted upon them as they wrote? What was the historical, the political, the philosophical, the economic, the cultural background? Was the writer accepting or rejecting the literary conventions of the time, or developing them, or creating entirely new kinds of literary expression? Are there interactions between literature and the art, music or architecture of its period? Was the writer affected by contemporaries or isolated?

Such questions stress the need for students to go beyond the reading of set texts, to extend their knowledge by developing a sense of chronology, of action and reaction, and of the varying relationships between writers and society.

Histories of literature can encourage students to make comparisons, can aid in understanding the purposes of individual authors and in assessing the totality of their achievements. Their development can be better understood and appreciated with some knowledge of the background of their time. And histories of literature, apart from their valuable function as reference books, can demonstrate the great wealth of writing in English that there is to be enjoyed. They can guide the reader who wishes to explore it more fully and to gain in the process deeper insights into the rich diversity not only of literature but of human life itself.

A. NORMAN JEFFARES

1
The Classical Age

Nothing is more remarkable in the history of literary criticism than the way in which theories launched in the classical age have kept a grip on people's minds. In the seventeenth and eighteenth centuries, writers were still hotly debating how far the authority of the ancients ought to determine literary practice. When in 1789 Thomas Twining (1735–1804) published what was to become for long the standard translation of Aristotle's *Poetics* (*Aristotle's Treatise on Poetry*), he accompanied it with *Two Dissertations on Poetic and Numerical Imitation* in the effort to rescue the Aristotelian concept 'imitation' from connotative confusions he detected as it was tossed about in argument between contemporary writers. In our own century, in 1955, when the Hungarian critic Georg Lukácz (1885–1971) made a celebrated critique of recent literary tendencies in a lecture, 'The Ideology of Modernism', he expounded his case on the basis of 'the traditional Aristotelian dictum' that man is a social animal. The dictum is 'applicable to all great realist literature', 'to Achilles and Werther, Oedipus and Tom Jones, Antigone and Anna Karenina'.

The literary critic allows his gaze to sweep the centuries. He has always done so, calling upon the names of Homer and Virgil, of Dante and Shakespeare, as readily as those of celebrated contemporaries. The reader who tries to take an overview of the literary criticism of the centuries cannot but repeatedly get the impression that from the days of Aristotle it is all of a piece. The classical education, of course, long kept alive this sense of the continuity of tradition. But had not the ancients produced a literature capable of standing up to the diligent scrutiny of the centuries, the continuity could not have been sustained as it was.

1

The intellectual activity which produced the earliest major texts of Western literary criticism was centred in Athens in the fifth and fourth centuries BC. The foundations of Athenian democracy had been laid towards the end of the sixth century BC. The fifth century saw Athenian forces warding off the threat from the East when Darius and his Persian army were defeated at the battle of Marathon in 490 and when his son Xerxes was overwhelmed at sea by the Greek fleet at Salamis in 480. The Delian League, the alliance of cities and islands which Athens founded in 478 BC as a defence against the Persians, was transformed into an Athenian empire as the threat from the East was lifted. Sparta was aroused to political and economic rivalry, and the Peloponnesian War, which began in 431, finally ended only when Sparta made a treacherous deal with Cyrus of Persia, and Athens was defeated in 404. After the defeat of Athens, Sparta assumed the role of dominant power in Greece until, in turn, Epaminondas of Thebes defeated the Spartans at the battle of Leuctra in 371 BC. It was Philip of Macedon (c.382–336) whose interference eventually put an end to the inter-city rivalries. He defeated the armies of both Thebes and Athens in 338.

A period of just over a hundred years contained the lives of both Plato (c.427–348) and Aristotle (c.384–322). They could look back on the glorious age of Pericles, a statesman of great vision and integrity, who attained a position of dominance about 460 BC in the hey-day of Athenian power. A man who numbered Sophocles and Herodotus among his acquaintances, he sought to establish an ideal democracy and to leave a legacy of public works. The Parthenon was erected between 447 and 438. But at least as relevant to us here as the great events of those days on the political and military scene is the rich literary inheritance which Plato's contemporaries received from the past. Homer's dates are not known, and scholars have variously placed him in the ninth and in the seventh century BC. Hesiod, the author of *Works and Days*, wrote a little later than Homer. It has been claimed that the history of literary criticism began when Xenophanes (b. c.570) took issue with the disrespectful representation of gods in Homer and Hesiod, and when Theagenes (*fl. c.525*) pressed for allegorical interpretation of Homer, seeing his gods and goddesses as symbols of human attributes and natural elements. Herodotus (*c*.484–*c*.420), known as the 'father of history', wrote his *Histories* in nine books, covering the struggle of Greece with Asia from mythical times to his own age. Meanwhile Greek drama was flourishing. Aeschylus (525–456), Sophocles (496–406), and Euripides (*c*.480–406) together made the fifth century BC perhaps the richest age in history for the production of tragic masterpieces, and Aristophanes (*c*.448–*c*.380) established a form of comedy which was to influence English writers such as Ben Jonson and Henry Fielding.

I Plato

The philosopher Plato (*c*.427–348 BC) was some twenty years younger than Aristophanes and was himself about twenty-one when Sophocles and Euripides died. A disciple of Socrates, he was deeply distressed when Socrates was condemned to death on a charge of having corrupted the young by his teaching. In fact Socrates had only made them critical of the existing order. His celebrated technique of instruction was by question and answer, to probe those he would educate and elicit from them admissions which, when analysed, revealed underlying ignorance and misunderstanding. This 'socratic' method was adopted by Plato. He presented his teaching in dialogues, using Socrates as the central spokesman. Socrates lures his listeners into expressions of opinion, then dissects them, and brings to light contradiction, absurdity, or shallowness inherent in what they have said. The utilisation of this method makes for entertaining reading, but it can easily mislead the inexpert reader. In the first place, there is often a heavy irony in what Socrates says as he leads his auditor step by step into clarifications which ultimately emerge as patently absurd. In the second place, we cannot automatically assume that the conclusion of an argument reached by Socrates necessarily represents Plato's own view. And in the third place, the prime purpose of this dialectical method is often rather to stimulate lively thinking than directly to indoctrinate.

Plato did not anywhere formally assume the role of literary critic, laying foundations for the evaluation of works of imagination and setting guide–lines for effectiveness in literary composition. Indeed, what we gather from his work is that he did not consider imaginative literature important enough to justify that kind of attention from the philosopher. It is largely due to his rather low estimate of the place of imaginative literature in the healthy society that he took the trouble to venture at all into what we call literary criticism. In his early dialogue, *Ion*, he introduces Ion, a rhapsodist, that is, a kind of actor or elocutionist who lives by dramatic recitation of poetry, in this case of Homer's *Iliad*. Ion is brought cheerfully and confidently into the company of Socrates, having just won first prize for his performance at the games. Socrates plays with him verbally like a cat with a mouse. Ion claims a special enthusiasm for Homer and a special ability in doing justice to his work. Is this just a matter of god-given inspiration, Socrates wants to know, or does Ion have a special understanding of Homer? The latter, Ion says. It is a matter of conscious art, not of untutored inspiration. Whereupon Socrates begins a stage-by-stage probe to try to elicit from Ion what the character is of the special skill he has and the range of the special knowledge he lays claim to as a Homeric recitalist. One by one Ion's pretensions are punctured. If Homer dilates on chariot-driving, will not the charioteer be the best judge of his work? Agreed. If Homer dilates on medical matters, on architecture, or on fishing, will not the physician, the architect, or the fisherman be the best judge of his work? Agreed. And is not Homer's concern with battle something that a general would best understand? By such questions Socrates leads Ion, in holding his corner, to the logical conclusion that if the rhapsodist's knowledge of Homer has the intellectual comprehensiveness he pretends it has, then as the greatest rhapsodist he will be the greatest general too – and indeed a man with mastery of medicine, architecture, fishing, and the like. In fact neither the poet nor the rhapsodist has that kind of mastery. Poetry is not a vehicle of learning but of inspiration.

For Plato the dichotomy between learning and inspiration, between what has intellectual validity and what is of mere aesthetic interest seems to be a sharp one. This accounts for the rather dismissive attitude to imaginative literature which emerges in his *Republic*. Here the significance of literature has to be dealt with, because Plato expounds a theory of education by which men can be trained to leadership in the ideal human society. The question of how their minds are to be formed and what will most healthily nourish their thinking is crucial. In short, literature comes up for consideration only because a curriculum of studies has to be defined. And the way in which Plato drew a distinction in *Ion* between the charioteer's first-hand concern with chariot-driving and the poet's second-hand concern with it gives us a key to his attitude to literature. It is all a kind of representation or imitation of the real thing.

For Plato, however, that 'real thing' – the chariot or the medicine or the fishing – is not the real thing. He formulated a doctrine of Ideas, or Forms, which has had a seminal influence on Western thinking because it tackled questions of the nature of reality and of temporal existence which press upon human beings in all ages. Plato recognised that prior to this circle I draw or that circle you draw (with whatever defects they may have as a result of our unskilfulness) is a notion or idea of circularity which is perfect, and against which the defects, however microscopic, of any given circle must be judged. Similarly milk or paper is judged to be 'white' by reference to a prior mental idea of 'whiteness' to which the colour of milk or paper approximates. What applies to 'circularity' or 'whiteness' applies to abstractions such as 'justice' and 'beauty'. We are continually defining acts as just, or objects as beautiful by reference to standards of perfect justice and perfect beauty excelling anything we can point to in our environment. The priority of the perfect form which is eternal to the imperfect manifestations of it which pass away with time is the keystone of the philosophy which came to be called 'Realism' as opposed to 'Nominalism'. The collision between these two doctrines was a dominant issue in the Middle Ages. For the 'realist' the concept 'beauty' is prior to any instance of the beautiful. For the 'nominalist' the universal concept 'beauty' is a mere name for what is recognised as common to all instances of the beautiful.

Now Plato's doctrine of forms reduces the status of what is around us, in that it is but an inadequate and ephemeral representation of what is perfect and eternal. The poet's representation or imitation of our world is thus a representation of what is itself an inadequate and ephemeral representation of the truly real. Literature stands, in other words, not at one remove from reality, but at two removes. The philosopher will try to discern through the world of phenomena that reality of which those phenomena are the reflection. The poet, on the other hand, by his imitation of the world of phenomena, moves in the opposite direction further away from reality. For Plato, truth is to be discovered, not by fictive reduplication of our world in narrative and description, but by insight into what our world itself mirrors and reduplicates.

Plato is not insensitive to literature. On the contrary, he is deeply responsive to the powerful appeal of Homer. His suspicion of literature is strengthened by his awareness of its power to move and to charm. For writers can demoralise readers by picturing human sufferings and disasters in such a way that divine goodness and justice are brought into question. They may project gods as responsible for strife and evil. They may project great heroes like Achilles as mean and self-indulgent. They may project a future life as a place of misery and torment. In all these ways writers present models which will damage rather than discipline the young. Plato would rigorously control the reading matter of the young élite. They must have courageous and noble models presented to them in literature.

The concept of imitation is crucial for Plato. It determines certain emphases by which he manages to give a questionable status to literature. The first is the emphasis which stresses that literature is a second-hand version of life. The second is the emphasis which regards writers as impersonators. The third is the emphasis on the unreliability of the writer's presentation of life. In all these respects Plato sheds around the world of imaginative literature an aura of falsity.

II Aristotle

Aristotle (384–322 BC) spent twenty years studying under Plato at Athens. His reputation was such that Philip of Macedon called him to Macedonia for eight years to act as tutor to his son, Alexander the Great. He eventually returned to Athens and established his own academy, the Lyceum. His habit of walking up and down in the grounds while discoursing with his disciples earned his school the label 'Peripatetic'. If Plato was the first thinker we need attend to for his commentary on the human influence of imaginative literature, Aristotle was the first thinker to produce a work of literary criticism, the *Poetics*, a work which has influenced theorising about literature ever since it was written. Aristotle's philosophical thinking diverged crucially from that of Plato. Where Plato's doctrine of universal Forms focuses primary significance on to the eternal, of which the natural is but a reflection or copy, Aristotle's thinking concentrates on the reality to be discerned in individual things. He sees a coming together in them of matter and universal form. Where Plato's thinking is poetic to the extent that his idealistic flights verge on mysticism, Aristotle's bent is scientific, and he endows natural phenomena with a validity that Plato transferred to the timeless.

Hence we have the paradox that the poetic idealist, seeking to discern the absolute mirrored in the natural world, should have propounded a rigorously 'puritanical' doctrine of literary value, while the more scientific thinker should have striven to give literature its due on its own grounds. Plato, of course, was concerned with the theory of education and the curricular impact of imaginative literature on growing minds. Aristotle was concerned to analyse the nature of imaginative literature in itself, and not as an educational tool.

The *Poetics* defines poetry and drama as 'modes of imitation',[1] as are music and dancing. So far so good, but Aristotle quickly goes on to make a very dubious distinction. Characters and their actions will be either good or bad, either superior to ourselves or worse than ourselves, and this is what distinguishes tragedy from comedy. But Aristotle does not proceed to press a theory of moral value on this basis. He is careful to explain that in comedy the imitation of men worse than ourselves does not mean worse 'as regards any and every sort of fault, but only as regards one particular kind, the Ridiculous'. And the Ridiculous may be defined as 'a mistake or deformity not productive of pain or harm to others'. Aristotle allows an aesthetic value even in descriptions of what is unpleasant, such as a putrefying corpse, because the informative accuracy of the account may give satisfaction.

A more lastingly influential element in the early pages of the *Poetics* is the distinction between three modes of literary representation. The first is the blend of narrative and dialogue, whereby the poet alternates between speaking in his own voice and speaking in the voices of his characters. This is what is found in Homer. The second mode of literary representation is that of sustained utterance by the single voice of the poet. The third mode is that which is used in drama, where the poet distributes all his utterance through the voices of his characters.

After some consideration of the origins of poetry and literary forms, Aristotle turns to make a systematic investigation of tragedy.

> A tragedy, then, is the imitation of an action that is serious and also, as having magnitude, complete in itself; in language with pleasurable accessories ... ; in a dramatic, not in a narrative form; with incidents arousing pity and fear, wherewith to accomplish its catharsis of such emotions.

Aristotle explains that in focusing upon tragedy, what he has to say will apply to epic too, because whatever is found in epic can be found also in tragedy, though the converse is not true. He goes on to spell out the six formative elements of tragedy: Spectacle (the appearance of the actors); Diction (the verse they speak); Melody (the chanting of the verse); Character (the personalities of the dramatis personae); Thought (the reasoning and motivation which determine their actions); and Plot (the combination of incidents). More specifically, he identifies 'Character' as 'what makes us ascribe certain moral qualities to the agents' and 'Thought' as being 'what is shown in all they say when proving a particular point or ... enunciating a general truth'. For Aristotle, Plot is the most important formative element of the six. 'Character gives us qualities, but it is in our actions – what we do – that we are happy or the reverse.' The action of a play is not there 'to portray Characters'. Characters exist for the sake of the action.

Aristotle's emphasis on Plot is crucial. He regards the Peripeties (sudden reversals of fortune) and Discoveries (sudden revelations of concealed or mistaken identities and unravelling of mysteries) as the most powerful of the various elements in a drama which fascinate the spectator. 'Tragedy is primarily an imitation of action', Character comes second in importance, Thought is third, fourth is Diction, fifth is Melody. Spectacle is the least important element of all because 'the tragic effect is quite possible without a public performance and actors'.

Two of Aristotle's terms require special emphasis. One is 'mimesis' which is translated as 'imitation'. It is evident from Aristotle's attention to plotting that he does not by 'mimesis' mean that art should be a 'literal' or 'photographic' representation of reality. Material from life has to be selected and carefully organised. With this proviso, it is obvious that imaginative literature will inevitably be imitative of real life. In Hamlet's advice to the players, he defines the purpose of drama as being at all times to hold the mirror up to nature, 'to show virtue her own feature, scorn her own image, and the very age and body of the time his form and pressure'. Aristotle's term 'catharsis' has become as much a part of critical vocabulary as has 'mimesis'. A catharsis is a purgation. Aristotle appears to regard it as a beneficial effect of tragedy that the emotions of pity and fear are aroused, expressed, and yet contained in such a way that the spectator is left in a more balanced and disciplined emotional state as a result of the experience. It is a pity that Aristotle did not elaborate this aspect of his doctrine. He left instead a simple statement that has aroused controversy ever since. The notion of purgation seems to be the nearest Aristotle comes towards a moral justification of imaginative literature which would refute Plato's criticism of poetry for its tendency to arouse feelings irresponsibly and perturb the heart to no rational end.

The central bulk of the *Poetics* concentrates on Plot. Aristotle's emphasis makes selection and organisation of material crucial in a work of art. A plot must have a beginning, a middle, and an end. That is to say, a haphazard or arbitrary arrangement of incidents will not do. There must be cogency, naturalness, and what De Quincey called 'sequaciousness' in the placing and sequence of events. This is not just a requirement of logic, but of aesthetics. The beauty of a living being consists both in the harmonious relationship of its parts and in the degree of its magnitude, which must be such as to allow it to be grasped as a whole. On this principle a rough general formula for a plot would confine it to 'a length which allows of the hero passing by a series of probable or necessary stages from misfortune to happiness, or from happiness to misfortune'.

Aristotle is critical of writers who assume that a story can be held together simply by the fact that it is concerned with the career of one man. Homer did not make his *Odyssey* by covering everything that ever happened to Odysseus. In other words, the eighteenth-century picaresque novel of Smollett and Defoe would not have satisfied Aristotle. He would have demanded the kind of organisation which Fielding gave to *Tom Jones*. His definition of a good plot is that:

> the story ... must represent one action, a complete whole, with its several incidents so closely connected that the transposal or withdrawal of any one of them will disjoin and dislocate the whole.

All that has been said about plot, Aristotle adds, indicates that the poet is required faithfully to record what has happened. That is the task of the historian. The poet is free of this responsibility.

> Hence poetry is something more philosophic and of graver import than history, since its statements are of the nature rather of universals, whereas those of history are singulars.

This does not, of course, mean that the poet cannot take his material from actual history. Historic occurrences may very well provide appropriate material for imaginative treatment.

Aristotle's insistence that poetry is 'more philosophic' than factual history, and involves rather what is universal than what is particular shows him diverging crucially from Plato. For Plato, the derivation of literature from life put it at one remove further from universal truth than life itself. For Aristotle, the freeing of literature from slavish adherence to the particulars of life lived gives it a greater accessibility to universal truth. It will be evident that Aristotle's distinction between the limitations of fact and the potentialities of fiction as vehicles of valid illumination was to become a cornerstone of critical theory.

Turning to a more technical aspect of what makes a good plot, Aristotle further elaborates what he meant by 'Peripety' and 'Discovery'. The incidents in a tragedy must arouse 'pity' and 'fear', and they will do so most effectively when there is a combination in them of what is unexpected and yet occurs in the logical sequence of things. The reversal of fortune ('Peripety') and the change from ignorance to knowledge ('Discovery') may occur in various forms. The most powerful dramatic effects are produced when a Discovery is itself attended by Peripeties. (We might reflect on Othello's discovery that Iago is a villain and that he has murdered an innocent wife.)

Another highly influential section of the *Poetics* tackles the question: What are the conditions on which the tragic effect of such transitions depends? Here Aristotle lists three forms of Plot to be avoided.

1. A good man must not be seen passing from happiness to misery or
2. a bad man from misery to happiness, or ...
3. an extremely bad man be seen falling from happiness into misery.

The first situation is odious, the second untragic, the third productive neither of pity nor of fear.

There remains, then, the intermediate kind of personage, a man not preeminently virtuous and just, whose misfortune, however, is brought upon him not by vice or depravity but by some error of judgment ...

Here again Aristotle throws out a definition which has survived in critical theory. It was later seized upon as summing up the recipe for an effective tragic hero, a man who is neither exalted above us by his virtue nor given to vice and depravity, but of such moderate moral quality that we can sympathise with him. And he comes to grief, not by any act of undiluted wickedness, but as a result of some flaw in his nature and some error of judgment.

Not everything in later critical thought that is labelled 'Aristotelian' can justly be derived from Aristotle's actual words. Just as he did not develop the theory of 'catharsis', which has since been elaborated by numerous writers, and just as he did not greatly expand his brief definition of the tragic hero, so too he did not lay down the full-scale theory of the 'dramatic unities' which later critics constructed on the basis of his remarks about the necessity for a single integrated plot to which every event in a drama is properly related.

There is a good deal in Aristotle's *Poetics* which must strike the modern reader as simply formulated common sense. There is also much that would have been relevant to the contemporary student of Sophocles and Homer, and seems remote from the practice of modern European literature. Yet there remains an extraordinary discerning substratum of critical analysis which has usefully survived his age, and he bequeathed a valuable critical currency to his successors.

III Horace

In turning from Plato and Aristotle to Horace (65–8 BC), we move from fourth century Athens to Rome in the first century BC: moreover, we turn our attention from two philosophers to a practising poet. The son of a tax-collector, Horace had a good education from a schoolmaster, Orbilius, whose penchant for administering corporal punishment left an indelible impression on him, and later he studied at Athens. Like many of the intelligentsia, the assassination of Julius Caesar led him to enrol under the revolutionary banner of Marcus Brutus, and when Brutus was defeated by Octavius and Mark Antony at the battle of Philippi in 42 BC, he fled back to Rome and took a job as a clerk in the civil service. The change in his fortunes came when he began to write poetry and gained the friendship of his greatest contemporary, Virgil (70–19 BC). With Virgil's help he was taken up by Maecenas, the distinguished patron of literary men, who had the ear of Augustus. Thus it was that he was received into the inner circle of poets enjoying imperial favour. The Augustan Age, represented as it was by writers of the distinction of Virgil, Horace, Ovid, and Livy, produced a body of literature of high quality and notable sophistication, reflecting the confidence of a stable and affluent society. Horace was given an estate in the Sabine Hills in which he took great delight. His poetic output included satires, odes and epistles. One of the epistles was addressed to a father and two sons called Piso, and it gives advice on the art of writing. This epistle was later labelled 'Ars Poetica' (The Art of Poetry).

Both by his own practice as a poet and through the advice given in the 'Ars Poetica', Horace has had a continuing influence of European literature. The 'Ars Poetica' was translated by Ben Jonson and published in his *Works* (1640). Pope used Horace as a model in various *Satires and Epistles of Horace Imitated*. But 'Ars Poetica' is not a systematic treatise. Nor is it a wholly original work. It is now accepted that Horace derived much of the material from a Greek handbook by Neoptolemus of Parium (third century BC). Nevertheless, though the epistle has been criticised for the haphazard and sometimes seemingly slapdash character of the observations it makes, it bears the stamp of Horace's personal charm. Above all, it is the work of a poet noted for the polish of his technique, the felicity of his style, and the unaffected naturalness of his self-projection.

Horace accepts that in human life and character the poet will find his material, and he must be faithful in representing it. But there is no Wordsworthian emphasis on stylistic fidelity to living conversation and no urge to the poet to give free play to what originates spontaneously from within. Horace is a classicist. He urges the would-be poet to study accepted models, Homer and the Greek tragedians. The ambition to be original can lure the writer into flashy excrescences ill-adjusted to the overall pattern of his work, and inimical to clarity and directness. The poet's task is to work hard at his text in order to produce verse that is felicitous, lucid and well-ordered. The place of natural inspiration is allowed for, but there is no escape for the poet from disciplined critical examination of all that is written.

There is a good deal in the 'Ars Poetica' which reads like common sense methodised. A writer must choose a subject within his powers and appropriate to his gifts; he must say at any given moment what needs to be said, and no more; he must choose vocabulary, metre and form that are right for his subject, whether noble, exciting, erotic or joyous. Horace has verse drama especially in mind in warning against extravagant implausibilities and incongruities. Indeed the prevailing emphasis throughout is on the need for consistency, coherence and seemliness. It is the writer's business so to refine and polish his text that the highest standards of propriety and artistry are maintained. One safeguard against sloppy workmanship is fastidiousness over the minutiae of scansion. Another is emulation of worthy models. 'Study the Greek masterpieces: pore over them night and day.'[2]

It may seem ironic, in view of Horace's emphasis on order and organisation, that his 'Ars Poetica' should itself be something of a hotch-potch. But it was never intended as a treatise. It is an epistle, and its charm lies in its casual air and inconsequential approach. Its effectiveness lies partly in its illustrative clarity and partly in its scattered apothegms. These apothegms give sparkle to the text and they represent its major critical illuminations for the modern reader. 'The secret of all good writing is sound judgment,' Horace avers, insisting that it is the well-formed and morally educative person who will have the right understanding to represent life faithfully in drama. Coming to the core of a since much-debated issue, he declares, 'The poet's aim is either to profit or to please, or to blend in one the delightful and the useful.' Then, after switching briefly to two of his favourite precepts – the need for brevity, which makes for memorability, and the need for plausibility – Horace presses home the need to blend instruction with delight. Older people complain if a work does not convey a useful lesson; younger people cannot bear too much gravity. 'The man who mingles the useful with the sweet carries the day by charming his reader and at the same time instructing him. That's the book to enrich the publisher, to be posted overseas, and to prolong its author's fame.'

Though market forces seem to be appealed to here as a primary basis for urging the mixture of profit and delight, the balance proposed is directly in keeping with Horace's overall insistence on proportion and propriety. His literary urbanity belongs with the graces and social polish of imperial Rome. He has no time for sentimentality, wordiness or technical laxity. A sensible critic, he tells us, will put his finger firmly on flaccid or harsh verses, on ugly lines and pretentious ornaments, on obscure passages or defective phrases. He ends his epistle with a satirical picture of the mad poet, given to frenzies and hallucinations, nursing wild passions, spouting his lines to the air, and stampeding scholar and dunce alike with his ravings.

IV Longinus

Manuscripts survive of a Greek work called 'On the Sublime', attributed to one 'Longinus', and dating from the first or second century AD. The identity of 'Longinus' is not known. The author was certainly not the third-century rhetorician Cassius Longinus (c.217–73) to whom the work was for long attributed. Modern scholarship has complicated matters further for the ordinary reader by concluding that 'the Sublime' is not the happiest label for what the book is about. A suggested alternative title is 'On Elevation of Style'. But 'Longinus on the Sublime' is a long-established marker in literary criticism.

Modern readers encounter in Longinus a writer far more akin to them than Plato and Aristotle, or even Horace. Longinus consciously looks back from a distance to a golden age of literature to which Homer, Demosthenes, and the great Greek dramatists belong. He addresses his subject in a way we find congenial. Faults of style are listed, and then a comprehensive analysis is made of those qualities which contribute to sublimity. Among the defects specified is bombastic verbal inflation which is the result of trying too feverishly to evade the obvious. The opposite defect is stylistic thinness and meanness produced when a pedestrian talent struggles for effect. Then there is misplaced sentimentality, overstrained figurative artifice, and many other cheap devices that spring from the craze for novelty, a craze of which Longinus finds his contemporaries especially culpable.

Longinus defines the ingredients of sublimity in turn. Firstly there is grandeur of thought. 'Excellence of style is the concomitant of a great soul.'[3] He cites examples from Homer and elsewhere to show that when a poet is at his best in descriptive writing, what he lays before the reader could have been conceived only by a man of noble spirit. The second source of sublimity is powerful emotion. Nothing, he argues, can be so effective as strong emotion when it is appropriate to the material, for it fills what is said with the breath of a seemingly divine exultation. These two constituents of sublimity, grandeur of thought and powerful emotion, derive largely from native gifts. The other three constituents are acquired by art. The third is a mastery of many and various devices of style and methods of presentation. The fourth is acute sensitivity to the qualities of words and to the potentialities of imagery. And the fifth constituent is the orderly placing of words, the ear for rhythm and cadence, sonority and roundedness, aural architecture and fluency. Indeed this fifth constituent seems to comprehend also everything that Horace recommended in his emphasis upon consistency and coherence in overall structure.

What for the modern reader differentiates Longinus from his predecessors is his eagerness to put his finger on those qualities of imaginative literature which resist codification by rule and precept, and which cannot be attained by technical expertise alone. He is sensitive to the need for individual genius in the poet. It has to be matched by quality of vision and understanding, and married to a fineness and grandeur of perception which have a moral and spiritual as well as an intellectual status. Longinus has none of Horace's prudery about flashes of inspiration and bursts of purple rhetoric. Though harsh in his judgments on cheap display and pretentious bombast, he recognises that the practice of literature cannot be reduced to a matter of hard work, persistent self-criticism, and the disciplined exercise of artistry. Without yielding an inch to literary self-indulgence, he manages to give due priority to qualities of inspiration, animation, and imaginative reach which can give birth to passages of exultant sublimity that flash upon the reader so as to electrify and entrance him. Longinus values the power of poetry at its most intense, not just to satisfy, but to astonish, to enrapture, and to exalt. Unlike Horace, he would value occasional bursts of sublimity far higher than a steady level of unexciting pedestrian competence.

In his essay on 'Heroic Poetry and Poetic Licence' John Dryden (1631–1700) seized upon this aspect of Longinus's thinking:

> And Longinus, who was undoubtedly, after Aristotle, the greatest critic amongst the Greeks, ... has judiciously preferred the sublime genius that sometimes errs, to the middling or indifferent one, which makes few faults, but seldom or never rises to any excellence.

The former is like someone very wealthy who looks after the main expenses but does not waste time on petty trifles. The latter is like someone of limited means who is so parsimonious that he or she never achieves a fine standard of living. In his 'Essay on Criticism', Alexander Pope (1688–1744) warmed to Longinus's balanced sensitivity to both the inspirational and technical aspects of poetry. Like many others, he found in Longinus's own work a model and justification of his theory.

> Thee, bold Longinus! all the Nine inspire,
> And bless their Critic with a Poet's fire,
> An ardent Judge, who zealous in his trust,
> With warmth gives sentence, yet is always just;
> Whose own example strengthens all his laws;
> And is himself that great Sublime he draws.

The achievement of a great inspirational writer such as Longinus is perhaps best measured by his influence upon others. And so far as English literature is concerned, that influence has been an inspiring one. Longinus is a critic who is eminently creative himself of those inspiring bursts of revelatory illumination which he rightly valued in others. He is an opener of doors. The great historian Edward Gibbon (1737–94) paid a tribute to him in his *Autobiography* (1794):

> I was acquainted with only two ways of criticising a beautiful passage; the one, to shew, by an exact anatomy of it, the distinct beauties of it and whence they sprung; the other, an idle exclamation or a general encomium, which leaves nothing behind it. Longinus has shewn me a third. He tells me his own feelings after reading it; and tells them with such energy that he communicates them.

This sensitivity to the reader's response to poetry helps to explain the excitement with which Longinus's work has often been received. In pinpointing it, Gibbon was drawing attention to an aspect of literary criticism which was to be increasingly cultivated during the nineteenth century; that of so vitally recording the delight of personal responsiveness to a work of art that the reader is infected with the writer's delight.

V Rhetoric

In observing the great influence of Longinus, we have referred naturally to seventeenth and eighteenth century men of letters to whom his work became a powerful inspiration. There was a very different branch of literary theorising in Classical times which was to exercise a strong influence much sooner than Longinus – in the Middle Ages – and then to fade from view. This was the study of 'Rhetoric'. Before we track further the history of literary criticism that is philosophically or inspirationally oriented, we must consider the growth of this more technical brand of literary theory.

The development of the art of rhetoric in Greece and Rome had been severely practical in origin, in that oratorical

ability was expected of all who wanted to hold positions of
authority in public life. Moreover the demands of litigation,
then as now, put a premium on the arts of clear exposition
and persuasive reasoning. In no case was the usefulness of
powerful oratory more evident than in that of Marcus
Tullius Cicero (106–43 BC) who made his name in the
Roman law-courts, and then achieved the highest possible
eminence in the political field by becoming consul in 63 BC.
Cicero was the greatest of the Roman orators. He mastered a
periodic style in which complex syntactical structure is not
only finely attuned to the ear in rhythm and cadence, but
also allows points to be planted in a cunningly appropriate
order. Moreover, he could play on the responses of his
audience with shrewd emotional appeals, with witty mockery, sarcasm or innuendo. And the flow of his exposition was
calculated to fix the attention and keep interest and
sympathy alive.

Cicero's influence was to be primarily that of a model of
elegance, lucidity and persuasiveness. But he contributed to
the theory of his subject with *De Oratore* (55 BC), a study of
oratory in general, *Brutus* or *De Claribus Oratoribus* (*c*.45), a
review of Roman orators, and *Orator* (46), an account of the
gifts and functions of the ideal orator. Cicero's technical
advice does not rise above the obvious. It is clear from what
he says that one of the charges which the orator had to
defend himself against was that he was not a specialist in any
of the fields in which he could be called upon to operate
persuasively in the courts. Though the *De Oratore* is written in
the form of a dialogue, it is not difficult to ascertain which
speaker's view represents Cicero's own. And he argues here
that the good orator has to be able to operate wisely and
persuasively *whatever* his subject. Indeed, Cicero insists that,
once he has been briefed by an expert, an orator will always
be a better exponent of the expert's specialism than the
expert himself.

Another specific charge against which Cicero had, seemingly, to defend himself was that his carefully contrived
oratory was over-elaborate and turgid. In reply, Cicero
appeals in *Orator* to the example of Demosthenes, and he
goes on to illustrate three styles of oratory: the plain, the

middle, and the grand. The plain style is unadorned and unrhythmic, but clipped and correct. A modest use of metaphor may be allowed, but all attempts at rhetorical contrivances and spell-binding delivery will be eschewed, though there may be occasions of wit and humour. The middle style has 'a minimum of muscle' and 'a maximum of sweetness'.[4] It is 'fuller than our concise type, more restrained than the ornate and copious style'. Stylistic ornaments are used to brighten the text, but the style 'flows gently and quietly'. The grand style is 'full, copious, weighty, and ornate'.[5] By its splendour and fullness it touches the emotions and influences opinions. But the exponent of the grand style, if he is not also master of the quieter, more restrained styles, will make a fool of himself. So what makes the perfect orator? 'That man is eloquent who can speak of humble things plainly, lofty things with gravity, middling things with the blended style.'

When Cicero comes down to more technical matters over the choice of words, the use of metaphor and figures of speech, his illustrations imply that what applies to rhetoric applies to poetry. Not that poets themselves were prepared to regard rhetoric as a sub-section of poetry. The first century poet Petronius protested against the idea that composing poetry was a suitable relaxation for an advocate after a period of hard work in the courts. And the poet Ovid (43 BC–c.17 AD), in one of his *Amores*, replied with dignity to the charge that he had wasted years that might have been spent in military, legal or political pursuits. 'What you are looking for is perishable; *my* aim is everlasting fame.'[6] Time can wear away rocks and ploughshares, but 'poetry is deathless'.

Rhetoric of course was Cicero's stock-in-trade in his two roles as barrister and statesman. The teaching of rhetoric at Rome as a salaried profession became a means to wealth for the Spanish-born Quintilian (35–c.95 AD), then he too worked in the law-courts and rose to be consul under the emperor Domitian and tutor of his grandnephews. He retired about the year 90 AD and composed his *Institutio Oratoria*, a treatise in 12 books dealing with the education of the orator. Quintilian works through the early and later phases of schooling (books I–II), then turns to technicalities of oratory, categorising subject-matter and examining the proper organisation of material (books III–VII). He deals with questions of style and delivery in books VII to IX; but the most fascinating section of his work has proved to be book X, in which is included a survey of the literature appropriate for an orator to study. Homer, Pindar, and the Greeks are dealt with and then Quintilian turns to Latin writers. His distribution of praise and disapproval when dealing with Virgil, Lucretius, Horace, Ovid, Sallust, Livy, Cicero and others constitutes a kind of 'literary criticism', but it is directed to the specific and limited purpose of refining the rhetorical technique of aspirants to a career in oratory. Book XI deals, among other things, with delivery, deportment, and the use of gesture, while book XII portrays the finished orator, 'the good man skilled in speaking'.[7] Here Quintilian insists on the importance of reading. 'Eloquence can never be mature and tough if it has not drawn strength from constant writing, and without the pattern supplied by reading effort devoted to writing will drift unguided.' In a similar vein, the poet Petronius declared that 'the mind cannot conceive or bring forth its offspring unless it is washed by a vast river of literature'.[8]

Both Petronius and Quintilian also had something to say about the practice of 'Declamation'. This was originally a practice for training speakers. Fictional legal cases were imagined and a speaker would be required to speak for the prosecution or the defence in a mock trial or debate. There was also a practice in which a speaker addressed a historical personage in a reconstructed situation. The unreality attendant upon these practices naturally tended to encourage the stoking up of emotion and the contrived utilisation of supposedly effective techniques of elaboration and persuasion. And as the occasions for public persuasion became less frequent in imperial Rome, oratory lost its roots in practical urgency, and declamation was practised for its own sake, becoming rather an exercise in histrionics and a form of entertainment than a practical discipline. Hence it was condemned as decadent. Nevertheless in parting with the world of law and politics, it came into the sphere of the artistic.

The elder Seneca (*c*.55 BC–*c*.37 AD), father of the more famous philosopher, collected *Controversiae*, that is exercises in presenting a legal case in respect of a civil or criminal charge, and *Suasoriae*, that is more general deliberations on some reconstituted historical situation. For instance, there is a surviving *Suasoria* in which various declaimers contribute advice to Cicero on whether he should appeal to Antony for clemency. (Cicero had delivered political speeches against Antony in 44–43BC, defending the republican cause, and lost his life as a result.) By about 95 AD Quintilian, who himself used the declamatory technique and believed that it could provide a good discipline, was nevertheless complaining in his *Institutio Oratoria*:

> Thanks to its teachers it has now so degenerated that the licentious ignorance of declaimers has become one of the principal causes for the corruption of eloquence.[9]

What was in Quintilian's mind is made clear in an even earlier work, the surviving fragments of the novel *Satyricon* by Petronius, who committed suicide in 65 AD after a false accusation had been brought against him to the emperor Nero. In the first fragment of *Satyricon* he mocks the declaimer's posturing in an imaginary situation of pathos:

> 'These wounds I received for the freedom of all; this eye I forfeited for you. Give me a guide to lead me to my children; my knees are hamstrung and will not support my body.'[10]

Petronius's spokesman goes on to criticise educational practices which cut the young off from real life by concern with melodramatic fictions – 'pirates in chains on the beach, tyrants writing edicts instructing sons to cut off their fathers' heads, oracles ordering that three or more virgins should be sacrificed to remedy a plague, honeyed balls of words, everything that's done or said coated with poppy-seed and sesame'.

Petronius condemns the foolishness of expecting to turn out sensible adults when boys are brought up to this kind of exercise. Moreover he laments the decay of genuine oratory that this cheap declamation represents. It encourages extravagant and shallow utterance, turgid and inflated loquacity. Under its decadent influence true eloquence disappears. It is clear that as the rhetoricians trained their pupils to the mechanical exploitation of contrived stylistic devices, a notion of rhetoric was encouraged which saw it as a training in the manipulation of descriptive flights, wordy amplifications, epigrammatic turns of phrase, exaggerated paradoxes and outlandish expressions.

This debased recipe for rhetoric was transmitted to later ages. The fifth century writer Martianus Capella wrote an influential extravaganza *De Nuptiis Philologiae et Mercurii*, the Marriage of Learning and Eloquence. The work is written in alternate prose and verse. It became a model for the high style, and C. S. Lewis called it 'the most agonisingly rhetorical book' ever written. It is basically a treatise on the seven liberal arts, and in the central books of the work they appear personified. The work as a whole is a hotch-potch, packed with indigestible learning, fantastic narrative, and encyclopaedic catalogues. What is notable about the book for the modern student is that the laborious extravagances of style match the author's theme, and his personification of Rhetoric underlines the decadent concept of what literature is all about. She was:

> a stately woman of lofty stature, and confidence greater than common, but radiantly handsome, helmed and crowned, weaponed both for defence and with flashing arms wherewith she could smite her enemies with a thundering coruscation. Under her armpits, and thrown over her shoulder in Latian fashion, was a vest, exhibiting embroidery of all possible figures in varied hue, while her breast was baldricked with gems of the most exquisite colour. As she walked her arms clashed, so that you would have thought the broken levin to rattle – with explosive hand-claps, like the collision of clouds, so that you might even believe her capable of wielding the thunderbolts of Jove. For it is she who, like a mighty queen of all things, can direct them whither she will and call them back whenever she chooses, and unbend men to tears or incite them to rage, and sway the minds of civic crowds as of warring armies. She brought beneath her sway the senate, the rostra, and the courts at Rome.[11]

Thus Rhetoric is a powerful force to arouse emotion and to inspire to action, but her vesture and equipment resemble a firework display. She is like a walking thunderstorm emitting kaleidoscopic coruscations.

2
The Middle Ages

The centuries between the fall of the Roman Empire in the west and the Renaissance are loosely called the 'Middle Ages'. Waves of barbarian invaders, Goths, Huns and Vandals, swept over the imperial frontiers in the last decades of the fourth century AD until Alaric, King of the Visigoths, eventually captured and sacked Rome itself in the last year of his life, 410. The submergence of Roman civilisation under the invading hordes was such that the period from the fall of Rome to the later eleventh century has been labelled the 'Dark Ages', and the term 'Middle Ages' applied more limitedly to the period from the twelfth century to the Renaissance. The Dark Ages were not uniformly dark. We caught a glimpse of the fifth-century literary mind in the last chapter when we cast our eyes forward to see the long-term effect of the decay of oratory into declamation in the first century AD. The Frankish King Charlemagne (c.742–814) was inspired to extend his rule in all directions with the hope of recreating the Christian empire of Constantine. Eventually he seized the crown of Lombardy and took the papacy under his protection. In 800 AD he was crowned by the Pope as Emperor of the Holy Roman Empire. His patronage was such that historians speak of the 'Carolingian Renaissance'.

England, as we shall see, had periods of significance in the history of European culture at the end of the seventh century in the days of Bede and in the ninth century in the reign of Alfred. It is generally assumed that the great Old English epic *Beowulf* dates from the eighth century. Somewhere about 940 Bishop Leofric copied Old English poems into the manuscript he presented to Exeter cathedral, known as the 'Exeter Book'. It includes the touching laments *The Wanderer* and *The Seafarer*. These are only some of the surviving texts which give the Anglo-Saxon period in England a literary status of its own.

In the Middle Ages proper, the spread of monasticism scattered centres of learning over Western Europe. It was an age of intense theological scholarship and related philosophical controversy. There was too an output of commentary on sacred texts which sometimes involved touching on questions of literary form or the distinction between the symbolical and the literal, fable and fact. There is, however, little for us to fasten on in this period in the way of literary criticism or even works in which the value of imaginative literature is at issue. But we have already seen that the value and function of imaginative literature are issues closely related, in the first place, to basic philosophical assumptions about the nature of reality, and in the second place, to the question of what things constitute healthy educative influences on people destined for authority over others. In so far as such questions continued to be aired by thinkers, presuppositions on which criticism of the arts is based were developed, clarified, and handed on to the future.

Mediaeval theology brought a new vitality to discussions about the nature of reality and a new urgency to questions of what conduces to spiritual and moral health. Much philosophical and moral thinking was channelled into concentration on the role of fallen and redeemed mankind in a divinely created and directed universe. It cannot be said that aesthetic theory benefited much from the consequent debates. But one or two thinkers, pagan and Christian, had influence on the direction of aesthetic theory when the Renaissance brought it to life again.

I Plotinus

A very early one was Plotinus (*c*.205–270), born perhaps in Egypt, who studied under Ammonius at Alexandria. Ammonius, a thinker who was born a Christian but reverted to paganism, had among his pupils the great Christian father Origen as well as Plotinus. The school of philosophy which Plotinus represented is known as 'Neoplatonism' because it expounded doctrines derived and developed from the metaphysics of Plato with its strong mystical orientation. Plotinus himself eventually settled in Rome to teach philosophy, and his pupil Porphyry edited and collected his philosophical essays in a series of six *Enneads* (sets of nine essays).

Plotinus develops the Platonic distinction between the world of appearance and true reality. The One is the primal ground of all being and the source of value. Plotinus's image for the nature of reality is an expanding series of concentric circles, each dependent on the one within it, and all produced by the spilling over of the eternal One. It is a hierarchy of the descending spheres of Reason, Soul, and Nature, and the principle of gradation is the degree of unity. Oneness disintegrates into multiplicity, unity into individuation. Men must discipline themselves to attain to the spiritual world of Being and unity, and not pursue what belongs to Negation and diversity.

No one, however, should be insensitive to evidences of symmetry and order in the world. Every manifestation of orderliness in nature is an image of that Unity and Beauty from which it springs. As for art, Plotinus does not accept the Platonic doctrine that depreciates it as being at one further remove from reality than the world it portrays. On the contrary, the artist enjoys an especially close participation in the divine Reason, for not only is he sensitive to the Beauty which the natural world reflects by imitation, he is also one who fashions beauty, improving upon nature itself. For Plotinus, man is a microcosm of the graded order of being, whose consciousness may operate by strict discipline at the ecstatic level of Reason, will generally operate on the level of Soul, and operates subconsciously at the level of Nature.

Plotinus hands on to later thinkers a concept of the Scale of Being crucial to much mediaeval scholarship. His emphasis on unity and its centrality in reference to natural or artistic beauty gives a microcosmic significance to every experience of the beautiful. The beauty of any whole seems to depend collectively on the beauty of its parts, yet the beauty of those assembled parts consists, not in their respective qualities, but in the way they work together to produce a comely total.

Centuries later, Coleridge made something like this one leg of his definition of poetry. A poem is a species of composition which, unlike works of science, has 'pleasure', not 'truth', as its immediate object, and 'it is discriminated by proposing to itself such delight from the *whole*, as is compatible with a distinct gratification from each constituent part'.

A celebrated example sheds further light on Plotinus's concept of what artistry can do to raw material. He compares an untreated block of stone and a finished work of sculpture. One is untouched by art, the other has been wrought by the craftsman into a beautiful statue.

> Now it must be seen that the stone thus brought under the artist's hand to the beauty of form is beautiful not as stone – for so the crude stone would be as pleasant – but in virtue of the form or idea introduced by art. The form is not in the material; it is in the designer before it enters the stone.[1]

Thus, if there is in Plotinus anything that can be called 'aesthetic doctrine', it is a by-product of concentration on more general philosophical issues.

II Augustine and Aquinas

We may take St Augustine (354–430) as representative of the historical development which was to push literary criticism out of the domain of intellectual life for several centuries. Born in North Africa, Augustine was brought up by a devoutly Christian mother, St Monica, but lost whatever faith he imbibed from her when he went to the university at Carthage. For many years he embraced Manicheeism, but as a professor at Milan he was greatly influenced by the preaching of St Ambrose, bishop of Milan, and after a severe internal struggle was converted at the age of 32 to become one of the profoundest theological scholars of the Christian Church.

The fact that Augustine's intellectual development was a progress from Manicheeism to Christianity gives him an almost symbolic status in relation to our present enquiry. The Manichees solved the intellectual problems posed by the

power of evil in the world by postulating a divided supernatural authority. Good and evil reigned as equal opponents.
There was unceasing cosmic conflict between the powers of
light and the powers of darkness. It was against such a
pessimistic dualism that Plotinus reacted in formulating the
doctrine which projected evil in terms of negation of the
ultimate reality. St Augustine was the thinker who above all
brought this kind of reasoning to bear on the Christian
account of the human situation since the Fall.

Augustine wrote at a time when civilisation was in a state
of decay and collapse. The new Christian church was at war
with paganism. Questions of aesthetic theory could but arise
as foot-notes to the immense programme of Christianising
Western Europe. The old literature was inextricably tied up
with the old polytheism, with the discreditable doings of
unrighteous gods. Dramatists and poets, Augustine argued in
The City of God, attribute vicious behaviour to gods 'to the
end that there might be sufficient authority, derived as it
were from heaven and earth, for men to commit all filthiness
by'.[2] The wickedness of gods implicitly authorised human
wickedness. Their vices gave the spectators and readers
'imitable example'. It was small wonder that Augustine
cited with approval Plato's exclusion of poets from the
well-governed city. His grounds are like Plato's, the question
of moral influence. For crimes will no longer be crimes, he
declares in his *Confessions*, when 'whoso commits them might
seem to imitate not abandoned men, but the celestial gods'.[3]
Pagan literature was thus sharply distinguished from the one
literature necessary to the Christian, the Scriptures. In the
first four books of his *De Doctrina Christiana*, Augustine lays
down the procedure for proper interpretation of the Bible.
Exploring how a text might be dealt with is, of course, the
one route by which the Fathers trespassed into the field of
literary criticism.

Augustine was no philistine. He was acutely sensitive to the
power of imaginative literature to perturb and enthral. He
describes in his *Confessions* how Virgil moved him to 'weep for
dead Dido because she killed herself for love'. But he has
learned to question such emotion as totally misdirected.
What can be more wretched than a man 'weeping the death

of Dido for love to Aeneas, but weeping not his own death for want of love to thee, O God'. Later he tells us how stage plays carried him away 'full of images of my miseries, and of fuel to my fire'. It is sheer wastefulness of grief over the fictional that he stresses. That is what we mean when we say that the birth of the Christian era so transformed the sense of proportion that there was scarcely room for the luxury of aesthetics. Everything, but everything became a moral and therefore a theological issue.

Yet there are no puritanical aridities in Augustine's address to God: 'Too late loved I Thee, O Thou Beauty of ancient days, yet ever new! too late I loved Thee!' It is the divine 'Beauty' that is the end of his search and his aspiration. And in reference elsewhere to the character of the beautiful, he speaks in a similar vein to Plotinus of the power of 'integrity and unity': 'Any beautiful object whatsoever is more worthy of praise in its totality as a whole than in any one of its parts.' Man judges one object as more beautiful than another by referring to an eternal standard of beauty. This is an aspect of the God-given reason which lifts man above animal kind. There is a sermon cited by Frederick Coplestone in his *History of Philosophy* (volume II: Mediaeval Philosophy) 'where the Saint depicts the human soul questioning the things of sense and hearing them confess that the beauty of the visible world, of mutable things, is the creation and reflection of immutable Beauty'.[4] When men go in search of what is immutable, Augustine declares, they arrive 'at knowledge of God the Creator by means of the things which He created'.

We spoke of St Augustine as a fit representative of the historical development which pushed literary criticism out of the domain of intellectual life for several centuries. We might regard St Thomas Aquinas (*c.*1224–74) as representative of the intellectual development which was to make literary criticism possible again. For Aquinas effected within the intellectual life of Christendom the full re-establishment of what was valuable and relevant in the philosophy of Aristotle. Metaphysical problems tussled with by Plato and Aristotle, Plotinus and the Neoplatonists were re-minted for Christian attention. Aquinas was able to rescue the insights of pre-Christian philosophy by his clear demarcation of the realm of reason and the realm of faith. 'Demarcation' is not the best word if it suggests contiguous but separate areas of human activity. The fundamental doctrines of Creation and the Fall, Incarnation and Redemption, are presented through the revelation recorded in Scripture. As such, within the province of faith, they make their call to the human will for obedient acceptance. This is a matter of moral choice, not of intellectual discovery. But in no sense does this primacy of faith produce a collision with the demand of the human reason. There are many truths about the existence of God as creator and sustainer of the world which the human reason can arrive at without recourse to revelation. And the revealed truths, to which the human reason could never have attained without the gift of revelation, are never offensive to reason. On the contrary, they fill up by enrichment and amplification what reason would presuppose on its own grounds: there is a perfect interplay of revealed truth with reason's own assumptions. Faith and Reason coalesce in the fabric of vision and understanding which God lays open to his creatures.

This was the door through which a flood of healthy rational speculation entered the realm of Christian theorising about God's world. It ensured that for centuries secular philosophical ratiocination could be accommodated within the Christian synthesis. It did not in Aquinas himself produce any systematic theory. Nevertheless he had something to say about the nature of beauty.

> A good thing is a beautiful thing, for both epithets have the same basis in reality, the possession of form; and this is why the good is esteemed beautiful. Good and beautiful are not however synonymous. For good, being what all things desire, has to do properly with desire... Beauty on the other hand has to do with knowledge, and we call a thing beautiful when it pleases the eye of the beholder.[5]

Thus the beautiful is the object of a non-possessive contemplation, whereas the good is something which we desire for ourselves. The beautiful is something we delight in recognising and appreciating. The good is the object of our desire.

Aquinas supplies a definition of what constitutes beauty:

> For in respect to beauty three things are essential: first of all, integrity
> or completeness, since beings deprived of wholeness are on this score
> ugly; secondly, a certain required design or patterned structure; and
> finally, a certain splendour, inasmuch as things are called beautiful
> which possess a pleasing colour.[6]

This is the definition which Stephen Dedalus quotes in
Joyce's *Portrait of the Artist*, using the terms 'wholeness',
'harmony' and 'radiance'. It seems to give to aesthetic
experience a status of its own, distinct from recognition of
the good and from intellectual understanding. But if we use
the word 'aesthetic' thus, we must be wary of attributing to
Aquinas anything like a theory of artistic appreciation such
as we might formulate today. For one thing, Aquinas does
not relate his definition to any consideration of art. For
another thing, if he had done so, he would not have meant
by 'art' what we mean today. The word 'arts' itself was used,
as we shall see, with a broad connotation now surviving in
academic usage ('Bachelor of Arts', 'Master of Arts'). As for
our more general use of the word, our categorisation of fine
arts as distinct from practical crafts would be alien to
mediaeval thinking. The mediaeval attitude to what we call
art has been compared to that voiced by the artist Eric Gill
in his book *Christianity and the Machine Age*. Gill laments that
we have nowadays 'come to think of art as though the word
did not mean all human works whatsoever, from drain-pipes
to cathedrals ... from sign-boards to Royal Academy
paintings ...'

Though Aquinas does not treat of art at all, as we
understand it, let alone of poetry, what he has to say about
beauty opens the way for a Christian aesthetic which others
were to formulate.

III The Trivium

While philosophical thinkers allowed their speculations about
beauty to hover around the fringes of 'literary criticism',
there was also throughout the Middle Ages a tradition of

technical linguistic instruction which concerned itself with questions of style that have become the province of the literary critic. The mediaeval educational curriculum was based on the 'Seven Liberal Arts', areas of study to be distinguished from mechanical arts such as carpentry. The Seven were divided into the Trivium, consisting of Grammar, Dialectic (or Logic), and Rhetoric; and the Quadrivium, consisting of Music, Arithmetic, Geometry, and Astronomy. The trivium was studied first and, being more elementary than the quadrivium, endowed the word 'trivial' with its pejorative flavour. We shall consider the parts of the Trivium in turn, beginning with Grammar.

As early as the second century AD, Apollonius Dyscolus, of Alexandria, had written a series of works on the parts of speech and on syntax, which were to influence later grammarians, including Priscianus. One of the great authorities accepted in the Middle Ages was Aelius Donatus, a fourth-century scholar who wrote a commentary on Virgil which might earn him the title of literary critic. He also wrote *Ars Minor*, a book introducing the parts of speech and using a catechetical form, and *Ars Major*, or *Secunda*, which goes on to analyse qualities and defects of style. Donatus's work *Ars Grammatica* was so widely used that the term 'Donat' or 'Donet' came to be adopted generally for any instructive manual. There is a celebrated passage in Langland's *Piers Plowman* where 'Covetise' confesses 'I joined the drapers to learn my donet', meaning to acquire the tricks of the trade. Donatus's work on Virgil was a considerable influence on the fourth-century grammarian and editor Servius, who wrote his own commentary on Virgil with his eye on educational use. Servius was concerned with matters of substance as well as of style, being anxious to establish Virgil as a poet of great learning as well as of masterly technique. He was liberal with quotations from other Latin writers, and he was ready to balance opposing views against each other; but the information he has to offer is of antiquarian rather than critical interest.

The cult of Virgil as a poet of supreme and unquestionable excellence, which was to be so influential in the Middle Ages, with Dante especially, was initiated by writers such as

Servius and Macrobius. The latter, who flourished about the turn of the century (400 AD), wrote a dialogue in seven books, *Saturnalia*, which focus eventually on Virgil, his learning, his poetic power, and his place in the Homeric tradition. One of Macrobius's disputants is Servius himself. (Boswell tells us that on Dr Johnson's arrival as a student at Oxford, he was making little impression on those who received him at Pembroke College until after a chance remark in conversation 'he suddenly struck in and quoted Macrobius'.)

Another mediaeval authority was the early sixth-century Priscianus who taught at Constantinople and wrote *Institutiones Grammaticae* in 18 books. They scarcely trespass into the field of literary criticism, confining themselves to questions of grammar and syntax, but the text is copiously illustrated by reference to classical literature.

It is clear that 'Grammar' covers a wider range of material than modern usage of the word would allow – except perhaps in the term 'Grammar School'. Indeed 'grammar' came to be used generally of 'learning'. Moving from questions of syntax or etymology to explanation of allusions or to textual observations, the grammarian enlarged his field of discourse and inevitably entered the field of 'literary criticism'.

Dialectic, the second section of the Trivium, is concerned with the art of argument: how to make your point; how to prove a case; how to disprove one. The basis of watertight disputational procedures is of course Logic, and the Trivium, as mentioned before, is often defined as consisting of Grammar, Logic, and Rhetoric. The study of Logic, especially of what exactly terms connote or denote, involves enquiry into the nature of meaning and thus inevitably involves metaphysical speculation. It was the study of Logic which eventually expanded during the Middle Ages into the seemingly all-embracing argument about the nature of meaning represented by the controversy between the Realists and the Nominalists. For long a standard mediaeval textbook of Logic was *Isagogue*, an introduction to Aristotle by the third-century scholar Porphyry (*c*.232–*c*.305) who was probably born at Tyre. Porphyry had studied under Longinus at Athens and under Plotinus at Rome. It was the Latin translation of Porphyry's *Isagogue* made by Boethius (*c*.480–524) that was current in the Middle Ages and sparked off controversy among the scholars about the nature of universals.

The study of Dialectic, or Logic, expanded beyond technical considerations of verbal cogency and coherence into the wider field of philosophy, but it scarcely trespassed into literary criticism. Only in the study of Grammar and Rhetoric can we find the ancestry of criticism. We have seen the study of Grammar widening into broader concerns as Donatus's work on Virgil was built on by Servius and Macrobius. Rhetoric, however, is concerned with questions of structure and style, methods of presentation and devices of literary embellishment. It might sound, on first hearing, very much like modern literary criticism: but it was not concerned with the human interest of literature which we call 'character-study' or the individual responsiveness of the writer which we call his 'imaginative sensitivity' or 'insight'. It concentrated on objective artistry and sheer eloquence.

IV The British scene

Little is known about how far the Roman conquest of Britain was accompanied by the introduction of Latin culture to the natives, and in any case the break in civilisational continuity which occurred with the departure of the Roman legions at the beginning of the fifth century and the subsequent invasions by the Anglo-Saxons was a bleak and thorough one. But the coming of Christianity to Britain and the establishment of monastic houses produced such a vast and swift cultural development that England, like Ireland, became by the end of the seventh century one of the strongholds of Latin learning in Europe. Nor was this flowering of scholarship centred chiefly in the south. A Benedictine abbey was founded at Wearmouth in 674 and a twin abbey at Jarrow in 682. Both foundations were the work of St Benedict Biscop, a man full of zeal for scholarship who visited Rome on several occasions and collected books for the monastic library at Jarrow. Hence it was that the most celebrated of early English scholars, Bede, spent most of his time in the cloisters at Jarrow. Bede (673–735) was not only a Biblical scholar but produced works in history and science. Best known is his *Ecclesiastical History of the English People*, which his thoroughness turned into an essential primary source for the early phase of English history. Among earlier and less mature works were his *De Orthographia*, a text-book for pupils in the form of an alphabetically arranged Latin glossary, and *De Arte Metrica*. In the latter, after analysing the various Latin metres, he turns to examine what he calls 'rhythm' (*rhythmus*) as opposed to 'metre' (*metrum*), distinguishing versification in which stressed and unstressed syllables, as opposed to long and short syllables, provide the basis of measurement. Finally Bede distinguishes three kinds of poetry; the dramatic, in which the voice of the poet is not heard; the narrative, in which only the voice of the poet is heard; and the mixed kind in which both the poet and his characters speak.

A third work of Bede's relevant to our study is his *On Figures and Tropes of Holy Writ*. By 'figures' he means variations in word-order and use of repetition. By 'tropes' he means figures of speech, such as metaphor, synechdoche, and onomatopoeia, as well as devices such as irony and sarcasm. Bede's work in literary theory has no great intrinsic significance. But in building as he does on predecessors such as Donatus, and in drawing his illustrations from Latin poetry (especially Christian poets), he inaugurated a branch of study in England and he made a notable development in applying critical theory to the books of the Bible.

It was a few years before Bede's death that his former pupil Egbert became Bishop of York and it was in the year of his death that the see became archiepiscopal. Egbert founded a school at York and taught theology there. His own most distinguished pupil, Alcuin (*c*.735–804) became its head-master in 766. After meeting Charlemagne at Parma in 781, Alcuin became the emperor's adviser on religious and educational matters and the most celebrated scholar in the Carolingian renaissance. Alcuin's brief was to improve educational standards in the interests of a proper under-standing of the Bible. He produced various text-books to this end. They include studies *On Orthography*, *On Grammar*, and

On Rhetoric. The first two of these are elementary manuals of
no particular distinction. There is evident indebtedness to
Donatus and Priscianus. In *On Rhetoric* the indebtedness goes
back to Cicero, who had defined the five constituents of
rhetoric in a formulation which the ancient world handed on
to the Middle Ages. These five constituents were: *inventio* (the
creative faculty), *dispositio* or *ordo* (form and structure),
elocutio (diction and style), *memoria* (memory), and
pronuntatio (delivery). Of the three major constituents,
Inventio, *dispositio*, and *elocutio*, the last tended to get the
greatest attention from mediaeval theorists. Alcuin classifies
the five elements and treats them in turn. He also defines the
three kinds of rhetoric, the forensic, the deliberative, and the
epideictic (histrionic). There is nothing distinctive in Alcuin's
work in this field, but it was a thread in the thin connecting
link which Bede had first stretched back between Anglo-
Saxon England and the old Latin culture.

There was another break in continuity when the Danish
invasions brought about the plundering of churches and the
destruction of libraries. King Alfred (849–99) did much to
rescue the remnants of culture and learning from oblitera-
tion. When he translated Pope Gregory's *Cura Pastoralis* into
English in 894, he described the sorry state of education in
the country, in particular the lack in the clergy of the
necessary ability to translate Latin into English. Alfred has
a special importance because of his emphasis on the need to
make Latin scholarship accessible in English translation. But,
in spite of the fact that Anglo-Saxon England produced some
fine examples of vernacular literature in both poetry and
prose, the English language was doomed to lose its status
after the Norman conquest of 1066, and more than two
centuries were to pass before a revived English literature
throve alongside a revived Latin scholarship.

A key figure in the latter revival was John of Salisbury
(*c*.1115–80), one of the finest Latin scholars of the period,
who was born in Salisbury and who went to France and
studied at Paris under Peter Abelard. Back in England he
became secretary to Theobald, Archbishop of Canterbury,
and then to Thomas à Becket. He was in fact present in
Canterbury Cathedral in December 1170 when the knights

burst in to murder Becket. John of Salisbury was deeply read in Aristotle and he wrote *Policraticus* and *Metalogicon*. *Policraticus*, a political and moral treatise sub-titled 'The Vanities of Courtiers and the Traditions of Philosophers' is satirical in its treatment of courtiers before turning to lay down a philosophy of government. *Metalogicon* is concerned with the study of logic. J. W. H. Atkins has praised John of Salisbury's achievement:

> first, in an attempt to claim for literature and literary study an essential place in a liberal education; secondly, in efforts made to expound those artistic principles that underlie good writing while also helping in an appreciation of literary values, and thirdly, in illuminating pronouncements on literature in general and on ancient classical literature in particular.[7]

John of Salisbury balances together the human faculties of reason and eloquence. As the study of logic is the foundation of reasoning, so the study of grammar and literature is the basis of eloquence. John has much to say on the value of eloquence which shows the influence of Cicero, Horace, and Quintilian. His recommendations for good writing lay stress on clarity, decorum, appropriateness, breadth of vocabulary, fluency, and a prevalent restraint.

More interesting to us today perhaps is John of Salisbury's evident enthusiasm for past literature. And there is no suspicion here of non-Christian classics. He writes feelingly of his own love for the classics, for the delight and consolation he has obtained from them, for the practical wisdom acquired from them. He is equally alive to the need to bring commonsense to bear on interpretation of the bizarre elements of classical literature, and the need to interpret the Bible with attention to metaphorical and allegorical as well as literal meanings. Moreover he recommends alertness in reading to felicitous stylistic touches and effects. But what is most attractive in John of Salisbury's attitude to literature is the flexibility of approach which does not limit itself to systematising technicalities or drawing boundaries around what is good for the soul, but which is acutely sensitive to the value inherent in a continuing literary tradition and sees it as a source of both enjoyment and enrichment, intellectual and moral.

V Style and substance

We must turn from this refreshingly congenial figure to a scholar of different breed who flourished about 1200, Geoffrey de Vinsauf. He produced a systematic study of poetic rhetoric, *Poetria Nova*, which established itself as a standard text-book. On the basis of the traditional formulation of the elements of rhetoric, which Alcuin also used (*inventio, dispositio, elocutio, memoria*, and *pronuntatio*), Geoffrey de Vinsauf develops his systematisation with the zeal of an enthusiast for codification. He defines two kinds of *ordo* (*dispositio*), Natural and Artificial. That is, you can begin at the beginning and go through the middle to the end. Or you can adopt one of three Artificial modes, beginning at the end, beginning in the middle, or beginning with some generalisation (*sententia*) or illustration (*exemplum*). A predecessor of Geoffrey's, Matthew of Vendôme, had written an *Ars Versificatoria* in about 1185, in which five methods of ending were laid down. The first was by Recapitulation of the *sententia*, the general moral of the piece (as in fact happens in Chaucer's *Miller's Tale* and his *Physician's Tale*). The second was by Emendation of the work, requesting readers to correct what was said where necessary. The third was by asking Pardon for any imperfections in the work. The fourth was a final flourish. And the fifth method of ending was by giving praise to God.

It is in Geoffrey de Vinsauf, however, that we find the fullest and most rigid systematisation of what he called *Amplificatio*, in other words, the various ways of spinning out one's material. There is *Descriptio*, in which a person or a scene is portrayed, *Exclamatio* or 'apostrophe', in which an emotional outburst is directed at some person or thing, *Conformatio* or 'personification', which endows objects or abstractions with capacity to speak, and *Expolitio*, or saying the same thing in a variety of different ways. There is also *Circumlocutio, Contrarium*, or 'contrast', *Similitudo*, or 'comparison', and lastly *Diversio*, or 'digression'. It is not difficult to work through the *Canterbury Tales*, pinpointing instances of these various stylistic devices. But of course Chaucer often used the literary formalities of the day with his tongue in his cheek and for comic effect. There is a celebrated passage towards the end of the *Nun's Priest's Tale* when the fox seizes Chaunticleer by the neck and runs off with him. At this crisis Chaucer inserts, firstly an Apostrophe to Venus, and then an Apostrophe to Geoffrey de Vinsauf himself.

> O Gaudfred, deere maister soverayn,
> That whan they worthy kyng Richard was slayn
> With shot, compleynedest his deeth so soore,
> Why ne hadde I now thy sentence and thy loore
> The Friday for to chide, as diden ye?

In fact Geoffrey de Vinsauf's *Poetria Nova* was published shortly after the death of Richard I and it used Richard's death as an occasion for providing an example of lamentation, singling out Friday, the day on which the King was wounded, for an especially poignant address.

When Geoffrey de Vinsauf comes to systematise methods of stylistic embellishment, *Ornatus*, he lists over sixty devices. Many of course are obvious devices, such as *superlatio* or exaggeration for emphasis, *translatio* or metaphor, and *transgressio* or transposition of words from their natural order. Some devices listed merely reduplicate each other. For instance Geoffrey classifies seven different species of *repetitio* or repetition of a word in different syntactical positions and for different effects. Other devices listed strike today's reader as instances of systematisation run riot, for instance *praecisio* or a sentence unfinished for effect, and *conclusio* or a brief summing-up. Likewise *divisio*, or the presentation of a dilemma, is categorised; and so are *effectio*, personal description of outward appearance, and *notatio*, personal description of character.

Geoffrey's more general observations on literature are conventional recommendations about appropriateness of style to matter (*decorum*), consistency of style, restraint in the use of figurative devices, and avoidance of awkward aural effects, strained images, and excessive syntactical complexity.

He warns against the respective risks in the three kinds of style distinguished by Cicero. The high style may become ostentatious and florid, the middle style flaccid and slack, the low style drab and anaemic.

The analysis of style under highly systematised headings seems by implication to ignore what later ages found to be the most stirring and illuminating aspects of imaginative literature. Historically the concern with 'substance' had been bedevilled by the collision between classical poetry and Christian revelation. The departure from literal 'truth' in great classical poetry obviously troubled theorists from Plato onwards. The problems surrounding the serious treatment of pure fiction was certainly not invented by the Christian Fathers. The first-century philosopher and biographer Plutarch (c.45 AD–c.120) left a series of miscellaneous treatises, the *Moralia*, which contain a study, *de audiendis poetis*. Here he tussled with the problem of falsity in poetry. Poets tell 'deliberate lies' because they believe truth more boring than fiction so far as their main aim is concerned, that of giving pleasure to the reader. 'Metre, trope, grand language, timely metaphor, harmony, and word-order possess nothing like the beguiling charm of a well-contrived plot.'[8] Poetry is an art of imitation. In imitation, accuracy demands that ugliness be represented as ugly, wickedness as wicked. When the poet therefore describes the words and deeds of vicious people, the reader is required to distinguish between disapproving of what is represented and approving the effectiveness of the representation. The poet may convey sound moral judgments on his characters directly or by representation of what happens to them. It is crucial that the young student should keep his feet on the ground when reading poetry, exercising careful discrimination in his judgment of the human behaviour portrayed.

If the dichotomy between truth and poetic fiction troubled pre-Christian thinkers, it became a larger and a graver issue for early Christian theologians. For them the Bible was the literary vehicle of truth. Secular literature was a totally different kettle of fish. Those theologians such as Aquinas, who dealt with the need to interpret Scripture on various levels, distinguishing especially the historical or literal sense from the spiritual sense, were consciously developing a technique for study of the truth, and it was not a technique which they might conceivably have considered relevant to secular poetry. But the boundary between secular and religious literature was inevitably blurred when poets produced works which were religious in substance even if remote from the kind of literature to which biblical exegesis seemed applicable. Verses of prayer or praise were one thing, but elaborate 'fictional' constructs such as Dante's *Divine Comedy* or Langland's *Piers Plowman* clearly raised new problems of the nature of literary truth.

In fact Dante (1265–1321) himself wrote a dedicatory letter to his *Paradiso*, introducing the *Divine Comedy* as a whole and making clear that the kind of interpretative technique applied to the Scriptures is applicable to his poem. It has many meanings.

> The first meaning is the one obtained through the letter; the second is the one obtained through the things signified by the letter. The first is called literal, the second allegorical or moral or anagogical.[9]

In order to illustrate his definition, Dante quotes Psalm 114 (1-2): 'When Israel went out to Egypt, the house of Jacob from a people of strange language; Judah was his sanctuary, and Israel his dominion.' He then exemplifies the various levels of meaning, the literal – the departure of the Israelites from Egypt; the allegorical – the redemption of mankind by Christ; the moral – the soul's conversion from sin to a state of grace; the anagogical – the soul's departure from the slavery of corruption to the freedom of eternal life. The three mystic meanings can all be called allegorical. So Dante declares that the literal subject of his poem is the state of human souls after death, but the allegorical subject is mankind as a whole, and the freedom man has been granted to opt for eternal salvation or damnation.

The application to poetry of interpretative techniques developed for the purpose of explaining the books of the Bible finally bridges the rift between the secular and the religious in the literary field. And as the work of Aquinas brought the best of ancient philosophy into the service of

Christianity, so the work of Dante affected a transference of theology into artistic equivalents. Giovanni Boccaccio (c.1313–1375), the poet and story-teller, in his *Commento* on Dante's work, pushed what Dante said in the Preface cited above to its logical conclusion. Just as the Scriptures present the divine truths of incarnation and redemption in narratives, visions, and the like, so classical poetry with its fictions of gods may convey moral truths. When poets tell us that 'Saturn had many children and devoured all but four of them' we are to understand that Saturn is time, which reduces everything to nothing except fire (Jove), air (Juno), water (Neptune), and earth (Pluto). The Old Testament visions of Daniel, Isaiah, Ezekiel and others are the vehicles of the Holy Spirit's instruction 'written by the divine pen'.

Thus Boccaccio concluded that 'theology and poetry can be called almost the same thing when they have the same subject'. There is plenty of 'poetic fiction' in the imagery and allegory of the Scriptures. Indeed, 'it plainly appears that not merely is poetry theology but that theology is poetry'.[10]

3
The Renaissance

The term 'Renaissance' is sometimes so vaguely used that it tends to represent a period of history rather than a historical development. In its strictest sense, at least for the literary world, the 'Renaissance' is the rediscovery of the ancient classics of Greece and Rome which scholars edited, translated, and wrote commentaries on. With the capture of Constantinople by the Turks in 1453 the drift of Greek scholars to Italy was accelerated. Increasingly manuscripts were transferred from Byzantium to the west and copied. It must be recalled that the Emperor Constantine (288–337) had transferred his capital to Byzantium in 328 and renamed the city 'Constantinople'. After the death of the emperor Theodosius the Great (c.346–395) the Roman Empire was split into two halves, one of Theodosius's sons ruling from Rome, the other from Constantinople. As Rome declined and ceased finally in 476 to be the seat of an emperor, Constantinople remained for nearly a thousand years an imperial centre capable of defending its culture against invaders.

The increasing influx of scholarship from Byzantium into western Europe came at a time when new impulses were already at work and, it may be argued, merely quickened and intensified an already inevitable reaction against the theological, philosophical, and artistic culture of the Middle Ages. The revival of Greek and Latin forms, first in Italy, and then elsewhere in west Europe, was not just a literary development, but affected architecture too. Economically Italy was especially ripe for change in that the fabric of feudalism had been weakened by the growing wealth and importance of trading cities such as Florence and Venice, and the growing power of the now urbanised middle class. This was, of course, to be the pattern of change in other European countries too. Currents of new vitality gave an impulse to cultural productivity and development just when a source of fresh inspiration was being tapped in the rediscovery of the classics.

Other currents of influence were brought to bear on this change in the cultural scene which we call the Renaissance. The rejection of the mediaeval synthesis involved puncturing the fabric of thought and practice which had tried to centre all human activity in the divine scheme of creation and redemption, and had made the future life of heavenly bliss the focus of obedient moral effort, and damnation the penalty for apostasy and disobedience. Classical writers had placed man in the centre of the universe, where the mediaeval scholastics had placed God. The movement of thinking, which veered at this time towards an upgrading of the purely human by virtue of the dignity due to individual rational man, became known as 'Humanism'. Thinking which thus called for a new estimate of the significance of human life might collide head-on with traditional Christian teaching about man's dependent status as God's fallen creature in need of grace. On the other hand, such thinking could be said merely to qualify and extend what Christian revelation taught about man as divinely created and God as one who had exalted humanity for all time through the Incarnation. Hence it is that the word 'humanist' was used of atheists and sceptics, such as Montaigne, and of Christians, such as Erasmus.

It is from the thinking of this period that the wider use of the word 'classical' (for instance as opposed to 'romantic') derives. Delight in newly-discovered Classical styles and genres created new models of artistic perfection, in which very often qualities of poise and polish, balance and decorum were highly prized. The tendency to codify the rules by which the perfection of the best Classical literature could be imitated and recaptured left a legacy of formulation which later ages – the eighteenth century in particular – were to emulate. This kind of systematisation had in it the seeds of aridity and ossification.

I The complete man

The Renaissance produced a number of books in which
thinkers laid down the law about what kind of men will be
fit to rule others and how they ought to be trained for
leadership. Castiglione (1478–1529) wrote a series of dialogues, *Il libro del cortegiano* (1528) which Sir Thomas Hoby
(1530–66) translated into English as *The Courtyer* (1561).
Contributors to the dialogues discuss what the virtues, talents
and interests of the ideal courtier should be. An English
specimen of this kind of literature is *The Book of the Governour*
(1530) by Sir Thomas Elyot (*c.1490-1546*). It is really the first
English book on education and what Elyot has to say about
the place of literature in education certainly expresses the
Renaissance spirit. In Book I, chapter X, *What order shulde be
in lerninge and which autours shulde be first redde*, Elyot
recommends especially Homer 'from whom as from a
fountaine proceded all eloquence and lernyng'. It is not
only that much can be learned from Homer about military
matters, but also that here is to be found 'incomparable
wisedomes, and instructions for politike governaunce of
people'. Aristotle was cunning enough to bring up Alexander the Great on Homer. From the *Iliad* Alexander gathered
'courage and strength agayne his ennemies, wysdome, and
eloquence for consultations, and persuations to his people
and army'. From the *Odyssey* he learned by Ulysses's example
to evade deceptions and treacheries, and how to sift good
characters from evil characters.

Turning to Virgil, Elyot writes lyrically of the variety of
delights to be found in his works of especial appeal to the
young. Moreover, there is a wealth of expert instruction
conjoined with sheer pleasure in reading about horticulture,
horses, astronomy, hunting, and the like. Youthful appetite
for the marvellous and the terrible can be satisfied by being
led alongside Aeneas into the underworld and seeing what
the rewards are of 'dissolute and vicious living'. Thereafter
there is the gladness of beholding in 'the pleasant fields of
Elysium the soules of noble princes and capitaines which, for
their vertue, and labours in advancing the publike weales of
their countrayes, do lyve eternally in pleasure inexplicable'.

The last book of the *Aeneid*, Elyot adds, contains matter likely to stimulate boldness, courage and adventurousness.

Elyot's preference for literature which can nourish morally as well as delight emerges again when he declares that, instead of spending overmuch time on Ovid's works in which there is little learning conducive to either 'vertuous maners or policie', it would be better to concentrate on Horace 'in whom is contayned moche varietie of lernynge and quickenesse of sentence'. Study of Horace may be interlaced with study of Homer's *Odyssey*, showing 'the wonderfull prudence and fortitude of Ulisses in his passage from Troy'. When dealing in chapter XI with more advanced studies for the teenager, Elyot prescribes Logic, Rhetoric, Cosmography, History and Moral Philosophy. There follow two chapters (XII & XIII) investigating the current decay of learning among gentlemen. And in chapter XIII Elyot is at pains to distinguish mere technical agility in Rhetoric from the true eloquence present where 'any mater or acte done or to be done is expressed in wordes clene, propise, ornate, and comely', so that those who hear are sympathetically won over or delighted. The true orator can unfold a weighty case with wisdom and can arouse or restrain the emotions of his audience. In the same way technical skill can make a versifier, but not a poet. The true poet is a philosopher whose poetry teaches us 'maners and naturall affections' and reveals 'the wonderfull werkes of nature', mingling what is serious in substance with what gives pleasure in presentation.

Elyot responds with vigour to the charge that in the works of poets 'is contayned nothynge but baudry'. In defence of his case he argues that even comedy can be a morally instructive 'mirrour of man's life'. It is no bad thing for people to be warned by witnessing on stage what can happen to the young who are prompt to vice and unable to resist the lure of harlots and deceitful servants. He defends Ovid, 'that semeth to be moste of all poetes lascivious' by citing 'commendable and noble sentences' that can be found 'in his mooste wanton bokes'. On this basis Elyot comes down firmly against censorship of what the young should read. A man walking in a garden treads the nettles underfoot while he gathers the good herbs. So the young reader will learn to discriminate the good from the bad. Not, Elyot adds, that he would recommend teaching the 'wanton poetes' to all pupils, but nothing should be excluded from those who are healthy-minded.

In Elyot this enlightened openness exists alongside the mediaeval notion of universal order. His book opens with a standard account of the hierarchical order governing the universe. It is the preservation of degree which distinguishes creation and order from chaos. The four elements, earth, water, air and fire, of which the natural order is compounded, must keep their proper place. Man, who is fashioned of the same elements, a microcosm of the whole, must order his life accordingly. Indeed, having dealt with academic studies and various forms of education, Elyot devotes several chapters to the defence of dancing. At the cosmic, social and personal levels the hierarchically ordered dance is the true expression of that Love which must govern all things. The association of man and woman in dancing, as the two match each other in rhythm and movement, is symbolic of the institution of marriage, and the various figures of the dance can be equated with qualities such as magnanimity, constancy, honour, wisdom, and continence – and these qualities together are what constitute nobility. (It is this chapter on Dancing which T.S. Eliot quotes at length in his 'East Coker' (*Four Quartets*).)

Sir Thomas Elyot's work exemplifies the fact that at this time such literary criticism as there is tends to be a by-product of enquiry into education, just as enquiry into education tends to be ancillary to study of good government. Thus when J. E. Spingarn turns to 16th-century writers in his standard *Literary Criticism in the Renaissance* (1897), he writes: 'But the most important figure of this period is Roger Ascham.' Roger Ascham (1516–68) was, like Sir Thomas More, an intimate friend of Sir Thomas Elyot. A classical scholar and a firm Protestant who nevertheless managed to hold the post of Latin Secretary under Edward VI, Queen Mary and Queen Elizabeth, Ascham left a treatise *The Scholemaster* which was published by his widow in 1570, two years after his death. Although another treatise on education, it does not have the grand philosophical dimensions of Elyot's work. It is a book of practical advice. Its composition was provoked by a situation which appealed to Ascham's humanity and good sense. He was at court one day in December 1563 when news came that a number of scholars had run away from Eton to avoid corporal punishment. The event became a topic of conversation at dinner, and Ascham was one to protest against cruel treatment of schoolboys. On the whole his advice about educating young boys does not rise above the conventional. The most quoted of his opinions is his protest against Malory's *Morte D'Arthur*. The whole pleasure of this book, he avers, 'standeth in two speciall poyntes, in open manslaughter and bold bawdrye; In which book those be counted the noblest Knightes, that do kill most men without any quarrell, and commit fowlest aduoulteries by sutlest shiftes'.

After the first book, 'teachyng the brynging up of youth', follows the second, 'teachyng the ready way to the Latin tong', and there is a substantial section headed '*Imitatio*', abounding in reference to authors. Ascham's thesis is that 'all languages, both learned and mother tonges, be gotten, and gotten onelie by *Imitation*' and therefore 'if ye would speake as the best and wisest do, ye must be conversant, where the best and wisest are'. We are told how Italian poets follow Virgil and how Virgil follows Homer, how Cicero follows Plato and Demosthenes, and what 'proprietie in wordes, simplicitie in sentences, plainnesse and light, is comelie' for writing history. Caesar and Livy are the ideal models. Cicero is the man for eloquence, Plautus (carefully selected) and Terence for purity of idiom and neatness of expression. Such generalities abound.

There is an occasional imaginative touch. Varro's treatise on husbandry *De Re Rusticana* does not display any great depth of eloquence. Varro is like the Rye or Yarmouth fisherman bringing a catch of herring from near the shore, not needing to deploy much seamanship but doing a useful job. Sallust's style suffers from artificiality because he did not have to address the common people as Caesar and Cicero did. But the conclusion is a climactic group of truisms: that you cannot stumble on mastery of the Latin tongue by accident; that there must be natural aptitude, love of learning, diligence, and so on.

II The art of poetry

We turn from Ascham to a writer whose concern is wholly with his mother tongue, George Gascoigne (*c*.1534–77), poet and dramatist, who appended to *The Posies of George Gascoigne* (1575) 'Certayne Notes of Instruction Concerning the Making of Verse or Ryme in English'. It is indeed largely a study of English versification, explaining the system of scansion in some detail, and adding notes on rhyming, on the use of figures, on word order, and on certain stanza forms. But all this he prefaced by preliminary insistence on the need for 'fine invention'. Rolling rhythms and resonant vocabulary are not enough. There must be 'invention' which eschews description that is trite and obvious ('christal eye' and 'cherrie lippe') but fastens on 'some supernaturall cause whereby my penne might walke in the superlative degree'. Similarly love must be expressed either in 'a strange discourse of some intollerable passion', or by pleading some historical parallel, or by veiling the disquiet allegorically, or by using 'the covertest meane' possible 'to avoyde the uncomely customs of common writers'. Gascoigne regards this pursuit of imaginative novelty and indirection as the most difficult and yet the most necessary poetic need. 'I would have you stand most upon the excellencie of Invention, and sticke not to studie deeply for some fine devise. For, that beyng founde, pleasant woordes will follow well inough and fast inough.' Emphasis is frankly laid on the need for poetic 'conceits', fanciful turns of thought, and contrived evasion of the obvious.

On the subject of scansion, Gascoigne illustrates the importance of placing accents correctly by contrasting the line

I understand your meanyng by your eye

with the quite unrhythmical

Your meanyng I understand by your eye

This subject is tackled also by King James VI of Scotland in 'Ane Schort Treatise Conteining Some Reulis and Cautelis to be Observit and Eschewit in Scotts Poesie', a contribution to *The Essayes of a Prentis in the Divine Art of Poesie* printed at Edinburgh by Thomas Vautrollier (1584). The predilection for jog-trot, evident in Gascoigne, is here too. Even thumping rhythms underpinned by alliteration have their uses:

> Let all your verse be *Literall* [alliterative], as far as may be, quhatsumever kynde they be of, but speciallie *Tumbling* verse for flyting ...
> *Fetching fude for to feid it fast furth of the Farie.*

There is a warning against obvious conventionalities. You must be wary of describing your lover's beauty or opening your poem with a sunrise. Better than praising your beloved's beauty extravagantly would be to say something very restrained and then remark that 'your wittis are sa smal, and your utterance sa barren, that ye can not discryve any part of hir worthelie'. As for descriptions of the sunrise, vary the terms; Sun, Titan, Phoebus, Apollo. Perhaps what is most interesting in King James's little treatise is his final section illustrating the way rhythm and vocabulary must be adjusted to the mood the subject requires, whether lengthy narrative, brisk feats of arms, grave and lofty themes, invective, or love.

Gascoigne's work and King James's are at first sight slight in substance when compared with the massive book *The Arte of English Poesie* published anonymously in 1589 and believed to be by George Puttenham (*c.*1529–91). Puttenham was the nephew of Sir Thomas Elyot, for his father Robert Puttenham had married Elyot's sister Margery. Indeed Sir Thomas dedicated his book *Education or the Bringing up of Children* to his sister Margery Puttenham. It does not seem to have been a very effective gesture, for her elder son Richard Puttenham was convicted of rape in 1561, and when the younger brother George was rumoured to be about to be placed on the commission of the peace in 1568, the Bishop of Winchester protested in alarm that he was a man of evil life and a notorious enemy of God's truth. (When George Gascoigne himself was elected MP in 1572 there was a petition of protest from his creditors accusing him of insolvency, manslaughter and atheism as well as of being 'a common rymer and a deviser of slanderous pasquits [lampoons] against divers persons of great calling'.) (Sidney Lee, *DNB*).

The Arte of English Poesie has a kind of pedestrian thoroughness. In the first section 'Of Poets and Poesie' we learn 'How Poets were the first priests, the first prophets, the first legislators and politicians in the world', and we move through a consideration of religious poetry, didactic poetry, satirical poetry, comedy and tragedy, pastoral, historical, love poetry, poetry of triumph, poetry of lamentation, and eventually reach epitaphs. And epitaphs, Puttenham insists, must be short and not require half a day's leisure for their perusal. Otherwise there is the danger of being 'locked into the Church by the Sexten as I myself was once served reading an Epitaph in a certain cathedrale'. There is little of true critical significance, though Puttenham has the sensitivity to praise Wyatt and Surrey as 'chieftains' of a new company of 'courtly makers' who were subjected to Italian influence and greatly 'pollished our rude & homely maner of vulgar Poesie, from that it had bene before, and for that cause may justly be sayd the first reformers of our English meetre and stile'. Chaucer is praised for the 'grave and stately' metre of *Troilus and Criseyde*, whereas 'his other verses of the Canterbury Tales be but riding ryme'. Gower is a 'good and grave' moralist, but there is little more to be said for him, his vocabulary being strained, his rhyme 'wrested' and 'in his inventions small subtillitie'. Sidney is praised for his pastoral poetry 'and that other Gentleman who wrate the late shepheardes Callender'. Ralegh has a lofty, passionate vein 'for dittie and amourous *Ode*': Dyer is the man for elegy. But of course 'last in recitall but first in degree is the Queene our soveraigne Lady' whose Muse easily surmounts everything written before her time or since in all genres whatsoever.

The second book, 'Of Proportion Poetical', devotes attention to the ocular appeal of stanzas shaped like lozenges, triangles, spheres, pillars, eggs, tapers, and even what looks like an egg-timer. When Puttenham turns to metre he proves inadequate to his subject. His ear is defective. His attempts at scansion reveal metrical insensitivity. The third book, 'Of Ornament', examines figures of speech with a dogged, lifeless persistence. For instance he gives four examples of *Apostopesis*, or breaking off in mid-speech, where the interruption is provoked by fear of offence:

> He said you were, I dare not tell you plaine:
> For words once out, never returne againe.

by shame or seemly reticence:

> And did ye not come by his chamber dore?
> And tell him that: goe to, I say no more.

by anger or by the need to threaten:

> If I take you with such another cast
> I sweare by God, but let this be the last.

and finally by some unexpected external cause of interruption:

> He told me all at large; lo yonder is the man.
> Let himself tell the tale that best tell can.

Puttenham enlivens his text from time to time with anecdotes and good-humoured digression, but his poetic sensibility is very limited and he is the last man to inspire a love of poetry by opening eyes to finer points of either substance or technique.

Nevertheless his level of sensibility was a good deal higher than that of William Webbe (*fl.*1568–91), put on display in his *Discourse of English Poetry* (1586). Its aim to 'to discerne betweene good writers and badde', and 'challenge from the rude multitude of rusticall Rymers, who will be called Poets, the right practise and orderly course of true Poetry'. For Webbe the standard is classical poetry, with its quantitative metres, and he was one of those who thought they could be imposed on English verse. He pays enthusiastic tribute to those who have tried to translate Latin poetry into English on this basis. And Thomas Phaet, the translator of Virgil's *Aeneid*, is 'without doubt the best'. In evidence Webbe cites examples which make nonsense of his claim, such as lines describing Dido's love for Aeneas in book IV:

> By this time perced sat the Queen so sore with love's desire,
> Her wound in every vayne she feedes, she fryes in secrete fire.
> The manhood of the man full oft, full oft his famous lyne
> She doth revolve, and from her thought his face cannot untwyne.

III The defence of poetry

In the late 1570s and 1580s a controversy arose about whether poetry, and more especially drama, had become a vehicle of moral degradation. Stephen Gosson (1554–1624) was in the forefront of a Puritan assault upon the contemporary theatre. In 1579 he published *The Schoole of Abuse, Conteining a pleasaunt invective against Poets, Pipers, Plaiers, Jesters and suchlike Catterpillers of a Commonwelth* ... Gosson argues that the theatre has become a hunting-ground for prostitutes and a place where 'every wanton and his paramour, every man and his mistress, every John and his Joan, every knave and his quean' first meet and make their assignations. This is scarcely a concern of literary criticism, but in pamphlets contributed to the ensuing controversy, Gosson attacks tragedies for their criminal subject matter, and comedies because their groundwork is 'love, cozenage, flattery, bawdry, sly conveyance of whoredom' and their characters are 'cooks, queans, knaves, bawds, parasites' and the like. (*Plays Confuted in five Actions*, 1582).

The first reply to Gosson's *Schoole of Abuse* came from Thomas Lodge (1558–1625) in *Defence of Poetry* (1579), an irritable outburst, abounding in lively invective. Lodge insists that pointing to wantonness and immorality in certain poets proves nothing.

> I reson not that al poets are holy, but I affirm that poetry is a heavenly gift, a perfit gift, then which I know not greater pleasure.

By some quirk of ignorance or bad taste, or both, Gosson dedicated *The Schoole of Abuse* to Sir Philip Sidney (1554–86).

This is what Edmund Spenser (*c*.1552–99) had to say in a letter to Gabriel Harvey (*c*.1550–1631) in October 1579:

> Newe Bookes I heare of none, but only of one, that writing a certaine Booke, called THE SCHOOLE OF ABUSE, and dedicating it to Maister SIDNEY, was for hys labour scorned, if at leaste it be in the goodnesse of that nature to scorne.

Indeed Gosson's importance in English literature derives entirely from the fact that his book is believed to have provoked Sir Philip Sidney to write his *Defence of Poesie* or *Apologie for Poetrie* (both titles were used), published in 1595 but probably written soon after Gosson's book.

To turn to Sidney's work from the works previously dealt with in this chapter is to enter a different world. Sidney has intellectual energy and stylistic vitality. Ideas flow from his pen. Apt illustrations, imaginative turns of thought and neat dialectical thrusts crowd his pages. And the prose, largely free of arid modish turgidities and superfluous contrivances, carriers the reader eagerly forward. Sidney speaks of the need to defend 'poore Poetry, which from almost the highest estimation of learning is fallen to be the laughing-stock of children'. It is sheer ingratitude for the learned to disparage poetry when poets were the first purveyors of knowledge, 'their Fathers in learning'. Philosophers such as Plato and historians such as Herodotus exploited the imaginative techniques of the poet as their 'passport' to the public ear. For the Romans the poet (*vates*) was a 'prophet', a role to be taken seriously if one reflects on the psalms of David. For the Greeks the poet was a 'maker'. And indeed the poet is not tied in subjection to what the world of Nature supplies, but outdoes what Nature does in what his imagination creates. Made by the Heavenly Maker in his own likeness, man shows his true status best when 'with the force of a divine breath' he brings forth things surpassing what is to be found in Nature.

Sidney then turns to Aristotle's definition. 'Poesie therefore is an arte of imitation, for so *Aristotle* termeth it in his word *Mimesis*, that is to say, a representing, counterfetting, or figuring foorth: to speak metaphorically, a speaking picture: with this end, to teach and delight.' (In fact this goes beyond

Aristotle and derives from Horace.) There are three kinds of poetry, religious, like the Psalms; philosophical (by which Sidney means 'instructive', citing Virgil's *Georgics* as natural philosophy); and 'right poets' who are not, like the 'philosophical' poets bound by the subject matter they have to convey. Sidney adds that 'it is not riming and versing that maketh a Poet'; it is 'fayning notable images of vertues, vices, or what els, with that delightfull teaching, which must be the right describing note to know a Poet by'.

The end of all learning is to draw us to as high a perfection as our degenerate souls are capable of. Since the end of all earthly learning is virtuous action, Sydney considers what intellectual pursuits can challenge poetry in serving this end. The chief rivals to the poet are the philosopher and the historian. The former teaches by precept without example, the latter by example without precept. Only the poet supplies both. He blends the universal with the particular. Sidney cites instances of heroic conduct in Homer and Virgil as well as the parables of Christ to corroborate his case that the imaginative range of the poet makes him the better teacher. Sidney tussles a good deal with the historian's servitude to fact as a limitation on effective moral teaching. Not being 'captivated to the truth of a foolish world', the poet can ensure that virtue is rewarded and vice punished. Moreover, the poet is able to bring to his instructive task the power to move, which is a far more effective means of persuasion than cold instruction. For the poet comes to you with what delights and entrances – 'with a tale which holdeth children from play, and old men from the chimney corner'. This sensitive awareness of the imaginative power of poetry is combined in Sidney with the basic notion that poetry's true function is 'the winning of the mind from wickedness to vertue'. It is impossible to read Sidney without being made aware of how persistent was the disquieting apprehension, dating back to Plato, that it was the falsity of poetry that made it suspect. After defending various genres of poetry against depreciative judgments, Sidney tackles this matter head-on. Far from being a principal liar, the poet is of all writers under the sun the least a liar. Astronomers and physicians make mistakes. Historians affirm so much that is uncheckable that they cannot possibly avoid lying at times. But the poet 'never affirmeth'. He never tries to trick you into believing that what he writes is true.

When Sidney comes to the charge that poetry corrupts by encouraging wanton sinfulness and lustful love, he demolishes it with a crisp rejoinder. Even if it were granted that many poets' works are so degraded, you would not have proved that poetry corrupts men; only that men corrupt poetry. All knowledge, all things can be well-used or ill-used. That which does most damage when ill-used is precisely what does most good when properly used. 'With a sword thou maist kill thy Father, and with a sword thou maist defend thy Prince and Country.' Then, turning to Plato's banishment of poets from his ideal realm, Sidney points out that Plato condemned the poets of his age for disparaging the gods by their fictions. Plato, in short, was only determined to 'drive out those wrong opinions of the Deitie (whereof now, without further law, Christianity hath taken away all the hurtfull beliefe) perchance (as he thought) nourished by the then-esteemed Poets'.

Having completed his case, Sidney makes some observations on English poets, praising especially Chaucer's *Troilus and Criseyde*, Surrey's lyrics, and Spenser's *Shepherd's Calendar*. He shows less indulgence to drama. Apart from *Gorboduc* he can find no tragedies to praise. He ridicules the neglect of the unities of place and time in contemporary drama, and objects to the mixing of tragic and comic material, 'mingling Kings and Clownes' and allowing the latter to interfere indecently in 'maiesticall matters', and conveying a mood proper to neither tragedy nor comedy. On contemporary lyrics and sonnets he complains of a lack of true passion in love poetry, and on the other hand of the artifices by which true Eloquence is 'apparelled, or rather disguised, in a Curtizan-like painted affectation'. Indeed Sidney reminds himself that the use of far-fetched and outrageous words defaces contemporary prose as much as contemporary poetry.

Sidney writes with the authority of the practised poet. There is a grand unaffectedness in the way he lays about him. It is the fault of poet-apes, not of poets, that poetry is not properly esteemed in England. His final peroration in praise of the power of poetry to infect with civility and virtue, to contain and convey great mysteries, to be the vehicle of divine inspiration, and to immortalise, has the air of a flourish by a man who knows that he is right and has no need of further self-justification.

Sidney was not of course an isolated apologist in European terms. It has been agreed that his account of the lofty role of poetry in the history of culture probably derives from Antonio Minturno's *De Poeta* (1559), one of a series of sixteenth-century books which retrod critical ground covered by Aristotle and Horace. A more evident indebtedness still is that to the French scholar, Julius Caesar Scaliger (1485-1558), the author of *Poetics* (1570) whose commentaries on classical writers exercised an enormous influence. Scaliger, as J. E. Spingarn writes, in *A History of Literary Criticism in the Renaissance*, 'was the first to regard Aristotle as the perpetual lawgiver of poetry'. He transmitted to later ages an excessively rigidified version of 'Aristotelian' regulations.

Another English defender of poetry who was indebted to Scaliger, Sir John Harington (*c*.1561–1612), prefixed 'A Brief Apology for Poetry' to his translation of Ariosto's *Orlando Furioso* published in 1591. The concession that poetry has been under attack recurs, Harington replying as Sidney replied to the charge that poetry is 'a nurse of lies ... and an inticer to wantonness'. He then illustrates the various levels of signification that poetry allows for: historical meaning, moral meaning, and allegorical meaning. And a distinction is drawn between natural allegory, heavenly allegory, and theological allegory. Plato may have faulted the poets of his time, but he himself used the 'principall part of Poetrie, which is fiction and imitation'. Subject having been dealt with, verse as a medium is defended for its memorability, for its forcefulness of expression, and for the 'pleasure and sweetnesse to the eare'. Harington cites Scaliger's praise of Virgil in insisting that 'a good Heroicall Poeme may make a man both wiser and honester'. Dante proves the point. When he wandered off the right way, it was Virgil who first made him 'look into himselfe and reclaim himselfe'.

Harington's translation of the *Orlando Furioso* was itself a landmark in being the first English version of the poem as a whole. Ludovic Ariosto (1475–1535) published *Orlando Furioso* in 1532. The poem centres on the noble knight Orlando – the heroic 'Roland' in the cycle of stories concerned with Charlemagne. Christian and Saracen are at war, and Orlando is driven mad by loss of his beloved Angelica. This is but one theme in a complex tangle of adventures and vicissitudes in battle and in love. The work established the pattern of the 'romantic epic', as opposed to the more formal and disciplined classical epic. Spenser was much indebted to it in writing the *Faerie Queene*, as his eighteenth-century critical advocates were to recognise.

IV Classical or native versification

One of the works which Sidney singled out for praise in his *Apology* was Spenser's *Shepheardes Calender* (1579). Although the Calendar exploits classical forms and pastoral artifice, an English ancestry was claimed for it in the Prefatory address by Spenser's Cambridge friend, Edward Kirke (1553–1613). The 'new Poet' is compared to Chaucer, and he is especially praised for his restoration of archaisms: 'that he hath laboured to restore, as to theyr rightfull heritage such good and naturall English words, as have been long time out of use and almost cleane disherited'.

The business of escaping the wrong kind of Latin influence on vernacular poetry was a taxing one. Conservative influences tried to fasten the rules of classical quantitative metre on to English verse. Even intelligent scholars seem to have been unable to see the total inapplicability to English of the fact that a Latin syllable ending in two consonants must be accounted 'long'. Clearly the accentual difference between the same syllable in 'enter' and 'moment', whether the words are used in verse or prose, makes nonsense of any attempt to apply the classical metrical system to English. There was some tussling with this problem in the published letters exchanged between Spenser and the Cambridge scholar Gabriel Harvey (*c.*1550–1631): *Three Proper and witty familiar letters* (1580) and *Two other very commendable letters* (1580). A movement had started under the impetus of Thomas Drant (d.1578), translator of Horace, to impose the rules of classical prosody on English verse. Thus the middle syllable of 'carp*enter*' would be reckoned 'long' because it ends with two consonants. Harvey rejects this, pointing out that the second syllable of 'merch*aund*ise', the third syllable of 'coven*aunt*eth' and the fourth syllable of 'appurten*aunc*es' must all be 'short' or weak in English. 'You may perceive by the *Premisses* (which very worde I would have you note by the waye to) the Latin is no rule for us.' Another tenet of the extreme supporters of classical prosody was hostility to rhyme, and this Harvey shared.

The question of the proper relationship of vernacular poetry to classical models was not an English one alone. The French poet Joachim du Bellay (1522–61) published his *Défense et illustration de la langue française* (1549) as spokesman for a group of poets, la Pléiade, including Ronsard, who believed that the French language was appropriate for handling any themes, however lofty. To this extent la Pléiade were opposed to excessive humanist idolatry of the classics. Nevertheless they accepted the classics as fit models and indeed believed that current French vocabulary required to be enriched by borrowings from Greek and Latin. They also recommended rhymeless verse. The dependence on the classics and the use of learned diction and idiom were thus encouraged only in the cause of nurturing a true vernacular literature. The main contentions were that the French language could attain perfection, but the route to perfection lay through imitation of Greek and Latin. Du Bellay's *Défence* was modelled on Dante's *De Vulgare Eloquentia* which was issued in Italian in 1529.

The question of the relative quality of Greek and Latin poetry may seem a remote issue compared to the more immediate question of the significance of the classics in general as models for English verse. But George Chapman (*c.*1559–1634), in presenting the second instalment of his translation of Homer's *Iliad* to the public as *Achilles Shield* (1578), let himself go in a preliminary address to the Reader on those who exalt Virgil way above Homer. In particular he lambasts 'soule-blind Scalliger' and his 'impotent braine', his 'exploded filcheries' ... 'so grossly illiterate' for his senseless disparagement of Homer:

the majestie he enthrones and the spirit he infuseth into the scope of his worke so farre outshining *Virgill*, that his skirmishes are but meere scramblings of boyes to *Homers*; the silken body of *Virgils* muse curiously drest in gilt and embrodered silver, but *Homers* in plaine massie and unvalued gold...

Perhaps nothing has been more fruitless in the history of literary criticism in England than the Elizabethan controversy about classical metres in English. And nothing has been more remarkable than the degree of metrical clumsiness sometimes displayed by writers attempting to scan English verse in terms of classical quantitative metres. Thomas Campion (1567–1620), skilled as both poet and musician, certainly could not be accused of having an insensitive ear. Yet his *Observations in the Art of English Poesie* (1602) show a deep-seated humanist bias against the Middle Ages. Learning declined with the Roman Empire, he tells us. Until Erasmus and Sir Thomas More came along to redeem the Latin tongue, learning was pitifully deformed 'in the hands of illiterate Monks and Friers'. Campion sees the perfections of classical verse as an integral aspect of the fact that 'the World is made by Simmetry and proportion'. And the 'unaptness of our toongs and the difficultie of imitation dishartens us' from emulating the Greeks and Romans. Campion protests that 'the facilities and popularitie of Rime creates as many Poets as a hot summer flies'. The case against rhyme is basically that subtly managed versification and harmonious cadences give such satisfaction that the addition of rhyme can only cheapen the total effect with a touch of absurdity.

Campion provoked his fellow-poet Samuel Daniel (1563–1619) to write his *Defence of Rhyme* (*c*.1603). Custom and nature are on the side of rhyme, he argues, 'Custom that is before all Law, Nature that is above all Arte'. Rhyme supplies an added excellence to metre. It is not an impediment to a poet's invention or conceit, but gives him wings to carry him 'to a far happier flight'. Daniel cites the sonnet as evidence of how formal limits operate without tyranny. 'Is it not most delightfull to see much excellentlie ordred in a small roome?' Indeed Daniel argues that the Greeks and Romans

can be outclassed in arrangement of matter, planting of
sentences, and neat conclusive cadences.

> Me thinks we should not so soone yeeld our consents captive to the
> authoritie of Antiquitie, unlesse we saw more reason; all our under-
> standings are not to be built by the square of Greece and Italie.

Daniel had the sense to protest against Campion's underestimate of the Middle Ages:

> Let us go no further than looke upon the wonderful Architecture of
> this state of *England*, and see whether they were deformed times that
> could give it such a forme.

We must build on our own past. All the classicist innovators
have done is to supply us with 'forraine Titles' for the metres
we already have. It is not rhyme, but foolish controversy,
that is discrediting poets.

V Bacon and Jonson

An erudite voice, from outside the field of technical controversy, was heard when Francis Bacon (1561–1626) wrote
his ambitious work *The Advancement of Learning* (1603 and
1605). It is in the second book that Bacon makes a systematic
survey of the various branches of learning. He argues that the
three parts of man's understanding are memory, imagination, and reason. History relates to his memory, poetry to his
imagination, and philosophy to his reason. Similarly theology
consists of history, parables (or poetry) and doctrine. Since
the imagination is not 'tied to the laws of matter', poetry has
such licence that it may 'at pleasure join that which Nature
hath severed, and sever that which Nature hath joined'. In
respect of style, Poetry is a technical matter belonging to 'arts
of speech'. In respect of substance, poetry is 'FEIGNED
HISTORY', which can be presented either in prose or in
verse. The events of true history cannot satisfy the human
mind. Poetry feigns acts and events that are 'greater and
more heroical' than history can supply, and distributes
reward and retribution to virtue and vice more justly than

life itself, and more in accordance with divine Providence. Poetry is judged to have 'some participation of divineness' because of the way it exalts and fulfils the aspirations of the mind, while 'reason doth buckle and bow the mind unto the nature of things'.

Poetry can be conveniently divided into that which is Narrative, a direct imitation of History, that which is Representative, or a visible presentation in dramatic form, and that which is Allusive or Parabolical, where narrative is directed to express some special message. And parabolical poetry may either convey wise instruction vividly as Aesop's Fables do, or may veil and obscure 'the secrets and mysteries of religion, policy, or philosophy'. Bacon says tribute to poets as surpassing philosophers in 'the expressing of affections, passions, corruptions, and customs' and being little inferior to orators in 'wit and eloquence'.

It is refreshing to turn from Bacon's detached analysis to the fervour of a writer to whom feigned history was not just a concept but meat and drink, the stuff of daily toil and heartbeat, Ben Jonson (1572–1637). Jonson, a poet and dramatist of great fertility, was also a scholarly, magisterial, and combative person, and it was in his blood to theorise about his trade. Such theorising is scattered about his work. There is a celebrated passage in the Prologue to *Every Man Out of His Humour* (1600) in which the doctrine of the comedy of humours is summed up. It is explained that the term 'humour' can be applied metaphorically to a person's general disposition:

> As when some one peculiar quality
> Doth so possess a man, that it doth draw
> All his affects, his spirits, and his powers,
> In their confluctions, all to run one way,
> This may be truly said to be a humour.

The theory of the comedy of humours has an ostensibly mediaeval base, but Jonson's model was the classical Roman comedy. He was a neoclassicist soaked in the literary traditions of the past, yet so alive to the contemporary world that in his comedies the portrayal of Elizabethan life, vulgar, boisterous and sourly satirical, throbs with vitality. The panoramic display of knavery and pretension, vanity and eccentricity, is disciplined by the dual control of the moral thrust and the grip of the plot. To have a theory of characterisation was as natural to Jonson as to have a pen to write with. In the Preface to his tragedy *Sejanus* (1605) he defends himself against the charge that he has not followed the strictest order of the ancients in such matters as the unity of time and the use of the Chorus, but claims that he has fulfilled the other obligations of a Tragic writer in respect of 'truth of Argument, dignity of Persons, gravity and height of Elocution, fullness and frequency of Sentence'.

The intellectual *gravitas* with which Jonson defends his work is only matched by the vituperative passion with which he lambastes those who bring disrepute on the poet and on poetry. In the Dedicatory Epistle to *Volpone* (1607) he pours scorn on contemporary peddlers of profanity and ribaldry who play to the gallery, and protests that his own satire has never been destructive of social order or public reputations. He has assaulted only mimicks, cheaters, bawds and buffoons, people deserving of censure, and only then without clear personal identification. The moral force of Jonson's outrage against 'the too-much licence of *Poetasters* in this time' depends on his rigorous conception of the poet's responsibility:

> For if men will impartially, and not a-squint, look toward the offices and function of a *Poet*, they will easily conclude to themselves the impossibility, of any man's being the good *Poet*, without first being a good *Man*.

Jonson left behind him a commonplace book *Timber, or Discoveries* written between 1620 and 1635. Scholars have tracked down the sources of about four-fifths of the material, and they include Cicero and Quintilian, the two Senecas, and recent writers such as Erasmus, Machiavelli, and Bacon. But what Jonson took and adapted and translated was presumably what he wanted to make his own. And the personal stamp can be recognised. The voice is that of abounding confidence, of perspicuity and commonsense:

The true Artificer will not run away from Nature, as he were afraid of her, or depart from life and the likeness of Truth, but speak to the capacity of his hearers.

Jonson scorns the flight from humanity which occurs when Tamberlaines strut and vociferate, though he allows that the restrained writer, who scorns such cheapness, may have to wait for another age for his wiser, subtler, sturdier, and ultimately more winning qualities to be appreciated.

There is an engaging forthrightness about Jonson's dicta. 'For rules are ever of less force and value than experiments,' he avers, 'but Arts and Precepts avail nothing, except Nature be beneficial and aiding.' He always speaks too with the voice of authority and does not wrap around his proclamations with qualifications:

To judge of Poets is only the faculty of Poets; and not of all Poets, but the best.

This was a fashionable seventeenth-century notion. Going back to Cicero and to Pliny, who averred that only the artist was equipped to judge the work of the painter and the sculptor, it was to surface plainly in Pope's *Essay on Criticism* ('Let such teach others who themselves excel') and to be demolished by Warton.

But many of Jonson's evaluations show a moderation which counter-balances his more oracular ordinances:

Nothing is more ridiculous than to make an Author a *Dictator*, as the schools have done *Aristotle*. The damage is infinite knowledge receives by it.

The advice on writing smacks of the experienced practitioner:

As we should take care that our style in writing be neither dry nor empty, we should look again it be not winding, or wanton with far-fetched descriptions: Either is a vice.

The advice to the reader is to begin with the 'openest and clearest' writers – Livy before Sallust, Sidney before Donne.

Jonson was prepared to do justice to his contemporaries. Sidney and Hooker in their diverse ways 'grew great masters of wit and language', men 'in whom vigour of invention and strength of judgment met'. And Jonson defended himself against any charge of malevolence over the celebrated reply he gave to a Player who praised Shakespeare because he never blotted out a line: 'My answer hath been, would he had blotted a thousand!' 'I loved the man, and do honour his memory on this side idolatry,' he added. And after Shakespeare's death he paid a notable verse tribute to him which stinted no praise: 'He was not of an age, but for all time.'

The birth of a literary offspring with so expansive a future before it as Shakespearean criticism perhaps merits a footnote. Shakespeare's reputation was well established by the time Jonson paid his tribute. In 1598 Francis Meres (1565-1647) published his *Palladis Tamia: Wit's Treasury*, an anthology of wise sayings, which included a *Comparative Discourse of our English poets with the Greeke, Latine, and Italian poets*. English poets, from Chaucer onwards, are considered in a series of artificially forced parallels with classical and Italian poets which do not say much for Meres as a critic. Shakespeare, however, is lauded as our best dramatist for both comedy and tragedy, matching Plautus and Seneca. Moreover, 'the sweete wittie soule of *Ovid* lives in mellifluous and hony-tongued *Shakespeare*, witnes his *Venus* and *Adonis*, his *Lucrece*, his sugred Sonnets among his private friends'.

The note of 'sweetness' was to re-echo in assessments of Shakespeare, and not just in reference to the poems. The reader may recall Milton's celebrated lines in 'L'Allegro' (written about 1630):

> Then to the well-trod stage anon,
> If Jonson's learned sock be on,
> Or sweetest Shakespeare fancy's child
> Warble his native woodnotes wild.

The contrast between Shakespeare and Jonson was also to become a recurring theme in critical comment. In making some notes about Shakespeare in his *Worthies of England* (1662), the historian Thomas Fuller (1608-61) was to see

Shakespeare as exemplifying that a poet is born and not made, and to describe conversational confrontations between the learned Jonson and the quick-witted Shakespeare in terms of encounters between a solid, heavily-built Spanish galleon and a less bulky but more agile English man-of-war.

4
The Seventeenth Century: Peacham to Dryden

In turning to the early seventeenth century we do not immediately take leave of the Renaissance. Some ninety years after the publication of Sir Thomas Elyot's *The Governour*, Henry Peacham (*c*.1578–*c*.1642) wrote a seventeenth-century version of the handbook for the governing class, *The Compleat Gentleman* (1622). 1622 was the year in which the architect Inigo Jones (1573–1652) completed the magnificent banqueting hall in Whitehall, and its opening was marked by the production of Ben Jonson's *The Masque of Augures*. Jones was influenced by the Italian Palladian style and is credited with having brought pure Renaissance architecture to England. The masque itself flourished increasingly in the later years of Queen Elizabeth and in the reigns of James I and Charles I. It gave free rein to the Renaissance taste for splendour. In the lavishness of its scenic display and the extravagance of its stage mechanisms, it epitomises the courtly opulence which the Commonwealth was to sweep away. And for practitioners such as Ben Jonson, the comprehensive artistic splendours of the masque conveyed an image of the eternal in a transient world. Jones and Jonson were two great artists inspired in their diverse ways by the Renaissance ideal of the Complete Man. There was a philosophical rift in the background when the collaboration of the two in the making of masques exploded into angry rivalry. Jonson poured scorn on the pretentious claim of the mechanical engineer to supplant in preeminence the poet, the true creator of the vision. It was a subversion of degree in the world of art when the mythic sovereignty of the poet was challenged.

English minds were soon to be preoccupied with matters other than these, for whatever else may be said of the mid-century upheavals, they did not encourage quiet reflection on works of literature such as we are concerned with. The Civil War of 1642–51, the execution of Charles I in 1649, the years of Commonwealth government and the Protectorate of Cromwell together represent a chasm so far as the history of literature is concerned. The Restoration of Charles II in 1660 brings a new literary age. No doubt for literary minds of the Restoration period, the intervening upheavals distanced the Elizabethan and Jacobean age and sharpened its identity. They might regard its literature enthusiastically or disapprovingly, but they could not escape the fact that it was essentially native, essentially English. The King, his court, and many royalist sympathisers had spent years in France. The culture and taste of the court of Louis XIV and the Paris of the mid-century left many English literary figures with rival criteria to those represented by native Elizabethan and Jacobean literature. The great dramatist Pierre Corneille (1606–84) was in full spate in the 1640s to 1660s, turning out grandiose rhetorical tragedies in which the heroic temperament is tested in situations of colliding demands, emotional and ethical. His highly stylised form evaded direct representation of action, and represented in some respects the antithesis of the boisterous Elizabethan drama with its stage battles and violent deaths. The contrast was such that it encouraged those who wished to high-light qualities of polish and sophistication over against native primitivism and crudity. And it so happened, as we shall see, that the period of Restoration productiveness in England was a period when the French were leading the way in literary criticism. Nicolas Boileau (1636–1711) was an exponent of a classicism which set the highest value on the role of reason in poetry, and his book *L'art poétique* (1674) won him a European reputation in the 'Age of Reason'.

In the course of the seventeenth century, the concerns of those who passed judgment on literature varied enormously. In the early decades, as theological controversy gathered force in public life, we naturally find anxiety to justify poetry by its educative usefulness. We hear claims for the poet as philosopher and sage which seem to anticipate Shelley. An exalted notion of the Christian poet is expounded by Reynolds and Milton, and touched on less persuasively by Davenant and Cowley. Then the respective roles of fancy and of reason are disputed. The respective authority of the ancients, of the French, and of the Elizabethans is brought into question. So is the respective value of stylistic plainness or of ornament, of rhyme or of blank verse, of the couplet or of the ode. Should there be rules or no rules? Should comedy be mixed with tragedy? Is the poet's duty to instruct or to delight?

Most of the significant issues receive their fullest treatment at the hand of Dryden. And it is impossible to read Dryden as a critic without a response of personal warmth – except when he begins to lay down the law as self-conscious spokesman for a cultural élite with an endowment of social graces and cultural refinements which those who lived in the unpolished days of Shakespeare could not be expected to possess.

I The gentleman and the Christian

Peacham's *The Compleat Gentleman* considers many activities appropriate to the cultivated country gentleman, including travel, fishing, and heraldry. Chapter 10, *Of Poetrie*, goes over ground covered by Puttenham and Scaliger, and, like so many writers of the period, Peacham finds it necessary to warn his readers against being infected with the common view in which poetry 'seemeth fallen from the highest Stage of Honour to the lowest staire of disgrace'. After an attack on aristocratic philistinism, Peacham analyses Virgil's qualities in terms of *Prudence, Efficacy, Sweetness,* and *Variety. Prudence* is the blend of learning and good judgment which makes for appropriate placing and relationship of events and style. *Efficacy* is the power to describe things vividly and imaginatively. *Sweetness* is the smoothness of versification which has spice and richness to ingratiate itself winningly with the reader. *Variety* is sheer imaginative and verbal range which makes every encounter in battle different from the others.

When Peacham turns to poets nearer home he deals first with those such as the Scot, George Buchanan (1506–82) and

Thomas More (1478–1535) who wrote in Latin. (Buchanan's *De Sphaera* advertised the Ptolemaic as opposed to the Copernican system.) A final brief survey of English poets gives Chaucer precedence. The antique style may put the reader off, but under its bitter and rough rind 'lyeth a delicate kernell of conceit and sweete invention'.

> What Examples, Similitudes, Times, Places, and above all Persons with their speeches and attributes, doe, as in his *Canterburie-tales*, like those threds of gold the rich *Arras*, beautifie his work quite thorough!

Gower's verses, however, are 'poore and plaine, yet full of good and grave Moralitie'. Then, after putting his foot in it by attributing 'that bitter Satyre of *Piers Plowman*' to Lydgate, Peacham allows his survey to degenerate into a list of names. (The error seemingly results from mis-reading a sentence of Puttenham's.) 'Thus much of Poetrie.'

As literary criticism this must be accounted ham-fisted stuff. By contrast the same decade saw the publication of a lively verse survey of English poets, *Epistle to Henry Reynolds, Esquire, Of Poets and Poesie* (1627), by Michael Drayton (1563–1631). We hear again the voice of the professional with its authority and perspicuity. Chaucer is acclaimed as the first to enrich English with poetry, to ransack the treasures of the Muses, work the mine of knowledge, refine it and turn it into valuable current coinage. He made the English language do as much as it was then capable of. Gower receives only a polite bow before Drayton moves on to recent times to praise Surrey and Wyatt for the 'many dainty passages of wit' in their songs and sonnets. Gascoigne and Churchyard are debunked. They were lucky to die when they did and be buried before their works were.

> Grave morall *Spenser* after these came on,
> Than whom I am perswaded there was none
> Since the blind *Bard* his *Iliads* up did make,
> Fitter a taste like that to undertake ...

Thus Spenser is praised for the richness of his invention and the excellence of his 'high knowledge'. And Drayton shows equal discernment in praising Sidney for showing how

English could go hand in hand with Greek and Latin in prose, and eschew extravagances and affectations.

These are the judgments of a sensitive fellow-practitioner, but perhaps the most perceptive of Drayton's estimates is that of Marlowe:

> Next *Marlow*, bathed in the *Thespian* springs,
> Had in him those brave translunary things
> That the first Poets had, his raptures were
> All ayr and fire, which made his verses cleare...
> For that fine madnes still he did retaine
> Which rightly should possesse a Poets braine.

So Drayton takes stock, giving their due to Shakespeare (for his 'strong conception'), to Jonson (for his learning), and to Chapman (for giving new life to Homer in English), while at the same time judging Daniel too prosaic.

Henry Reynolds (*fl.*1627–33), the friend to whom Drayton's epistle is addressed, was a scholar with a different mission. His *Mythomystes, Wherein a Short Survey is taken of the nature and value of true Poesie, and depth of the Ancients above our Moderne Poets* (1632) is little concerned with what English poets may have done but rather almost exclusively with what they failed to do. We live in a time when 'the world is decrepit', the soul of the universe is bedridden and near to death, for we have lost all knowledge of the 'Truth of things'. So, after a few sentences of commendation for Chaucer, for 'the generous and ingenious Sidney', and for 'the learned Spenser', and rather grudging mentions of Daniel's *Civil Wars* and Drayton's *Polyolbion*, Reynolds is rather dismissive of recent 'pretenders to Poesy'.

His main thesis is that the 'never-enough honoured Auncients' were not just Poets but 'Prophets and Privy-counsellors of the Gods... or sounes of the Gods'. The disparity between modern 'mountibanke Rimers' and these exalted seers is analysed under three heads. In the first place, the ancient poets aspired to contemplation of the 'Beauty of Supernall and Intellectuall thinges'. They attained a rapture of spirit which blinded them to 'all things of triviall and inferiour condition'. Modern poets by contrast scorn disinterested study and fawn flatteringly on the great and wealthy. In the second place, modern poets lay all their cards on the table. They have nothing to hide or to veil, no understanding of mysteries so profound and meanings so precious that they must be protected from the vulgar eye. The story of Orpheus and Eurydice tells how Truth was recovered from the darkness of barbarism but lost again on the way to upper earth. It remains lost to us because we do not have that '*Art* of Numbers that should unlocke and explane his Mysticall meanings to us'. Allegorical-mystical interpretation can discover that the 'full and entire knowledge of all wisdome, both divine and humane, is included in the five bookes of the *Mosaicke* law'. By contrast modern poets (and Reynolds grants a few exceptions in the case of prose-writers) possess no such mysteries as would be worth concealing.

In the third place, modern poets are totally ignorant of 'the mysteries and hidden properties of Nature'. We have philosophers who explore these matters, performing the true function of poets, while poets are peddlers of trivia more appropriate to plain prose. Fallen man lives in a mist, blind and benighted. His duty is to refine and advance his rational 'part' in the effort to regain his 'lost felicity'. The ancient poets are valued for their openness to mystical-allegorical interpretation. And the Christian is enjoined by St Paul to seek the evidence of the 'invisible things' of God in the things he has made. For Reynolds classical myth, the material of classical literature, incoherent and immoral as it may be on the literal level, on the allegorical level is a treasure-house of knowledge of the nature of things. He is passionately scornful of those who would write off this vast literary inheritance as a legacy of old wives' tales. He has a sacramental sense of the human duty to explore the world and its mysteries as a 'book' of divine revelation like the Scriptures, whereby we can more properly fit ourselves for the 'land of our eternall Heritage and Beatitude Hereafter'.

Some ten years after Reynolds's essay, John Milton (1608–74), in his tractate *Of Education* (1644), recapitulated Reynolds's doctrine of the combined intellectual, moral, and spiritual function of learning in relation to fallen mankind:

The end, then, of learning is, to repair the ruins of our first parents by regaining to know God aright, and out of that knowledge to love him, to imitate him, to be like him, as we may the nearest, by possessing our souls of true virtue, which, being united to the heavenly grace of faith, makes up the highest perfection.

What the transcendental approach to the function of poetry and the vocation of the poet meant for Milton personally, he explained in *The Reason of Church Government Urg'd Against Prelaty* (1641). He chose to write in his native tongue 'to be an interpreter & relater of the best and sagest things among mine own Citizens throughout this Iland in the mother dialect'. He wanted to do for his own country what the greatest writers of Greece, Rome, Italy, and the Hebrews had done for theirs. Milton goes on to make a covenant with his reader to spend some years in fulfilling his poetic vocation. It is a question first of devout prayer to the Holy Spirit 'who can enrich with all utterance and knowledge'. It is then a matter of 'industrious and select reading, steady observation, insight into all seemly and generous arts and affairs'. And prose-pamphleteering such as he is now engaged upon is a personally unwelcome interruption of this great work.

A year later in another pamphlet in the controversy about episcopacy, *Apology for Smectymnuus* (1642), Milton has a few autobiographical reflections on his poetic enthusiasms and tells how he learned to admire the art of certain poets and at the same time to deplore their characters. And he comes to Ben Jonson's conclusion that a man who wants to write well and worthily 'ought himself to be a True Poem; that is, a composition and pattern of the best and honourablest things; not presuming to sing high praises of heroick men or famous Cities, unless he have in himself the experience and the practice of all that which is praise-worthy'. This lofty concept of the poet's role is clearly more relevant to the production of an epic such as *Paradise Lost* than to the throwing off of lyrics or satires to answer the moods of the moment. And we can understand why in the tractate on *Education* Milton advised that the young should study the 'sublime art' deriving from Aristotle, distinguishing the laws of true Epic, Dramatic, and Lyric poetry. For this training, he assures us, would make the young 'soon perceive what despicable creatures our common rimers and playwrites be, and shew them what Religious, what glorious and magnificent use might be made of Poetry, both in divine and humane things'.

The references to poetry and to poets scattered over Milton's prose works are of a philosophical character. A more technical issue is raised in his Preface to *Paradise Lost* (1668), where he defends his use of blank verse. Looking back, we are inclined to take the use of blank verse for granted in serious poems of epic proportions, having Wordsworth and Tennyson and many others in mind. But, with Chaucer and Gower to look back to, a seventeenth-century writer might more naturally be on the defensive in eschewing rhyme. Milton is rightly impatient with those who use rhyme 'to set off wretched matter and lame Meeter', and notes that the best English tragedies are written in blank verse. For Milton what matters is:

> apt Numbers, fit quantity of Syllables, and the sense variously drawn out from one Verse into another, not in the jingling sound of like endings...

The verse of *Paradise Lost* is indeed built on principles totally antithetical to the use of rhyme. For rhyme gives emphatic pressure to the last words or syllables of the lines. Milton's poetic technique exploits a system of keywords, which are echoed and re-echoed, with subtle intensifications or changes of connotation, so as to create a pattern of music and meaning throughout the poem. And the placing a keywords (e.g. 'guile', 'fraud', 'Author', 'adorned') at various points along the line produces a flexible music which rhyme would utterly destroy. It is this significant echoing of words and phrases which determines the poetic architecture.

Milton's one other significant preface in this connection is that to *Samson Agonistes* (1671), where he finds it desirable to 'vindicate Tragedy from the small esteem, or rather infamy, which in the account of many it undergoes at this day'. The reason for the poor current reputation of tragedy is the popular error of mixing the comic with the tragic, and the absurdity of introducing 'trivial and vulgar persons'. Milton makes clear that in plot and design he is working in the tradition of the great Greek tragedians, and observing the unities.

II Some Royalist critics

Milton's prefaces to *Paradise Lost* and *Samson Agonistes* were but brief explanatory notes. By contrast Sir William Davenant (1605–88), the dramatist said by some to be Shakespeare's illegitimate son, wrote a substantial Preface to his 'Heroick Poem', *Gondibert* (1650), though the work was far from complete. Few have had a good word to say for this chivalrous romance of some 1700 quatrains, highly mannered in style. Davenant begins his preface with a brief survey of heroic poets from Homer to Spenser. And Spenser gets his due of praise, except that his use of archaisms and of a stanza requiring excessive rhyming is censured. Davenant then lists his own prerequisites for a successful epic poem. Mere imitation is no guide because it forestalls originality and prevents us from improving on our predecessors. His characters, he says, will be 'Christian persons' because the 'Principles of our Religion conduce more to explicable vertue, to plain demonstrative justice, and even to Honour ...than any other Religion'. The story will be placed in a 'former age than the present', far enough removed, in fact, to free the poet from the shackles of the historian.

> Truth narrative and past is the idol of Historians, who worship a dead thing, and truth operative, and by effects continually alive, is the Mistris of Poets, who hath not her existence in matter but in reason.

He has chosen a foreign setting also as being more to the taste of the reading public. And his characters are schooled in Courts and Military Camps: they provide 'patterns of such as will be fit to be imitated' by men of blood, education, and magnanimity. As for evil characters, they will show 'the distempers of Love and Ambition' in action.

Davenant next proceeds to defend a form of the heroic poem in five books which is closely modelled on the five acts of a drama, and to defend his interwoven iambic quatrains on the grounds that they are pleasing to the ear. Finally, he turns from outer frame and furniture to the essential material of which is work is made. That is 'Wit' – not just 'luck and labour, but also the dexterity of thought, rounding the world, like the Sun, with unimaginable motion, and bringing swiftly home to the memory universall surveys'. It is the 'Soul's *Powder*'; it can burst through all bonds and shed light on all dark places, and it emanates from God.

> It is the Divines Humility, Exemplariness, and Moderation; in Statesmen Gravity, Vigilance, Benign Complacency, Secrecy, Patience, and Dispatch; in Leaders of Armies, Valor, Painfulness, Temperance, Bounty, Dexterity in punishing and rewarding, and a sacred Certitude of promise. It is in Poets a full comprehension of all recited in these, and an ability to bring those comprehensions into action, when they shall so far forget the true measure of what is of greatest consequence to humanity (which are things righteous, pleasant, and usefull) as to think the delights of greatness equall to that of Poesy, or the Chiefs of any Profession more necessary to the world than excellent Poets.

In elaboration of this seemingly extravagant claim, Davenant makes a sustained analysis of the utility of poetry. His premiss is that the masses are unruly, feverish with disobedience, consumed with an appetite for 'Liberty', which is a 'license of Lust'. In turn Davenant argues that Divines, Leaders of Armies, Statesmen, and Makers of Laws are envious of each other and each incapable of effectively authoritative control of the people. Martial art requires an assault on the weaker part, 'and the weakest part of the people is their minds, for want of that which is the mindes only strength, *Education*'. Poetry is the one means of persuasion which works by charm and not by menace. It can make virtue attractive. So, in the last resort, for Davenant both drama and poetry are a means of education.

Davenant dated his Preface from Paris, where a number of English Royalists had sought refuge. Among them was the philosopher Thomas Hobbes (1588–1679) to whom Davenant's Preface was addressed. When *Gondibert* was published in England there was prefixed to it, not only Davenant's

Preface but also Hobbes's *Answer* to it. No doubt French influence contributed to this outburst of theorising. (There was lively critical controversy in France in the 1630s and thereafter from a generation of critics who predated Boileau. A dominant figure among them was the classicist, Jean Chapelain (1595–1674).) Hobbes thought so highly of *Gondibert* as to give Davenant a place beside Homer and Virgil. Nevertheless he concentrates in his *Answer* on generalities. He equates the three kinds of poetry '*Heroique*, *Scommatique*, and *Pastorall*' with the three regions of mankind, Court, City, and Country, and the three levels of humanity, the lustrous nobility, the moody, unreliable city-dwellers, and the plain, dull, yet not unwholesome, rural population. Since each of these kinds of literature can be sub-divided according to whether it is narrative or dramatic in presentation, we are left with six kinds of poetry: epic and tragedy, satire and comedy, pastoral and pastoral comedy. For epic, Hobbes approves of English pentameters which compensate for the neglect of classical quantity by 'the diligence of Rime'. A longer line than the decasyllabic 'is not far from ill Prose, and a shorter is a kind of whisking, you know, like the unlacing rather than the singing of a Muse'. Hobbes also approves of Davenant's motive, 'to adorn virtue and procure her Lovers', as of his initiative in abandoning the traditional invocation to the Muse.

What is most interesting in Hobbes's piece is his summary of the creative process. 'Time and Education begets experience; Experience begets memory; Memory begets Judgement and Fancy; Judgement begets the strength and structure, and Fancy begets the ornaments of a Poem.' Judgment is 'severer' than her sister Fancy. Judgment soberly and strictly seeks out the appropriate material; then Fancy swiftly orders and enriches it 'in copious Imagery'. Fancy indeed works the work of 'true Philosophy' in producing the glories of architecture, mechanical invention, and whatever distinguishes civilisation from barbarism. Where the guidance of Philosophy is lacking – as in 'the doctrine of Moral vertue', there Fancy must itself assume the mantle of Philosophy. Thus, in the making of an epic poem duly extolling virtue, the writer 'must not only be the Poet, to place & correct, but also the Philosopher, to furnish and square his matter, that is, to make both Body and Soul, colour and shadow of his Poem out of his own Store'.

Many years later Hobbes published his own translation of Homer's *Odyssey* (1675), and prefaced it with an address to the reader 'concerning the *Vertues* of an *Heroique Poem*', in which he lists the qualifications needed to make an epic poem pleasurably readable. In the first place, vocabulary must avoid foreign words and names of 'instruments' and 'tools' and the like. (This is in direct contradiction of Davenant, who was prepared to accept terminology for 'any Science, as well mechanicall as liberall', and argued that in ensuring correctness in the use of technical terms, the poet got an added bonus of learning from his labours.) Hobbes's rather remarkable motive for his recommendation is that it is 'Persons of the best Quality' who make up poetry's reading public, and the vocabulary must be within their reach. Moreover women have as much right to be catered for as men, and they do not have the same 'skill in Language' as men. In the second place, style must be natural and not distorted in the interests of metre of rhyme. In the third place, the mode of presentation, whether narration by the poet or by his characters, and the order of events in the narration must be appropriately contrived. For his fourth requirement, Hobbes returns to the role of Fancy. And here he reinforces his case against those who exalt Fancy 'above Judgement or Reason, or Memory, or any other intellectual Vertue'. It is wrong to reserve the word 'Wit' for Fancy alone, and to devalue the function of reason and judgment. Hobbes brings the philosopher's mind to bear on this issue. The poet's 'sublimity', the 'poetical Fury' which readers clamour for, will militate against all decorum unless its extravagances are restrained by reason and judgement. This remains one of Hobbes's most crucial emphases. He had protested in his *Answer* against fantastic implausibilities like invulnerable bodies and flying horses, arguing that 'beyond the actual works of nature a Poem may go; beyond the conceived possibility of nature, never'. This is all of a piece with his emphasis on naturalness of style. Hobbes's last three requirements are truth to fact in not disparaging historical figures, originality and fitness in the use of imagery, and variety in presentation.

Another English writer who was a royalist refugee in Paris along with Davenant and Hobbes was the poet and essayist Abraham Cowley (1618–67). When he published his collection of *Poems* (1656), he followed the new fashion by prefixing a Preface. Much of it consists of rather undistinguished reflections on his work as a poet. The volume included his incomplete biblical epic 'Davideis', telling the story of David. Introducing it, he gives vent to the conviction that the Bible is rich in potential poetic material. What worthier subject could a poet have than the greatest Monarch that ever sat on the most famous throne, and the highest person ever to honour the profession of poethood? The neglect of scriptural subjects in favour of flattery of the great, idolising of foolish women, and recounting of shallow fables, provokes Cowley's scorn. His attachment to the concept of the 'Christian Poet' may lack the philosophical dimensions which it had for Reynolds, and even Davenant, but it is fervently argued:

> Amongst all holy and consecrated things which the *Devil* ever stole and alienated from the service of the *Deity*...there is none that he so universally and long usurpt as *Poetry*.

He would bid poets prefer Noah to Deucalion, Jeptha's daughter to Iphigenia, Samson to Hercules, the passage of Moses into the Holy Land to the voyages of Ulysses or Aeneas. But he insists that such subjects require no less poetic skill and artistry than any others. Indeed, being superior material, biblical subjects would produce even more deformed results than profane subjects if not competently treated.

Cowley, however, gave cause indirectly for the publication of what has been reckoned the first English literary biography to give prominence to the writer's work as well as his life. Cowley's friend, Thomas Sprat (1635–1713), as his literary executor, attached a biographical and critical essay to the collected edition, *The Life and Writings of Cowley* (1668). Sprat was one of those involved with the Royal Society, which was established in 1662, and in particular with the movement within it for starting an English Academy of Letters. In his *History of the Royal Society* (1667) he pressed the need for a body to regulate vocabulary. He was highly critical of the superfluities and extravagances in current usage, and urged a rejection of 'all amplifications, digressions, and swellings of style' and a return to 'primitive purity and shortness'. The campaign was directed towards encouraging 'a close, naked, natural way of speaking, positive expressions, clear senses, a native easiness, bringing all things as near the Mathematical plainness as they can, and preferring the language of Artizans, Countrymen, and Merchants, before that of Wits and Scholars'. Sprat's Academy was not only to be an arbiter over linguistic usage, but also to form a 'fixt and *Impartial Court of Eloquence,* according to whose Censure all Books or Authors should either stand or fall'.

When Sprat turned to sum up the achievement of Cowley, he proved to be an initiator giving due recognition to another initiator. For Sprat initiates in blending an account of the writer's personal experience with a consideration of his literary achievement. This was to be Samuel Johnson's formula for the *Lives of the Poets* and to become established as a literary genre. Thus Sprat tells us how Cowley experienced the worlds of University and Court, as man and as poet skilfully making the best of what was to be found in both:

> In his life he join'd the innocence and sincerity of the Scholar with the humanity and good behaviour of the Courtier. In his Poems he united the Solidity and Art of the one with the Gentility and Gracefulness of the other.

Sprat goes on to praise the lack of affectation in Cowley's vocabulary. And, in the age of the smooth-flowing couplet, he defends Cowley against the charge of metrical roughness, insisting on the need for variety of tone in verse comparable to the variety in natural scenery, where 'a Rock, a Precipice, or a rising Wave is often more delightful than a smooth, even ground or a calm Sea'. Those who opt for perpetual gentleness and smoothness in verse need to learn that different subjects require different verbal 'colouring'. There is such a thing as masculine poetry, strong and sinewy, as well as feminine poetry, smooth and beautiful.

Sprat argues that Cowley's swift flow of Fancy is restrained by the balance of his Judgment. He has learned the hardest secret of good writing: he knows where to stop. Powerful and large as his imaginative invention is, it always seems to grow naturally from his subject. Above all, the scope and variety of Cowley's range is applauded. Whether he is inflaming the reader's emotions, indulging in good-humoured raillery, presenting the familiar social scene, the profundities of philosophy, or the heroic figures of religion, he has the right idiom and the 'proper measure of Wit'. Sprat is especially perceptive in dealing with Cowley's use of the 'Pindaric Ode'. This form has indeed become known as the 'Cow-leyan Ode'. It is a form in which the stanzas, or verse paragraphs, are immensely varied in size, line-length, and rhyme scheme. The form was to be brilliantly exploited by Dryden in the 'Cecilia's Day' ode and by Wordsworth in the 'Immortality' ode. It was scarcely calculated to appeal to those late seventeenth-century literary men for whom the smooth couplet was the poetic norm. Sprat moves logically from his praise of Cowley's variety to a defence of a form which can be adapted to contrasting subjects, cheerful or serious, amorous or heroic, moral or religious. The reader can be delighted by 'the frequent alteration of the Rhythm and Feet' which can have the naturalness of prose. Sprat recognises Cowley's work in this genre as perhaps 'rather a new root of Writing than a restoring of an Ancient'.

In turning to Cowley's Essays, Sprat commends his capacity in prose to restrain 'Curiosity of Ornament' and to adopt 'a lower and humbler style'. When the occasion is right, it requires just as much art to limit oneself to 'plain Conceptions' as to indulge 'extraordinary Flights' on other occasions. There is appropriate restraint too in Cowley's letters; clarity, conciseness, plainness, and 'a peculiar kind of Familiarity'. The style has been called the 'familiar style'. Cowley was a pioneer in practising it. Sprat was a pioneer in appreciating it. And above all he was a pioneer in connecting the 'Natural easiness and unaffected Grace' of Cowley's style, where 'nothing seems to be studied, yet everything is extraordinary' with the 'perfect natural goodness' of his personality, his firmness of mind, freedom from vanity, 'great integrity and plainness of Manners'.

III The debate about drama

The Royal Society represented a stirring to life of the scientific and literary communities which was encouraged by the Restoration of Charles II in 1660. The Restoration also brought about the re-opening of the theatres and consequently the renewal of dramatic criticism. The poet and dramatist Richard Flecknoe (d.*c*.1678) wrote 'A Short Discourse of the English Stage' as preface to *Love's Kingdom, a Pastoral Tragi-Comedy* (1664). Flecknoe is a character who stirs curiosity. Seemingly an Irishman and a Roman Catholic priest, he spent time on the continent, and when Andrew Marvell encountered him in Rome he commented on Flecknoe's appetite for reciting his own poetry. Marvell treated him to a satire, 'Flecknoe, an English priest at Rome', and Dryden poured scorn on him in *MacFlecknoe* as the writer who

> In prose and verse was owned, without dispute,
> Through all the realms of nonsense, absolute.

Flecknoe's preface, however, is not absurd. Looking back on Elizabethan dramatists, he finds the main native fault that of 'huddling too much matter together', the fabrication of excessive intrigue. The audience should be led into a maze from which it is possible to find the way out, and not into an impenetrable mist. A good play has to be carefully and evenly designed. The dramatic poet is to the stage what the pilot is to the ship, and to the actors what an architect is to builders. 'He is to be a good moral Philosopher, but yet more learned in Men than Books.' Flecknoe's poet will be wise, witty and good, but not above enjoying a drink. '*Shakespear* excelled in a natural Vein, *Fletcher* in Wit, and *Jonson* in Gravity and ponderousness of Style'. Indeed, he says, Jonson mixed up too much erudition in his plays. If you compare

him with Shakespeare you see the difference between Nature
and Art, and if you compare him with Fletcher you see the
difference between Wit and Judgment. Wit is an exuberant,
overflowing thing: but Judgment is a restrained, well-poised
thing. Flecknoe gives us his definition of Wit. It is the 'spirit
and quintessence of speech, extracted out of the substance of
the thing we speak of'. There is nothing redundant, nothing
lifeless, nothing cheap in the way of verbal devices. It is to
pleasant and cheerful discourse what eloquence is to grave
and serious discourse. You can acquire wit, not by 'Art and
Precept, but by Nature and Company'.

In an interesting comparison between the comparatively
bare stage of the Elizabethan theatre and the magnificent
and costly trappings of the Restoration theatre, Flecknoe
allows himself to question whether perhaps 'that which
makes the Stage the better makes our Playes the worse' –
the emphasis on spectacle rather than on dialogue.

Among other prefaces to plays published in the 1660s were
two from the dramatist Sir Robert Howard (1626–98), a
preface of *Four New Plays* (1665) and a preface to *The Great
Favourite, or the Duke of Lerma* (1668). The reader must be
warned at this point that arguments began to be conducted
between dramatists in successive prefaces as plays were
published: in particular Howard and Dryden (who married
his sister Elizabeth) conducted such a controversy. The
literary historian therefore must choose between threading
his way through a particular argument from writer to writer
and back again, or dealing with the thinking of each writer
in turn. Since the various prefaces contain a good deal more
than appertains to the points of dispute, the method chosen
here is to deal in turn with the work of each writer
separately. Thus Howard's 1665 preface replies to Dryden's
defence of rhyming verse for drama in his dedicatory epistle
to *The Rival Ladies* (1664). Dryden came back to the topic in
his *Essay of Dramatic Poesy* (1668). Howard responded in his
1668 preface, and Dryden rounded off the exchange in his
Defence of an Essay of Dramatic Poesy (1668).

The controversy over rhyme or blank verse is not the only
much-debated current issue that Howard touches on in his
prefaces. Indeed he brings a fund of commonsense to bear on

several matters. He stoutly defends English drama against those who press for servitude to classical rules. The ancients, with their stories of scattered limbs, self-immolation, magical rejuvenation and the like, were compelled by this material to substitute indirect narration for direct presentation. Howard quotes Horace, 'that everything makes more impression Presented than Related'. It follows, he argues, that for a dramatist to choose a subject which precludes presentation and compels relation is culpable. Howard does not give his blessing to the English practice of mixing the tragic and the comic, on the grounds that though actual life may present us with such contrasts, the style of a play ought to be consistently adapted to either the serious or the comic vein.

His most cogent logic is directed to dismantling the reasoning of those who argue for rhymed verse in drama on the French model. A poem is accepted by the reader as a 'premeditated form of Thought' and therefore no means of making it harmonious to the ear should be neglected. But a play presents situations which are supposed to have arisen naturally. Dialogue ought not to sound so artfully contrived that speakers appear to be aware in advance of what each other will say. He tackles the defences of rhyme in drama which see it as a convenient discipline upon the writer's fluency, causing him to take careful stock of what he is saying. Such reflections are irrelevant to the argument, which is not about what style suits a poet best, but what style suits best the subject he is writing on. To treat rhyme as a check on bad writing is absurd. The bad writer will write badly, rhyme or no rhyme. Verse may adorn great thoughts, but it is itself 'unbeautified' by mean thoughts. Howard cites the absurdity of calling for a servant or asking for a door to be shut in rhyme.

He takes up this subject with more thoroughness in his second preface, which follows on Dryden's reply to his first. Anything Dryden may have said about the naturalness of rhyme to a grave and serious drama is beside the point. 'Naturalness' of this kind is not at issue, since Howard himself prefers rhymed poetry to blank verse or prose. The question rather is what is most 'natural' in being 'nearest the nature' of what is presented: that is, the living dialogue of persons assumed to be speaking *ex tempore*. Dryden provided an example from Seneca of a loftily dignified request to shut the door (*Reserate clusos regii postes laris*) which proves nothing except that 'nothing can seem something by the help of a Verse'. From this matter Howard moves to a forceful attack on the attempt to lay down formal rules for drama. To ridicule the practice of crowding two separate countries into one stage or the events of many years into two hours and a half is absurd. To imagine that the unities restricting time and place are nearer to what is natural is illogical. It is just as impossible for the stage to represent two rooms as two countries; just as impossible for 24 hours to be compressed into two hours as a thousand years. Attempts to formulate what practices are appropriate in this respect and what practices are not, to measure the 'degrees in impossibilities' may make useful 'propositions', but certainly not binding laws or rules.

A fellow-dramatist, Thomas Shadwell (*c*.1642–92) also contributed two prefaces to the ongoing debate about drama, the preface to *The Sullen Lovers, or The Impertinents, A Comedy* (1668) and the preface to *The Humorists, A Comedy* (1671). Shadwell was to get rough treatment from Dryden, who lampooned him as Og in *Absalom and Achitophel*:

> The midwife laid her hand on his thick skull,
> With this prophetic blessing – *Be thou Dull*;

and made him Flecknoe's only fit successor in *MacFlecknoe*:

> The rest to some faint meaning make pretence,
> But Shadwell never deviates into sense.

It is difficult to rescue a personality from this degree of superlative denigration, but to read Shadwell's prefaces is not to read nonsense. His comedy *The Sullen Lovers* was based partly on Molière's *Les Fascheux*. Shadwell boats that in it he has as nearly as possible observed the unities of Time, Place, and Action. He professes himself a disciple of Ben Jonson, developing the comedy of humours. This makes a faithful representation of human life possible, and is thus preferable to 'wild Romantick Tales' exaggerating themes of love and honour to the point of burlesque. Shadwell claims that in pin-pointing a humour, far more 'wit and invention' are required than in writing backchat for stand-up comics. For the dramatist has to discipline his material exactly to his characters, a discipline sadly lacking in the dramatists who turn out the crude current stereotypes and make bawdy and profanity their chief subject.

In his later preface (to *The Humorists*) Shadwell takes issue with 'those who seem to insinuate that the ultimate end of a Poet is to delight without correction or instruction'. (Dryden had argued that 'delight is the chief, if not the only, end of poesy: instruction can be admitted but in the second place, for poesy only instructs as it delights'. This scarcely 'insinuates' what Shadwell asserts it does.) A poet must not reduce himself to the level of the fiddler or the dancing master. His business is to 'adorn his Images of *Vertue* so delightfully to affect people with a secret veneration of it in others, and an emulation to practice it in themselves: And to render their Figures of *Vice* and *Folly* so ugly and detestable, to make people hate and despise them, not onely in others, but (if it be possible) in their dear selves'. Jonson is Shadwell's ideal in formulating his doctrine that satirising human follies and vices realistically is the prime purpose of comedy. An interesting sidelight is thrown on social thinking when he argues that comedy is more useful in this respect than tragedy, because the vices and follies of courts are a minority issue, whereas the cheats and villainies among the masses are relevant to all.

IV John Dryden

John Dryden (1631–1700) is the dominating figure around whom the lesser critical writers of the age group themselves. The controversy with Sir Robert Howard over the use of rhyme in verse drama began when Dryden addressed a dedicatory epistle to Roger Boyle (1621–79), Earl of Orrery, a fellow poet and dramatist, in publishing his tragi-comedy *The Rival Ladies* (1664). Dryden makes the point that he has tried to write English distinguishable from 'the tongue of pedants and that of affected travellers' and he regrets excessive current borrowing of foreign vocabulary. The use of rhyme is recommended. In this respect 'shall we oppose ourselves to the most polished and civilised nations of Europe?' Waller and Denham have perfected a technique for couplets which has sweetness and dignity, and in which the sense flows smoothly, and Davenant has used the same technique in drama. Rhyme aids the memory, and it demands of a poet a degree of application which puts a brake on excess.

Howard's preface to *Four New Plays* (1664) was clearly not the only thing to spark off Dryden's composition of his celebrated *Essay of Dramatic Poesy* (1668), for it is only in the last quarter of the essay that the controversy about rhyme is dealt with. Indeed Dryden's preliminary note 'To the Reader' begins:

> The drift of the ensuing discourse was chiefly to vindicate the honour of our English writers, from the censure of those who unjustly prefer the French before them.

The essay is cast in the form of a dialogue. Four friends take a barge on the Thames and engage in conversation. Some light-hearted mockery of fashionable poetry, especially that of Cleveland (1613–58) and Wither (1588–1677), leads to a more formal presentation of views which ultimately covers four topics: Are the modern poets as good as the ancients? Are the contemporaries as good as the Elizabethans? Are the English as good as the French? And is rhyme better than blank verse for drama? The agreement to restrict the argument to the subject of drama is suggested by Crites, who thinks it will be easiest to prove the superiority of the ancients to the modern and of the Elizabethans to the contemporaries with this genre. The four speakers are Crites, representing Sir Robert Howard, Lisideius, representing Sir Charles Sedley, Eugenius, representing Lord Buckhurst, and Neander, representing Dryden himself.

Crites opens the discussion on behalf of the ancients. All we achieve in drama is achieved by building on the foundations laid by the ancients and by copying their models. The ancients were 'wise observers of that nature which is so torn and ill-represented in our plays'. Structurally the ancients formulated and obeyed those rules of the three unities which so much modern drama fails lamentably to observe. As for style, the greatest of the moderns, Ben Jonson, gave the ancients undisputed preeminence and indeed derived an immense amount of material from them. Eugenius replies to Crites on behalf of the moderns. Imitation of the ancients would lead to nothing but dullness. We represent life from nature not from the rules of the ancients, and knowledge of nature has progressed so much since the days of Aristotle that poetry and the arts must necessarily derive advantage from the fact. Eugenius goes on to criticise classical rule and practice as defective. The recurrent use of hackneyed plots made for tediousness. The range of characterisation was very limited. The unities were not always observed. The lessons conveyed by the savage deeds represented were often immoral. As for 'wit', Eugenius does not find a lot of praise in the ancients in the way of dressing great thoughts in easily understood words. And in respect of the tenderer and softer passions – as opposed to lust, revenge, and bloodthirstiness – their tragedies cannot match those of Shakespeare and Fletcher, and in most of their comedies lovers have little to say to one another.

Lisideius introduces the question of the relative merits of French and English dramatic poets. He grants that forty years earlier, when Beaumont and Fletcher and Ben Jonson were just at the end of their careers, England would have had preeminence. Since then French drama, led by Corneille, has become the best in Europe. The unities are observed. The French dramatists eschew the absurd complications of English plots, which are such that half the actors in a given play are not known to the other half. English tragi-comedy vainly tries to combine incompatibles such as mirth and compassion. French plots may use known historical material, but they are pleasingly interwoven with plausible fiction, whereas Shakespeare's historical plays romp through decades of public life in a few hours. It is like looking through the wrong end of a telescope. French dramatists give coherence to their plays by focusing on one major character in relation to whom all others have a subordinate role. The French use narration for major clashes such as duels and battles which English dramatists struggle to represent directly with absurd consequences. 'For what is more ridiculous than to represent an army with a drum and five men behind it?' The same applies to tragic deaths. 'I have observed that in all our tragedies, the audience cannot forbear laughter when the actors are to die; it is the most comic part of the whole play.' Moreover a third-person description of a death can be far more moving than the attempt to represent it. Lastly Lisideius protests against eleventh-hour conversions of villains in the dénouement, and against carelessness in providing reasons for stage entrances and exits.

Neander now speaks, representing Dryden's own views. Accepting that French drama has more regularity of plot and exactness in stage 'decorum' does not establish superiority over English drama. The 'lively imitation of nature' is the business of drama, and it is therefore by approximation to nature that drama must be judged. The beauties of French poetry, as described, are the 'beauties of a statue' not of living humanity. In characterisation and representation of 'humours', French drama cannot compare with English. In this respect there is more substance and variety in one play of Ben Jonson's than in the whole of recent French drama. Neander then defends the mixing of comedy and tragedy as perfectly acceptable. We glance from a pleasant object to an unpleasant one in a flash. Our spirits are not less adaptable than our senses in this matter. Indeed mirth and gravity set each other off by contrast. Neander finds French plots barren but English plots full of variety and copiousness. A neatly related sub-plot but adds to that variety. He also finds the French concentration on a single theme productive of tediousness, for the speeches in French drama are lengthy and wearisome declamations. Corneille's *Cinna* and *Pompey* are not so much plays as 'long discourses of reason of state'. It may suit the sprightly French people to be thus rendered more serious, but we English are a more sullen people and need to be stirred up in the theatre. In any case short speeches and quick exchanges are apter to touch our emotions and rouse our sympathy than lengthily protracted outbursts of passion. And there is no need to restrict the number of significant persons surrounding the protagonist, provided that due proportion and overall unity of design are sustained, as is the case in Beaumont and Fletcher's *The Maid's Tragedy* and Jonson's *The Alchemist* and *The Silent Woman*.

In turning to the question of the use of narration, Neander insists that English audiences revel in the direct representation of combats and calamities, before yielding the point that deaths may be better off stage. But 'if we are to be blamed for showing too much of the action, the French are as faulty for discovering too little of it'. The French too, by servile observation of the unities, have paid the price in 'dearth of plot, and narrowness of imagination'. In fact we have many plays as regular as the French with greater variety of plot and character as a bonus superadded. And where our drama is by that standard 'irregular' – Shakespeare and Fletcher, for instance – there is 'a more masculine fancy and greater spirit in the writing' which more than compensate. On this theme, through the mouth of Neander, Dryden rises to a noble and celebrated declaration of Shakespeare's qualities:

> To begin, then, with Shakespeare. He was the man who of all modern, and perhaps ancient poets, had the largest and most comprehensive soul. All the images of nature were still present to him, and he drew them, not laboriously, but luckily; when he describes anything, you more than see it, you feel it too. Those who accuse him to have wanted learning, give him the greater commendation: he was naturally learned; he needed not the spectacles of books to read nature; he looked inwards, and found her there. I cannot say he is everywhere alike; were he so. I should do him injury to compare him with the greatest of mankind. He is many times flat, insipid; his comic wit degenerating into clenches, his serious swelling into bombast. But he is always great, when some great occasion is presented to him ...

Beaumont and Fletcher are praised for their lively representation of the passions, especially love, for the 'perfection' of the English language in their hands, for the gaiety of their comedies and the pathos of their tragedies. As for Jonson, he was 'the most learned and judicious' of writers. 'One cannot say he wanted wit, but rather that he was frugal of it.' He knew what he could do well, and made little attempt in his plays to move passions. He drew copiously and openly on the ancients. 'He invades authors like a monarch; and what would be theft in other poets is only victory in him.'

> If I would compare him with Shakespeare, I must acknowledge him the more correct poet, but Shakespeare the greater wit. Shakespeare was the Homer, or father of our dramatic poets; Jonson was the Virgil, the pattern of elaborate writing; I admire him, but I love Shakespeare.

Neander concludes his tribute to Elizabethan drama with a detailed examination of the qualities of Ben Jonson's *The Silent Woman*. He has praise for the coherence and unity of the plot, for the range and effectiveness of the characterisation, and for the skilful unfolding of the action to its climax.

It is seemingly almost as an afterthought that the topic of rhyme is raised. Crites rehearses the arguments again which Howard presented in his Preface. Neander then analyses the case point by point, but makes clear that he is thinking of tragedy. Comedy is excluded from his defence. In the first place, it is just as easy to point out the faultiness of much blank verse as to point out defects in rhymed verse. With sharp logic, Neander tells Crites that he must either prove that rhyme interferes with naturalness in poetry or else establish that rhyme is specifically unfitted to drama. On the first point he argues that the 'necessity of rhyme' never forces any but a bad poet to say what he would not otherwise say. As for its fittedness to drama, rhymed verse can be as natural as blank verse. And blank verse, which is 'but a poetic prose', is the appropriate medium for comedies. The crucial argument of Crites – that rhymed dialogue is unnatural and suggests prior collusion between characters on stage who employ it, for people do not rhyme *ex tempore* – provokes Neander to a sharp differentiation between what is more natural to comedy, 'which is the imitation of common and ordinary speaking', and what is nearest the nature of a serious play, which 'is indeed the representation of nature', but 'nature wrought up to a higher pitch'. This argument, that the intensity of the representation of life requires a comparable intensity of poetic utterance, is central to Dryden's thinking. And therefore, quite logically, he argues that the case against rhymed verse in drama must apply to poetry too. Moreover the argument that rhyme in dialogue is too contrived must logically apply, for instance, to a dance in which partner responds to partner. If the hand of art is evident in rhyme it is evident in all verse.

Howard's reply to Dryden's *Essay* in his Preface to *The Great Favourite, or The Duke of Lerma* provoked an immediate response from Dryden, *A Defence of an Essay of Dramatic Poesy* (1668). Some slips on Howard's part in quoting and translating Latin, in grammar and in use of words, give Dryden the opportunity for some amusingly ironic dialectical knockabout, which is all the more effective because of the tone of respectful deference prevalent alongside it. Since Howard admits that he would rather read verse than prose, Dryden argues that his case is lost, for 'delight is the chief, if not the only, end of poetry'. (This was an expression which, as we have seen, Shadwell was to seize upon.) Granted that 'bare imitation' of life in drama will not do, there can be no arbitrary limit in serious drama on the degree to which the conversation of the day may be heightened by art. Dryden pounces on a careless remark by Howard, that 'in the difference of *Tragedy* and *Comedy*, and of *Farce* itself, there can be no determination but by Taste', to emphasise that tragedy and comedy would be what they are irrespective of anyone's opinion or taste. He then seizes on another loose statement, that it is 'not necessary for Poets to study strict reason, since they are so used to a greater latitude than is allowed by that severe Inquisition', to insist that 'they cannot be good poets who are not accustomed to argue well' ... and that 'moral truth is the mistress of the poet, as much as of the philosopher'. For the rest, Dryden concentrates on defending the classical unities against Howard's attack on them. Not that Dryden recommends slavish adherence to them. But he ridicules the notion that since the stage cannot exactly approximate to actuality in representation of duration or location therefore no restraints are needed:

But as it is an error on the one side to make too great a disproportion betwixt the imaginary time of the play, and the real time of its representation; so on the other side, it is an oversight to compress the accidents of a play into a narrower compass than that in which they will naturally be produced.

An artistic chasm seems to be opened up whenever Dryden moves from talking of tragedy to talking of comedy. In his preface to the successful comedy *The Mock Astrologer* (1671) he makes a useful distinction between farce, which relies on the totally implausible, and comedy, which 'presents us with the imperfections of human nature'. The effectiveness of farce is like the effectiveness of a mountebank who happens to prove successful, and the effectiveness of comedy is like the effectiveness of the genuine physician. Dryden declares himself more suited to tragedy than to comedy and seems to disparage comedy for the need it imposes on the writer to observe the follies of the vulgar. Indeed he confesses himself embarrassed by the laughter his successful comedies have provoked. (This seems to be an occupational hazard for writers of comedy. Bernard Shaw spoke disparagingly of *You Never Can Tell* when its audiences rocked with laughter.) In analysing the nature of comedy he distinguishes between the element of 'wit' or 'sharpness of conceit' and the element of 'humour' which is the natural imitation of folly. Where Jonson had too little of the former, Shakespeare had too much of it. As for the moral effect of comedy, Dryden does not believe that the rules of tragedy apply to it in respect of the need for just distribution of punishment for vice and reward for virtue. Tragedy has to instruct as well as delight, but 'the first end of comedy is delight, and instruction only the second'.

In the Prefatory Essay to *The Conquest of Granada* (1672) we find Dryden's enthusiasm for the heroic drama of the Restoration stage forcefully expressed. Again he defends rhyme. If you stop at the poetic half-way house of blank verse 'you have lost that which you call natural, and have not acquired the last perfection of art'. In praising Sir William Davenant as a pioneer in post-Restoration literature, he makes a point which is very revealing. Davenant 'takes the image of an heroic poem from the drama'. Dryden reverses this dependence. He models his 'heroic plays by the rules of an heroic poem'. There is a profound confidence about Dryden's citation of Homer and Virgil, Ariosto and Tasso, Spenser too, in displaying how heroic literature can embrace the supernatural, as there is in his citation of Shakespeare to defend his own representation of battles. Dryden the critic writes like a master consciously inhabiting the great tradition.

The confidence seems to acquire a note of defensiveness in the Defence he wrote soon after of the Epilogue to the second part of *The Conquest of Granada*. Basically the argument is that the heroic drama such as Dryden wrote was in some respects superior to the drama of the Elizabethan age. And this is not because Dryden and his contemporaries are greater writers than Shakespeare, Jonson, and Fletcher, but because there has been a leap forward since the Elizabethan age in two or three crucial respects. To begin with, English vocabulary has been refined by the rejection of unsatisfactory words and the admission of 'more proper, more sounding, and more significant' ones. Shakespeare and Fletcher had verbal faults in plenty of expression and meaning, but 'the times were ignorant in which they lived' and poetry was in its infancy. Hence the absurdly implausible and indigestible plots of plays such as *The Winter's Tale*, *Measure for Measure*, and Beaumont and Fletcher's *Philaster*. As for incorrectness in sense and language, examples are cited from Ben Jonson, who offended least in this respect. In the second place, there has been a 'refinement of Wit' which in Shakespeare tends to dullness and vulgarity, and even in Jonson to puns and cheap word-play. The Elizabethans had wit but it was 'not that of gentlemen', rather it was somewhat 'ill-bred and clownish'. Lastly, the Elizabethans lived in an 'unpolished age'. Ben Jonson apart, they had no experience in courts and therefore lacked the 'greatest advantage of our writing, which proceeds from *conversation*'. Dryden thus ends with a tribute to Charles II who has been 'conversant in the most polished courts of Europe', and whose influence has now reformed the manners of his compatriots 'by mixing the solidity of our nation with the air and gaiety of our neighbours'.

The modern reader is likely to be perplexed by the contrast in Dryden between passages of enthusiastic praise of Shakespeare and passages of half-hearted commendation or even carping denigration of his work, more especially in relation to Shakespeare's plots and his style. In his own day John Wilmot, the Earl of Rochester (1647–80) took Dryden to task in *An Allusion to the Tenth Satyr of the First Book of Horace* (*c*.1677–9). For while he grants that Dryden's excellencies exceed his faults and that he deserves his fame, he adds:

> But does not *Dryden* find ev'n *Johnson* dull?
> *Fletcher* and *Beaumont* uncorrect and full
> Of lewd Lines, as he calls 'em? *Shake-spear's* stile
> Stiff and affected, to his own the while
> Allowing all the justness that his Pride
> So arrogantly had to these deny'd?

The sense that Dryden is engaged in a living dialogue with opponents is felt throughout his early critical essays and prefaces. And indeed his sometimes rather prickly defence of heroic drama could not but be influenced by the publication in 1672 of the Duke of Buckingham's play *The Rehearsal* which ridicules contemporary heroic tragedy for its excesses. The burlesque contains parodies of passages in Dryden, and in *The Conquest of Granada* especially. But the defence of heroic drama it helped to provoke proved to mark something of a turning point in Dryden's critical output, in that the role of the combatant engaged in running battles seems to give place gradually to that of the philosophically minded thinker able to detach himself from current controversies and take the wider view. Thus in his Author's Apology prefixed to *The State of Innocence and Fall of Man* (1677), Dryden's adaptation for the stage of Milton's *Paradise Lost*, he pays tribute to Milton's epic as being 'undoubtedly one of the greatest, most noble, and most sublime poems which either this age or nation has produced'. He then defines the function of criticism as 'a standard of judging well; the chiefest part of which is, to observe those excellencies which should delight a reasonable reader'. And he cites Longinus's view that the sublime genius who sometimes errs is preferable to the faultless plodder who never touches the heights.

Dryden's defence of 'heroic poetry' as 'the greatest work of human nature' appeals not only to the authority of Aristotle, Horace, and Longinus, but also to French critics, Boileau (1626–1711) and Rapin (1621–87). Boileau began as a satirical poet in the tradition of Juvenal and Horace, and then made a reputation by his lively critical observations of contemporary poets. His *L'art poétique* (1675), which stressed the importance of artistic craftsmanship, established him as an arbiter of critical taste in the classical school to which Molière and Racine belonged. For Dryden, as for Pope, the canons of taste and the critical guide-lines he laid down were to be treated with the utmost respect. The weight of authority is called upon by Dryden in order to counter the current notion that the poetic grandeurs of epic are bombastic and unnatural. His case expands into a defence of poetic devices which have been used to heighten style in representing passion. He is impatient with those who regard only what is dull, insipid, and sinewless in poetry as truly natural. In fact the essay becomes a plea for poetic inclusiveness which embraces the fantastic and the supernatural in subject, and all kinds of imagery and rhetorical devices in style.

Meanwhile Dryden had been rethinking his theory of heroic drama. In his Prologue to *Aureng-Zebe* (1675) he confesses that he 'grows weary of his long-loved mistress Rhyme'. And comparing himself with Shakespeare, he feels 'secret shame':

> Awed when he hears his Godlike *Romans* rage,
> He in a just despair would quit the stage!

So it was that he wrote *All for Love* (1678), his version of the story of Antony and Cleopatra, in blank verse and again introduced it by a Preface. He reveals his reverence for the classics, he tells us, by observing the unities of time, place, and action, but he moulds his blank verse on Shakespeare's. He now regards French drama as deficient in 'the genius which animates our stage'. French playwrights are so afraid of making you laugh or cry that they send you to sleep. And, claiming that in literature practitioners make the fittest critics, he rounds on those who presume to pass judgment on tragedy when they are only fitted to appreciate comedy. Notwithstanding the bow to Shakespeare ('In my style I have professed to imitate the divine Shakespeare'), the general gist of Dryden's preface is that his play improves on *Antony and Cleopatra* both in structure and in moral implication.

The conviction that the work of the great Elizabethan dramatists cried out for refinement led Dryden next to make a revised version of Shakespeare's *Troilus and Cressida* (1679). Once more the work was prefaced. The coarseness of the original, the bad grammar and the excessive imagery all call for treatment. The fact that 'Cressida is false, and is not punished' is another defect, so Dryden decided to re-model the play, removing the 'heap of rubbish', throwing out redundant characters, restricting the leaping between Troy and the Grecian camp, and refining the language. Having done so, he raises the question how far Shakespeare and Fletcher are just models for imitation when judged by the principles laid down by Aristotle, Horace, and Longinus. Thus Dryden recapitulates central tenets on the need for a single line of action in tragedy, for unity of tone, for shape, plausibility, and for combining instruction with delight. It is again clear that Dryden has been reading the works of Boileau's contemporaries and fellow-critics, Rapin's *Réflexions sur la Poétique d'Aristote* (1674) and Le Bossu's *Traité du Poème Epique* (1675), and he cites him as authority (a 'judicious critic') in setting out how tragedy should move us to fear and pity. In revealing that even the greatest can experience terrible misfortune, it both frightens us and abates our pride. In revealing that even the most virtuous can come to grief, it stirs our pity and our tenderness to the distressed. Dryden's message is that Shakespeare and Fletcher ought to be imitated only in so far as they have 'copied the excellencies of those who invented and brought to perfection Dramatic Poetry'. But when he actually examines the works of Shakespeare and Fletcher, he gives us the feeling that he is never quite comfortable with the canons of judgment he tries to apply to them. 'Shakespeare moves more terror and Fletcher more compassion.' The former had a fiery, masculine genius, the latter a softer, feminine one. And when it comes to analysis of characterisation – of the temperaments, the virtues and vices motivating people – the handling of this is one of Shakespeare's excellencies, whereas the characters in French drama are so standardised as to be, whatever their supposed age and nation, 'wholly French' and fresh from Versailles.

Dryden makes much of the need to avoid inappropriate displays of wit and verbal artifice by characters supposedly in situations of emotional tension. 'No man is at leisure to make sentences and similes when his soul is in an agony.' And he confesses himself culpable in this respect in his earlier work. No doubt we can detect here again the rippling effect of Buckingham's burlesque *The Rehearsal*. 'Now here she must make a simile,' says the author Bayes (representing Dryden), and when asked why, he retorts, 'Because she's surprised. That's a general rule; you must ever make a simile when you are surprised; 'tis the new way of writing.' Whereupon Cloris embarks upon an eight-line epic simile ('As some tall pine, which we on Aetna find ...') which directly parodies one in Dryden's *The Conquest of Granada* ('As some fair tulip, by a storm opprest ...').

Dryden's later critical prefaces are much concerned with the art of translation, but there are points where more general matters are raised. In his 'Epistle Dedicatory' to *The Spanish Friar, or The Double Discovery* (1681) Dryden concedes that his taste has matured since the days when, as a young man, he relished the extravagant bombast of Chapman's *Bussy D'Ambois* and, as a boy, thought poorly of Spenser. Indeed he confesses himself now ashamed of some of the rhetorical extravagances in his plays *The Conquest of Granada* and *Tyrannic Love*. It is the offence against Nature of which he now disapproves:

> As in a room contrived for state, the height of the roof should bear a proportion to the area; so, in the heightenings of Poetry, the strength and vehemence of figures should be suited to the occasion, the subject and the persons. All beyond this is monstrous: 'tis out of Nature, 'tis an excrescence, and not a living part of Poetry.

The fact that such excesses pleased his audience leads him to conclude that the fitness of 'thoughts and words, which are the hidden beauties of a play' cannot be properly judged in the lively atmosphere of stage performance. They emerge only in reading. So 'as 'tis my interest to please my audience, so 'tis my ambition to be read'. The student of Dryden's critical output is made repeatedly aware of an element of conflict between the man who had to earn his living and the true artist. He wants to be read, yet he writes to be listened to on stage. His temperament and taste are for tragedy, yet he writes comedy. Even here his defence of his new tragicomedy is that audiences grow weary of the unbroken melancholy in pure tragedy, yet at the same time he insists that the true literary genius must be master of both the tragic and the comic modes.

By 1685, in the Preface to *Sylvae*, the second part of his *Miscellany Poems*, a collection of translations of classical poets, we find Dryden confessing that he has for half a year been 'troubled with the disease... of translation'. He has been stimulated to his efforts by the appearance of the *Essay on Translated Verse* (1684) by Wentworth Dillon, the Earl of Roscommon (*c*.1633–85), who had translated Horace's *Ars Poetica* and now laid down the rules of the game in heroic couplets. Roscommon insists that the English can beat the French:

> But who did ever in *French Authors* see
> The comprehensive *English Energy*?

His practical advise is not remarkable. The translator must select a poet whose genius has a personal appeal for him; he must take pains to explore the 'genuine Meaning', and so on. What gives the poem its memorability is a final passage, added in 1685, in which Roscommon forsakes couplets for a blank verse tribute to Milton that shows real critical sensitivity to the quality of Milton's rhetoric. Though Roscommon impressed Dryden, he recommends in translation a closeness to the original which Dryden did not emulate.

Before we turn to Dryden's later observations on this topic, it is worthwhile to look at his *Examen Poeticum*, the dedication to his third *Miscellany Poems* (1693). For in this we hear a note of disgruntlement from the aged poet who recognises that the kind of brain power and application which have made him a name in poetry, if otherwise exploited, might have gained him the maximum public distinction. Stung, it seems, by hostile attacks, he contrasts contemporaries with those true critics of the past who saw it as their duty to shed light on the poems they considered, bringing out hidden beauties and correcting misinterpretation. His contemporaries pay reverence to the names of Shakespeare, Fletcher, and Jonson only as a means of denigrating their true successors. And he takes up vigorously the defence of Elizabethan and contemporary dramatists alike. Many English tragedies were utterly superior to those of Sophocles and Euripides. English drama has built upon the achievements of the ancients and improved upon them. Moreover English drama is superior to French drama. English audiences demand a multiplicity of character and action. The French follow the classical rules too servilely; the English perhaps use too much licence in neglecting them. But if English audiences demanded observation of the unities, English dramatists could easily comply, whereas French dramatists could never rise to the 'sublimity of our thoughts or to the difficult variety of our designs'. And once more Dryden repeats that it is the writer's duty 'to please those whom we pretend to entertain'.

The full range of Dryden's critical acumen and the odd streak of critical insensitivity come together finally in his Preface to *Fables Ancient and Modern, Translated into Verse from Homer, Virgil, Boccace, and Chaucer* (1700). The preface contains another discerning comparison of Homer's genius with Virgil's, of Homer's impetuosity and fire with Virgil's 'propriety of thoughts' and verbal ornament. Dryden challenges Hobbes's view that 'the first beauty of an epic poem consists in diction; that is, in the choice of words, and harmony of numbers'. Words may indeed be the first thing to strike the reader, but it is 'the design, the disposition, the manners, and the thoughts' which have prior importance. However, it is in judging Chaucer that Dryden's vast qualities and odd limitations most forcefully emerge. He recognises the magnitude of Chaucer's achievement in the portrayal of his characters, the distinctiveness and vividness of their living presence on the page. He is scathingly dismissive of critics who lament Chaucer's lack of 'conceits and jingles'. Chaucer is better without them. And thus Chaucer leads Dryden to one of those magisterial pronouncements which are unforgettable:

> In the first place, as he is the father of English poetry, so I hold him in the same degree of veneration as the Grecians held Homer, or the Romans Virgil. He is a perpetual fountain of good sense; learned in all sciences; and, therefore, speaks properly on all subjects. As he knew what to say, so he knows also when to leave off ...

Dryden marvels at the compass of Chaucer's imagination in comprehending the 'various manners and humours' of the whole English nation in his age, and at the extraordinary aptness with which the stories are fitted to their narrators in both style and substance. The variety is astonishing. "Tis sufficient to say, according to the proverb, that *here is God's plenty.*' Side by side with these tributes stands the belief that the verse of the *Canterbury Tales* is 'not harmonious', that 'Chaucer is a rough diamond, and must first be polished ere he shines'. The view hangs on that seemingly unshakeable conviction of Dryden that the progress of English versification reached its peak in the smooth couplets of Waller and Denham. Dryden has of course heard the argument that it is 'little less than profanation and sacrilege' to tamper with Chaucer's text. But he argues that it is pointless to talk of preserving the beauty of verse which is simply no longer understood.

New genres in literature have sometimes sprung to life and rushed to maturity with astonishing rapidity. The rise of Elizabethan drama was a case in point. So too was the rise of the novel in the eighteenth century. Fielding, Richardson, and Smollet issued their *fiats* and the magnificent progress of the English novel began to unfold. Dryden is the man who seems almost singly to have launched English literary criticism on its way. Before him the genre scarcely exists. After him it has bulk and substance.

5
The Seventeenth Century:
Rymer to Dennis

It is easy to oversimplify in defining the character of the
Restoration period, because the comedies of the age stamp in
our minds the picture of a frivolous society ready to trivialise
human relationships, to treat love and marriage flippantly,
and to show scant regard for the virtues of hard work,
sobriety and unselfishness. Indeed the public that supported
the London theatre was a very different public from the
seemingly mixed cross-section of the populace who attended
the Globe theatre in Shakespeare's day. The Restoration
theatre provided amusement for a leisured and dissolute
society taking their cue from a dissolute court. Puritans
naturally shunned it. The respectable Londoners who
earned their livings by honest trade or craft could scarcely
be expected to throng to see themselves made butts of upper-
class mockery. The court of Charles II certainly contained
more than its fair share of cynical libertines who made a
mockery of virtue and assumed all its advocates to be
hypocrites. This was the public which relished the antics of
Horner in Wycherley's *The Country Wife* (1675) when he
passed himself off as a eunuch in order to gain admission to
feminine circles and seduce women under the noses of their
husbands and guardians. But *The Country Wife* was certainly
not representative of the spirit of the kingdom as a whole.
Milton's *Paradise Lost* was published in 1667 and Bunyan's
Pilgrim's Progress in 1678. The civil struggle may have been
settled politically in favour of the monarchy and the Church
of England, and against the puritans, but the moral and
theological struggle continued in literary productivity and in
commentary upon it.

The Restoration age was not a period weak in artistic or scientific achievement. It was in 1666 that a falling apple focused Isaac Newton's attention on the fact of gravitation. In the 1660s Sir Christopher Wren was designing the Sheldonian Theatre at Oxford and by 1675 he began directing the rebuilding of St Paul's Cathedral. In 1667 the Earl of Clarendon went abroad to work on his massive historical masterpiece *The History of the Rebellion* which was published posthumously in 1702–4. In 1677 Henry Purcell, at the age of eighteen, was appointed 'Composer in Ordinary' at the Chapel Royal. Not that these were publicly calm decades in all respects. The Great Plague of London in 1665, the Dutch War and the Fire of London in 1666, the Titus Oates plot in 1678, the murder of Archbishop Sharp by Scottish Covenanters in 1679, and James II's brief reign from 1685–8 provided a turbulent prelude to the establishment of the more tolerant and settled regime of William and Mary. William was the son of Charles I's daughter Mary, and Mary was the daughter of James II. The Bill of Rights of 1689 not only settled the question of succession to the throne, but also protected the liberties of the subject.

One of the effects of the accession of William and Mary was to put an end to the ascendancy of the royal court as the place where the fashions were set, where the arts were fostered, and where public positions and reputations were to be obtained. The court became the place where royalty lived in comparative privacy at a distance from their subjects. People now had to turn to ministers, members of Parliament, and the landed aristocracy in search of patronage.

I The standing of the Elizabethans

In the Preface to his *Troilus and Cressida*, Dryden drew attention to a formidable defender of the ancients in the ongoing controversy with the moderns: 'How defective Shakespeare and Fletcher have been in all their plots Mr Rymer has discovered in his criticisms ...'

Thomas Rymer (1641–1713) was a scholarly man of letters who had translated Rapin's *Reflections on Aristotle's Treatise of*

Poesie (1674) and added a preface stoutly defending the
neoclassical position with the dogmatic assurance of one to
whom the rules enunciated were a matter of plain commonsense. He accepts Rapin's view that the English have a
natural genius for tragedy, but rejects Rapin's argument
that this is due to the English delight in cruelty and blood-
sports. Rymer attempts to display the unfortunate consequences for English poets of neglecting Aristotelian rules.
Spenser chose to follow Ariosto instead of Homer and Virgil,
and 'blindly rambling on *marvellous* Adventures', lost all basis
of probability. Thus the Italians debauched 'great Spenser's
judgment' so that he used a totally inappropriate stanza and
superstitious allegory. Davenant's *Gondibert* comes likewise
under judgment for its lack of a definable 'great action',
for its tangled substance, and for the strains imposed by its
stanza form. Cowley's *Davideis* comes off better, and indeed
Rymer is at pains to insist that English poetry is not inferior.
To prove the point he juxtaposes passages from a number of
poets whose common theme is a description of the night.
Apollonius Rhodius, Virgil, Tasso, Marino, Chapelain and
Le Moyne are all represented by examples which Rymer
subjects to critical appraisal. He finally quotes some lines
from Dryden's *The Indian Emperor*, claiming that they surpass
all the other specimens quoted:

> All things are hush'd, as Nature's self lay dead:
> The mountains seem to Nod their drowsie head,
> The little birds in dreams their Songs repeat,
> And sleeping flowers beneath the Night-dew sweat:
> Even Lust and Error sleep.

A few years later, in *The Tragedies of the Last Age* (1678),
Rymer submitted Beaumont and Fletcher's *The Maid's
Tragedy* to a detailed examination by reference to what he
called 'the practice of the ancients' and 'the common sense of
all ages'. His emphasis being what it is – on the plot, its
questionable coherence and plausibility – it is not difficult for
him to do a thorough demolition job on the play, and indeed
to make his points with vividness and humour. The lack of a
true centre to the over-ramified sequence of events and the

improbability of so much that happens is brought into sharp focus. In the first place, the King tries to protect his mistress Evadne from scandal by marrying her to a faithful subject, Amintor, and enjoining her not to sleep with him. Amintor's unhappy acquiescence is only one of a tangle of absurdities which Rymer submits to devastating ridicule. His analysis is both shrewd and entertaining. Where he falls down is in failing to recognise any of the emotional qualities of the play, which somehow compensate for what is indeed a hotch-potch of indigestible plotting. And in this respect Rymer differs from Dryden who never wearied of applauding Fletcher's management of the tenderer passions.

Rymer pressed home his theorising at the expense of English drama in *A Short View of Tragedy, Its Original, Excellency, and Corruption, with some Reflections on Shakespeare and other Practitioners for the Stage* (1693). He takes as his model Aeschylus's tragedy *Persians* (472 BC). Its subject and the design of the action are duly described and applauded. Then Rymer proposes that an ideal English tragedy could be written on the same model with the Spanish Armada as its subject. With great solemnity and total confidence, Rymer supplies a detailed act-by-act synopsis of *The Invincible Armada*, and hands the idea over free gratis to Mr Dryden as a recipe for finally displacing Shakespeare from his preeminence in the theatre.

It is in this work that Rymer makes a full-scale onslaught on *Othello*. He selects it as Shakespeare's most popular play, and brings to bear upon it the judgment in terms of 'common sense' which had some effect when applied to *The Maid's Tragedy*. He is ruthless in its application. Whoever heard of a Moor so exalted as Othello is? Whoever heard of a Senator's daughter so taken in as to run off and marry a blackamoor without her parents' consent? What civilised state would promote a negro to general and entrust him with its defence?

With us a *Moor* might marry some little drab or small-coal Wench; Shakespeare would provide him the Daughter and Heir of some great Lord or Privy Councellor: And all the Town should reckon it a very suitable match.

If Othello is an implausible study as a soldier, Iago is a nonsensical one. As for Desdemona, it is absurd to imagine that a noble woman could be won over by talk such as Othello's to treat black as white. Rymer makes great sport of the way Brabantio is awakened by night to be warned of Desdemona's elopement, also of Othello's defence of himself before the Senators, and he projects the picture of a negro staking his claim to a peer's daughter before the House of Lords. But where his criticism really does strike home is in his analysis of some carelessness in the time-sequence touching the development of Othello's jealousy, Cassio's supposed part in it, and Iago's manipulation of it. At the end of his scathing analysis of offences against reason and decorum, he concludes that 'the tragical part is plainly none other than a Bloody Farce, without salt or savour'. Rymer did not go in for finesse. His assertiveness is not tempered with the kind of logical dialectic which makes Dryden so persuasive. 'Dryden's criticism has the majesty of a queen,' Dr Johnson said, 'Rymer's has the ferocity of a tyrant.'

Rymer was no fool, but he was remarkably insensitive to poetry. His view was that some of the supposedly most moving high points in Shakespearean tragedy would be improved if the words were left out. The rich poetry that delights us he regarded as bombast. 'In a Play one should speak like a man of business,' he says, and later:

> In the *Neighing* of an Horse, or in the *growling* of a Mastiff, there is a meaning, there is as lively expression, and, may I say, more humanity, than many times in the Tragical flights of *Shakespeare*.

It is not surprising that Rymer made plenty of enemies in the theatre. Addison tells us how it was the custom to manufacture stage snow showers by shredding the rejected manuscripts of unsuccessful playwrights, and when Rymer offered his play *Edgar, or The English Monarch* (1678) for production, it was used to 'fall in snow at the next acting of *King Lear*', a play which Rymer had denigrated.

Perhaps the most characteristically 'English' reply to Rymer came from the satirical poet, Samuel Butler (1613–80), whose *Hudibras* (1662–80) had shown him to be the bitter foe of academic pedantry and pomposity. He wrote some verses *Upon Critics Who Judge of Modern Plays Precisely by the Rules of the Antients* (1678), in which native commonsense bristles with outrage against those who want to reduce the composition and judgment of poetry to matters of strict rule and regulation. He makes ridiculous the attempt to bring the Muses to heel by court verdict, to impose choruses and episodes on modern tragedy, and to insist

> That not an Actor shall presume to Squeak
> Unless he have a Licence for't in Greek,
> Nor Whittington Henceforward sell his Cat in
> Plaine vulgar English, without Mewing Latin...

An English poet should be tried by his fellow-poets, not by pedants and philosophers who, most intolerably of all, are foreigners applying a foreign code. Plainly Rymer's treatment of Beaumont and Fletcher was a major aggravation to Butler,

> When all their worst miscarriages Delight
> And please more than the Best that Pedants write.

'What Reformation may not we expect, now that in *France* they see the necessity of a Chorus to their Tragedies?' That was the challenging sentence which opened Rymer's *Short View*. For him the Chorus was 'the root and original' and 'always the most necessary part' of a tragedy. Twenty years earlier Edward Phillips (1630–96), Milton's nephew, had ventured to question whether re-installation of the Chorus might revive 'the pristine glory' of tragedy. Phillips had written a collection of rather undistinguished biographical accounts of poets, arranged them in alphabetical order, and published them as *Theatrum Poetarum, or a Compleat Collection of the Poets* (1675). The publication is remembered today only for its Preface, which makes a plea for comprehensive consideration of the work of poets, whether celebrated or forgotten. The awareness of a community of poets, not all of whom may have attained eminence, is an aspect of Phillips's sense of the literary tradition which gives the Preface its importance. Phillips goes back to Chaucer and deals with the objection that the language of the period before Henry VIII is unattractively uncouth, by pointing to the danger of making the language of one's own day a criterion. This too will be superseded and become obsolete. Phillips's determination to put temporary 'fashion' in its place is another aspect of his developed historic sense. He does justice too to Spenser's stanza as 'an Improvement upon *Tasso's Ottava Rima*'. He is sensitive enough to question the appropriateness of either the heroic couplet or Davenant's quatrain for epic poetry. Indeed, as befits Milton's nephew, he suggests that dispensing with rhyme altogether may offer the epic poet greater scope in relation to both 'style and fancy'. A heroic poem concerns itself with 'the unbridled passions of Love, Rage, and Ambition, the violent end or downfalls of great Princes, the subversion of Kingdoms and Estates'. As such, it will require a style 'not ramping, but passionately sedate and moving'.

A more workmanlike exercise in the new critical approach essayed by Phillips was *An Account of the English Dramatick Poets* (1691) by Gerard Langbaine (1657–92). The book includes a full-scale assault on Dryden as a plagiarist. The study is sprinkled with accusations of theft, robbery, plunder and pillage, so that subsequent critics have not always exercised much patience in examining exactly what Langbaine says. Once more we are faced by a formidable scholar, and in so far as he is angry, it appears to be because he deeply resents those remarks of Dryden which amount to cool disparagement of Shakespeare, Fletcher and Jonson. What especially riles Langbaine is that Dryden has frequently pressed home the indebtedness of other writers to their sources. But Dryden, he maintains, is far more deeply indebted, not just for plots in general, but for the detailed substance of episodes, and not just to the ancients, but to Italian, Spanish and French writers. Langbaine subjects Dryden's plays to careful scrutiny, tracking down indebtednesses. There are times when the thoroughness of his exploration of parallelisms is enlightening and persuasive. For instance, he digs out this parallel between Milton's *Samson Agonistes* and Dryden's *Aureng-Zebe*:

> *Dalila*: I see thou art implacable, more deaf
> To prayers than winds and seas; yet winds to seas
> Are reconcil'd at length, and sea to shore:
> Thy anger unappeasable still rages,
> Eternal Tempest never to be calm'd.

> *Emperor*: Unmov'd she stood, and deaf to all my prayers,
> As Seas and Winds to sinking Mariners;
> But Seas grow calm and Winds are reconcil'd;
> Her Tyrant Beauty never grows more mild.

II The ancients and the moderns

The question of how contemporary writers stood in relation to those Elizabethans they claimed to have outclassed was a byway of literary controversy compared to the question of how the 'moderns' (which embraced Elizabethans and contemporaries alike) stood in relation to the 'ancients'. Many scholars deeply versed in the classics could be outraged that the question should ever arise. Sir William Temple (1628–99), the diplomat who went to the Hague to arrange the marriage of William of Orange and Mary, and in whose household at Moor Park Swift met 'Stella' (Esther Johnson), was moved to write *An Essay Upon the Ancient and Modern Learning* (published in *Miscellanea*, the *Second Part*, 1690). His position was that 'whoever converses much among the old books will be something hard to please among the new'. He first demolishes the idea that we must necessarily possess more knowledge than the ancients because, however small we may be, we stand on their shoulders. His argument is that the ancients too had the shoulders of their predecessors to stand on. 'The advantage we have from those we call the Ancients may not be greater than what they had from those that were so to them.' In any case the dependence of modern scholarship on the pioneering thought of the Greeks is indisputable. He grants that modern learning far surpasses the understanding of the Dark Ages, but this does not mean that it surpasses the understanding of the ancients. Indeed evidence from the history of scholarship but confutes the notion of inevitable progress implicit in the dwarf-on-the-shoulders image. Temple's argument culminates in a series of rhetorical questions. Has Boileau surpassed Virgil and Davenant surpassed Homer? Does a Welsh or Irish harp outclass Orpheus's instrument or the pyramid in London those of Memphis?

In an interesting parenthesis, Temple allows that the Reformation may have damaged learning by diverting such massive intellectual energies into feverish controversy, theological and ecclesiastical. He also regrets the decay of patronage in favour of the pursuit of wealth. And he concludes his good-humoured thesis by quoting a saying attributed to Alphonsus the Wise of Aragon:

> That among so many things as are by Men possessed or pursued in the Course of their Lives, all the rest are Bawbles, Besides Old Wood to Burn, Old Wine to Drink, Old Friends to Converse with, and Old Books to Read.

Temple turns literary critic more specifically in another section of the *Miscellanea, Of Poetry*. It is the business of poets both to profit and to please, he begins. Though Greek and Latin terminology implies the operation of divine creativity and of the prophetic spirit in the work of the poet, Temple insists that there is no supernatural dimension to the making of poetry. Its origins are purely natural. But undoubtedly poetry can work powerfully on human passions, incorporating as it does the emotive resources of 'eloquence, of music, and of picture', each of which might transfix with love, or disturb with joy or grief. Invention is, of course, the mother of poetry, but the many gifts of nature needful for its composition have to be supplemented by learning and art, by a fertile, wide-ranging imagination, and by that poetic insight which discerns images and similitudes hidden over the world. Temple piles up the adjectives in a strenuous effort to convey the need for a balancing of the 'heat of Invention and liveliness of Wit' with 'the coldness of good Sense and soundness of Judgment'. There has to be 'a great agitation of Mind to invent, a great Calm to judge and correct'.

After an eloquent tribute to Homer and Virgil, voiced in the familiar vocabulary ('Spirit, Force, and Life' in Homer; 'Design, Proportion, and Grace' in Virgil), Temple turns to answer the rigid claims for the Aristotelian rules made by French critics such as Boileau and Rapin. Here he reveals a delightful vein of commonsense. 'The Truth is there is something in the *Genius* of Poetry too Libertine to be confined to so many Rules.' To formulate rigid regulations for poets is like cutting off the wings of bees and restricting their power to roam, in the attempt to improve the honey. The most that can be claimed for rules is that they might prevent some men from becoming bad poets without helping anyone to become a good one. It is by the power of the poet to work on your feelings that he can be judged.

At this point Temple embarks on a brief survey of the history of poetry. We make the familiar journey from the ancient world, through the fall of Rome, the unhappy disintegration of classical Latin, and the Middle Ages, to the Renaissance and the revival of poetry. Since for Temple the epic is central to the poetic tradition, he makes an attempt to do justice to Spenser. He argues that the 'true religion' sits less comfortably in heroic poetry than did the false one. Spenser tried to solve the problem by his moral allegory, making 'instruction instead of story the subject of an epic poem'. His 'execution was excellent, and his flights of fancy very noble and high, but his design was poor, and his moral lay so bare that it lost its effect'. Modern poets have tried to give greater value to the small coinage of shorter poems. To this end they have exploited two distinctive veins – the use of 'conceits' intended to give spice and vitality to the verse, and the use of 'ridicule'. Both veins have been overworked, in Temple's view.

Temple concludes his study by turning to drama. Here is a genre in which we English have excelled ancients and moderns alike. The secret of our success is our vein of 'humour', by which he seems to mean the capacity to represent striking but not unnatural characters of great variety in their temperaments and their oddities. Temple regards the English as having this peculiarly developed gift partly because political liberty gives English individualists plenty of scope, partly because the comparative wealth of the English preserves them from the uniformity which is imposed upon the masses of poorer countries, partly because they are brought up in a climate so unreliable and unpredictable, and partly because our fierce religious and political factions have bred a generation of controversialists, fanatics, and hypocrites, not to mention libertines and debauchees, toadies and self-seekers.

Temple makes good company. He is a courteous polemicist who neither snarls nor bites, but maintains an easy, equable relationship with his reader.

Temple's thesis was taken up by William Wotton (1666–1726) in *Reflections Upon Ancient and Modern Learning* (1694). Wotton was enough of a prodigy to have been reading Greek at five years of age and to have been examined in Greek, Latin and Hebrew by the time he was six. In his *Reflections* he is anxious to modify the position adopted by Temple. He accepts that the works of the ancients have been wrapped in reverence for us by their distance from us and by the dependence of so much modern literature on them. These facts are conducive to a blind admiration for the ancients, and true appreciation of their work needs to be established on a more rational basis. To begin with, he sees Greek and Latin as having a beauty and expressiveness that lend themselves to great poetry. Indeed 'if *Homer* and *Virgil* had been *Polanders* or *High-Dutch-Men*, they would in all probability never have thought it worth their while to attempt the Writing of Heroick Poems'. Moreover the ancient commonwealths allowed of a degree of liberty conducive to the development of oratory. If the moderns enjoyed the same advantages, they might match the achievements of the greatest of the ancients.

The controversy was not restricted to this country. Fontenelle (1657–1757), French thinker and poet, and a nephew of Corneille, had taken up the cudgels on behalf of the moderns in *Digression sur les Anciens et les Modernes* (1688). Charles Perrault (1628–1701) challenged the views of critics such as Boileau in his poem *Le Siècle de Louis le Grand* (1687) by also claiming superiority for the moderns. Wotton takes issue with Perrault in his *Reflections*. He rejects Perrault's assumption that the progress of civilisation gives the later poet or orator superiority to the earlier one. He finds this basic premiss naive. It fails to allow for the possibility of decay as well as improvement. He makes short work of Perrault who found fault with Virgil for not carrying on his poem to the marriage of Aeneas with Lavinia. Perrault too made much of the progress since the time of the ancients in polish and politeness, failing to recognise the value of the simplicity of the ancients, which is now mistaken for crudity, and praising modern niceties of manner which might be more properly condemned as strained and artificial. But the most forceful thing in Wotton's case is probably his point that the French critics have relied on French translations of the ancients in passing judgment. They have poured the 'spirits of ancient poetry from one bottle into another' and 'lost the most subtile parts'.

III The moral debate

Controversy was naturally provoked by the way in which the moral laxity of Restoration society infected contemporary poetry and drama with a vein of licentiousness. The notorious Earl of Rochester came under attack for his libertinism in life and in letters. When John Sheffield, the Earl of Mulgrave (1642–1721), one of Dryden's patrons, attacked him in his *Essay Upon Satire* (*c*.1680), published anonymously, Rochester assumed Dryden to be the author and employed ruffians to assault him. Mulgrave (Sheffield) showed himself another of Boileau's disciples in *An Essay Upon Poetry* (1682), whose couplets rehearse familiar arguments about 'Fancy' and 'Judgment'.

> Fancy is but the Feather of the Pen;
> Reason is that substantial, useful part,
> Which gains the Head, while t'other wins the Heart.

Mulgrave deals with the various poetic forms in turn, and it is while dealing with 'Songs' that he raises the moral issue:

> Here, as in all things else, is most unfit
> Bawdry barefac'd, that poor pretence to Wit, –
> Such nauseous Songs as the late Convert made,
> Which justly calls this censure on his Shade.

The 'late Convert' is Rochester, an account of whose death-
bed repentance had been published shortly after his death by
Gilbert Burnet (1643–1715) who later wrote *The History of
My Own Times* (1724, 1734).

Mulgrave won support from the Earl of Roscommon, to
whose *Essay on Translated Verse* (1684) we have already
referred.

> *Immodest words* admit of no defence,
> For want of *Decency* is want of *Sense*,
> What mod'rate *Fop* would rake the *Park* or *Stews*,
> Who among Troops of faultless Nymphs may choose?

And Dryden in the *Preface to Sylvae* (1685) echoed Mulgrave's
words:

> 'Tis most certain that barefaced bawdry is the poorest pretence to wit
> imaginable. If I should say otherwise, I should have two great
> authorities against me.

The 'great authorities' are Mulgrave's *Essay* and Cowley's
Ode concerning Wit.

> Much less can that have any place
> At which a virgin hides her face.

Pope too was later to applaud Mulgrave in his *Essay on
Criticism* as one of those who rehabilitated the fundamental
laws of Wit:

> Such was the Muse, whose rules and practice tell,
> 'Nature's chief Masterpiece is writing well.'

But heavy artillery was directed against Mulgrave by
Robert Wolseley (1649–97). After Rochester's death he
edited for publication in 1685 his 'improved' version of
Fletcher's tragedy *Valentinian*, and prefixed a substantial
Preface to the publication. It sheds light on the thinking of
the age that Wolseley takes it for granted that Rochester has
great advantages over Fletcher in 'a nicer knowledge of Men
and Manners, an Air of good Breeding, and a Gentleman-

like easiness in all he writ, to which *Fletcher's* obscure
Education and the mean Company he kept made him
wholly a Stranger'. This, however, is tangential to the
central issue of Wolseley's Preface, which is a vigorous
defence of Rochester against Mulgrave's charges. The
praises he heaps on Rochester mark him as a fervent
admirer, and the anger against the anonymous author is
that of an outraged devotee. Had Rochester been alive to
speak for himself, it would have been of no avail 'to pick up
scraps of Bossu, Rapin, Boileau, Mr Dryden's Prefaces and
Table-Talk ... and send 'em out in the World as a new *Art of
Poetry*'. The vanity of small-minded versifiers was kept in
check during Rochester's life 'by the general dread' of his
pen. But now satire has degenerated into all manner of mud-
slinging and injustice.

When Wolseley turns to analyse Mulgrave's charges phrase
by phrase, he wins the limited dialectical combats, if not the
overall moral one. Mulgrave had called 'barefaced bawdry' a
'poor pretence of Wit', and Wolseley makes high sport of the
notion that wit can be measured by the worth of its subject.
He makes much of the theory that poetry is *Pictura loquens*
and painting is *Poema silens*. On the basis of Mulgrave's
charge, he argues, the most admired statuary of the ancient
world would have to be condemned as obscene in its nudity.
Is nudity a 'poor pretence' to sculpture as bawdry is a 'poor
pretence' to wit? And what of the great classical poets who
on this basis would fall under condemnation? Wolseley grants
that bawdry for its own sake, pointless obscenity, makes a
poor pretence to wit. But Rochester is free of such crudity.
Wolseley defines 'poetical wit' as 'a true and lively expression
of Nature', and them emphasises that Mulgrave 'brands not
Bawdry for being indecent and immoral, but for being
unwitty', a case which plainly cannot be sustained. Moreover he tackles another charge made by Mulgrave:

> But obscene words, too gross to move desire,
> Like heaps of fuel do but choak the Fire.
> That Author's Name has undeserved praise,
> Who pall'd the appetite he meant to raise.

Wolseley dissects this passage with devastating effect. Bawdry has always been assumed to be offensive because it is an incentive to unlawful desires, and if 'barefaced bawdry' does not thus offend, but on the contrary 'flattens and stifles' them, then it is innocent indeed. What it amounts to apparently is that Mulgrave dislikes Rochester's bawdry because it does no damage! Wolseley does not claim that Rochester is faultless in relation to Mulgrave's charge, but he argues that the 'careless gaieties' of his pen can be excused as the effervescence of youth. And he insists that poems must be judged in accordance with their proper purpose and the particular public to which they are addressed. Rochester did not design the offending songs 'to be sung for Anthems in *King's-Chapel*'. They were for limited private consumption. Thus, supported by critical dissection of some of Mulgrave's turns of phrase and even his scansion, Wolseley's onslaught may be said to have convincingly exposed crucial weaknesses in Mulgrave's argument.

Wolseley was so doughty a controversialist that he fought a duel over a 'poetical' dispute with Thomas Wharton's younger brother, who died from his wounds.

Another aggressive controversialist was Sir Richard Blackmore (1654–1729), who served both William III and Queen Anne as physician and who was a great manufacturer of lengthy poems. His *Creation: a philosophical poem demonstrating the Existence and Providence of God* (1712) was to win praise from Addison and Dr Johnson and to be compared favourably by Dennis with Lucretius's *De Rerum Natura*. His *Prince Arthur, An Heroick Poem* (1695) was accompanied by a *Preface* in which the account of current decadence is more impressive than the standard neoclassical recommendations for poetic composition. The aim of poetry, to give pleasure and delight, is subordinate to the prime end which is to instruct. Tragedy is designed 'to scare men, comedy to laugh them out of their vices'. On these terms Blackmore looks out on a situation in which the right use of poetry has been perverted on an unprecedented scale. The typical hero of current comedy is a witty, idle, extravagant, pleasure-loving libertine who debauches women and derides religion. The typical heroine is brazen, shameless, and profane in her chatter; she is mistress of intrigue, she scoffs at female modesty, despises the wise advice of her elders, and disobeys parents and guardians. Clergymen are represented as objects of contempt, pimps, blockheads, or hypocrites. Citizens' wives are induced to despise their husbands and accept the favours of the rakish heroes. As chastity and fidelity are thus derided, so diligence and frugality are undermined by making the well-to-do citizen a contemptible fool. Nor is the attack limited to the stage. 'Monstrous, lewd, and irreligious books of poems' are also under fire. And the purpose of the present epic is directed 'towards rescuing the Muses out of the hands of these ravishers, to restore them to their sweet and chaste mansions, and to engage them in an employment suitable to their dignity'.

Several writers had a go at Blackmore. John Dennis (1657–1734) responded with *Remarks on a Book, entitled Prince Arthur, An Heroick Poem* (1696), accusing Blackmore of failing to represent the classical rules accurately either in his preface or in his poem. Blackmore returned to the fray in his preface to *King Arthur* (1697), but he was mocked in the burlesque poem *The Dispensary* (1699) by a fellow-physician, Sir Samuel Garth (1661–1719). Finally Blackmore wrote his *Satyr against Wit* (1700) in which he lambasted all the literary corruptors who were undermining virtue in private life and decency in public life. He gives 'wit' a thoroughly pejorative connotation. The English were vigorous, brave, virtuous, and sober in those 'unpolished times' that were free of knavery and wit. If only wits had been rounded up and isolated in the pest-house when they first began to infect society with their plague, the contagion might have been controlled. As it is, alas, houses and streets are littered with thousands of terminal cases. Wits are not only licentious,

> For next to Virtue, Learning they abhor,
> Laugh at Discretion, but at business more.

They are idle fools who scoff at 'all Liberal and Mechanick Arts'.

Blackmore calls for all the bogus poets to be melted down and reminted into genuine coinage.

'Tis true that when the coarse and worthless Dross
Is purg'd away, there will be mighty Loss.
Ev'n Congreve, Southerne, Manly Wycherly,
When thus refin'd will grievous suff'rers be.
Into the melting pot when Dryden comes,
What horrid Stench will rise, what noisome Fumes!
How will he shrink, when all his lewd Allay
And wicked Mixture shall be purg'd away.

It is not surprising that Blackmore made his share of enemies.
His early days as a schoolmaster were trotted out against
him. There was a lampoon ending:

In vain his drugs as well as birch he tried,
His boys grew blockheads and his patients died.

The most thorough and hard-hitting analysis of the
indecency and licentiousness of Restoration drama came
from Jeremy Collier (1650–1726), a bishop and one of those
'non-jurors' who believed that if they took the Oath of
Allegiance to William and Mary they would be betraying
previous allegiance to James II. Collier was a prolific
polemicist. He was twice imprisoned and was finally out-
lawed for giving absolution on the scaffold to two men who
tried to assassinate William III. Collier's *Short View of the
Immorality and Profaneness of the English Stage* (1698) deals in six
chapters with the immodesty of the stage, the profanity, the
treatment of the clergy, and the immoral influence; then
subjects some contemporary plays to a moral critique, and
finally surveys some classical and mediaeval views of the
theatre. It is in the fourth and fifth chapters that Collier's
crucial charges of immorality are presented and illustrated,
and it is of course in pressing his case with detailed
exemplification that he functions as a literary critic.

In Collier's Introduction he nails his colours to the mast:

The business of *Plays* is to recommend Vertue, and discountenance
Vice; to shew the Uncertainty of Humane Greatness, the sudden
Turns of Fate, and the Unhappy Conclusions of Violence and
Injustice: 'Tis to expose the Singularities of Pride and Fancy, to

make Folly and Falsehood contemptible, and to bring every Thing that is Ill under Infamy, and Neglect.

Collier's platform is thus something more than a negative assault on current liberties. His sense of the playwright's responsibilities is based on a philosophical grasp of the nature and function of drama. Some prior respect is perhaps due to him for the comprehensiveness of understanding which saw drama as related to the lives of the public at the deepest level. But when Collier gets down to particulars, the modern reader is bound to squirm over the dogged humourlessness which mars his work. He launches into a survey of the 'rankness' and 'indecency' of language, the 'smuttiness of expression', the swearing and profanity, the lewd treatment of religion and the clergy, and then turns to the topsy-turvy values by which heroes are turned into vicious libertines who are finally rewarded for their debaucheries. Thus Collier examines plays be Dryden, Wycherley, and Congreve in order to prove that 'A fine Gentleman, is a fine Whoring, Swearing, Smutty, Atheistical Man ... The Restraints of Conscience and the Pedantry of Virtue are unbecoming a Cavalier.'

Collier develops Blackmore's charges. Learning, industry, and frugality are ridiculed in comedy. Fine ladies are rude to their seniors, given to sauciness, indecency and profanity. He ridicules the vast difference Dryden makes between tragedy and comedy, particularly Dryden's view of the necessity to punish vice in tragedy because the persons involved are 'great' and of the less serious nature of the follies exposed in comedy. Dryden's maxim, 'that the chief end of comedy is delight' is contrasted with Rapin's view that 'delight is the end that poetry aims at, but not the principal one'.

Collier's case in general had substance. Dryden recognised the fact two years later in his Preface to *Fables Ancient and Modern* (1700), 'I shall say the less of Mr Collier, because in many things he has taxed me justly.'

But he added that Collier had also often perverted his meaning by misinterpretation. And when we look at Collier's exemplifications rather than at his general premisses, we are astonished at the lack of literary sensitivity. His detailed analysis of Vanbrugh's *The Relapse* is irritating, not because it is fallacious, but because it is irrelevant. We do not need to have the implausibilities of the plot or even the clumsinesses of the construction put under the microscope. They are self-evident. And to apply the measuring-rod of moral judgment with strict censoriousness to the antics of Young Fashion, Lord Foppington and Sir Tunbelly Clumsy is as absurd as to query their strict realism. All the positive things in the play, the riotous satiric caricature, the ironic exaggerations, the humour, the vitality and the wit might as well not be. Thus where Collier's work ought to have had its chief merit – in the application of general principles to actual texts – it collapses into absurdity.

Sir John Vanbrugh (1664–1726) was stung to reply in *A Short Vindication of the 'Relapse' and the 'Provok'd Wife' from Immorality and Profaneness* (1698). He argues that it is the business of comedy 'to shew People what they shou'd do, by representing them upon the Stage, doing what they shou'd not'. The stage is a mirror in which people ought to see themselves as they are, with clean or with dirty faces. It will fail of its purpose if it does not lay open the vices as well as the virtues. Collier's outburst did in fact produce an official reaction in the form of a proclamation against immorality backed up by the imposition of fines on offending playwrights and actors.

William Congreve (1670–1729) was also sufficiently disturbed by Collier's attack on him to publish a reply *Amendments of Mr Collier's False and Imperfect Citations* (1698) which A. N. Jeffares has described as 'an example of how not to reply in anger'. Congreve was not at his best when he turned critic. He had responded in 1695 to a request from John Dennis that he should say something about '*Humour* in Comedy'. His letter 'Concerning Humour in Comedy' scarcely advances critical theory. Congreve's notion of 'humour' has not escaped from the Jonsonian connotation. He describes it as:

A singular and unavoidable manner of doing or saying anything, Peculiar and Natural to one Man only; by which his Speech and Actions are distinguished from those of other men.

For Congreve all figures of caricature are 'humorous' provided that they do not simply represent either unfortunate personal defects which ought to raise compassion, or externals of dress or accent or manners which appertain rather to whole classes of people and are the product of custom rather than of disposition. (Sailors, traders, jockeys etc. have their special 'cants'.) Congreve's complaint that people tend to speak of 'humour' when they really mean 'wit' shows how the connotation of 'humour' was undergoing change. He takes the view that there is more humour in English comic writers than in others because humour seems to be 'almost of English growth' and perhaps a by-product of the great freedoms the common people of England enjoy. (There is surely something piquant in the asseveration of one who was virtually an Irishman by his upbringing that humour is a specifically English product.)

IV John Dennis

A critic who lived long enough to bestride the ages of both Dryden and Pope was John Dennis (1657–1734). His earlier work *The Impartial Critic* (1693) was written specifically in reply to Rymer's *Short View of Tragedy*. It is presented in the form of an introductory 'Letter to a Friend', followed by five dialogues in which two old friends, Beaumont and Freeman, discuss Rymer's work. Dennis has some sensible things to say against Rymer's advocacy of the use of the Greek Chorus in modern tragedy. Strict adherence to Greek practices which were closely linked to the religious and cultural notions of the day would be an absurdity in modern drama. He gives examples of turns of thought which made sense to the Greeks and would make nonsense in his own day, and instances the neglect of love themes and scenes on the Greek stage as something which modern drama cannot accept. Dennis also disapproves of the 'pleasantry' pervading Rymer's work. The tone is out of place in a sphere of argument where style should be direct, succinct, unaffected, and have that gravity which conveys an assurance that proceeds from reason and authority. He takes up Rymer's criticism of the *Oedipus* Dryden wrote in collaboration with

Lee. He is ready to accept that Dryden's Oedipus is so virtuous and his act of parricide so totally the consequence of ignorance that, instead of compassion, the audience can respond only with horror. Sophocles's Oedipus, by contrast, has that degree of culpability in vanity and rashness which, while not sufficient to alienate an audience, is enough to involve them with him.

> For how can an Audience choose but tremble, when it sees a Man involv'd in the most deplorable Miseries only for indulging those Passions and Frailties which they are but too conscious that they neglect in themselves?

The arousal of compassion and terror alike is dependent on a capacity for fellow-feeling with the hero. If the hero is perfect, compassion turns to horror. If (and this must follow) his misfortunes are due to accident, the audience's sense of immunity is not disturbed. But Dennis is careful to insist that he cannot therefore join Rymer in denigration of Dryden, whose poetic power mesmerises the audience into blindness to any such defects.

In the third dialogue Dennis cunningly applies Rymer's technique of critical dissection to Waller's poem 'To the King, on his Navy' in order to bring to light defects of expression. It is an effective piece of critical surgery, all the more so because Dennis insists that his aim is not to denigrate Waller, whose work he genuinely admires, but to show how biassed and unscholarly Rymer had been in seeing only the merits of Waller and only the faults in Shakespeare. The fourth and fifth dialogues tackle more thoroughly Rymer's insistence on the necessity of the Chorus in tragedy. Dennis argues convincingly that a Chorus is necessary neither to the structure nor to the substance of a tragedy, and that it can add nothing in the way of moral instruction or commentary on the action which cannot be directly conveyed in its absence. It must be understood that Dennis's critique of Rymer is totally different in its basis and inspiration from the critiques of those such as Butler who utterly rejected the neoclassical stance. Dennis was himself a neoclassical critic. For him 'The rules of Aristotle are nothing but Nature and Good Sense reduc'd to a Method'. But he was far too sensitive to the cultural gap separating classical Greece from modern Europe to be able to take over outdated formulations uncritically.

Dennis was not content merely to contribute to the field of criticism in a piecemeal fashion. He was not satisfied merely to take his part in the ongoing literary conversation. He was interested in current controversy only because he had the itch to establish basic principles of the theory of literature. There are passages in his book *The Advancement and Reformation of Modern Poetry* (1701) where he ventures to lay foundations for a systematic and comprehensive philosophy of poetry. He gives us a definition: 'Poetry, then, is an imitation of Nature by a pathetic and numerous speech.'

Poetry must in the first place be 'pathetic', that is, passion is necessary to it. In the second place it is 'numerous', that is rhythmical. 'Harmony' (that is versification) distinguishes the 'instrument' from prose; but 'passion distinguishes its very nature and character'. Good metrical verse, if it lacks passion, is only 'measured prose', whereas prose discourse which is 'everywhere extremely pathetic...bold and figurative' is 'poetry without numbers'. Passion must be 'everywhere' in poetry, but it is not the ordinary passion of real life, which is something 'clearly comprehended'. It is passion that Dennis calls 'enthusiasm', passion whose 'cause is not clearly comprehended'.

Dennis developed this line of thought later, notably in *The Grounds of Criticism in Poetry* (1704). His plan in this work was to explore the nature of poetry, and to establish reliable standards of criticism by making clear the rules proper to epic, dramatic and lyric poetry. He makes a good case for 'rules'. Poetry is 'either art, or whimsy and fanaticism'. If it is an art, it has definable end and means. If its end is 'to instruct and reform the world', this is a matter of replacing irregularity and confusion by rule and order, indeed of bringing man's work into line with God's in the creation of an orderly universe. This is one aspect of restoring 'the decays that happened to human nature by the fall'. Thus Dennis recapitulates Milton's doctrine that 'the end of learning is to repair the ruins of our first parents'.

Dennis spells out his basic position. Poetry is an art which excites emotion ('passion') in order to please and reform the mind. Its subordinate end is pleasure, its final end instruction. All instruction has an emotive element in the sense that even a dry moral philosopher will make 'vice odious and virtue lovely'. Poetry instructs more powerfully than philosophy because it 'makes the very violence of the passions contribute to our reformation'. The 'greater poetry' (epic, tragic and lyric) 'excites great passion'; the 'less poetry' (comedy, satire, elegies and pastoral) 'excites less passion'. Dennis now proceeds to clarify the concept of 'passion' or emotion. There is the 'vulgar' passion of day-to-day anger, pity and admiration. But the 'enthusiastic passion' peculiar to poetry is, as he explained in *The Advancement*, a different matter. It is more intense, able to be relished by the mind in the act of experiencing it, and proceeds from causes hidden from us. These emotions, or 'passions' (admiration, terror, horror, joy, sadness, desire) are aroused by contemplation of ideas, not by the kind of direct reference to them found in ordinary life. A conversational mention of thunder, with the idea of a black cloud and a big noise, makes little impression on us. But 'the idea of it occurring in meditation sets before us the most forcible, most resistless, and consequently the most dreadful phenomenon in nature'. The kind of 'terror' produced is what Dennis calls 'enthusiasm'. It is the business of the poet to work on both the 'vulgar' passion which all men can respond to and the more subtle 'enthusiastic' passion available to the few. Wordsworth who, like Coleridge, had read and admired Dennis's work, seems to have been influenced by him in his Preface to the *Lyrical Ballads*, where he claims that the poet has 'a disposition to be affected more than other men by absent things as if they were present; an ability of conjuring up in himself passions, which are indeed far from being the same as those produced by real events'.

A crucial thesis now emerges. Since the intensest and most exalted emotions are to be stirred by great poetry, and since their arousal must be consonant with reason, it follows that the highest and worthiest ideas of all, those of religion, are the most fitting material for poetry. Dennis makes a systematic defence of this thesis, citing Aristotle, Hermogenes and Longinus as authorities, and illustrating his case by detailed reference to *Paradise Lost*. The purpose is to establish that a poet who seeks to give the maximum elevation, gravity and majesty to his work can derive his ideas from nothing so fitting as God. In effect the modern reader is likely to be more impressed by the imaginative sensitivity Dennis reveals at many points to the power of Milton's verse than by the accompanying critical rationale. For Dennis *Paradise Lost* is 'the greatest poem that ever was written by man', yet he considers it an artistic blunder that whereas in the first eight books we are 'divinely entertained' with the 'wondrous works of God', in the later books, and especially in the last one, Milton 'makes an angel entertain us with the works of corrupted man'.

For Dennis modern poetry has fallen from dignity and excellence into contempt through 'divesting itself of religion'. Christianity and Poetry have a common aim in delighting and reforming mankind. The conviction that religion gives warmth and 'passion' to poetry leads Dennis to the impossible conclusion that the less religion is mixed in poetry with anything profane and human, the greater will be its effect. Yet Dennis was a formidable critic. Though he seems to have degenerated in his later days into the kind of aggressive dogmatic pedant who provoked ridicule and mockery from Pope and other poets, he deserves credit for the way he gave neoclassical rules respect without literal servitude, for his emphasis on the essential role of emotion in poetry, and for his determination to corroborate his judgments with detailed scrutiny of the literature he criticised.

6
The Eighteenth Century: The Age of Addison and Pope

The early decades of the eighteenth century represent a period of calm and prosperity after the dissensions and turmoils of the previous century. The lively picture of the state of the country given by Daniel Defoe (1660–1731) in his *Tour through the Whole Island of Great Britain* (1724–6) shows a nation busily and contentedly at work. It was an age when industry and commerce were expanding, when agriculture, sheep-farming and woollen manufacture prospered. 'Puritanism' was taking on a different guise. Energies which had gone into religious controversy were being devoted to trade and industry. In this respect the dissenter Defoe himself seems to represent a new breed. With his heroine Moll Flanders, spiritual self-examination and financial accountancy go hand in hand as she repeatedly takes stock of her sins and her income. The same Defoe had been sent as an agent to Edinburgh in 1706 by the arch-political intriguer Robert Harley, Earl of Oxford (1661–1727). His brief was to pose as a disinterested friend of the Scots ('a hardened, refractory, and terrible people', he called them) and persuade them that union with England would be in their best interests. The Union was achieved in 1707.

Queen Anne (reigned 1702–1714) was a conscientious woman, exemplary in private life, but saddened by the deaths of all her seventeen children, and perturbed by the consequent question of the future succession. Anne, like Mary, was the daughter of James II by his first marriage (to Ann Hyde), and was a convinced Anglican. But there was a son by James II's second marriage, James, a Catholic (the 'Old pretender'), whose claim to the throne in succession to Anne was apparently supported by the powerful Tory ministers, Harley and Henry St John Bolingbroke (1675– 1751). Queen Anne's unexpected death in 1714 apparently forestalled their plan for Jacobite succession. The Act of Settlement, passed by the Whig government in 1701, had catered for the situation caused by the childlessness of both William III and Anne, and had settled the succession on James I's granddaughter, Sophia, Electress of Hanover, whose son became George I. This act thus guaranteed the Protestant succession. Bitter hostility between Whigs and Tories, whose party identities became firmly established by the turn of the century, was fuelled by the problem of the succession. The Whigs were low churchmen and Hanover- ians, the Tories high churchmen and Jacobites. Echoes of political controversy are scattered over the literary produc- tivity of the age. Gifted writers were in demand, their services sought by powerful ministers in an age of prolific pamphleteering.

The reign of Queen Anne was the age of the military victories in Europe won by the great Duke of Marlborough (1650–1722). He was of course duly rewarded. The reign saw work in progress on the enormous baroque mansions, Blenheim and Castle Howard, designed by the architect and playwright Sir John Vanbrugh (1664–1726). Blenheim Palace was a present to the Duke of Marlborough from a grateful nation. The trees in the grounds were placed so as to recreate the positioning of the English forces at the battle of Blenheim. The reigns of George I (1714–27) and George II (1727–60) saw successively George Frideric Handel's (1685– 1759) prolific output of opera in the 1720s and 1730s and of oratorio in the 1740s. In the literary field the development of periodical journalism gave a new outlet for writers and soon provided a platform for literary criticism. The *Tatler* was launched in 1709 and the *Spectator* in 1711. At the same time clubs and coffee-houses increasingly provided centres of talk and sociability for those interested in politics or literature. The use of the term 'Augustan Age' to identify the period implies that in English literary history it has the kind of distinction which Virgil, Horace and Ovid gave to the reign of the Emperor Augustus. Certainly Pope, Addison and Swift were keen admirers of the classical writers, and when they translated or imitated their great predecessors, they seemed to claim a parallelism of purpose and stature.

It is not surprising that in the new century the development of the genre of literary criticism gathers pace. In the seventeenth century much of the critical output fastened on topical issues arising out of current publications. Gradually, as we saw in the work of Dryden and Dennis, a more comprehensive concern with the function of literature emerged, and critics began to reflect self-consciously on the criteria and techniques of criticism. The literary critic as a figure in his own right begins to disentangle himself from the surrounding company of poets and dramatists jostling to defend themselves and attack their rivals.

I Joseph Addison

Joseph Addison (1672–1719) thus made a conscious effort to produce prescriptive essays laying down lines of guidance which might both clarify controversy and aid composition. He was not, however, a professional writer like Dryden, but a man who pursued a political career as a Whig, holding various posts. Writing was a side-line. Nevertheless his tragedy *Cato* (1713) was one of the most celebrated dramas of the age. It was chiefly in articles for the *Spectator* between 1711 and 1714 that his criticism appeared. In all about fifty articles could be classed as literary criticism. The output deserves attention under three heads. Firstly, there are the papers on separate critical issues; secondly, the papers on *Paradise Lost*; and thirdly, the papers on 'The Pleasures of the Imagination'.

In the first category Addison wrote a series of papers on English tragedy, on wit, and on ballads. He had something to say about 'Poetic Justice' in *Spectator* No. 40, ridiculing the 'modern doctrine' that there must be 'an equal distribution of rewards and punishments' in tragedy. Life is not like that. Good and evil happen alike to all men. Addison also takes the opportunity for a side swipe at tragicomedy as a monstrous invention. But perhaps the most perceptive passage in this paper is that where he illustrates how 'just and natural thought', spoken without vehemence, can be far more moving to an audience than ranting extravagance.

In his papers on wit Addison has a lot to say about various forms of 'false wit'. He decries as 'false wit' artifices such as those employed by George Herbert and others in shaping poems visually to represent a pair of wings or an egg, as well as devices such as puns and acrostics. In *Spectator* No. 62 he takes a definition from Locke's *Essay on Human Understanding* as his starting-point. For Locke, wit lies chiefly in 'the assemblage of ideas, and putting those together with quickness and variety wherein can be found any resemblance or congruity'. Addison amends this definition. The likeness brought to light by wit must not be obvious. It must 'delight and surprise the reader'. 'Thus when a poet tells us the bosom of his mistress is as white as snow, there is no wit in the comparison; but when he adds, with a sigh, that it is as cold too, it then grows into wit.' The resemblance must reside in the 'ideas', not in the words, letters, or assonances. That is 'false wit'. Resemblance of ideas is 'true wit'. Resemblance which is partly the one and partly the other is 'mixed wit'. Cowley is cited as the arch-proponent of the last. While Addison echoes Dryden in criticism of Cowley, he rightly points to the inadequacy of Dryden's definition of wit as 'a propriety of words and thoughts adapted to the subject' ('The Author's Apology' prefixed to *The State of Innocence and the Fall of Man*). This is 'not so properly a definition of wit as of good writing in general'.

In two celebrated papers on the ballad 'Chevy Chase', Addison took his cue from a famous passage in Sidney's *Apology for Poetry*: 'Certainly I must confess my own barbarousness: I never heard the old song of Percy and Douglas that I found not my heart moved more than with a trumpet.' There is boldness and candour about Addison's praise of 'Chevy Chase'. His thesis is that this poem fulfils the conditions laid down by neoclassical criticism, such as that of Le Bossu, for the 'heroic poem'. It is 'founded upon an important precept of morality adapted to the constitution of the country in which the poet writes'. It celebrates 'persons and actions which do honour to their country'. But above all the poem exemplifies Addison's preference for 'the essential and inherent perfection of simplicity of thought' above what he calls 'the Gothic manner in writing'. For Addison the 'Gothic' is exemplified by the ornate formal irregularities and fine stylistic elaborations of a Cowley ode. Over against this kind of pretentious artifice Addison praises the 'majestic simplicity' of the ballad, the 'greatness of the thought', the dignity and beauty of the poetry, all of which justify direct comparison with Homer and Virgil. Herein lies its appeal.

> Had this old song been filled with epigrammatical turns and points of wit, it might perhaps have pleased the wrong taste of some readers, but it would never have become the delight of the common people, nor have warmed the heart of Sir Philip Sidney like the sound of a trumpet ...

We have to remember, of course, that the ancient version of the ballad rescued by Bishop Percy was not yet published and Addison was speaking of an updated Elizabethan version. But we can well admire his repeated insistence on 'the great force which lies in a natural simplicity of thought to affect the reader', as he puts it in his paper on 'Taste' (No. 409), where he once more decries the 'Gothic' attachment to 'turns of wit and forced conceits'. In the same paper too he insists that for a reader to acquire a 'finished taste' it is not only necessary that he should be 'well versed in the works of the best critics both ancient and modern', for he needs something more than a familiarity with mechanical rules. He must be able to 'enter into the very spirit and soul of fine writing' and elucidate what it has to offer.

In the eighteen papers on the subject of Milton's *Paradise Lost*, which appeared in the Saturday *Spectators* between January 5 and May 3, 1712, Addison may be said to have broken new ground in subjecting a great literary masterpiece to systematic and appreciative critical scrutiny. There are six papers on generalities, followed by twelve papers, each devoted to one of the twelve books of *Paradise Lost*. What strikes the modern reader, if he comes to these papers without prior study of the critical environment from which

they spring, is the persistent dependence upon the ancients as
providing the criteria for judgment. Aristotle is appealed to
as the authoritative theoretician on general principles, and
reference is continually made to Homer and to Virgil in the
detailed examination of Milton's text.

The first paper considers how well *Paradise Lost* stands up
by the classical rules of Epic poetry, and whether it matches
up to the *Iliad* and the *Aeneid* in this respect. Addison starts
with the Fable itself. The action should be unified, complete,
and great. Judged by these criteria *Paradise Lost* can be
praised for its structure, its coherence, and above all for
'an unquestionable Magnificence' far in excess of anything
that could have emerged from 'any Pagan system'. The
second paper examines the characters ('Actors'). Addison
has high praise for the sheer variety of characterisation.
Milton did the maximum that was possible, given the
subject and its restriction to two human beings.

> We see Man and Woman in the highest Innocence and Perfection,
> and in the most abject State of Guilt and Infirmity. The two last
> Characters are, indeed, very common and obvious, but the two first
> are not only more magnificent but more new than any Characters
> either in *Virgil* or *Homer*, or indeed in the whole Circle of Nature.

Moreover there could not be a reader of the poem, of any
nation, who is not related to these two principal actors. They
are not only our Progenitors, they are also our Representatives.

The third paper considers the *Sentiments* of *Paradise Lost*.
Milton's 'chief Talent, and indeed his distinguishing Excellence, lies in the Sublimity of his Thoughts'. Anything in a
heroic poem which detracts from naturalness or sublimity is
to be accounted a defect. Anything which leads to mirth can
offend in this respect, and Addison protests against the
unloading of comic puns and quibbles by the fallen angels
after their successful use of artillery on the second day of the
battle in Book VI. The fourth paper specifies 'Perspicuity'
and 'Sublimity' as the prerequisites of the epic style.
Unnaturalness and affectation may detract from perspicuity, and Addison finds Shakespeare sometimes guilty in

this respect. Meanness may detract from sublimity, and that is characterised as reliance upon phrases 'debased by common use'. Milton is not found to be often at fault here. Indeed Addison gives Aristotle as authority for the various verbal devices for avoiding the 'Idiomatick Style' which Milton uses. These include metaphor, foreign idioms, transposition of word order, the careful management of syllables, and the use of coinages. By such means and 'by the Choice of the noblest Words and Phrases which our Tongue could afford him', Milton has carried 'our Language to a greater Height than any of the *English* Poets have ever done before or after him'. Addison is sensitive to the fact that where verse is not built on rhyme, 'Pomp of Sound, and Energy of Expression' are indispensable to keep the verse from lapsing into the flatness of prose.

A fifth paper is devoted to the qualifications of a critic, who must be well-read, a clear and logical thinker, and a master of his native tongue. The true critic 'ought to dwell rather upon Excellencies than Imperfections, to discover the concealed Beauties of a Writer and communicate to the World such things as are worth their observation'. This proclamation proves to be a prelude to a paper on the defects of *Paradise Lost*. Here Addison begins to show his limitations, for the first defect he detects is that 'the Event is unhappy'. The hero of the poem is 'unsuccessful, and by no means a Match for his Enemies'. This fact, Addison tells us, 'gave occasion to Mr Dryden's reflection that the devil was in reality Milton's hero'. Addison will have none of this. Looking for an epic hero of that brand in *Paradise Lost* is looking for something which Milton never intended. In so far as anyone can be called a hero, ''tis certainly the Messiah'. But plainly the kind of misunderstanding which causes Dryden to deny to Adam the role of hero is exactly the same as that which causes Addison to define the 'Event' as 'unhappy' because the 'Hero' (Adam) is beaten by his foes. The confusion over this issue indicates an insensitivity to the presentation of the theology of Redemption in Michael's prophecy, which overwhelms Adam by the sheer goodness of it all. For the rest, Addison shows his hand most clearly of all when, following the neoclassical rule-book, he defines

Milton's digressions (on his blindness, etc.) as a defect, and then proclaims them so beautiful that he would not wish to see them removed. The other blemishes listed are the inappropriate allusions to heathen fables, excessive display of learning, and the use of laboured stylistic devices, of jingles, and of technical terms.

To restore the balance it is necessary to emphasise that the twelve succeeding papers, exploring the books of *Paradise Lost* in turn, are largely enthusiastic encomiums on Milton's achievement. It would be tedious to recapitulate the substance of Addison's tributes. Much of it tends to employ a vocabulary of generalised praise such as we should now associate with the essays submitted by the more pedestrian candidates in English Literature examinations. Things are 'finely imaged' or 'wonderfully beautiful', 'in every way suitable' or 'exquisite in their kind'. Sometimes an expression cannot but draw a smile, as when, speaking of the war of the angels, Addison writes, 'The Author's Imagination was so inflam'd with the great Scene of Action, that wherever he speaks of it, he rises, if possible, above himself.'

What is notable, however, is the distribution of praise over the whole work in relation to such a variety of episodes, descriptions, and incidents. There can be no doubt of Addison's sensitivity to the multifarious qualities of *Paradise Lost*. His stance is that from which so much of the best literary criticism has sprung; the stance of the reader so entranced with what he has read that he must willy-nilly share his delight with others.

Between June 21 and July 3, 1712, in numbers 411 to 421 of the *Spectator*, Addison published a series of papers on 'The Pleasures of the Imagination'. These represent another innovation on Addison's part. He read the philosophers as well as the critics. He had praised Locke's *Essay on the Human Understanding* (1690) while discussing the critic's need to 'learn the Art of distinguishing between Words and Things' in the paper on the Critic which interrupted his series on *Paradise Lost*. His papers on the Imagination lay philosophical foundations before fastening on literature specifically. They thus constitute what we would now call an 'aesthetic'. Addison begins by proclaiming the superiority of sight over all other senses, and it is from sight that the pleasures of imagination arise. The primary pleasures of the imagination derive from direct observation of objects before our eyes. The secondary pleasures of the imagination derive from recollection of objects no longer actually present. This recollection may arise in the mind without external stimulus, or may be provoked by a picture or a verbal description. (Addison tells us that for him the words 'imagination' and 'fancy' are interchangeable. 'Imagination' has not yet acquired the kind of transcendental overtones which it had for the Romantics.)

Addison accepts that the pleasures of imagination are not so refined as those of understanding, but they are more moving, more vivid, and less strenuous. And he categorises what pleases the imagination as what is great, what is new, and what is beautiful. In the first case he makes an interesting connection between the mind's distaste for restraint and its delight in the immensity of spacious scenery. The philosophical basis, however, of human delight in the great, the new, and the beautiful, lies in the fact that God 'has so formed the soul of man that nothing but Himself can be its last, adequate, and proper happiness'. In order to stimulate in us a proper desire for that contemplation of Himself, He has made us so that we take a natural delight in the immense, and to incite us to further exploration of the wonders of his creation, He has added a sweet pleasure in anything new or uncommon.

It is in the last six of the papers that Addison has most to say about literature. He first makes it clear that the imagination's power to recollect does not depend on our having previously seen exactly what is described in words, so long as we have experienced what bears a resemblance, 'or at least some remote analogy', with what is described. And well-chosen words are so powerful 'that a description often gives us more lively ideas than the sight of things themselves'. The poet improves on nature, giving a landscape more vitality and heightened beauty. Developing his earlier categorisation of the sources of imaginative delights, Addison tells us that Homer makes a special impact on the imagination with what is great, Virgil with what is beautiful, and Ovid with what is strange. And if he were asked to name a poet who is 'perfect master in all these arts of working on the imagination', then Milton is the man.

At this point Addison turns to deal with a matter that might be said to prove difficult to accommodate with his theory as so far expounded. It is the fact that it is not only pleasant sights but thoroughly unpleasant sights which can please when received by the imagination. Literature does not always fasten on beautiful scenery. There are descriptions of dung-hills and corpses, of torments and bloodshed. From these things we shrink in reality: but we can take pleasure in them when described because we do not then focus simply on the horrors presented but rather on our own immunity and well-being. From literature's concern with the unpleasant, Addison moves on to its concern with what is unreal, such as 'fairies, witches, magicians, demons, and departed spirits'. He defines it as 'the kind of poetry which Mr Dryden calls the fairy way of writing', and indeed Dryden defended 'the use of spectres and magic in heroic poetry' in his *Prefatory Essay to 'The Conquest of Granada'* (1672) and of 'hippocentaurs and chimeras', 'fairies, pigmies', not to mention angels, in his *Apology Prefixed to 'The State of Innocence and the Fall of Man'* (1677). Dryden's position was that popular belief in such beings was enough to justify their representation in poetry. Addison's view is that we cannot regard the representation of spirits and the like as impossible. Childhood memories and the superstitions of our ancestors all dispose us anyway towards conniving at the idea that fairies and ghosts exist. Indeed he believes the English have a special disposition towards fanciful poetry of this kind. Being naturally gloomy and melancholy, we are peculiarly susceptible to 'wild notions and visions'. Poetry enlarges its scope by not limiting itself to the natural for its province but seeking 'new worlds of its own'.

Addison writes of 'imagination' in his last paper in such a way as to make us feel that the connotation of the word has been enriched since he first took it up and defined it. 'It sets off all writings in general, but is the very life and highest perfection of poetry.' Whatever beauties a work may have, it will be 'dry and insipid' if it lacks this quality. 'It has something in it like creation; it bestows a kind of existence and draws up to the reader's view several objects which are not to be found in being. It makes additions to nature and gives greater variety to God's works.' In his peroration Addison moves from considering the influence exercised by one man over another through the imagination to grasp at a conception of what the use of this faculty can be in the hands of God. 'He can so exquisitely ravish or torture the soul through this single faculty as might suffice to make up the whole heaven or hell of any finite being.'

Flights of this kind provide a corrective to any patronising view of Addison. He may have lacked profundity and analytical precision when judged by the standards of later criticism, but literature moved him, and he sought to understand why. In pursuing his quest he could admit his esteem for Aristotle and Longinus, Horace and Quintilian, Boileau and Dacier, and at the same time lambaste contemporaries who postured as learned critics by borrowing the terminology of neoclassicism and advertising its regulations. Addison insists that there are deviations from artistic rules in the works of the greatest masters. Critics need to learn that 'there is more beauty in the works of a great genius who is ignorant of the rules of art than in those of a little genius who knows and observes them.'

> Our inimitable Shakespeare is a stumbling-block to the whole tribe of these rigid critics. Who would not rather read one of his plays where there is not a single rule of the stage observed than any production of a modern critic where there is not one of them violated?

II The battle of the books

Addison's work seems to set the scene for the critical output of the Augustan period. But early in the century a work appeared which brought to a brilliant climax a controversy of the Restoration period. This was *The Battle of the Books* (1704) by Jonathan Swift (1667–1745), a satire in which the Ancients battle against the Moderns. Swift's sympathies were with his former patron Sir William Temple, whose comrades in arms are Homer, Euclid, Plato and Aristotle, Herodotus and Livy; but the effect of the fable is to render critical controversy itself absurd. Momus, the patron of the moderns, flies off to 'the region of a malignant deity called Criticism'. She sits in her den devouring volumes.

> At her right hand sat Ignorance, her father and husband, blind with age; at her left Pride, her mother, dressing her up in the scraps of paper herself had torn... About her played her children, Noise and Impudence, Dulness and Vanity, Positiveness, Pedantry, and Ill-manners. The goddess herself had claws like a cat; her head, and ears, and voice, resembled those of an ass; her teeth fallen out before, her eyes turned inward, as if she looked only upon herself...

That is Criticism. Ugly monsters suck at her teats, and she claims that it is she who gives wisdom to infants and idiots, makes children wiser than their parents, turns beaux into politicians and schoolboys into philosophers. 'It is I who have deposed wit and knowledge from their empire over poetry, and advanced myself in their stead.' She encourages her darling son Wotton to the fray. Among the encounters is one between Virgil, in shining armour and mounted on a dapple-grey steed, and Dryden on a massive, lumbering, worn-out cart-horse, his head buried in a helmet nine times too big. Dryden absurdly claims kinship and proposes an exchange of armour and horses, but in the upshot is too terrified to try to mount the steed. Wotton is rendered equally ridiculous in an encounter with Temple. A fable-within-the-fable is provided by the encounter of a spider, representing the moderns, with a bee, representing the ancients, an encounter between a creature feeding on the insects and vermin of the age and one getting what it can by 'infinite labour and search, and ranging through every corner of nature'. The one creature accumulates 'dirt and poison', the other honey and wax which furnish mankind 'with the two noblest of things, which are sweetness and light'.

Swift was not the man to write with the coolness and detachment, the steady appraisal of pros and cons, which we have come to associate with the critical mentality. When he had a point to make, he wielded a literary sledge-hammer. But his concern for literary standards emerged from time to time in squibs and throwaways like the piece 'On the Corruption of the English Tongue' contributed to the *Tatler* (No. 230, September 28, 1720). It is a protest against vulgarisation of the language by transferring careless conversational elisions and abbreviations to paper, by use of slang and neglect of syntax. 'Can't', 'do't', and 'tho't' come in for ridicule; innovations like 'banter' and 'bamboozle', and also affected polysyllables introduced during 'the War'. The latter sound harmless enough today ('speculations', 'operations', 'preliminaries' etc.), but the general positive recommendation is a very healthy call for simplicity, and equally a condemnation of that false rejection of supposed pedantry which produces cheap slang in sermons.

The impatience of the genius with the follies of littler men gives thrust and venom to Swift's satirical output. Another Irishman who found it difficult to control his impatience with the littleness of those he disagreed with was the dramatist George Farquhar (1678–1707). He had known both success and failure with his comedies on the London stage when he published 'A Discourse upon Comedy, in Reference to the English Stage' (1702). Farquhar's impatience is the impatience of the fruitful practitioner with arid theoreticians. The modern reader who has ploughed through the mass of critical works of the period, from which the names of the great classical and neoclassical critics are never long absent, is apt to welcome Farquhar's outburst against the whole tribe of theoreticians like a blast of fresh air.

In divinity, law, or mathematics, he argues, everyone defers to the specialist. Only in poetry does everyone claim to be an expert fit to judge the practitioners. Everyone thinks he can set himself up as a dramatic critic. The poor dramatist has to adjust his work so as to please his audience; then the scholar comes down on him like a ton of bricks, quoting Aristotle or Scaliger, Horace or Rapin, and flinging about the jargon of their trade. And when plays are actually modelled on their system, they prove lifeless. So Farquhar demands that people lay aside their 'superstitious veneration for antiquity'. Our age is not an age of decadence. Why should we drag about with us the fetters of the discredited thinking of the past? What have the rules designed for Aristotle's Athens got to do with Drury Lane, London? Why is poetry, unlike other specialisms, regarded so cheaply that any Tom, Dick or Harry can prescribe for poets? Poets are rare birds. Greece and Rome could supply hundreds of philosophers, but only one Homer and one Virgil. Moreover 'Aristotle was no poet, and consequently not capable of giving instruction in the art of poetry'.

Seeking the origin and purpose of comedy, he defines it as 'a well-framed tale handsomely told as an agreeable vehicle for counsel or reproof'. The end is to give both profit and pleasure, instruction and delight. And the people to be instructed are neither French nor Spanish, neither ancient Greeks nor Romans. 'An English play is for the use and instruction of an English audience' possessed of all the follies and weaknesses peculiar to them. As for giving delight to the audience, which means amusing them, the English represent such a medley of temperaments and dispositions, oddities and humours, that only a richly variegated story can divert them. It is no good turning up a rule book or studying history, if we want to succeed as playwrights for such audiences. Far better to concentrate on how our forbears, Shakespeare and Fletcher amused them – in defiance of classical regulations. Farquhar ends by rehearsing the standard arguments against the 'unities' and against the demand for 'probability'. The world of the drama is a world of pretence. The theatre is only a theatre, the actors only actors. Arbitrary limitations on movement of place or time are nonsensical.

> 'But it must be so, because Aristotle said it.' Now I say it must be otherwise because Shakespeare said it, and I am sure that Shakespeare was the better poet of the two.

Farquhar is an attractive writer. The reaction against Restoration licentiousness gave a very different tone to the London stage. In Farquhar's comedies the hot-house atmosphere of metropolitan wit and sophistication is disturbed by the arrival of provincial characters who are no longer mere butts for ridicule: and though the sexual interest remains powerful, the cynicism and callousness of rakes and debauchees gives place to good-natured decency and generosity. At the same time, in the world of letters the grandiose moralism of Sir R. Blackmore's epics was often winning lip-service approval where it did not arouse enthusiasm.

III Poetry: sacred vocation and disciplined art

Claims for 'Christian literature' were reinforced from the sphere of evangelical piety by the poet Isaac Watts (1675–1748). As a hymn-writer Watts has had a vast and continuing influence on church worship. Hymns such as 'O God our help in ages past', 'Jesus shall reign' and 'When I survey the wondrous cross' testify by their continuing popularity to his skill and sensitivity in a form of verse in which it is none too easy to reconcile the requisite demands of simplicity and vitality. In 1709 Watts added a Preface to the second edition of his *Horae Lyricae* (1706). It is an eloquent and fervent plea to reform the situation in which 'the stage and licentious poems have waged open war with the pious design of church and state'. Watts is no 'puritan'. Was it for this, he asks, that poetry was given her allurements and her intellectual charms – 'that she might seduce the heart from God?' This was not why man was given 'those sweet and resistless forces of metaphor, wit, sound, and number'. In Watts's eyes Collier performed a needed task when he projected the final end of the 'lewd and profane versifiers' who will face the Judgment with the blood on their hands of the many souls their writing destroyed.

Watts laments that the profanation and debasement of poetry should have deceived weaker Christians 'to imagine that poetry and vice are naturally akin'. The subject excites Watts to an enthusiastic exploration of the powerful imagery of the Old Testament. The grandeur, the pomp, and the stylistic beauty of books such as *Job*, the *Psalms*, and *Isaiah* are acclaimed in rapturous rhetorical phrases. Dennis is praised for having proclaimed the superiority of poetry on sacred subjects to all other. Rapin is quoted for having recommended the preacher who aims at eloquence to read the prophets incessantly. (See *Réflexions sur l'usage d'éloquence*, 1672.) Cowley's *Davideis* and Blackmore's *Prince Arthur* are cited as proof that Christian poetry is practicable. For Watts the wonders of our religion are such that they readily acquire grandeur, dignity and beauty when simply expounded. The 'naked themes of Christianity' far outclass and outshine the dazzling falsities of heathen poetry. They lend themselves readily to the muse:

> With how much less toil and expense might a Dryden, an Otway, a Congreve, or a Dennis furnish out a Christian poem than a modern play!

If the 'trifling and incredible tales' of tragedies can so move us, what a conquest 'over the wild world' might be effected by presenting the 'scenes of religion' in their due majesty, sweetness and terror.

Even where Watts seems to us to be wrong-headed, there is a cogency and directness about his thesis which testify to the strength of his faith. Among the learned, however, the early eighteenth century was an age in which Deism flourished. There was a tendency to accept God the Creator, to regard him as the Supreme Being whose existence could be rationally established, but to treat with varying degrees of scepticism the body of supernatural revelation which to believers like Watts was the heart and core of the Christian religion. It was natural that an emphasis on tolerance and free inquiry should accompany a movement of thought which tended to prefer all-embracing vagueness in spelling out the historic relationship (if any) of God to man, to the divisive doctrinal clarities of sectarian Christianity. John Locke (1632–1704), whose *Essay concerning Human Understanding* (1690) exercised a great influence, combined the empiricist's attitude to the human mind as a 'tabula rasa' and its knowledge as wholly derived from experience, with acceptance of God's existence on rational grounds.

Among thinkers into whose mental world the revelatory certainties of a Watts could never enter, and yet who pondered uneasily whether Locke had not abolished, along with the Ideas of Plato, the foundations of man's value-system, was Anthony Ashley Cooper, the third Earl of Shaftesbury (1671–1713) who published a series of specula-tive books and gathered them together as *Characteristics of*

Men, Manners, Opinions, Times (1711). The sweeping inclusiveness of the title gives a true impression of Shaftesbury's work in general. There is none of the clarity and cogency to be found in Watts. The book is neither systematic nor lucid. In flaccid prose Shaftesbury rambles on with an air of affected conversational ease which projects the persona of the patronising aristocrat. From time to time his reflections impinge on the sphere of literary criticism. In giving advice to authors, he contrasts the way the ancient poets hid themselves from sight, giving the stage to their characters, with the modern author's use of all possible devices to cut a figure before the reader. The whole machinery of prefaces, dedicatory epistles and the like is designed to focus attention on the writer himself. He 'caresses and cajoles' the reader.

> And as in an amour or commerce of love letters, so here the author has the privilege of talking eternally of himself, whilst he is making diligent court and working upon the humour of the party to whom he addresses.

Shaftesbury sees modern poets as an 'insipid race'. We call them poets merely because they have 'attained the chiming faculty of a language with an injudicious and our use of wit and fancy'. The true poet is 'a second *maker*, a just Prometheus under Jove'. He can 'imitate the Creator' by fashioning a well-structured whole and justly represents passion, sentiments and action, distinguishing 'the beautiful from the deformed, the amiable from the odious'. As for Shakespeare and Fletcher, Jonson and Milton, they represent poetry in an infant state. They 'lisp as in their cradles' and stammer out puns and quibbles. Nevertheless, rude as they were, these bards have provided us with 'the richest ore'.

> To their eternal honour they have withal been the first of Europeans who, since the Gothic model of poetry, attempted to throw off the horrid discord of jingling rhyme.

So Shaftesbury grants that 'our natural genius' outshines that of the neighbouring French, for all their attention to order and proportion.

On two topics Shaftesbury is especially memorable, that of rules and that of the importance of the critic. He regrets the fashionable attacks on critics. They are not the enemies of the commonwealth of wit and letters 'but the props and pillars of the building'. In a little dramatised episode Shaftesbury links scorn of critics with scorn of rules. He pictures the poet or dramatist surrounded by a group of fans in the coffee-house. Suppose you ask him why something is not more exactly written.

> The answer would be, 'We Englishmen are not tied up to such rigid rules as those of the ancient Grecian or modern French critics.'

As the dialogue continues, the critic is dismissed out of hand by the writer because he has himself written nothing and is therefore unfit to judge. Rymer's *Edgar* is cited as evidence that the critic of tragedy couldn't write one himself. For Shaftesbury this is nonsense. 'Can no one judge a picture but who is himself a layer of colours?' He quotes an angry rebuttal of critics by Dryden in his preface to *Don Sebastian* as evidence that he was not unjustly burlesqued in the study of Bayes in Buckingham's *The Rehearsal*. (The reader perhaps needs to recollect how Dryden pictured Shaftesbury's grandfather in *Absalom and Achitophel*.)

The controversy about rules recurs with tedious persistence. The neoclassical position was restated by Joseph Trapp (1679-1747) who, as the first Professor of Poetry at Oxford, delivered *Lectures on Poetry* which were published in Latin in 1711, 1715, and 1719, and translated into English in 1742.

> That Poetry is an Art is sufficiently plain ... It observes certain Laws and Rules, is brought to the Test of right Reason, and lastly, it aims at some particular End.

This had been Dennis's view, and it was to be echoed again by Charles Gildon (1665–1724) in his *Complete Art of Poetry* (1718).

> Poetry is an Art.... No Body can doubt so evident a Truth, that in all Things, where there may be a Right and a Wrong, there is an Art, and sure Rules to lead you to the former, and direct you to avoid the latter.

Trapp's lectures, by the way, include a definition of 'Wit' as

a thought formed so agreeably to nature and right reason, and impressed upon the mind with such clearness, vivacity, and dignity, as excites pleasure or admiration.

Trapp explains that he is taking 'wit' in the larger sense, not just jokes and 'pointed turns' but 'every conception of the mind that is beautiful, whatever eloquence or sublimity the imagination is capable of'. He insists on two requisites; there must be 'ingenious thought' and it must be well-founded on truth, nature, and reason. He exemplifies various kinds of false wit. There is the French poet Théophile de Vian (1590–1626) in whose tragedy *Pyrame et Thisbé* (1623) we are told that 'the sword, when dyed with the blood of the unhappy lover, blushed from a consciousness of its crime', and an unnamed poet who 'tells us that lovers always abound with wit because Venus sprang from the salt ocean'. Trapp quotes Boileau. 'Wit is not wit but as it says something everybody thought of, and that in a lively, delicate, and new manner', and goes on to cite the example Boileau gave. When it was suggested to Louis XII that he might punish some people who had opposed him before he came to the throne, he replied, 'A King of France revenges not the injuries done to a Duke of Orleans.'

While Trapp engaged himself somewhat fruitlessly in rehashing again the staple neoclassical formulations, the poet and essayist John Hughes (1677–1720) was trying to do for Spenser something of what his friend Addison had done for Milton. Hughes, a contributor to the *Spectator*, published his edition of Spenser's works in 1715. It included a biographical sketch as well as 'An Essay on Allegorical Poetry', 'Remarks on the *Fairy Queen*' and 'Remarks on the *Shepherd's Calendar*'. In the first of these Hughes notes that no men of learning have thought it worth while to spell out rules for allegory as they have done for epic, and himself suggests four prerequisites. The fable should be interesting, appropriate, and self-consistent, and the moral should be clear. In the second essay he praises Spenser's rich vein of 'fabulous invention' and the 'poetical magic' of his imaginative fecundity. His faults are by-products of his abundance – the lack of overall unity in the story and the independence of the separate books. But Hughes is most perceptive when he emphasises that to judge the *Faerie Queene* by the standards of the classical epic is irrelevant. The author 'never designed it by those rules'. He wanted a structure appropriate to his remarkable 'range of fancy' and found it in Ariosto. Spenser's stories, if superficially trifling, are yet justified by the symbolism. Hughes is not happy with the ambiguous concept of 'fairies' who are not distinguishable in character or magnitude from the human beings. And he would have preferred a Prince Arthur with some solid historic substance to his record. But his essay is perhaps most memorable for his insistence that comparing the *Faerie Queene* with classical epic would be like comparing the beauty and ornamental variety, if also the 'barbarism', of Gothic architecture with the majestic grandeur and simplicity of Roman architecture. He praises Spenser too for the sublimity of his thought, and for his freedom from the 'mixture of little conceits and that low affectation of wit' which has infected English verse and prose since his day. In the third essay, on the *Shepherd's Calendar*, he again shows himself aware of differences of genre: 'There seems to be the same difference between *The Fairy Queen* and *The Shepherd's Calendar* as between a royal palace and a little country seat.'

In commenting on the current controversy about how far pastoral poetry can afford to have its artifices and conventions tempered by rural realism, he defends the practice of Spenser and Ambrose Philips (though he does not like the intrusion of moral satire). This was one of the issues heatedly taken up by Pope.

IV Alexander Pope and his victims

For critical influence during this period the only other major writer to have the status of an Addison or a Dryden was Alexander Pope (1688–1744). This is not because he wrote many critical essays substantial enough to be compared with those of Addison and Dryden, but because, as a poet, he threw himself into the controversies of the day and into lively commentary upon the social and literary scene in such a way that the fruits of a critical mind are scattered over his output. Studied critical generalisations as well as throwaway personal jibes can be found giving sparkle to many a piece of topical commentary. The fullest formal statement of a critical position is provided by *An Essay on Criticism* (1711). This is a poem in the tradition of Horace's *Ars Poetica*. Scattered here and there over the text are frank paraphrases of lines from Virgil, Cicero and Quintilian, and evidence of reliance on the French critics, Boileau and Rapin.

The *Essay* is neither notably systematic in its approach nor thorough in its analysis, but the sheer polish of Pope's couplets is such that the whole has an air of authoritative guidance from a master who is vastly superior to his subject and exudes commonsense. Pope's opening declaration is that it is just as ignorant to judge badly as to write badly, and even more damaging because it is a matter of misleading readers instead of merely boring them, and there are ten bad critics to one bad writer.

> Let such teach others who themselves excel,
> And censure freely who have written well.

Pope thus seemingly embraces the doctrine that only poets are fit to be critics, and after some fairly rough treatment of the fools and failed writers who turn critic, he sets out the qualifications of the true critic. He must know his own limitations, and he must 'follow Nature' – 'At once the source, and end, and test of Art'. Wit must be restrained by judgment and this is where the ancient rules can help.

> Those Rules of old discovered, not devis'd,
> Are Nature still, but Nature methodiz'd.

For they were not imposed arbitrarily in a theoretical vacuum. They were derived as just precepts from the great examples, and the critics who formulated them did a direct service to poetic inspiration. A thorough knowledge of the ancients is thus a prerequisite of criticism. Virgil is cited as a young poet determined to write a world masterpiece and discovering that 'Nature and Homer were ... the same'.

Pope, however, distances himself from those who recommend a slavish adherence to the ancient rules and models. In poetry there are 'nameless graces which no methods teach', and the end may justify the means when 'lucky Licence' goes beyond what the rules permit. Indeed when poetic inspiration breaks through the 'vulgar bounds' to 'snatch a grace beyond the reach of art', it can go straight to the heart and possess it.

> Great Wits sometimes may gloriously offend,
> And rise to faults true Critics dare not mend.

On this theme (by which, one feels, Pope manages to recover the cake he has eaten) he rises to a paean of praise for the great poets, begging a spark of inspiration from them in his modest task:

> To teach vain Wits a science little known,
> T'admire superior sense, and doubt their own.

At this point there is a break, and the reader may naturally feel that the neoclassical critics, in spite of having started out as favourites, have lost the first round on points. Pope turns now to examine the various impediments to true critical judgment: pride, inadequate knowledge ('A little learning is a dang'rous thing'), and piecemeal judgment instead of survey of the whole. Thus there are critics who measure only in terms of elaborate conceits, ignoring the fact that

> True Wit is Nature to advantage dress'd,
> What oft was thought, but ne'er so well express'd.

Others focus only on the style, ignoring the fact that

> Expression is the dress of thought, and still
> Appears more decent, as more suitable.

But most judge only by the degree of metrical smoothness, ignoring the fact that

> 'Tis not enough no harshness gives offence,
> The sound must seem an Echo to the sense.

In exemplifying this point Pope displays his verbal and metrical virtuosity in contrasting descriptions of smooth breezes, toilsome labours, and swift-footedness. It is characteristic of his method that his images are inspired both by phrases from the Italian poet Marco Girolamo Vida (1485–1566) and by lines from Dryden's *Aeneid*.

Pope also directs his fire at critics obsessed with sectarian defence of the ancients or of the moderns, critics who adapt their views to the topical trend, and those who fawn on the output of aristocrats. And he ends his second section with an attack on those envious writers who, having got to the top of the tree, do their best to disparage others, and with the demand that there should be no tenderness about harsh condemnation of literary obscenity.

In the third section of the poem Pope lays down rules for the good critic. He must be frank and truthful, hold his peace when he is not sure of himself, and speak diffidently even when he is confident. It is no good voicing truths bluntly, for people must be taught without their sensing that they are being instructed. The critic must not be niggardly with his advice nor restrain himself so politely that he is unjust. There is no need to fear that fair criticism will anger wise writers, Pope adds, and takes the opportunity to pillory John Dennis:

> But Appius reddens at each word you speak,
> And stares, tremendous, with a threatening eye ...

There is no doubt that Dennis eventually became touchy and irascible. Pope calls him 'Appius' disparagingly, for his tragedy *Appius and Virginia* (1709) was a failure, in spite of the fact that it exploited his new method of making thunder. When later Dennis found the management using his invention in a production of *Macbeth*, he protested in anger that they had 'stolen his thunder'.

Pope argues that some poets are so bad that it is best to restrain comment on them. There are blockheads among the critics too. Having demolished both, Pope characterises the good critic: unbiassed, learned, well-bred, sincere, 'modestly bold and humanly severe', and the portrait leads him to survey great critics of the past; Aristotle, Horace, Dionysius,

Petronius, Quintilian and Longinus. Their age of learning was succeeded by an age of superstition, and eventually by the revival represented by Erasmus, Raphael and Vida. It is at this point that Pope shows his allegiances again. As learning advanced over the northern world, he claims, it was mostly in France that 'critic-learning' flourished, where Boileau ruled in the lineage of Horace. But we Britons, independent as usual, continued to repel Roman conquest, despising foreign laws and preferring to remain 'unciviliz'd'. Nevertheless among the 'sounder' minority of the less presumptuous, better instructed critics, there were one or two who dared to defend the 'juster ancient cause' and managed to restore here in England too 'Wit's fundamental laws'. Those honoured by name are Mulgrave (see p.114), Roscommon (see p.100), and William Walsh (1663–1708), the author of an *Essay on Pastoral Poetry* (1697) whom Dr Johnson was to describe as 'known more by his familiarity with greater men, than by anything done or written by himself'.

As early as 1704, at the age of sixteen, Pope had turned critic with a 'Discourse on Pastoral Poetry' which was published in 1709 as a preface to his 'Pastorals'. These are highly conventional, and in his 'Discourse' Pope defends thoroughgoing imitation of the classical models of Theocritus and Virgil. The character of Pastoral consists in 'simplicity, brevity, and delicacy'. But illusion is essential, for 'pastoral is an image of what they call the golden age', and the miseries of real life and the crudities of true rusticity cannot be allowed.

In this respect Pope was decisively with the ancients against the moderns; for the moderns advocated a policy of updating the Pastoral form by adapting it more realistically to the life and even the climate of modern England. In 1713 Steele's journal the *Guardian* published some essays on pastoral poetry, the last of which traced the true pastoral lineage from Theocritus and Virgil through Spenser to Ambrose Philips (c1675–1749). Quite apart from being guilty of insipidity and triviality, Philips had disfigured his Pastorals, in Pope's view, with incongruous concessions to realism and modernity. He therefore wrote an anonymous essay for the *Guardian* which was published in No. 40 on April

27, 1713. This takes the form of an ironic critique ostensibly illustrating the superiority of Philips's pastorals to Pope's. Philips has 'excelled both Theocritus and Virgil', for Virgil's diction was too courtly. 'Mr Pope hath fallen into the same error with Virgil. His clowns do not converse in all the simplicity proper to the country...' Daphnis and Thyrsis are introduced on British terrain, whereas Philips has the 'delicacy' to name his characters Hobbinol, Lobby, Cuddy, and Colin Clout. When comparisons are made between stanzas by Philips and stanzas by Pope the irony turns hilarious. Doggerel by Philips is quoted side by side with lines by Pope in which the author unfortunately 'deviates into downright poetry'. The sarcasm escalates as Pope ventures to cite passages in Philips 'in which no one can compare with him':

> O woeful Day! O Day of Woe! quoth he;
> And woeful I, who live the Day to see!

In climax Pope refers to *A Pastoral Ballad* he has found among some old manuscripts which seems to him to stand truly in the tradition of Spenser and Philips:

> CICILY: Rager go vetch tha kee, or else tha Zun
>   Will quite be go, be vore c'have half a don.
> ROGER: Thou shouldst not ax ma tweece, but I've a be
>   To dreave our Bull to Bull tha Parson's Kee.

The most sustained of Pope's serious literary criticism is his 'Preface to the Translation of the *Iliad*' (1715). It is one of those critical statements which are at once lucid and persuasive in analysis and heart-warming in the enthusiasm it communicates. To turn to it after reading, say, the turgid prose of Shaftesbury, is to realise how closely clarity of thought and clarity of style are related. For Pope, Homer is preeminent because he excels in the most fundamental respect – in 'invention'. Invention is the source of all the materials on which art operates. It is the sheer abundance and power of Homer's creativity ('invention') which stokes up the 'fire and rapture' energising his work. This creativity permeates every aspect of Homer's work. And Pope illustrates this by examining Homer's qualities under the accepted headings: fable, characters, speeches, sentiments, imagery, style, and versification. Thus Pope praises the fecundity and comprehensiveness of Homer's inventive genius, the variety and vitality of his characterisation, the grandeur of his sentiments, the rich profusion of his imagery, the vividness of his style, and the flexibility of his versification. He writes like a man enraptured with his subject, time after time reiterating that it is in 'invention' that Homer is supreme, and from this all his virtues derive. No author can ever excel all the world in more than one faculty, 'and as Homer has done this in invention, Virgil has in judgment'. This does not mean that Homer was deficient in judgment or Virgil in invention. The two authors can be said to have 'less' only when compared with each other.

> Homer was the greater genius, Virgil the better artist. In the one we most admire the man, in the other the work. Homer hurries and transports us with a commanding impetuosity; Virgil leads us with attractive majesty. Homer scatters with a generous profusion; Virgil bestows with a careful magnificence.

In dealing with Homer's 'defects', Pope for the most part defends him against the cavillers, especially those who would exalt Virgil above Homer, ignoring the fact that Homer wrote first. In a companion piece to this essay, the 'Postscript to the Translation of the *Odyssey*' (1726), Pope turns to refute those who judge the *Odyssey* as though it were a continuation of the *Iliad*, seek in it for exactly the same qualities, and then proclaim it the work of 'old age'. Even Longinus is taken to task for finding less of sublimity and fire in the *Odyssey* than in the *Iliad*. Pope insists that the subject of the *Odyssey* made different demands upon Homer, and that when this is accepted the epic will be found to have the same qualities of invention, description, characters, and versification as its predecessor.

The reader who has warmed to Pope's jealous fervour in praise of Homer will be a little disappointed by the editorial 'Preface' he wrote to *The Works of Shakespeare* (1725). Shakespeare provides 'the most conspicuous instances of beauties and faults of all sorts', and Pope does justice to some of the former. Shakespeare was more 'original' than Homer.

> The poetry of Shakespeare was inspiration indeed: he is not so much as imitator as an instrument of nature, and it is not so just to say that he speaks from her, as that she speaks through him.

Every single character in Shakespeare 'is as much an individual as those in life itself'. Shakespeare not only gives variety and vitality to his characters, but he preserves each individuality throughout each play. Pope displays again the enthusiasm he had for Homer when he speaks of Shakespeare's power over the passions. It was supreme and unique. Without any strain or evident effort Shakespeare produces the situation where the 'heart swells and tears burst out just at the proper places'. If he excels in the range of joyful or grievous passions he has control over, he is no less perspicacious in the reflections, the reasoning, and the judicious sentiments expressed. The 'penetration and felicity' displayed is 'perfectly amazing from a man of no education' or experience of public life. He 'seems to have known the world by intuition, to have looked through human nature at one glance, and to be the only author that gives ground for a very new opinion: that the philosopher, and even the man of the world, may be born, as well as the poet'.

After this tribute, the prejudices of Pope's age emerge. Shakespeare had to write for a living and to please the box-office. The audience 'was generally composed of the meaner sort of people', and Shakespeare had to appeal to them. Hence the bombast in the tragedies, and the buffoonery and ribaldry in the comedies. As Shakespeare gained the applause of the court, his 'productions improved in proportion to the respect he had for his auditors'. But he remained a player. 'Players are just such judges of what is right as tailors are of what is graceful.' Taking up the charge that Shakespeare lacked learning, Pope points to evidence of considerable reading; and, having dealt with some technical editorial problems, he concludes by comparing Shakespearean drama with 'more finished' plays. It is like 'an ancient majestic piece of Gothic architecture compared with a neat modern building'. We have greater reverence for the former fabric, even though 'many of the parts are childish, ill-placed, and unequal to its grandeur'.

The notion that Shakespeare achieved literary status accidentally as a by-product of making money recurs in the 'Epistle I' which Pope wrote in imitation of Horace's 'Epistle to Augustus'. In it Pope addresses George II with an ironic appeal for the claims of literature on his interest. His thesis is regret that a poet has to have been dead some time before he gets recognition. In surveying the literary scene, Pope pin-points aspects of various poets' works in memorable epigram, as when he declares of Milton:

> In Quibble Angel and Archangel join,
> And God the Father turns a school-divine.

The Cavalier wits of Charles I's reign are summed up as:

> The Mob of Gentlemen who wrote with Ease.

There are brief throwaway comments on the 'pert, low Dialogue' of Farquhar, the moral laxity of Aphra Behn, and the cheap farce of Colley Cibber.

It is for telling couplets which sum up poetic characters in unforgettable phrases that we feel most indebted to Pope the critic:

> Waller was smooth; but Dryden taught to join
> The varying verse, the full-resounding line,
> The long majestic March, and Energy divine.

Pope's most interesting foray into criticism was a treatise he contributed to a volume of *Miscellanies* (1728) under the pseudonym, Martin Scriblerus. The 'Scriblerus Club', which included Swift, Arbuthnot, and Gay, collaborated to mock 'all the false tastes in learning'. Pope called his treatise '*Peri Bathous*, or The Art of Sinking in Poetry'. He had paid tribute to Longinus in his *Essay on Criticism*:

> Thee, bold *Longinus*! all the Nine inspire,
> And bless *their Critick* with a *Poet's Fire*.

Here he modelled his work on Longinus, ironically twisting the word *bathos* ('profundity') to mean 'a ludicrous descent to the commonplace', a meaning which has stuck. The treatise has its place in the long struggle between the Ancients and the Moderns. What seems to have stung Pope to its composition was the tasteless over-estimate of certain contemporary writers, disrespect for the great classical models, and especially misapplication of the notion of 'sublimity' in the cult of enthusiasm and passion at the expense of reason, and of elaborate stylistic affectation at the expense of commonsense. Pope was not himself unappreciative of 'fire and rapture' in poetry. He praised Homer for the fact that these qualities are so forceful in him 'that no Man of a true Poetical Spirit is Master of himself while he reads him'. But he was as offended by the false splendours of poets such as Sir Richard Blackmore as he was by the false simplicities of Ambrose Philips.

Throughout his treatise Pope maintains the pose of the poker-faced instructor. It is accepted, he argues, that the moderns far excel the ancients and yet there has been no systematic study of Bathos (the 'Profound') which is their *forte*. And Bathos is the natural taste of man, the taste of the majority, who have to be forced into appreciation of the Sublime. There is an Art of Bathos, the Art of Sinking in Poetry. It has its own rules. First among them is an abhorrence of commonsense, the foe of cant. The principle of wrong-headedness (*'Gout de travers'*) must be acquired by the poet.

> And since the great Art of all Poetry is to mix Truth with Fiction, in order to join the *Credible* with the *Surprising*; our author shall produce the Credible, by painting nature in her lowest simplicity; and the Surprising, by contradicting common opinion.

Pope illustrates this point by quoting from Blackmore's *Prince Arthur* a description of the acclamation of the angels at the creation of the universe which reads like an account of a Lord Mayor's Show with huzzaing crowds and a firework display.

As the detailed analysis of aspects of 'the Profound' proceeds, Blackmore is the poet most frequently quoted. However, some of the funniest quotations are unattributed and were probably invented by Pope himself. Such is the image of the frightened stag in chase who

> Hears his own feet, and thinks they sound like more;
> And fears the hind feet will o'ertake the fore.

Judicious words of praise are distributed as appropriate techniques of 'Amplification' and 'Imitation' are illustrated from the poets, and a systematic survey is made of 'Tropes' and 'Figures' and the 'several Sorts of Style'. Although one must suspect that the modest request of two absent lovers, 'Ye Gods! annihilate but Space and Time,/ And make two lovers happy' is another of Pope's concoctions, there are passages from the poets scarcely less absurd, such as Blackmore's

> The gaping clouds pour lakes of sulphur down,
> Whose livid flashes sickning sunbeams drown

or Ambrose Philips's

> Teach me to grieve with bleating moan, my sheep.

The treatise is a tour de force in ironic spoofery and, in spite of its evident topicalities, the survey of cheap poeticisms constitutes sober instruction in how not to write.

One of the writers ridiculed was the poet Leonard Welsted (1688–1747), who had married the daughter of Henry Purcell. He had translated Longinus with a commentary in 1712. Pope and he kept up a running literary battle.

> Lewd without lust, and without wit profane!
> Outrageous and afraid, contemned and vain!

So Welsted wrote of Pope, and in the *Dunciad* Pope proclaimed:

> Flow, Welsted, flow! like thine inspirer, Beer,
> Tho' stale, not ripe; tho' thin, yet never clear.

In fact Pope's ridicule of Welsted in *Bathos* is intensified by misquotation which transforms an infelicity into a *double entendre*:

> Behold the Virgin lie
> Naked, and only *cover'd* by the Sky.

What Welsted had actually written was:

> Now, *Acon*, the coy Nymph is wholly thine:
> Nor will her Fame permit her to decline
> His suit, who saw her, with familar Eyes,
> Asleep, and only cover'd with the Skies.

Welsted had attacked neoclassicism in *A Dissertation Concerning the Perfection of the English Tongue, and the State of Poetry* (1724). Pope's enemies were rarely such fools as he made them out to be, and the *Dissertation* deserves attention. Welsted regards his own age as one in which the English language has reached perfection and, most conveniently, at a time of commercial prosperity, peace and enlightened government. The situation is ripe for the dawn of a 'classical age'. In an earlier work, *An Epistle to the Duke of Chandos* (1720), Welsted had written, 'I see arise a new Augustan Age', and should perhaps therefore be recognised as the originator of that usage. Welsted's case against the classical rules is that they emerge 'as comments to the work of certain great authors who composed those works without any such help'. Most of the critical treatises in the classical tradition are trite and commonplace.

> The truth is they touch only the externals or form of the thing, without entering into the spirit of it; they play about the surface of poetry but never dive into its depths.

You can't get at the 'soul' of poetry through such 'mechanic laws'. Its beauties are to be felt, not described. You can't instruct a man pedagogically into appreciation of poetry. A special faculty, that of 'taste', has to be superadded to his ordinary faculties. The true enchantment of poetry, to which the fortunate few who are born with taste are susceptible, is no more reducible to measure and analysis than is the loveliness of a beautiful woman. This does not mean that the composition of poetry is something wild and lawless. It is as dependent upon reason as is everything else. But 'poetical reason is not the same as mathematical reason'. The 'truth' of poetry is not susceptible to proof, for it depends greatly on imagination, but that does not make it less rational 'for imagination is as much a part of reason as is memory or judgment'. Rules have nothing to do with that gift by which the heightened imagination of the poet conceives images and turns of thought whose beauty could never have been attained by study.

Nevertheless, Welsted adds, 'when I speak of rules in poetry as useless, I do not mean that experience, know-ledge, application, and every method by which excellency is attained in other things are not necessary'. In illustrating what he *does* object to, Welsted displays a nice sense of humour. He quotes actual critical maxims (mostly drawn from Mulgrave's *Essay Upon Poetry*) giving advice to poets and parodies them in rules for a painter ('Display not a crocodile among a flock of sheep...') which suggest that the maxims are too obvious to be worth recording. And when he turns to give positive advice, it consists of sensible, if also obvious, recommendations:

> The great general rules of poetry are: to think justly ... to imagine beautifully; and to distinguish well what sort of writing suits one's genius.

Welsted then turns to the English poetic scene to lament the prevalence of 'servile copiers after others'. This is the weakness of English poetry. 'Imitation is the bane of writing' and nothing has done more to 'swell the throng of ill-writers' than those critical essays on poetry which he has attacked. Poetry is equal to the other branches of learning in its usefulness: it instructs while it pleases. Among Welsted's notorious misjudgments are his criticism of Dryden for 'his way to say everything that came into his head, and only for the sake of saying it', his criticism of Addison for having too many short sentences 'that do not run cleverly into one another', and his tribute to Ambrose Philips (as a prose writer) for avoiding this pitfall.

Another writer to have his verse ridiculed in *The Art of Sinking* was Lewis Theobald (1688–1744). Pope cited a line, from his play *Double Falshood* (1728), which became a focus of general ridicule: 'None but Himself can be his Parallel'. Pope suggested that it might have been inspired by a Smithfield Showman's advertisement: 'This is the greatest Elephant in the world, except Himself'. The animosity between Pope and Theobald was such that in the first, anonymous, version of the *Dunciad* (1728) Theobald was hero. Colley Cibber replaced him in the *New Dunciad* (1742). The animosity took heat from Theobald's *Shakespeare Restored* (1726) which displayed the defects in Pope's edition of Shakespeare. Pope had determined his text from the various readings in the Quartos and Folios by an arbitrary application of personal preference. Some quite celebrated lines disappeared from the text altogether, others were tastelessly altered, and others simply misunderstood. Theobald, however, got little thanks for his efforts, and he sharpened the vendetta with Pope in his own edition of *Shakespeare* (1733–4).

Whatever his capacity as a poet, Theobald was no fool as an editor or as a critic. As early as 1715 he was writing on Shakespeare in his periodical *Censor* (1715–17), and showing an imaginative sensitivity that was to edge Shakespearean criticism forward. In one issue he surveyed the 'real history of King Lear' and a week later, in issue No. 10 (May 1715) he examined Shakespeare's treatment of this material, showing how it was determined by the intention to draw two morals from the fond old father's transfer of his cares to his children and their response. The first is 'a caution against rash and unwary bounty; the second against the base returns and ingratitude of children'. In tracing what Shakespeare did with his sources, he praises the exquisite poetic mastery revealed at high points in Lear's agony. Although the study is marred by his frank wish that Cordelia and Lear should have survived, as they do in Tate's version, Theobald shows remarkable insight in laying bare the psychological consistency and insight revealed in the character of Lear. It is Shakespeare's skill in the convincing registration of emotional crises that sets Theobald reaching out to concepts and idioms which we now recognise as the coming currency of Shakespearean criticism.

In a later paper on 'The Character of Tragic Heroes' (No. 36. January 12, 1717) Theobald takes up the question of the degree of culpability tolerable in a tragic hero, disputing Corneille's view that Oedipus is not guilty of any fault, because of his ignorance, and is therefore no fit model for moral generalisation. On the contrary, Oedipus's fault was 'being too rashly transported to anger'. It was his 'curiosity, rashness, and impetuous temper' which led him into the terrible calamities. The mix of virtue and vice must determine human character in literature as in life. Theobald regrets the fashion of representing crimes on the stage perpetrated by villains with whom one can have no sympathy. In this respect *Othello* is excellent. 'For the crimes and misfortunes of the Moor are owing to an impetuous desire of having his doubts cleared, and a jealousy and rage native to him, which he cannot control...' Otherwise Othello is a brave, open, generous, loving person. There is equal subtlety of analysis in a paper Theobald wrote on *Julius Caesar*. Taking up a point made by Dryden in his 'Preface' to *Troilus and Cressida*, praising the quarrel scene between Brutus and Cassius, Theobald makes a detailed analysis of the collision of temperaments and the swelling up of mutual accusations. It is alive with sympathetic insight into Shakespeare.

It is this quality of sympathy which brought distinction to Theobald's edition of Shakespeare (1733–4). He applied to Shakespeare's text the techniques of emendation which were familiar in editions of the classics. Where the text from the Quarto and first Folio made sense he was reluctant to interfere with it on mere grounds of good taste. Where passages were unintelligible he was prepared to consult known sources or usages elsewhere in Shakespeare or other Elizabethan literature which might help in elucidation. All editors since have been indebted to him for seemingly inspired conjectures about cruxes. The most celebrated is Mistress Pistol's description of Falstaff's death in *Henry V* (II, iii, 14): 'for his nose was as sharp as a pen and a table of green fields', which Theobald rendered 'and 'a babbled of green fields'.

V Uniformity and simplicity

While Shakespearean editors applied rival principles of textual emendation, philosophers argued about the nature and significance of aesthetic experience and the basis of the moral sense. Yet philosophical debate has always borne down upon literary criticism, and in the 1720s the debate continued which Hobbes initiated by his emphasis on man's drive for self-preservation as basic to his political and moral motivation. Shaftesbury had rejected Hobbes's view of self-preservation as the basis of conduct. Man, he argued, is gifted with a moral sense by which he distinguishes good from evil; and since his own good is inextricably involved with the general good, the self-regarding impulse is not in competition with the concern for society. An influential contribution to this debate came from a Dutch physician who settled in England, Bernard de Mandeville (1670–1733). He was rash enough to plead the cause of feminine education and at the same time to urge public control of brothels. In his part-verse, part-prose work *The Fable of the Bees* (1714 and 1723) he attacked Shaftesbury's cheerful estimate of human altruism. The driving force of a flourishing society is individual acquisitiveness which creates demands that boost trade and increase the general wealth. Among those who replied to Mandeville was Francis Hutcheson (1694-1746), an Irish scholar who became Professor of Moral Philosophy at Glasgow University, where Adam Smith was one of his pupils.

Hutcheson wrote *An Inquiry into the Original of Our Ideas of Beauty and Virtue* (1725) in which he claimed to be vindicating the principles of Shaftesbury 'against the author of the *Fable of the Bees*'. Hutcheson argued that when objects are perceived by the senses, the experience is registered in the mind by an 'idea' – a simple idea, such as sweetness or redness, or a *complex*, or compound of simple ideas. The idea may be pleasant or unpleasant. In some cases what is pleasant to one man may be unpleasant to another because of peculiar experiences. Thus the idea of wine might be associated with sickness instead of with good fellowship. Complex ideas give rise to more pleasure than simple ideas, a face more than a colour, a sunset more than a clear sky, a piece of music more than a single note. The reason why not all people with the same external senses derive the same pleasure from complex ideas is that they may not possess that extra sense, the *internal* sense which appreciates the beauty and harmony revealed in them.

Hutcheson distinguishes two kinds of beauty, *absolute* and *relative*. Absolute (or 'original') beauty does not proceed from any comparison with something it is supposed to imitate. The basis of beauty is 'uniformity amidst variety' and the greater the uniformity, the greater the beauty. This is illustrated by reference to geometrical figures, animals, birds, and so on. Relative (or 'comparative') beauty is founded on conformity between the original and the copy. It can exist even where there is no beauty in the original. When Hutcheson applies this to poetry, he repeats what Theobald said. We have 'more lively ideas of imperfect men, with all their passions, than of morally perfect heroes such as never occur to our observation'. This principle of conformity makes 'probability' a requisite. It also makes 'similitudes, metaphors, and allegories' beautiful. Metres and cadences are further instances of harmony. Hutcheson extends this principle in showing how we incline to make, say, a storm at sea 'an emblem of wrath' or a withering flower a symbol of a hero's death. The whole doctrine is based on the recognition of the regularity and uniformity pervading the created universe, and on the assumption that man has an innate sense of beauty antecedent to custom or education.

In the same year that this study was published, Hutcheson contributed some papers to the *Dublin Journal*. Two of them, 'Reflections on Laughter' (no. 10, June 5, 1725 and no. 11, June 12, 1725) very cogently point out the inadequacy of Hobbes's thesis that laughter is the sudden 'glory' of recognising some 'eminency' in ourselves by comparison with the infirmities of others or with our own past infirmities. Hutcheson produces examples to support his case. Who are we feeling superior to when we laugh at *Hudibras*? Homer or Butler? And why don't the miseries of the poor make us laugh, if laughter derives from the feeling of superiority? Hobbes's view is on a par with the theory that we enjoy a tragedy because we witness distress from a vantage point of security. The real cause of laughter is incongruity; 'the bringing together of images which have contrary additional ideas as well as some resemblance in the principal idea'. Overstraining of wit makes us laugh because it brings together 'resemblances from subjects of a quite different kind from the subject to which they are compared'.

Hutcheson's attempt to define beauty takes its place among a series of ventures into aesthetic theory which a little later, as we shall see, involved artists such as Reynolds and Hogarth. And there was a critic active in the 1720s, Joseph Spence (1699–1768), who was to explore the relationship of Roman painting and sculpture to Roman literature in *Polymetis* (1747). Spence was Professor of Poetry at Oxford and a friend of Pope's: scattered remarks of his that the student comes across are likely to endear the man as a friend to commonsense and a foe to affectation. He said he would 'as soon think of dissecting a rainbow as of forming grave and practical notions of beauty'. And writing to Samuel Richardson about the reaction of critics to his novel *Clarissa Harlowe*, he said, 'For Heaven's sake, let not those sworn enemies of all good works destroy the beauty you have created.'

Spence wrote an *Essay on Pope's Odyssey* (1726) after the publication of the first half of the translation, and added to it after the second half came out. The form of the essay is a dialogue between Philypsus, an enthusiast, and Antiphans, a man with a 'clear head' and given to precision in his thinking. Spence's aim was to defend Pope, but he does not hesitate first to examine the faults of the poem, and much of what Philypsus has to say reflects Spence's soundness of judgment. His main charge is that the 'simplicity of Homer' is lacking in the translation. He cites example after example in which a simple statement in Homer is transformed into something elaborate and highly-coloured. In Homer Circe tells Ulysses to stay the night and set sail next morning. In Pope she gives him leave to:

> Spread his broad sails, and plough the liquid way,
> Soon as the morn unveils her saffron ray.

Depth and clarity, Spence argues, are sacrificed to smooth versification, 'and as the ancients valued thought more than sound, we seem to be taken with sounds more than thought'. The whole essay develops the case that plainness and strength in the original give place to what is 'fine and artificial'. Instances are quoted of highly contrived antithesis, of mixed metaphor and elaborate circumlocution. The citations include a couplet about the disorder in the court of Penelope:

> And these indulge their want, and those their woe;
> And here the tears, and there the goblets flow.

Spence quotes Quintilian that when the intention is to stir pity, nothing is 'more odious than a show of eloquence', and emphasises that his purpose is not to discredit 'the use of art' but 'the appearance of it'.

Entertaining as Spence's illustrations are, what is most impressive about the essay is the awareness it shows of the excessive finery and affectation cultivated by poets as a feature of the age like the 'profusion of lace and embroidery'. The modern hero delights too much in his wardrobe. Antiphans laughingly recalls a portrait he has seen: 'The Duke of Marlborough in the heat of an engagement, with a full-bottomed wig very carefully spread over his shoulders!'

While Spence thus brought contemporary taste into question, there appeared a work which marked a break with the urban sophistication of Pope. James Thomson (1700–48) published his poem *Winter* in March 1726 and the other books of *The Seasons* were out by 1730. We find in Thomson's poetry that sense of how the natural world reflects its Maker in its harmony and uniformity which Hutcheson had imbibed from Shaftesbury. And the fact that Thomson's work anticipated attitudes to nature to be adopted by the Romantics gives it a special position in the history of English literature. The style is not free from the artifices of the period and of the imitators of Milton, but in its descriptive passages it often shows a welcome degree of exact observation. Thomson was a Scot by birth and education, and he had a healthy readiness to do justice to bad weather:

> At last the muddy deluge pours along,
> Resistless, roaring, dreadful down it comes
> From the chapt mountain, and the mossy wild ...

Plainly this is a far cry from the pastoralism of Pope.

In a Preface to the second edition of *Winter* in June 1726 Thomson enters the fray about the status of poetry – 'the most charming power of imagination, the most exalting force of thought, the most affecting touch of sentiment, ... the very soul of all learning and politeness'. The 'present contempt' of it is an affront to the taste that has been charmed by Moses, by Milton, by the Bible itself. Thomson was on the defensive, outraged by the fact that William Law (1686–1761), in *The Absolute Unlawfulness of the Stage Entertainment* (1726) had just tried to do for the 1720s what Jeremy Collier had done for the 1690s. Law is referred to as 'the present sulphureous attacker of the stage'. Thomson does not deny that poetry, like everything else that is good, has often been abused, yet, given a subject that is neither trifling nor vulgar but useful, magnificent, and divinely inspired, then the most inveterate critics will be silenced and poets become 'the delight and wonder of mankind'. A prerequisite of such a development is that a great poet must arise who will turn his back on 'all the pomp and pride of fortune', scorn all the flatteries and fopperies of a 'tasteless age' and devote himself utterly to the cause of virtue, learning, and humanity.

The one thing that can revive poetry, Thomson urges, is 'the choosing of great and serious subjects' to amuse, enlighten, and stimulate, and the eschewing of the forced fancies and 'glittering prettinesses' which are to native poetry what buffoonery is to sound thought. No subject can more readily meet these demands than 'the works of nature'. The best poets have always seemed happiest in their contemplation, far from the busy world.

Thomson's concern for poetry to be rescued into the service of high religious ends is echoed in a Preface written by an Oxford fellow, John Husbands (1706–32), to *A Miscellany of Poems by Several Hands* (1731). He is scathing about the way the contemporary '*beaux esprits*' mistake profanity for wit, sneering at religion and offending the virtuous by their smut. They write less like Christians than the ancient heathen writers with their 'moral reflections, manly sentiments, and serious addresses to the Deity'. The divine art of poetry was dedicated once to a religious purpose. Yet now, though we are surrounded by evidence of God's goodness, divine poetry is neglected. Yet this is the loftiest and most inexhaustible subject for poetry. The Scriptures provide the noblest examples for us. 'We have not only a religion, but a language from heaven.' Husbands is eloquent upon this theme, and he shows taste and understanding in illustrating the poetic techniques used in the Old Testament. He praises especially the 'simplicity and sublimity', the rejection of 'all dross and adventitious ornament'. And he emphasises the need, when reading either the literature of the Hebrews or that of the Greeks and Romans, to take into account the background from which they spring, the particular 'genius and customs of the people'.

This is also the theme of another academic, Thomas Blackwell (1701–57), Professor of Greek at Aberdeen University, in *An Inquiry into the Life and Writings of Homer* (1735). His initial question is: How do you account for the remarkable phenomenon of Homer? He was the product of a happy combination of cultural conditions. The climate, the terrain, the recent history of Greece, the stage of civilisation reached, the spectacle of peace and liberty, and the naturalness of prevailing manners all favoured the appearance of the genius. Homer gives us minute descriptions of how people lived, but 'when we consider our own customs, we find that our first business when we sit down to poetize in the higher strains is to unlearn our daily way of life, to forget our manner of sleeping, eating, and diversions'. The trouble is that 'we live within doors covered, as it were, from nature's face'. The moderns, in admiring nothing but pomp and wealth, 'exclude themselves from the pleasantest and most natural images that adorned old poetry'.

VI Henry Fielding

Lively critical campaigning may by-pass the genre of 'literary criticism'. Buckingham's *The Rehearsal* and Pope's *The Art of Sinking in Poetry* show critical minds at work to an invigoratingly healthy purpose. The same is true of *The Tragedy of Tragedies, or Tom Thumb the Great* (1731) by Henry Fielding (1707–54). It is a rollicking mock-heroic farce that burlesques the affectations of Restoration and post-Restoration heroic drama with all its bombast and extravagance. To heighten the fun, Fielding wrote a tongue-in-cheek Preface, examining the piece under the traditional Aristotelian heads, with solemn appeals to Horace, Cicero, and Longinus. Moreover he supplied copious footnotes showing his indebtedness to writers such as Dryden, Lee, and Thomson. Thus we can see how an image from Lee's *Gloriana* has been metamorphosed into:

> Daughter, I have observed of late some grief
> Unusual in your countenance; your eyes
> That, like two open windows, used to show
> The lovely beauty of the rooms within,
> Have now two blinds before them.

Fielding brought a blast of fresh air into the world of criticism, not only because he so cheerfully exposed pretentiousness, but because he came representing a new genre of literature which was eventually to transform the arena of critical studies. Fielding's *Joseph Andrews* and *Tom Jones*, Richardson's *Pamela* and *Clarissa* were all published in the 1740s. It may be doubted how far Richardson's novels (or for that matter, Defoe's) arose from any sense of that tradition emanating from the ancients to which almost the whole of the criticism so far studied in this book was either deeply attached or paid lip-service. But Fielding enters the literary world dragging all the paraphernalia of neoclassicism behind him. Yet for all that indebtedness, he knows how much of an innovator he is.

> For as I am, in reality, the founder of a new province of writing, so I am at liberty to make what laws I please therein. (*Tom Jones*, Bk II, ch i)

In the Preface to *Joseph Andrews* (1742), however, Fielding had appealed to Homer and Aristotle as authorities for his own 'species of poetry'.

> Now a comic romance is a comic epic poem in prose: differing from comedy, as the serious epic from tragedy: its action being more extended and comprehensive; containing a much larger circle of incidents, and introducing a greater variety of characters.

This genre has a 'light and ridiculous' fable instead of a 'grave and solemn' one, persons of inferior rank and manners instead of superior ones, and in its sentiments and diction it substitutes the 'ludicrous' for the 'sublime'.

Joseph Andrews, however, was marked by ambiguities of artistic purpose, for the early chapters are a parody of Richardson's *Pamela*. Fielding's full-scale effort in the new genre was *Tom Jones* (1749) and he presented it in eighteen books, each equipped with an introductory chapter in the form of a commentary on the work. In Book IX, chapter i he gives a list of the qualifications required by a novelist of his kind ('historian' is the word he uses). The passage refers to Horace and Homer, Milton, Jonson and Shakespeare, indicating the company to which he felt he belonged. The requisite qualities are: Genius, Learning, Conversation, and a Good Heart. Genius is operative in two faculties, 'Invention' and 'Judgment'. 'Invention[2] is a 'quick and sagacious penetration into the true essence of all the objects of our contemplation', and 'Judgment' is 'the discernment of differences' therein. Since 'nature can only furnish us with the tools of our profession', learning is necessary to fit them for use and contribute to the needed substance. And since book-knowledge alone is not enough, the 'historian' must know humanity at first hand. 'This conversation must be universal, that is, with all ranks and degrees'. Lastly (a 'Good Heart'), the 'historian must be capable of feeling'. 'No man can paint a distress well which he doth not feel while he is painting it.'

So who are the 'historians'? Fielding tells us:

> Homer and Milton, who, though they added the ornament of numbers to their works, were both historians of our order, were masters of all the learning of their times.

Fielding's claims are certainly to be taken seriously. Nothing is more remarkable than the fact that in the long story of the English novel the two most innovatory writers, Fielding and James Joyce, should have found the basis for their innovation in Homer. Arthur Murphy (1727–1805), the playwright who wrote a biography of Fielding (1762), writes:

> *Amelia* has the same proportion to *Tom Jones* that the *Odyssey* of Homer bears, in the estimation of Longinus, to the *Iliad*. A fine vein of morality runs through the whole: many of the situations are affecting and tender; the sentiments are delicate; and, upon the whole, it is the *Odyssey*, the moral and pathetic work of Henry Fielding.

Another critic, Lord Monboddo (1714–99), the enthusiastic Rousseauist, touched on the same comparison in *Of the Origin and Progress of Language* (1773–92).

> There is lately sprung up amongst us a species of narrative poem, representing likewise the characters of common life. It has the same relation to comedy that the epic has to tragedy... It is therefore, I think, a legitimate kind of poem ... The reason why I mention it is, that we have in English a *poem* of that kind (for so I will call it) which has more of character in it than any work, ancient or modern, that I know. The work I mean is, *The History of Tom Jones* by Henry Fielding.

Lord Byron was to call Fielding 'the prose Homer' and Coleridge was to class him with Sophocles and Ben Jonson: 'What a master of composition Fielding was! Upon my word I think the *Oedipus Tyrannus*, the *Alchemist*, and *Tom Jones* the three most perfect plots every planned.'

There seems to be a special ironic justice about the fact that, while so many poets and dramatists, scholars and essayists, were pontificating year after year about the glories of the Homeric tradition and the extent to which contemporary literature did or did not live up to it, a man who had little time for critics (whose role he compared to that of the 'common slanderer') and less for any kind of pedagogical pretentiousness, should have quietly taken a leaf out of Homer's book to become, in a totally new prose form, the most fruitfully influential English writer since Shakespeare and Milton.

7
The Eighteenth Century: Dr Johnson and his Successors

The age of Pope, Swift and Addison has been regarded as the great classical age of English literature. It became known as the Augustan age because writers themselves saw a parallel between the great age of Virgil, Horace and Ovid and their own period of stability and cultural health. The self-conscious complacency was not wholly unjustified. After his visit to England in 1726–9, Voltaire (1694–1778) was moved by his experience of the freedom and justice of English society to attack the *ancien régime* at home in his *Lettres Philosophiques* (1734). It is, however, the bulky figure of Dr Johnson who represents for many readers the archetype of the eighteenth-century spirit, and his literary productivity belongs especially to the 1750s, 1760s and 1770s. Though, strictly speaking, the 'classical' label attaches less fittingly to Johnson than to his Augustan predecessors, if faithful attachment to ancient classical formulations is the criterion, yet the label belongs supremely to him in connoting the central fount of literary influence in the century of stability and the age of reason. There is a familiar portrait of Dr Johnson sitting in post-prandial chairmanship, surrounded at table by the admiring faces of the musician Dr Burney, the statesman Edmund Burke, the dramatist Oliver Goldsmith, the actor David Garrick, the painter Joshua Reynolds, and the biographer James Boswell. The gathering indicates over what intellectual brilliance Johnson's ascendancy was sustained.

When we actually fasten on Johnson's contemporaries and successors in the literary field, we find fundamental changes in taste and sensibility, indeed in traditional literary allegiances too, eroding the fabric of Augustan classicism. It is not surprising that, while some literary historians have presented the first decades of the eighteenth century as a transition phase between the Restoration age and the age of Johnson, others have represented the 1740s to 1770s as a transition phase between the Augustan age and the age of Romanticism.

We cannot look back at the age of Johnson without sensing that it represents a period of calm before the storm. The momentous events at the end of the century were to mark one of the major turning points in the history of western civilisation. Meanwhile, at home, William Pitt the Elder (1708–78) was Prime Minister from 1757 to 1761 at a time when British prestige abroad was raised to new heights. In the decades of Johnson's maturity, Robert Clive (1725–47) was laying the foundations of British imperial rule in the East. James Wolfe (1727–59) died while gaining his celebrated victory at Quebec in 1759. This was one of the far-flung fields of combat in the Seven Years War (1756–63), which left Great Britain supreme as a naval power and colonising nation. On the other hand, Johnson lived long enough to see the American Declaration of Independence promulgated in 1776 and eventually accepted by the British government in 1785 at the end of the War of Independence.

It has to be accepted that too much of the criticism of the Augustan age looked backwards, while the criticism of Johnson's age often points forwards. Not that there was any improper neglect of the past. Indeed in 1764, musing among the ruins of the Capitol at Rome, the young Edward Gibbon (1737–94) conceived the plan of writing the massive work *The Decline and Fall of the Roman Empire*, which began to come out in 1775. But for the literary historian the most momentous development of Johnson's life-time was the virtual invention of a new literary form, the novel. Within a few years of the deaths of Pope and Swift, Richardson's *Clarissa Harlowe* (1748), Smollett's *Roderick Random* (1748) and Fielding's *Tom Jones* (1749) had transformed the literary landscape.

I Dr Johnson

Samuel Johnson (1709–84) holds a magisterial status among English literary critics. Many of his utterances are crammed with illumination and entertainment. The comment is so wide-ranging that it cannot be neatly summed up under a few heads. We can but select from this material some samples of Johnson's critical acumen in action. The most relevant output is largely contained in three branches of Johnson's work: periodical essays in the *Rambler* and the *Idler*; the edition of Shakespeare; and the *Lives of the Poets*.

There is, however, plenty of critical comment outside these works. Indeed one of Johnson's most striking general statements about poetry is put into the mouth of the old philosopher, Imlac, in his novel *Rasselas* (1759), 'The business of a poet ... is to examine, not the individual, but the species; to remark general properties and large appearances ...'

Thus Imlac begins, echoing Fielding's introductory chapter to Book III of *Joseph Andrews*, ' ... I declare here, once for all, I describe not men, but manners; not an individual, but a species ...'

In portraying nature, Imlac continues, the poet must exhibit 'such prominent and striking features, as recall the original to every mind':

> But the knowledge of nature is only half the task of a poet; he must be acquainted likewise with all the modes of life. His character requires that he estimate the happiness and misery of every condition; observe the power of all the passions in all their combinations, and trace the changes of the human mind as they are modified by various institutional and accidental influences of climate or custom, from the sprightliness of infancy to the dependence of decrepitude. He must divest himself of the prejudices of his age and country; he must consider right and wrong in their abstracted and invariable state; he must disregard present laws and opinions, and rise to general and transcendental truths, which will always be the same: he must therefore content himself with the slow progress of his name; contemn the applause of his own time, and commit his claims to the justice of posterity. He must write as the interpreter of nature, and the legislator

of mankind, and consider himself as presiding over the thoughts and manners of future generations; as a being superior to time and place.

There is an anticipation here of the rhetoric to be used in the Romantic Age by Shelley and Wordsworth. And what makes Johnson's such a refreshing output in the history of criticism is that it immediately lifts him above his age and above his predecessors. The mere fact that here is a critic who is obsessed neither with literary allegiance to the ancients nor with defensive rejection of the ancients is indicative of his independence and self-confidence. His attitude to the race of contemporary critics in general was scornful. In *Rambler* No. 3 (27 March, 1750) he sees them as men who, out of either duty or amusement, make it their business to impede the reception of 'every work of learning or genius'. And he constructs an allegory of how Criticism, 'the eldest daughter of labour and truth', brought her torch to earth whose light would show up the true quality of works of art, and confer immortality or oblivion as appropriate. But increasingly the works of art tended to have a mix of qualities and defects, and she decided to hand over her judicial function to time. The 'slaves of flattery and malevolence' seized fragments of her broken sceptre, and tried to take over the role of conferring immortality or condemning to oblivion.

In a very different vein Johnson wrote two papers for the *Idler* (nos 60 and 61, June 9 and 15 1759) celebrating the theme that 'criticism is a study by which men grow important and formidable at very small expense'. Johnson's aim, he says, is to instruct those living in obscurity 'how easily distinction may be obtained'. In short, one must turn literary critic. In that role you can give vent to malignity without doing any damage because it is always ineffective. Johnson then illustrates his case by tracing the career of 'Dick Minim', a poorly educated brewer's apprentice suddenly enriched by the death of an uncle, who decides to become a man of wit. He frequents the coffee houses near the theatres, reads a few books, and then begins to pontificate. In rehearsing Dick's views, Johnson supplies a neat summary of some of the most hackneyed critical clichés and prejudices of the day on Shakespeare, Jonson, Sidney, Waller, Dryden, and so on. When specific instances are provided of Dick's influence and his special discoveries, they are of course absurd. Some doggerel from *Hudibras* is solemnly quoted to instance 'striking accommodation of the sound to the sense': 'When pulpit, drum ecclesiastic,/ Was beat with fist instead of stick ...'

More serious observations on the role of the critic occur in *Rambler* no. 93 (February 5, 1751) on 'The Prejudices of Critics'.

> There are few books on which more time is spent by young students than on treatises which deliver the characters of authors, nor any which oftener deceive the expectation of the reader or fill his mind with more opinions which the progress of his studies and the increase of his knowledge oblige him to resign.

The qualities of good writing do not lend themselves to ready systematisation in a list of regulations. Johnson warns therefore against undue reliance upon critics, whose views are likely to be partly influenced by vanity, negligence, lack of reading, and a 'thousand extrinsic and accidental causes'. Self-interest may play its part even with the most distinguished critics. Dryden wrote dissertations 'only to recommend the work upon which he happened to be employed' and 'Addison is suspected to have denied the expediency of poetic justice because his own Cato was condemned to perish in a good cause'. When Johnson turns to adjudicate between the supposedly arrogant offences of critics and the demand of writers that critics should learn to know their inferior status, he implies that there may be six of one and half-a-dozen of the other. Perhaps the critic ought to deal gently with writers who have 'committed no other offence than that of betraying their own ignorance and dulness'. But there is no such general obligation for critical indulgence. By turning writer, you issue a general challenge, for 'to commence author is to claim praise, and no man can justly aspire to honour but at the hazard of disgrace'.

In an essay in *Rambler* no. 125 (28 May, 1751), Johnson sweeps away a mass of ill-digested critical lumber on the nature of comedy and tragedy. He insists that it is wrong to categorise comedy and tragedy in terms of the kind of people represented, mean and bad, noble and good. A lot of nonsense would have been avoided if it had been recognised that comedy and tragedy can be defined only in terms of 'their effects upon the mind'. Comedy is a matter of raising mirth, and a man does not need to be either mean or corrupt to raise mirth. In a scathing indictment of the bombast that passed for tragedy, Johnson mocks the poets who imagine that all that is necessary for tragedy is 'that they should crowd the scene with monarchs, and generals, and guards; and make them talk, at certain intervals, of the downfall of kingdoms, and the rout of armies'. With an equally whole-some application of the disinfectant of commonsense Johnson discredits slavish adherence to the rules of the ancients in two papers in *Rambler* nos 156 and 158 (Sep 14 and Sep 21, 1751). Some rules for writing are indispensable, some merely useful; some based on reason, others merely on 'despotic antiquity'. Rules prescribing five acts for a play and limiting the period of time covered are purely arbitrary. So is the prejudice against mixing tragedy and comedy. The stage is supposed to be the mirror of life, and the mingling of the important with the trivial is a fact of life. Criticism is not a science and the 'rules hitherto received' have no firm basis, but derive from the whims of self-appointed legislators who put brakes on the natural adventurousness and innovative-ness of wit and genius.

Johnson was not infallible. The papers on Milton's *Samson Agonistes* in *Rambler* nos 139 and 140 (June 16 and July 20, 1751) reveal imaginative limitations. He condemns 'allusions to low and trivial objects' and to unsuitable Greek legends in the Old Testament scene. Moreover Johnson's insensitivity to the development of moral and spiritual tensions in the central acts of the tragedy leads him to the conclusion that, by Aristotle's criteria, the drama is deficient in having a beginning and an end but no middle.

The work of Johnson was central to the establishment of Shakespeare's reputation in eighteenth-century literary scho-larship. Johnson's estimate of Shakespeare was one which above all did justice to Shakespeare's imaginative range.

Each change of many-colour'd life he drew,
Exhausted worlds, and then imagin'd new:
Existence saw him spurn her bounded reign,
And panting time toil'd after him in vain.

So he spoke of Shakespeare in the Prologue he wrote for David Garrick to deliver at the opening of the Theatre Royal, Drury Lane, in 1747. Nearly twenty years later, in 1765, Johnson's edition of Shakespeare was published. In his Preface Johnson claims for Shakespeare the status of an 'ancient'. He has already stood the test of time. All other motives, personal or ulterior, for acclaiming him, but that his works give pleasure, have passed away, and he keeps his appeal. He is above all the 'poet of nature', holding up a 'faithful mirror of manners and of life'. His characters 'act and speak by the influence of those general passions and principles by which all minds are agitated'. Johnson drives this point home by a forceful contrast. For, under any other direction than that of Shakespeare, the theatre 'is peopled by such characters as were never seen, conversing in a language which was never heard, upon topicks which will never arise in the commerce of mankind'. Lamenting the artificial excesses of emotion and posture in contemporary drama, he insists that Shakespeare's characters act and speak in such a way that 'his drama is the mirror of life'. Rebutting the charge of Dennis and Rymer that Shakespeare's Romans are insufficiently Romans, he replies that Shakespeare 'always makes nature predominate over accident ... His story requires Romans or Kings, but he thinks only on men'.

Johnson once more defends Shakespeare's mingling of the tragic and the comic, praising his capacity to work on whatever feelings he chooses. Since 'the end of writing is to instruct' and 'the end of poetry is to instruct by pleasing', since 'mingled drama' is truer to life, and anyway 'all pleasure consists in variety', the case is irrefutable. What is universal in the motives and feelings of Shakespeare's characters transcends what is historically ephemeral. 'The stream of time, which is continually washing away the dissoluble fabricks of other poets, passes without injury by the adamant of Shakespeare.'

On the subject of Shakespeare's defects Johnson betrays some of the prejudices of his age. He complains that Shakespeare 'seems to write without any moral purpose'. There is lots that is worth while in his moral teaching, but it is casual and adventitious and amounts to no clear judgment of good and evil. The plots are loosely constructed and the dénouements often careless. There are anachronisms and incongruities over what properly appertains to a given age or nation. The comic backchat is often crude and indecent. Shakespeare's narration has an excess of artifice and circumlocution. Above all he will introduce 'some idle conceit or contemptible equivocation' where it is totally inappropriate. 'A quibble was to him the fatal Cleopatra for which he lost the world and was content to lose it.'

Johnson defends Shakespeare's readiness to move from place to place and from year to year. All arguments on behalf of the unities of time and place presuppose that a stage representation can be mistaken for reality. But the spectators are always in their senses, aware that 'the stage is only a stage, and the players are only players'. We could not enjoy tragedies were we not aware of the fiction. And Johnson takes Voltaire to task for expressing surprise that a nation which had seen *Cato* could tolerate Shakespeare's extravagance. 'Let him be answered, that Addison speaks the language of poets, and Shakespeare of men.' *Cato* is a mass of artifices. '*Othello* is the vigorous and vivacious offspring of observation impregnated by genius.' Johnson marvels at how exactly a man with Shakespeare's personal background could understand so many modes of life; for he always shows plainly 'that he has seen with his own eyes'. No other author except Homer has 'invented so much as Shakespeare'. On Shakespeare's style Johnson at once applauds the 'smoothness and harmony' of his verse and protests against the presence of what is 'ungrammatical, perplexed and obscure'.

Johnson surveys the record of recent previous editors, Rowe, Pope, Theobald, Hanmer and Warburton, and explains his own methods of textual editing and emendation. 'I have always suspected that the reading is right, which requires many words to prove it wrong; and the emendation wrong that cannot without so much labour appear to be right.' Finally, Johnson shows where his allegiance lies by aligning himself with Dryden, quoting in full Dryden's eloquent tribute to Shakespeare in the *Defence of Dramatic Poesy* (see p.91).

Johnson's *Lives of the English Poets* was originally commissioned as a series of biographical prefaces to an edition of English poets published in ten volumes (1779–81), and was then issued separately in 1781. In a reference to the *Lives* in *The Use of Poetry and the Use of Criticism* (1933), T. S. Eliot distinguishes the Scylla and Charybdis between which the critic of poetry must sail. The danger is that if he concentrates on moral, social, or religious aspects and implications of poetry, then the poetry becomes little more than a 'text for a discourse'. But if he concentrates on the 'poetic' aspects of the work to the neglect of what the poet is saying, then he will empty it of significance. The critic can keep his true status as a critic only if he steers clear of turning into a philosopher or sociologist or psychologist. 'Johnson, in these respects, is a type of critical integrity. Within his limitations, he is one of the great critics; and he is a great critic because he keeps within his limitations ... I view Johnson's *Lives of the Poets* as a masterpiece of the judicial bench.'[1]

Words like 'judicial' come appropriately to mind when describing Johnson's critical attitude. There is a massive authoritativeness about it, a strenuous straining to be just, and yet a refusal to blanket plain defects from exposure. Since no critic is infallible, the clarity and candour of Johnson's *dicta* are such that when he is right he floods the mind with illumination, and when he is wrong he is thoroughly wrong. The illuminations do not represent scattered prescriptions from a critical code that can be formulated as Johnson's manifesto. His critical premises do not have that kind of priority. When Johnson applies himself to a given poet, the poet and his work take over. The flow of aphorisms and judgments belongs to that context only. As a result there is neither a critical posture to be defined nor a cultural crusade to be summed up. There is only a fount of critical wisdom to admire as it plays on diverse personalities and their works.

Among the more substantial lives are those of Dryden and Pope. Dryden, Johnson declares, is 'the father of English criticism' who 'taught us to determine on principles the merits of composition'. And Johnson recognises that 'the criticism of Dryden is the criticism of a poet'; in short, it was not based on formulae, but was always alive to what it was dealing with. It is in this respect that Johnson proclaims the 'majesty' of Dryden's work. In particular he praises the sheer verbal opulence and imaginative vitality of the *Essay on Dramatic Poesy*. He regards Dryden's account of Shakespeare as a 'model of encomiastic criticism' and an 'epitome of excellence'. And it is notable that, although Johnson recognised in Dryden's prose style the lack of that 'formality of a settled style, in which the first half of the sentence betrays the other', the lack of balanced clauses and modelled periods, he acknowledged the vigour and animation of the seemingly casual word order, the overall spiritedness, and the touches of splendour.

As a poet, Dryden is praised for having established the new versification so firmly that since his time English poetry has shown no tendency to relapse 'to its former savageness'. Johnson's notion of poetic diction distinguishes it clearly from prose. He protests against the intrusion of nautical terms like 'okum', 'marling', and 'tarpawling' into Dryden's description of the naval engagement in *Annus Mirabilis*. While allowing for the financial pressures which turned Dryden into a perhaps too prolific and too hasty writer, Dr Johnson does justice to poems such as *Absalom and Achitophel* which have stood the test of time. But he finds the use of animal allegory for the purpose of theological polemic in *The Hind and the Panther* 'injudicious and incommodious; for what can be more absurd than that one beast should counsel another to rest her faith upon a pope and council?'. In summing up Dryden's qualities he recognises that 'strong reason' rather than 'quick sensibility' was his predominant intellectual power. Dryden 'studied rather than felt, and produced sentiments not such as Nature enforces, but meditation supplies'. The simple elemental passions he seems to know little of, and deals with them only when 'they are complicated by the various relations of society, and confused in the tumults and agitations of life'.

These are the observations of a critic with his mind locked into contemplation of his subject and not predisposed to make that subject a platform for himself. In dealing with Pope, he does not hesitate to give a busy sketch of his weaknesses and eccentricities, the excessive demands he made on servants and hosts, his way of pampering himself at table, his love of intrigue and sly indirection, his fretfulness and readiness to take offence, his fondness for wealth and his liking for the aristocracy, and above all the false affectations like his pretended indifference to criticism of his work. But hard on the heels of a forceful, if superficially temperate, register of his personal failings, Johnson praises Pope's intellectual good sense about what was right for him to tackle, and the ambitious aspiration which drove him towards ever greater achievements. He emphasises Pope's retentive memory, his devoted application to his craft, his thoroughness, his patience, and his careful method of composition by continual improvement and refinement of his first drafts.

In this matter, of course, Pope contrasted strongly with Dryden, and Johnson inserts in his 'Life of Pope' a passage comparing and contrasting the two which has been celebrated for its shrewdness and insight. Both poets had 'integrity of understanding and nicety of discernment'. But Dryden was content to write to satisfy his public without straining to uncover new resources in himself. He did not struggle to make what was good better. He wrote spontaneously as the occasion required, and then dismissed the product from his mind. Pope, however, 'was not content to satisfy; he desired to excel'. He did not spare himself, but amended what he had written with painstaking punctiliousness. He brooded over what he had written before submitting it for publication. And he continued to watch over his works after their publication, correcting further with a diligence which Dryden lacked. Dryden, however, was the more scholarly of the two with a larger intellectual range. 'Dryden knew more of man in his general nature, and Pope in his local manners.' Comprehensive speculation was the basis of Dryden's notions, and minute attention of Pope's. As for their prose:

The style of Dryden is capricious and varied, that of Pope is cautious and uniform; Dryden obeys the motions of his own mind, Pope constrains his mind to his own rules of composition. Dryden is sometimes vehement and rapid; Pope is always smooth, uniform, and gentle. Dryden's page is a natural field, rising into inequalities, and diversified by the varied exuberance of abundant vegetation; Pope's is a velvet lawn, shaven by the scythe, and levelled by the roller.

So far as genius is concerned, that energy which gives life and order to everything, Dryden just has the superiority. That does not mean that Pope lacked poetical vigour. If Dryden 'has brighter paragraphs, he has not better poems'. 'Dryden's performances were always hasty, either excited by some external occasion, or extorted by domestic necessity...' He gave whatever his mind 'could supply on call', and left it at that; whereas Pope cautiously worked up his material with the maximum care:

If the flights of Dryden therefore are higher, Pope continues longer on the wing. If of Dryden's fire the blaze is brighter, of Pope's the heat is more regular and constant. Dryden often surpasses expectation, and Pope never falls below it. Dryden is read with frequent astonishment, and Pope with perpetual delight.

Johnson himself, in the Preface to his edition of Shakespeare, issued a warning against the practice of illustrating a poet's quality by select quotations. The person who tries thus to recommend Shakespeare 'will succeed like the pedant in Hierocles, who, when he offered his house to sale, carried a brick in his pocket as a specimen'. Yet the quality of Johnson's critical work can be justly conveyed only by piling up instance after instance of his apothegmatic judgments. How can the sense of humour be illustrated if not by the way Johnson deftly puts a person in his place for one of his failures? In the case of Pope it is the *Essay on Man* on which he exercises his gift for the magisterial put-down. Pope, he insists, was not sufficiently master of his subject. Metaphysical morality was a new subject to him, 'he was proud of his acquisitions, and, supposing himself master of great secrets, was in haste to teach what he had not learned':

Having exalted himself into the chair of wisdom, he tells us much that every man knows, and much that he does not know himself ... This essay affords egregious instance of the predominance of genius, the dazzling splendour of imagery, and the seductive power of eloquence. Never was penury of knowledge and vulgarity of sentiment so happily disguised.

Johnson hammers his victim into the ground, summarising the argument of the poem in a series of trite truisms, and then adding:

Surely a man of no very comprehensive search may venture to say that he has heard all this before; but it was never till now recommended by such a blaze of embellishment, or such sweetness of melody.

In the 'Life of Addison' Dr Johnson seems concerned to rescue a reputation that has posthumously slumped. He frankly defines the qualities of verbal distinction and of emotional force that are lacking in Addison's poetry. 'He thinks justly, but he thinks faintly.' His poetry has clarity and polish, it is 'the product of a mind too judicious to commit faults, but not sufficiently vigorous to attain excellence'. But Johnson turns on those who depreciate Addison the critic for his lack of the 'scientific' approach and for his appeal to taste rather than to established principles. He reminds his readers that there was not in Addison's day any general diffusion of knowledge in this respect to which a writer could appeal. And he thereby illustrates the importance of a critical maxim which he had propounded in his 'Life of Dryden':

To judge rightly of an author, we must transport ourselves to his time, and examine what were the wants of his contemporaries, and what were his means of supplying them.

On this basis Johnson now defends Addison the critic: he was catering for an uninformed public who might have admired a more scholarly approach but would not thereby have paid any more attention to *Paradise Lost*. As it is, 'by the blandishments of gentleness and facility', Addison has made

Milton 'an universal favourite'. Moreover Addison's essays on 'Wit' and on the 'Pleasures of Imagination' display both skill and elegance in examining the psychological basis of the 'principles of invention'. But on the subject of Addison's praise of 'Chevy Chase', Johnson quotes Dennis's scathing judgment that there are three ways of deviating from nature; by bombast or tumour which magnifies nature, by affectation which forsakes nature, and 'by imbecility, which degrades nature'. In 'Chevy Chase', Johnson adds, 'there is not much of either bombast or affectation; but there is a chill and lifeless imbecility.' Johnson concedes that it is 'as a describer of life and manners' that Addison stands in the first rank. His fidelity to reality in picturing the domestic scene and daily life acquires an air of novelty from his distinctive sense of humour. Addison's style Johnson regards as 'the model of the middle style', evading the heights and depths of rhetoric and vulgarity. Perhaps he is sometimes too wordy or too conversational, but he is always clear and fluent, without touches of special warmth or acuity.

> Addison never deviates from his track to snatch a grace; he seeks no ambitious ornaments, and tries no hazardous innovations ... Whoever wishes to attain an English style, familiar but not coarse, and elegant without ostentation, must give his days and nights to the volumes of Addison.

When Johnson is out of sympathy with his subject he can drive a critical steam-roller. In the 'Life of Gray' he shows his scorn for the 'Ode on the Prospect of Eton College' as saying nothing worth saying, 'His supplication to father Thames to tell him who drives the hoop or tosses the ball, is useless and puerile. Father Thames has no better means of knowing than himself!' As for the grand pindaric odes, 'The Progress of Poetry' and 'The Bard', those lofty pre-Romantic ventures into the sublime, Johnson makes nonsense of the imagery ('Criticism disdains to chase a schoolboy to his commonplaces') and uses logic to puncture imaginative sequences. He devotes several paragraphs to a hatchet job. There is 'a kind of cumbrous splendour which we wish away'. The odes are 'marked by glittering accumulations of ungraceful ornaments; they strike rather than please; the images are magnified by affectation'. But after this devastating exercise Johnson turns to concur with the popular acclamation accorded to the 'Elegy in a Country Churchyard': 'The *Churchyard* abounds with images which find a mirror in every mind, and with sentiments to which every bosom returns an echo.'

The 'Life of Milton' tested Johnson's impartiality in that Milton's political opinions were anathema to him. Johnson makes no attempt to disguise the fact. Milton's 'political opinions were those of an acrimonious and surly republican'. His republicanism was 'founded in an envious hatred of greatness, and a sullen desire of independence; in petulance impatient of control, and pride disdainful of superiority'. 'He thought women made only for obedience, and men only for rebellion...' But the venom does not infect Johnson's treatment of the poetry, though there is one celebrated instance of profound misjudgment in the case of 'Lycidas'. Johnson finds 'its diction is harsh, the rhymes uncertain, and the numbers unpleasing'. Plainly he resented the incongruous combination of the artifices of the pastoral with the gravities of religious polemic, 'trifling fictions' with 'the most awful and sacred truths', and the condemnation is wholesale: 'In this poem there is no nature, for there is no truth; there is no art for there is nothing new.'

Yet 'L'Allegro' and 'Il Penseroso', 'two noble efforts of imagination', stir him to detailed exploration of their contrasting characteristics. And when Johnson turns to *Paradise Lost*, he shows the deepest admiration for Milton's achievement. The epic is subjected to examination by reference to the neoclassical categories. The *moral* is 'the most useful and the most arduous; *to vindicate the ways of God to man*' and show the necessity for obedience to God. The *fable*, that of the Fall of Man, equals that of any other poet. It involves the 'fate of worlds', and indeed 'before the greatness displayed in Milton's poem, all other greatness shrinks away'. The *characters*, angelic and human, are appreciatively surveyed. In respect of the *probable* and the *marvellous*, the theme of *Paradise Lost* is such that 'the probable ... is marvellous, and the marvellous is probable', for the 'sub-

stance of the narrative is truth'. The supernatural *machinery* is
not arbitrary but essential to the action. The two *episodes*
(Raphael's narration and Michael's prophecy) are equally
central to the action as warning to Adam and as consolation.
As for the *integrity* of the design, 'there is perhaps no poem, of
the same length, from which so little can be taken away
without mutilation'. The poem must be judged *heroic* and the
sentiments are just.

While Johnson pays tribute to the vast scope of Milton's
vision and his resourcefulness in feeding the reader's imagination, he accepts Dryden's view that Milton saw Nature
'through the spectacles of books'. Milton's 'moral sentiments'
of course 'excel those of all other poets'. In turning to
Milton's defects, Johnson observes that *Paradise Lost* 'com-
prises neither human actions nor human manners'. There is
an obstacle in the way of reader-identification and sympathy
with a man and woman placed in a situation the reader can
never experience. But, after reference to one or two other
lesser deficiencies, Johnson concludes that they are such that
anyone who thought it worthwhile to weigh them in the
balance against the vast beauties of the poem would deserve
to be pitied for his insensitivity.

There is material here and there in the *Lives of the Poets*
that could be seized upon, and has been seized upon, by
detractors for the purpose of denigrating Johnson's achievement. The 'Life of Cowley' contains an attack upon the
metaphysical poets as writers who pursued novelty at the cost
of truth, and went in for 'violent and unnatural fictions' and
'enormous and disgusting hyperboles'. To Donne's celebrated
image of the compasses 'it may be doubted whether
absurdity or ingenuity has the better claim'.

Johnson's tone of voice has been sometimes misunderstood,
and the hints it can convey of a twinkle in the eye or a
raising of the eyebrow are not perhaps always accessible to
the insensitive. There is no doubt more than a hint of self-
parody about pronouncements which have been declared
over-ponderously dogmatic. Johnson enjoyed himself when
he was talking, and T. S. Eliot has observed that the style of
the *Lives* 'reads often like the writing of a man who is more
habituated to talking than to writing; he seems to think aloud'.

II The rejection of neoclassicism

In his 'Life of Pope' Johnson recommends the *Essay on the Genius and Writings of Pope*, published in part in 1756 and in whole in 1782, the work of Joseph Warton (1722–1800). For Johnson it was 'a book which teaches how the brow of Criticism may be smoothed, and how she may be enabled, with all her severity, to attract and to delight'. Warton had contributed papers to the *Adventurer* (1752–4), the journal which succeeded the *Rambler*. Among them were papers on *The Tempest* and *King Lear* in which new emphasis was laid on characterisation. The *Essay on the Genius and Writings of Pope* fully justifies Johnson's praise. Warton's thesis is that Pope excelled all others in his particular 'species' of poetry, but that species is not 'the most excellent one of the art'. He differentiates between the man of wit, the man of sense, and the true poet. No amount of intellectual acuity and clarity can make a poet. No degree of elegance and beauty in observation can make poetry. What alone makes a poet is 'a creative and glowing *imagination, acer spiritus ac vis*'. To illustrate his point Warton quotes the first fourteen lines of Pope's *Moral Essays*, 'Epistle I':

> Yes, you despise the man to Books confin'd,
> Who from his study rails at human kind...

He paraphrases them in prose and shows how fully the paraphrase does justice to the original. But if one tried to take ten lines of the *Iliad* or *Paradise Lost* and apply the same test to them, the quality of the original would be lost. 'The sublime and the pathetic are the two chief nerves of all genuine poetry and in these two qualities Pope was deficient.'

In his careful survey of Pope's poetry, Warton often impresses by his freshness of judgment. Of the Pastorals he laments that 'there is not a single rural image that is new'. And he finds the inadequate, half-hearted adaptation of background and mythology to the British environment and climate rather absurd. He shows how much better this new problem was solved by Milton in 'Lycidas'. And indeed Warton repeatedly turns aside to comment on the work of other poets. It is in some of these comparisons that his insight emerges most clearly as representative of the new direction criticism was taking. For instance, he quotes from 'Windsor Forest':

> Here waving groves a chequer'd scene display,
> And part admit, and part exclude the day;
> As some coy nymph her lover's warm address
> Nor quite indulges, nor can quite repress.

The reflection is condemned as false, 'Far-fetched and forced'. 'The fallacy consists in giving design and artifice to the wood as well as to the coquette, and in putting the light of the sun and the warmth of a lover on a level.' By contrast Warton cites instances from Virgil and from Dyer of pathetic reflection appropriately and enrichingly introduced into descriptive poetry, and the exploration of descriptive techniques leads to an enthusiastic illustration of the imaginative power displayed by Milton in the 'Ode of the Nativity of Christ'.

Warton shows himself even more strikingly to be of a new school when he turns to the descriptive work of James Thomson. Here was a man who actually wandered in the country for days and weeks, observant and attentive, while other poets lived always in the Strand, and their descriptions suffered accordingly from 'nauseous repetition' and an artificial 'set of hereditary images'. Thomson is praised for the accuracy and novelty of his observations, his exactness and resourcefulness in escaping the descriptive conventions and bringing the detailed life of nature vividly before the reader. He is praised too for his imaginative ingenuity in recording the effect on the mind of the spectator of the scenes described. While 'Pope, it seems, was of opinion that descriptive poetry is a composition as absurd as a feast made up of sauces'.

When Warton turns to the *Essay on Criticism* he quotes Dr Johnson on the subject of rules; in particular the need 'to distinguish nature from custom, or that which is established because it is right, from that which is right only because it is established' (*Rambler* no. 156). Warton again adopts a progressive position. He attacks the concept of 'correctness' as a proper criterion for criticism: 'It is perpetually the nauseous cant of the French critics, and of their advocates and pupils, that the English writers are generally incorrect.'

Reflections on the influence of critics leads Warton to a forthright declaration: 'In no polished nation, after criticism has been much studied and the rules of writing established, has any very extraordinary work ever appeared.'

Unaccountable as it may be, the effect of authoritative, regulatory criticism on literary productivity has been damaging. In evidence, compare the current understanding of the rules of the drama with the 'uninteresting, though faultless tragedies' lately staged.

Whatever Warton looks at, he seems to illuminate. He sets the record straight by a thorough reconsideration of Addison's *Cato*, that tragedy constantly overrated at the time. He attributes its success to its topical political allusions. It is pure sententious declamation. Its pompous sentiments are facile. It lacks action and pathos. It is deficient in characterisation. The love episodes are 'vicious and insipid' and debase the dignity of the drama. The issue leads Warton to a fascinating digression on the excessive concentration on the passion of love in 'modern' drama. Too many pieces are 'emasculated with this epidemical effeminacy'. There is no doubt that to read Warton is to be in touch with a personality as independent in his thinking as Dr Johnson himself. At one point a reflection on the representation of madness in literature leads him to declare that the most interesting example he knows is that of Clementina in Richardson's *Sir Charles Grandison*. He is not sure whether even Lear's madness reveals so many 'strokes of nature and genuine passion', then adds: 'Shall I say it is pedantry to prefer and compare the madness of Orestes in Euripides to this of Clementina?'

And the thought leads Warton to suggest that, as in Rowe's *Jane Shore*, dramatists might be well advised to forsake Greek and Roman stories and seek for subjects 'in the annals of England'.

Summing up at the end of the essay, Warton remarks that Pope's successes in didactic, moral and satiric poetry were not successes in 'the most poetic species of poetry'. Imagination was not his predominant talent. He stuck to dealing with modern manners, which are no subject for lofty treatment. He became one of the most correct poets, polishing assiduously, yet he rarely ravished or transported his reader or affected him with the strong emotions that Homer or Milton can stir.

Warton dedicated his essay to Edward Young (1683–1765), the poet of the massive, sombre and reflective work *Night Thoughts* (1742–5). Young himself, towards the end of his long life, turned critic in *Conjectures on Original Composition* (1759), an essay written in the form of a letter to the novelist Samuel Richardson. It represents a further shift of critical theory away from the neoclassical school, and it attacks the subject far more comprehensively than Warton did. Young distinguishes 'originals' from 'imitations', the former deserving far more admiration than the latter, though the latter are many and the former few. The ancients could not choose but be original whereas the moderns have the choice to make, and if they make the right choice they need not be so inferior to their ancestors. The ancients deserve their tribute, but there is a right and a wrong way to emulate them. 'The less we copy the renowned ancients, we shall resemble them the more.' It is within human reach to match and even surpass our predecessors.

Young lays great emphasis on the distinction between 'genius' and 'learning'. 'A genius differs from a good understanding, as a magician from a good architect: that makes his structure by means invisible; this by the skilful use of common toils.' Learning, without genius, loves rules and models; it condemns the 'natural unstudied graces, and small, harmless inaccuracies' and fetters the liberty which is the supreme glory of genius. Genius is characterised by 'unprescribed beauties, and unexampled excellencies' which are outside the 'pale of learning's authorities and laws'. Genius is often most deserving of praise when it is most sure to be condemned. Young distinguishes between 'adult' and 'infantine' genius. Shakespeare was an adult genius in that he was endowed with it at birth. Swift's was an infantine genius in that he had to nurse and tutor it to bring it to fruition. And genius is not confined to poets. In possessing this gift Shakespeare and Aquinas are of the same party. Young will have no disparagement of learning, and has no time for 'self-taught philosophers' who fancy they have a genius which makes them superior to both learning and revealed truth. But the suppression of genius is damaging; it deprives the 'liberal and politer arts' of the advantage the 'mechanic' arts enjoy, of progressing beyond their predecessors. Moreover it fails to cooperate with Nature, which makes us all originals, with no two faces or two minds alike. Lastly it impoverishes our productivity in quality while increasing it in quantity.

For Young the powers of the moderns are equal to those of the ancients, but they are not properly extended. We underestimate our potentialities. There is no cause for us to prostrate ourselves in thoughtless admiration before assumed superiority in any walk of life, turning ourselves into pedestals for others to pose on. 'Imitators and translators' go in for that kind of thing. The proper way to beat Homer is to do what Milton did, not what Pope did; and Pope is all the more to blame for putting Achilles in petticoats (rhyming couplets) in that Milton had already shown the way with his masculine blank verse. Might Pope have succeeded better by trying to write something original? Young asks.

Talents untried are talents unknown ... Imitation is inferiority confessed; emulation is superiority contested, or denied; imitation is servile, emulation generous; that fetters, this fires ...

Had Pope indeed possessed 'a strong imagination, and the true sublime', then we might have had two Homers instead of one.

Young cites Shakespeare as a genius equalling the greatest of the ancients, but criticises Jonson for being overloaded with learning, where Shakespeare was master of two books often neglected by deep readers, 'the book of Nature, and that of man'. Dryden he regards as unfitted for drama.

He was a stranger to the pathos, and, by numbers, expression, sentiment, and every other dramatic cheat, strove to make amends for it; as if a saint could make amends for the want of conscience; a soldier for want of valour; or a vestal, of modesty.

In epic poetry rhyme is 'a sore disease', in tragedy it is 'absolute death'. As for Addison, though he had what Jonson and Dryden lacked, 'a warm and feeling heart', he was too reticent to let it show in *Cato*.

Young's *Conjectures* has some interesting incidental attractions. It is the source of the once much-quoted story that, on his death-bed, Addison called for a young relative, seized his hand and said 'See in what peace a Christian can die'. And it includes a memory of a walk with Swift just outside Dublin, when Swift stared in seeming transfixion at an elm whose uppermost branches were withered and decayed, and said 'I shall be like that tree, I shall die at the top'. Perhaps the most ironic aspect of Young's essay for the modern reader is that its very readability and the solidity of its substance contrast so sharply with the pretentious turgidities of his *magnum opus*, *Night Thoughts*.

A more formidable figure in the history of literary criticism than either Edward Young or Joseph Warton was Warton's younger brother, Thomas Warton (1728–90), Professor of Poetry at Oxford and eventually Poet Laureate. It was his lot to move critical thinking further in the direction which eventually led to the Romantic movement, and at the same time to attempt a comprehensive work of literary history. The seed of his later achievement was sown in *Observations on the Faerie Queene of Spenser* (1754). It surveys the merits and defects of the poem and does not hesitate to follow where the argument seems logically to lead, into comment on other writers and on historical factors relevant to the case he is making. Above all, Warton insists that the reader of an earlier poet has to take into account the 'customs and manners' prevailing in the age when the poet wrote. We have to put ourselves in that poet's position, and consider how his ways of thinking were influenced by an environment totally different from our own. This insistence was to be the hall-mark of Warton's literary surveys. He was an erudite scholar, he was thorough in research, and he was able for the most part to detach himself from the prejudices and misconceptions of his own age and generation.

Thus Warton argues that, although Spenser follows the epic tradition in constituting Prince Arthur as his hero, the model of the perfect knight, and involving him in the grand quest of service to Gloriana, this unity of design is not matched by unity of action, for the adventures of the knights who represent the individual moral virtues are separately complete in themselves, and in each case the role of Prince Arthur is a subordinate one. A better plan might have been to have either 'twelve knights without an Arthur, or an Arthur without twelve knights'. However Warton accepts that the *Faerie Queene* is a good deal less confused and irregular than Ariosto's *Orlando Furioso*; and he insists that the deficiency in organisation is no obstacle to enjoyment of the poem. 'In reading Spenser, if the critic is not satisfied, yet the reader is transported.' Among aspects of the historic environment which the reader of Spenser must take into account are the fact that the cultivation of Chivalry was very much alive in Spenser's day, and that the practice of literary allegory acquired vitality from the popularity of public pageants and dramas in which virtues and vices were personified. Warton shows imaginative sensitivity in his estimate of Spenser's allegory, but he complains that the sacred and the profane are mingled and confused. He instances the echoes of the book of Revelation in the description of Duessa, the evil enchantress, and in the horrors of Orgoglio's castle in Book II. It is an impropriety to apply the 'visions of God' to allegorical fiction.

Consideration of Spenser's place in English literature leads Warton to make a brief survey of his predecessors from the days of Chaucer, Gower and Lydgate. After referring to the beginning of the revival of classical literature in the reign of Henry VIII, he turns aside to observe that Skelton contributed nothing compared with his elegant contemporaries, Wyatt and Surrey, but that in Scotland David Lindsay and William Dunbar were 'animated with the noblest spirit of allegoric fiction'. The brief literary restrospect is directed to establishing that 'allegorical poetry through many gradations at last received its ultimate consummation in the *Faerie Queene*'. After Spenser allegory declined into 'a species of poetry whose images were of the metaphysical and abstracted kind'. Warton traces the process by which 'imagination gave way to correctness, sublimity of description to delicacy of sentiment, and majestic imagery to conceit and epigram'. 'Poets began to be more attentive to words than to things and objects.'

In a substantial 'Postscript' Warton includes a rebuke to Pope for mocking the attention Theobald gave in editing Shakespeare to:

All such reading as was never read (*Dunciad* IV, 250). These books, strange and odd maybe, were the very books Shakespeare himself read. Reading them saved Theobald from the editorial howlers Pope committed. The labour of a Theobald contributes to true taste and does not merit relegation to 'The Temple of Dulness'.

The study of Spenser clearly whetted Warton's scholarly appetite and he started work on *The History of English Poetry* (vol I, 1774, revised 1775; vol II, 1778; vol III, 1781). He began his survey after the Norman Conquest and continued up to the Elizabethan Age. He gave illustrated accounts of the poets' works and often shed light on their sources. He filled out the background by going into historical questions, social, religious, political, philosophical and technical. This practice of course resulted in lengthy digressions, not all of them strictly relevant: but the disproportion is mitigated by the continuing awareness it brings of the interaction between literature and life. Warton was plainly fascinated by this interaction, by the way English poetry developed under the changing historical conditions, by the way its movements and fashions were interlinked with adjustments in practical and intellectual life, and reflected concurrent developments abroad.

For instance, in a section on the Age of Elizabeth he defines the great features of the poetry of the period as 'the predominancy of fable, of fiction and fancy, and a predilection for interesting adventures and pathetic events'. And he assigns this predominancy to six specific causes which operated sometimes singly, sometimes together. They include the revival and translation of the classics, the importation and translation of Italian models, the prevalence of superstition, and the popularity of 'allegoric exhibition'. In illustrating his points Warton is entertainingly lavish. The way classical learning took hold of people under Elizabeth is exemplified in vivid snapshots. When Queen Elizabeth paid a visit to a noble house, she would be greeted in the hall by the Penates and led to her room by Mercury.

Even the pastrycooks were expert mythologists. At dinner select transformations of Ovid's *Metamorphoses* were exhibited in confectionery, and the splendid icing of an immense historic plum cake was embossed with a delicious *basso-relievo* of the destruction of Troy.

Outside in the grounds Tritons and Nereids covered the lake and footmen gambolled on the lawns as satyrs. 'This inundation of classical pedantry soon infected our poetry.' Even Shakespeare's Mrs Page can talk of being a giantess under Mount Pelion. The fashion was fed by a flood of translations from the classics. The restoration of the classics opened up a new world of fiction. But alas, what first made an impression was not the 'regularity of design and justness of sentiment' to be found in the classics but their 'fabulous inventions'. 'A rude age beginning to read these writers imitated their extravagances, not their natural beauties.'

In the year of Warton's death there appeared his Preface to an edition of *Milton's Minor Poem* (1790), in which he traced the unjustified neglect of these poems, overshadowed as they were by *Paradise Lost*. In 1738 *Comus* was produced at Drury Lane with music by Arne, and in 1741 Handel set 'L'Allegro' and 'Il Penseroso' to music. These events, and the increasing interest in *Paradise Lost* helped to bring the whole of Milton's poetry to an eager public.

A visible revolution succeeded in the general cast and character of the national composition. Our versification contracted a new colouring, a new structure and phraseology; and the school of Milton rose in emulation of the school of Pope.

Thus Warton annotates the revolution in taste to which he himself contributed.

Richard Hurd (1720–1808) played a notable part in rehabilitating Elizabethan literature, Spenser especially, in the reaction against neoclassicism. His *Letters on Chivalry and Romance* (1762) generalises the question about the status of the *Faerie Queene* into an issue over the difference between the 'Gothic' and the classical tradition. Hurd's argument is that, had Homer been able to compare the manners of his own age with the manners of the feudal ages, he would have preferred the latter as the basis for his poetry. Even the old romances, rude as they are, give evidence that the gallantry prevalent in feudal times provides better material for poetry than 'the simple and uncontrolled barbarity of the Grecians'. Alongside similar bloodthirstiness, the romances display the gentler emotions of friendship and exalted love. Thus they have a variety, a beauty, a novelty, a pathos, and indeed a dignity and magnificence not found in Greek epic. As for the 'religious machinery' and the use of the preternatural, the advantage is again with the 'Gothic' over the classical. There is awe and horror in the Gothic exploitation of witchcraft and incantation, while the 'mummeries of the pagan priests were childish'. Shakespeare and Milton, when they touched the magical and the supernatural, had at their disposal traditions of superstition and belief which enabled them to convey fancies far more sublime, terrible and alarming than the stuff of classical fables.

On the structure of the *Faerie Queene*, Hurd tackles the problem of the seeming confusion of two different designs, the one aiming at classical unity around the figure of Prince Arthur, the other at Gothic diversity in the adventures of the separate knights. He insists that the *Faerie Queene* is to be read as a Gothic poem. If an architect examined a Gothic structure by reference to Grecian rules, he would find it a mass of deformities. The same applies to a Gothic poem such as the *Faerie Queene*. The notion of the 12-day feast and the 12 knightly adventures is based in actual historic chivalrous practice. It was just as logical and necessary for the *Faerie Queene* to be built around the adventures of 12 knights as it was for the *Odyssey* to be confined to a single hero. Classical ideas of unity are irrelevant to the *Faerie Queene*. Its unity resides in the common end of the separate adventures in fulfilling the Queen's injunction. It is a unity of design, not of action. But Spenser's appreciation of classical practice led him to weave interconnections between the separate actions and also to give Prince Arthur a part in each. In Hurd's view, this was where Spenser went wrong. For it was an attempt 'toally two things in nature incompatible, the Gothic, and the classic unity'. Spenser should have stuck to his guns and been satisfied with unity of design. For the whole narration is subservient to the moral plan of exemplifying twelve virtues in twelve knights, and composing one illustrious character who partakes of all twelve. It is in the moral scheme that the unity of the *Faerie Queene* consists. Judge the *Faerie Queene* either as an allegory governed by the moral or as a narrative poem conducted on the 'ideas and usages of chivalry', and its plan is defensible; but the combination of the two designs causes an element of confusion which is the only serious defect in the poem.

Hurd's importance lies in the way his work brings to a culmination the various uneasinesses of critics before aspects of the neoclassical dogmatism. In his defence of the 'Gothic' or the 'romantic' he gives concreteness and definition to that strand in the literary tradition whose qualities could not be respectably accommodated so long as everything mediaeval was considered 'barbaric'. He had a genuine historical appreciation of the need to consider past literature in the light of the social and intellectual conditions obtaining at the time. When he turned, some years after writing the *Letters*, to write *A Dissertation on the Idea of Universal Poetry* (1766) he adopted a more strictly philosophical approach to the subject. His starting-point was a pronouncement in Bacon's *Advancement of Learning*, that poetry ministers to 'magnanimity, morality, and to delectation'. It 'doth raise and erect the mind, by submitting the shows of things to the desires of the mind; whereas reason doth buckle and bow the mind unto the nature of things'. Hurd accepts that whereas in every other kind of literature 'pleasure is subordinate to use, in poetry only, pleasure is the end'. Whatever rules are formulated for poetry, they can only be means to that end, the art of pleasing. On this basis Hurd justifies the ingredients of poetry. Firstly, there must be expressiveness, variety and novelty in the choice of words, and generous use of figures and images. Secondly, poetry must shy away from plain and simple delineation of reality, and rather 'outstrip nature', appealing to our 'wildest fancy rather than to our judgment and cooler sense'. Poetry will make the most of whatever wonders are to be derived from fable or religion: for the 'two requisites of universal poetry' are 'that licence of expression which we call the style of poetry and that licence of representation which we call fiction'. Thirdly, poetry will not be what it pretends to be unless it exploits too the charm of metre. Verse is essential to poetry. And here Hurd takes to task those like Fielding who produce 'novels or romances ... constructed on some private and familiar subject' that are 'wholly destitute of measured sounds'. Whether dramatic or narrative, prose pieces can only be regarded at best as 'hasty, imperfect, and abortive poems'. Hurd, somewhat short-sightedly, proclaims all such pieces as ephemeral. 'Good sense will acknowledge no work of art but such as is composed according to the laws of its kind.' It seems a pity to take leave of so attractive a writer as Hurd on a rather sour note but, alas, his strictures on prose poems are followed by an insistence on the desirability of rhyme and a claim that, a few prejudiced scholars apart, most people would agree that Milton's epic would have been better if it rhymed.

The supremacy of classical models came increasingly under question as the taste for the 'Gothic' or the 'Romantic' spread. It was natural, especially after the way in which Milton had drawn on both the Hellenic and the Hebraic traditions in *Paradise Lost*, that Hebrew poetry, as represented in the Old Testament, should eventually be recognised as offering authoritative inspirational models from the ancient world alternative to those provided by Homer and Virgil. Robert Lowth (1710–87) who was Professor of Poetry at Oxford before eventually becoming Bishop of London, delivered a series of 34 lectures on Hebrew poetry which were published in 1753 as *De Sacra Poesi Hebraeorum*, and went through several editions before being issued in English as *Lectures on the Sacred Poetry of the Hebrews* (1787). The sheer amount of attention given to Hebrew poetry is symptomatic of the changing critical environment. Lowth analyses the various stylistic devices used in the Old Testament and examines the various genres – prophetic, elegiac, didactic, lyric and dramatic.

In Lowth's eyes Hebrew poetry excels all other poetry in sheer 'sublimity'. He appeals to the authority of Longinus and defines sublimity as both the quality 'which exhibits great objects with a magnificent display of imagery and diction' and 'the force of composition ... which strikes and overpowers the mind' and 'excites the passions'. The cool temperate language of reason is contrasted with the way in which, in the language of the passions, 'the conceptions burst out in a turbid stream'. 'In a word, reason speaks literally, the passions poetically.' Lowth speaks eloquently of the way in which the passions amplify, magnify, and exaggerate whatever the mind is dwelling upon, and have recourse to 'animated, bold, and magnificent terms'. Thus the splendid imagery and the extraordinary forms of expression are a true representation of the 'state of the soul'. In this matter Lowth has no time for the pompous theories of rhetoricians who attribute to art what is 'due to nature alone'. He makes a clear distinction between Hebrew prose, which is 'plain, correct, chaste, and temperate', regular in word order, direct and smooth in its progress, and Hebrew poetry of which the *Book of Job* supplies an example. It is not just a matter of the unrivalled force, beauty, and sublimity of the sentiments, but the vividness of the diction, the packed, abrupt, explosive sentences, the syntactical freedoms, the forcefulness and impetuosity of the utterance, and the intimate contact it produces with personal tension and agitation – all these are aspects of that poetic grandeur which strikes the reader with rapt admiration and awe.

It is illuminating to set beside Lowth's scholarly work a work far less rigorous in intellectual content, but equally representative of the widening critical outlook. Hugh Blair (1718–1800), a Scottish minister and Professor of Rhetoric at Edinburgh, was so impressed by the poems which Macpherson published as supposed translations of the ancient poems of Ossian that he published *A Critical Dissertation on the Poems of Ossian, the Son of Fingal* (1763). His fellow Scot, Hume, as well as Dr Johnson, was highly sceptical of the work's authenticity. But Blair was enthusiastic. In its glowing and undisciplined imaginative power, the poetry 'carries a remarkable resemblance to the style of the Old Testament'. Blair details the authentic characteristics of antiquity it displays: no artful tricks of style, no sophisticated organisation of material, but 'a style always rapid and vehement' and a narrative conciseness and abruptness which leaves much to the reader's imagination.

> The two great characteristics of Ossian's poetry are tenderness and sublimity. It breathes nothing of the gay and cheerful kind; an air of solemnity and seriousness is diffused over the whole.

Ossian is a poet who never lapses into 'the light and amusing strain', but stays aloft in the 'high region of the grand and the pathetic'. Against the wild, romantic scenery we find the events recorded all serious and grave. The mind is attuned to solemnity by the picture of mountain and torrent, scattered oaks 'and the tombs of warriors overgrown with moss'. There are no 'gay trifles' to tickle the fancy. Indeed Ossian's poetry, 'more perhaps than that of any other writer, deserves to be styled "the poetry of the heart"'. So here is *Fingal*, celebrated as a regular epic and eliciting a praise that testifies to the new taste for the primitive. The declamatory, repetitive, rhythmic prose of Ossian throbs with urgent sonorities and captivates the ear with its haunting incantations. There was a growing public waiting to be told that poetry flourished best among the uncultivated, and for all the justified scepticism of Dr Johnson, Blair's encomium aroused widespread enthusiasm both at home and on the continent.

As a footnote to this survey of changing taste in the second half of the eighteenth century, attention should be drawn to a book produced by Walter Whiter (1758–1832), a fellow of Clare College, Cambridge, a classicist and philologist. Its title indicates its drift: *Specimen of a Commentary on Shakespeare, Containing I. Notes on As You Like It. II An Attempt to Explain and Illustrate Various Passages, on a New Principle of Criticism, Derived from Mr Locke's Doctrine of the Association of Ideas* (1794). As Scott Elledge has pointed out, the work is curiously anticipatory of some twentieth-century trends in Shakespearean criticism. The exploration of the effect of unconscious associations between words and ideas certainly takes eighteenth-century criticism into a new field. Connections between a given subject and a particular metaphor or expression that are already established in the poet's mind by previous usage may surface when thought recurs to the subject. Verbal echoes and ambiguities may trigger off metaphorical associations that are not necessarily conceptually justified. Clusters of imagery arise from aspects of the poet's own experience; and understanding of his age and environment may be necessary to recognition of these groupings. Whiter illustrates his point by showing how the conditions of Elizabethan dramatic presentation reinforced the use of certain repeatedly connected images. He is especially interesting when he explains how certain references to figures in classical legend and mythology may take their inspiration rather from how they were represented on tapestries and wall-hangings than directly from literature. Thus he devotes several pages to a celebrated crux over Atalanta's special virtue in *As You Like It*.

> Helen's cheek but not her heart,
> Cleopatra's majesty,
> Atalanta's better part,
> Sad Lucretia's modesty.

III Theorists on aesthetic experience

Those writers such as Thomas Warton and Hurd who emphasised the critic's duty to take into account the fashions and notions prevailing at the time of its composition when passing judgment on a literary work, were touching on a question that had been tussled with at the philosophical level by David Hume (1711–76). In his essay 'Of the Standard of Taste', published in *Four Dissertations* (1757), he struggled to find a rationale of aesthetic taste. However hard we try to fix a standard of taste and explain away the varying reactions of different people to the same work of art, there will always remain two causes of such variations: 'The one is the different humours of particular men, the other, the particular manners and opinions of our age and country.'

The critic can do his best to free his mind from prejudice and survey a work of art from the point of view of those to whom it was originally addressed. Nevertheless, Hume argues, these obstacles stand in the way of establishing firm criteria of taste. The literary taste of a young man of twenty will differ from that of a man of forty, and his again from that of a man of fifty. 'One person is more pleased with the sublime; another with the tender; a third with raillery.' As for the gap separating the attitudes of the ancients from those of the moderns, Hume distinguishes between what it is proper for the critic to discount – the changes in ephemeral fashions and manners – and the differences in 'ideas of morality and decency' which can constitute real deformity in literature.

Hume will not allow the simplistic theory that sharply distinguishes the province of judgment from the province of sentiment. With the former, conformity to objective fact is the standard of reliability. But with the latter, 'a thousand different sentiments excited by the same object are all right, because no sentiment represents what is really in the object'. If beauty belongs not to objects but to the contemplating mind, then everybody's sentiment is a matter of private response inapplicable to anyone else. Over against this extreme relativism Hume asserts that commonsense issues a corrective:

> Whoever would assert an equality of genius and elegance between Ogilby and Milton, or Bunyan and Addison, would be thought to defend no less an extravagance than if he had maintained a molehill to be as high as Teneriffe, or a pond as extensive as the ocean.

It is of course an unfortunate irony that Hume should have judged attribution of literary quality to Bunyan to be an absurdity. The virtue of his theorising lies rather in his thorough exploration of the problem of taste than in incidental literary judgments. He relied in this field on the work of the French critic Abbé Jean-Baptiste Dubos (1670–1742), whose influential book *Réflexions critiques sur la poésie et sur la peinture* (1719) had been translated into English in 1747. In the matter of ultimate aesthetic evaluation it laid stress on the intuitive response of the general public.

Hume was indebted again to Dubos in his essay 'Of Tragedy', another of the *Four Dissertations*. It tackles the question why we enjoy watching the painful events and sufferings represented in tragedy. Is it just, as Dubos had suggested, that any kind of excitement is preferable to the 'insipid languor which arises from tranquillity and repose'? Common liars exaggerate all kinds of danger and horror in order to gain attention. Yet if the kind of thing represented in tragedy were represented to us in reality, it would cause the maximum uneasiness even though it relieved us from languor and repose. Hume's theory is that delight in the artistic qualities of the play subsumes and overpowers all feelings of sorrow, distress or terror that the events arouse in the audience. The movements of the imagination predominate over the painfulness of what is witnessed, effecting its conversion to what is pleasurable. The converse would apply in real life. If a parent had just lost a child and you tried to comfort him by a magnificent elocutionary display on the subject, the painful reality would still predominate and convert the eloquence into an intensification of despair.

The two questions which these essays of Hume tackled were also tackled by Edmund Burke (1729–97) in *A Philosophical Enquiry into the Sublime and the Beautiful* (1757). Burke was one of Dr Johnson's close friends and valued by Johnson as the disputant who made the greatest demands upon him in argument. 'That fellow calls forth all my powers,' Johnson said one day when he was ill. 'Were I to see Burke now it would kill me.' He regarded Burke's essay as an example of 'true criticism'. In his section 'Of Taste' Burke rejects the thesis that whereas there is a universal standard of reason, taste is such a nebulous faculty that it cannot be tried by any test or regulated by any criterion. People have had strong motives for systematising the maxims of reasoning, but have been loth to apply themselves to the task of formulating a 'logic of taste'. He defines taste as the faculty of the mind affected by works of art and forming judgments on them. The senses, the imagination, and the judgment are the natural human powers concerned with external objects. We accept that the matter of reception of external objects by the senses is roughly universal. We agree about such concepts as sweetness and bitterness. Even a man who comes to prefer tobacco to sugar, or vinegar to milk, does not lose his precise sense of which is sweet and which is sour. But if a man could not accept this differentiation, we should regard him as totally deficient in taste. It is the same with visual responses to light and darkness, to summer and winter, to beautiful creatures or plants. Addiction may nourish an acquired taste for tobacco or opium, but it does not affect the basic differentiation between sweetness and bitterness. The pleasure of the senses is the same in all people.

The imagination, the domain of pleasures and pains, fears and hopes, derives its images from the senses, and the pleasure or displeasure it takes in those images must be consonant with those found in the realities. In the imagination, of course, there is an added pleasure from recognition of the resemblance between the imitation and the original. Locke distinguished between the activity of wit in tracing resemblances and the activity of judgment in finding differences. Burke argues that the human mind takes greater delight in the former activity, for which it has a ready aptitude, than in the latter more irksome activity. All men are roughly equal in the appeal of resemblance to the imagination, but they differ in the amount of knowledge of the things which are represented, and thus arises what we loosely call difference in taste. Burke illustrates his point by the story of how a Turkish emperor responded to a picture of St John the Baptist's severed head. He was able to point out an inaccuracy in the way the skin edged the wound. But this did not really reveal a superior natural taste to that of the painter. It was simply due to his extensive experience of decapitation. Thus it is only when our examination of things brings us within the province of judgment that disagreement arises. There can be general agreement about distinguishing smoothness from roughness. Only if there were a difference of opinion about which of variously but highly polished tables were the smoother, would it require the expertise of the marble-polisher to adjudicate.

As long as we are concerned with artistic representation of sensible qualities of things we are almost entirely within the province of imagination. And the representation of human passions is largely contained within the same province. But when representation involves human attitudes, motives, purposes, and relationships, virtuous or vicious, then this comes within the province of judgment, and whatever degree of certainty there is in the theory of human behaviour will apply in the representation as it does in the reality. What we call taste is an amalgam of responses to the pleasures of the senses, of the imagination, and of the reason. The principles of taste are uniform, 'but the degree in which these principles prevail, in the several individuals of mankind, is altogether as different as the principles themselves are similar'. This is because the two constituents of taste, sensibility and judgment, vary enormously from person to person. A degree of sensibility is a requisite of good judgment, but the soundness of judgment will not automatically be commensurate with the liveliness of sensibility. A very lively sensibility may make a poor judge easily satisfied with what is inferior. But the pleasures of the imagination are higher than those of correct judgment, and judgment may interfere with these pleasures by being hypercritical and consciously superior. The acute sensibility of the young finds the most pleasurable delights at an age when judgment is faulty and immature. Burke will not accept the notion that taste is some separate faculty of the mind, some sixth, intuitive sense. Reason may be little involved in the sphere of the imagination and the passions, but as soon as questions of fitness, decorum, and arrangement are involved, the understanding comes into operation, and this is where the distinction between good and bad taste arises.

On the subject of the sublime, Burke's theorising overlaps with Hume's because Burke is much concerned with the reasons why the representation of what is terrible or painful can give pleasure. In the first place, he insists that whatever is terrible or awe-inspiring may be a source of the sublime and thus productive of the strongest emotion of which the mind is capable. Torments can affect the body more intensely than any pleasures. Pain is stronger than pleasure, and death is the supreme terror. These things cannot but terrify when they press nearly upon us, yet when distanced and modified they can become delightful to us. That is the question to be explored. And Burke does not accept the received view that the pleasure we derive in witnessing tragedy is due firstly to our awareness that what is represented is fiction and not reality, and secondly to our awareness of our own freedom from the sufferings represented.

Burke finds the matter more complex than that. The contrast between reality and fiction cannot be the basis of our pleasure for the simple reason that we read authentic historical accounts of calamities with as much delight as fictional ones. Moreover when we hear of a rare and grievous disaster we eagerly want to see it. The nearer the tragedy approaches to reality and the further it is removed from fiction, the more powerful its appeal is. If an audience were engrossed by the most sublime and affecting tragedy performed with the richest resources of spectacle and poetry, and news were to reach them of a public execution of a notorious aristocratic criminal nearby, the theatre would empty in a few moments. The notion of contrast between pain in a reality and pleasure in a representation is not tenable. The crucial distinction is between what we would never want to do and what we should be most eager to see if it were already done.

In a summary of the distinction between the sublime and the beautiful, Burke insists that basically they are very different ideas, the one rooted in pain, the other in pleasure. The sublime embraces the vast, the rugged the dark, the gloomy, the solid and the massive. Beauty embraces the comparatively small, the smooth, the polished, the clear, the light and the delicate. Though the qualities of the sublime and the beautiful are sometimes blended, this does not prove that they are closely related. They are more impressive separately. What affects the mind most powerfully are things with a predominant quality in which the numerous aspects corroborate and intensify that quality.

Some idea of the kind of discussions which took place on the subject of critical theory in Dr Johnson's circle can be gained by comparing what Johnson had to say with what Burke and the artist Sir Joshua Reynolds (1723–92) left behind. A couple of years after the publication of Burke's *Enquiry into the Sublime*, Reynolds helped Johnson out by supplying three papers for the *Idler* in 1759 (nos 76, 79 and 82). Reynolds attacks the notion that application of rules will get a critic very far in appreciating 'sublime beauties in works of genius'. It is more likely to encourage that propensity to disparagement which Burke warned against. Reynolds mocks the man who prides himself on being a connoisseur, has mastered the current clichés about line and composition, and finds fault with everything. Then he tries to correct misunderstanding about what the universal rule, 'Imitate nature', really means. Faithful mechanical copying is a fruitless drudgery making no appeal to the imagination. This applies alike to poetry and to painting. Reynolds regards the work of the Dutch school, with its petty peculiarities and its minutely exact literalism, as of a lower order of beauty than the work of the Italian masters. Michaelangelo's works would lose their grandeur and nobility if they had the same kind of mechanical accuracy. As it is, they are 'all genius and soul'. For Reynolds, Michaelangelo is 'the Homer of painting'. Reynolds's praise is for what is 'in the highest degree sublime'.

The contrast between Dutch and Italian painting is for Reynolds a contrast between attention to what is particular and individual, and what is general and universal. In his third paper he explores how far our notion of beauty is determined by custom and education rather than by universal principles; for he believes that in so far as the painter concentrates on the 'particular and the accidental' at the expense of the 'invariable and general ideas of nature', his work will deviate from beauty into deformity. Reynolds was to take up these topics more fully in his addresses given to the students of the Royal Academy, of which he was the first President when it was founded in 1768. The lectures were published as *Discourses* (1769–90). When Reynolds speaks about the need to possess the vision of the 'Ideal Beauty' which is supreme over all the productions of nature, and what this involves for the artist, there are sentences which echo the words of Imlac in *Rasselas*:

> ... the whole beauty and grandeur of the art [of discovering perfection] consists, in my opinion, in being able to get above all singular forms, local customs, particularities, and details of every kind
> ...
> ... the painter must divest himself of all prejudices in favour of his age or country; he must disregard all local and temporary ornaments, and

look only on those general habits which are every where and always the same ...

Reynolds, of course, is at pains to insist that nothing of what he says should be taken as encouragement for carelessness and indiscipline in painting, but his enthusiasm for the 'great style' and the sublime, and his lofty conception of the artist's role were to have their influence in the Romantic period. Wordsworth shared in sympathy with Sir George Beaumont when he erected an urn in memory of Reynolds in his grounds. Wordworth supplied the tribute:

> Admiring, loving, and with grief and pride
> Feeling what England lost when Reynolds died.

A more scholarly philosophical thinker, Henry Home, Lord Kames (1696–1782), a Scottish judge, published a work *Elements of Criticism* (1762) which was to be several times reprinted and which drew the psychological theory of empiricist philosophers into the sphere of critical thinking. Kames was one of that group of distinguished men representing the remarkable Scottish Enlightenment which coincided with the buildings of the New Town of Edinburgh. The group included Hume, Lord Monboddo, and Hugh Blair, three writers to whose work we have already referred. Kames's book belongs to the sphere of aesthetics. He directs his inquiries 'to such attributes, relations, and circumstances as in the fine arts are chiefly employed to raise agreeable emotions'. His chapters have such headings as 'Grandeur and Sublimity', 'Novelty', 'Risible Objects', 'Resemblance and Contrast', 'Uniformity and Variety', 'Wit', and so on.

In a section headed 'Emotions Caused by Fiction' Kames distinguishes the actual experience of an object or event from what the memory recaptures of it when a conscious effort is made to bring it vividly to mind. For this purpose Kames uses the terms 'real presence' and 'ideal presence', making clear that a cursory recollection of an event unaccompanied by any effort to image it distinctly does not constitute 'ideal presence' but only 'reflective remembrance'.

In contradistinction to real presence, ideal presence may properly be
termed a waking dream because, like a dream, it vanisheth the
moment we reflect upon our present situation.

This 'ideal presence' of things to the mind can be produced
either by the activity of the memory or by the impact of a
recreation in words or art. The power of language to raise
emotions depends entirely on the raising of vital and distinct
images of this process. It follows from this account of the
matter that the impact of the 'ideal presence' will not be in
the least affected by whether the 'subject be a fable or true
history'. Authentic history stands on the same footing as fable
in affecting our passions only through the medium of the
'ideal presence'. And here Kames neatly clears up a matter
which earlier critics had stumbled over. The reflection that a
story is pure fiction affects our sympathy in the same way as
the reflection that 'the persons described are no longer
existing'.

Such is the kind of reasoning that Kames sets before us; but
the modern reader will find much that is congenial when
Kames turns his attention to Shakespeare in exemplification
of his theorising about the impact of literature upon the
human mind. He laments that too much criticism has been
devoted to the 'mechanical' aspect of the plays and such
matters as the classical unities and the mixing of tragedy and
comedy. Shakespeare's greatness lies in his profound understanding of the human heart and the ability to represent the
subtlest and most complex movements of the emotions. In
illustrating his thesis, Kames investigates Shakespeare's
characterisation, its fidelity to life and the way characters
reveal themselves by what they say and do. He objects to the
intrusion of conceits, quibbles and hyperboles into situations
of agony or terror, but in most respects his freedom from
neoclassical prejudice and his sensitivity to Shakespeare the
psychologist give what he has to say a refreshing congeniality.

While Kames and Hume were at work in Edinburgh, there
was a group of scholars at Aberdeen whose philosophical
studies impinged on the field of aesthetics. George Campbell
(1719–96), who became Principal of Marischal College in
1759, published *The Philosophy of Rhetoric* (1776), a compre-

hensive treatise designed to explore the workings of the human mind by studying the impact of poetry and oratory on it. His aim was to investigate the means by which the use of language can please, inform, and persuade. A close acquaintance of Campbell's, Alexander Gerard (1728–95), Professor of Divinity at Marischal College and later at King's College, Aberdeen, published a work on aesthetics, *An Essay on Genius* (1774), which includes a section 'On the Influence of the Passions on Association'. It fastens on Shakespeare's plays in order to illustrate how the passion of the moment generates distinctive associations of ideas. In showing how an emotional complex suggestively triggers off associations of ideas, Gerard, like Kames, explores the relationship between character and utterance which subsequent criticism was to illuminate ever more fruitfully. He makes a shrewd point when he exemplifies the difference between the kind of speech which is a natural *representation* of passion, something actuated by the passion itself, and the kind of speech which sounds more like a laboured, third-party *description* of passion.

Another close acquaintance of George Campbell's was James Beattie (1735–1823), Professor of Moral Philosophy and Logic at Marischal College, the poet whom Boswell introduced to Dr Johnson in 1771. He published his *Essay on the Nature and Immutability of Truth* (1770) in refutation of Hume and Berkeley, and carried his reasoning into the aesthetic field in *Essays on Poetry and Music, as They Affect the Mind* (1776). The study includes a chapter 'Of Sympathy' in which Beattie argues that since our sympathetic feelings are the source of much of the pleasure we derive from poetry, the 'philosophy of sympathy' ought to be a part of the 'science of criticism'. After analysing the various objects, characters and modes of behaviour that move our sympathy, Beattie goes on to declare that the conveying of appropriate feelings by poets and writers can be 'a powerful instrument of moral discipline'. In this respect he is critical of excessive recourse to themes of 'romantic love' on the grounds that 'the frequent contemplation of its various ardours and agonies, as exhibited in plays and novels, can scarce fail to enervate the mind and to raise emotions and sympathies unfriendly to innocence'. In addition, he was convinced of the bad moral effects of horror novels, 'dreadful tales that only give anguish'.

Beattie ventured more extensively into the literary field in his *Dissertations Moral and Critical*(1783). The book includes a section 'On Fable and Romance' which, after looking at the history of mediaeval romance, points to the 'final extirpation of chivalry and all its chimeras' achieved by Cervantes's *Don Quixote*. He then turns to the 'new romance' and defines two categories, 'serious' and 'comic', each of which is sub-divided into two sub-categories according to whether they are chronological narratives ('historical') or structured plots ('poetic'). Thus Defoe's *Robinson Crusoe* is a serious historical romance, and it wins praise from Beattie as a work which the rigid moralist can recommend, a work that can be read with pleasure and profit, breathing as it does throughout 'a spirit of piety and benevolence'. The modern serious romance that is poetical in arrangement is exemplified by Richardson's *Sir Charles Grandison* and *Clarissa Harlowe*. Beattie accepts that the epistolary technique leads Richardson into detail that is tedious, and that the pathetic scenes are so overcharged and lengthy that the reader's spirits droop. Moreover Richardson 'has given too much prudery to his favourite women and something of pedantry and finicalness to his favourite men', while the villainous Lovelace has been given 'intellectual and bodily accomplishments' that are dangerously attractive to the susceptible.

Of the new romance that is comic, Smollett's *Roderick Random* and *Peregrine Pickle* are cited as examples. Though 'humorous and entertaining', Beattie finds them in many ways objectionable. Smollett is often 'inexcusably licentious'. Profligates, bullies, misanthropes and the like people his pages. But turning to Fielding, whose novels exemplify the comic romance that is poetically constructed, Beattie is plainly at some pains to reconcile his rigorous moral criteria with his enthusiasm for Fielding's accomplishment. In wit and humour, and in knowledge of mankind, Fielding among modern writers is second only to Shakespeare, and his natural abilities were refined by taste based on sound classical study. Though Beattie has some minor moral reservations about *Joseph Andrews*, he pays high tribute to

Tom Jones and to *Amelia*. 'Since the days of Homer the world has not seen a more artful epic fable' than that of *Tom Jones*. The same may be said of *Amelia*. But Beattie is a little apprehensive about the effect of what he has said. 'Let not the usefulness of romance writing be estimated by the length of my discourse upon it. Romances are a dangerous recreation.' Only a few of the best are 'friendly to good taste and good morals'.

Back in England in the 1770s there was one writer whose emphasis on the aesthetic function of sympathy anticipated Beattie's. Sir William Jones (1746–94), an eminent scholar and jurist who ended his days as a judge in Calcutta and who had been a member of Johnson's club, distinguished himself by his reputed fluency in thirteen languages. Certainly he mastered Sanskrit, and his translations of oriental poems were to have their influence on romantic poets such as Moore and Byron. Byron fell naturally into quoting one of Jones's translated songs in a letter of 1811 rejoicing in a good review by Gifford. It was more welcome than 'all Bokara's vaunted gold, than all the gems of Samarkand'. Jones's *Poems, Consisting Chiefly of Translations from the Asiatic Languages* came out anonymously in 1772 with two essays appended to it. One was 'On the Arts Commonly Called Imitative'. In it Jones, then aged twenty-six, supplied a nice riposte to one of the cherished principles of neoclassicism. Whatever poems, pieces of music, and paintings derive from, it is certainly not imitation. Poetry probably first arose out of praise of God for the created world, love between the sexes, grief on bereavement, hatred of vice, and love of virtue. In none of these cases is imitation at work. It is the passions which provide the main impulse of poetry and music. Jones looks at the lamentations and songs of joy in the Old Testament. A man who is joyful or afflicted does not *imitate* joy or affliction; he expresses it. We may speak of descriptive poetry and descriptive music, but in fact 'words and sounds have no kind of resemblance to visible objects'. Jones has a good deal to say about music which suggests dissatisfaction with prevailing baroque and contrapuntal styles: but aside from some questionable technicalities in this sphere, he makes a cogent point about poetry. The artist gains his end, 'not by imitating the works of nature, but by assuming her power and causing the same effect upon the imagination which her charms produce to the senses'. So poetry, like music and painting, is 'expressive of the passions'. It operates on our minds 'by sympathy'.

IV The practitioners speak

As the reader makes his way through the critical works by scholars whose main discipline was philosophy or theology, philology or oriental languages, he naturally thirsts to hear something from creative writers themselves. The poets, novelists or dramatists who turn aside to enter the sphere of literary criticism have for us something of the appeal of oases in a desert. Even if they do not break new ground, their voices reach us with a special authority. And there were one or two critical efforts from practising creative writers in the 1770s and 1780s which have freshness, if not great depth. Oliver Goldsmith (1730–74) contributed an 'Essay on the Theatre' to the *Westminster Magazine* in January 1773, and its sub-title was 'A Comparison between Sentimental and Laughing Comedy'. Since the success of Steele's play *The Conscious Lovers* (1722), the moralistic sentimental comedy had held the stage with its tear-jerking emphasis on heroes and heroines whose virtuous resolves are tested and proven, or whose domestic happiness survives the assaults of conspiracy or calamity. Goldsmith's own rollicking comedy of incident, *She Stoops to Conquer*, was to be produced later in the year and to make a triumphant challenge to the prevailing fashion. In his 'Essay' Goldsmith attacks sentimental comedy as 'bastard tragedy'. Almost all the characters are good, generous, sensitive people, so good-hearted that their faults or foibles can be not only pardoned but applauded. There is no real ridicule of folly. There is an attempt to work on the feelings, but no real pathos. In short, the comic poet is invading the territory of the tragic muse. It is profitable, but it leaves the comic muse high and dry.

All this is admirable, yet it is marred for us today by the fact that Goldsmith takes as the basis of his case the old classical definitions of genre. Tragedy exhibits the misfortunes of the great, while comedy pictures the 'frailties of the lower part of mankind'. It is not the business of comedy to detail the calamities of low or middle life but to excite laughter 'by ridiculously exhibiting the follies of the lower part of mankind'. Boileau is cited as authority for excluding all tragic distress from comedy. The comic writer has no business to exalt his characters 'into buskined pomp' and make what Voltaire called a *tradesman's tragedy*.

A writer who turned critic to better effect was the Scottish novelist Henry Mackenzie (1745–1831) whom Scott called 'the Addison of the North' for his work on the periodicals the *Mirror* (1779–80) and the *Lounger* (1785–87). His essays in literary criticism point as surely forwards in their handling of texts as Goldsmith's theoretical assumptions (unlike his theatrical practice) point backwards. In May 1786 Mackenzie wrote two papers on the character of Shakespeare's Falstaff from which apologetic nods towards the classics are excluded. Shakespeare has the most fertile imagination of all poets and is more than Homer's equal. In respect of incident, character, and imaginative power there is nothing in the *Iliad* to match *The Tempest* or *Macbeth*. In Greek tragedies the 'delineation of manners' is excellent and just, but the wisdom displayed is derivatively conventional, whereas Shakespeare's wisdom 'marks the knowledge of intimacy with mankind'. It goes almost without saying that in his study of Falstaff's character, imaginative insight and analytical penetration are conjoined. The essay concludes with a perceptive contrast of Falstaff with Don Quixote.

> The ridicule in the character of Don Quixote consists in raising low and vulgar incidents, through the medium of his disordered fancy, to a rank of importance, dignity, and solemnity, to which in their nature they are the most opposite that can be imagined. With Falstaff it is nearly the reverse; the ridicule is produced by subjecting wisdom, honour, and other most grave and dignified principles, to the control of grossness, buffoonery, and folly.

Mackenzie was discerning enough at the end of the same year (1786) to give a warm welcome to Burns's first volume of poems, praising his power in representing the passions, in drawing the scenery of nature, and in catching aspects of human character and human manners.

A third writer to turn critic in the 1780s was the dramatist and novelist Richard Cumberland (1732–1811), one of the playwrights whose early sentimental comedies such as *The Brothers* (1770) and *The West Indian* (1771) provoked Goldsmith's ire for their flattering human portraiture. As the model for Sir Fretful Plagiary, the blustering, pretentious ass of Sheridan's *The Critic*, Cumberland has suffered historical disparagement which he scarcely merits. Between 1785 and 1790 he published five volumes of essays called *The Observer*. Among the literary pieces in this collection is an essay on Milton's *Samson Agonistes* (no. 76) in which Cumberland refutes Dr Johnson's claim that the drama lacked a middle between its beginning and its end. Cumberland quotes Johnson's claim that 'nothing passes between the first act and the last that either hastens or delays the death of Samson', and shows that whatever plays upon Samson's mind to discourage or encourage the decision to bury himself with his enemies is relevant to the catastrophe. Thus the interviews with Manoah, Dalila, and Harapha constitute a 'middle', and Samson's response to them brings about his refusal to listen to the idolaters and his determination to obey God's call.

If the insensitivity of Sir Fretful Plagiary consorts ill with this critical independence and thoughtfulness, it seems absurdly out of key with the Cumberland who wrote three substantial papers on Rowe's tragedy *The Fair Penitent*. The reputation of this play, first produced in 1703, kept it before the public throughout the century. Dr Johnson thought its longevity justifiable for the interesting plot and the 'exquisitely harmonious' diction. Rowe took the plot from Massinger's *The Fatal Dowry*. Cumberland explores the two plays side by side. There is nothing injudicious, hasty, or unbalanced in the exercise. Cumberland examines in detail each fundamental change that Rowe made from his original. The effect of each change is illustrated in detailed reference to the texts. Cumberland argues that Rowe tended to sacrifice 'nature and the truth of character for stage effect'. Step by step, with the utmost good temper, he quite cogently establishes the total inferiority of Rowe's play in terms of 'real nature, dramatic character, moral sentiment, tragic pathos, or nervous diction'. This is literary criticism as we have since come to know it. What is being discussed, on every page, is not the relationship of this or that aspect of the play to critical dogma of any kind, but the relationship of characters' emotional responses, turns of thought, decisions and acts to the ways in which men and women think and feel and behave in real life. The characters are discussed as though they were living people. The grip of neoclassicism seems finally to have been shaken off.

8
The Romantic Age

The Romantic age was an age of revolution, social and technological, philosophical and literary. The harnessing of steam-power, the consequent development of mass-production, and the movement of population from rural areas to the growing urban areas of industry and commerce, marked one of the crucial turning-points in modern history. Cities were built, fortunes made, and workers' lives rendered dismally laborious in applying the *laissez-faire* principles of the economist Adam Smith (1723–90), whose study *The Wealth of Nations* (1776) encouraged the pursuit of individual profit as the route to national prosperity. The Industrial Revolution transformed the face of the countryside and thrust workers together in the new urban environments, packed and smoky.

When we read how Sir Charles Grandison looked after his tenants in his mini-welfare-state, we realise that the picture is a highly idealised one, but at the same time we get the genuine feel of the settled society for which eighteenth-century literature catered. We cannot but sense that the critical controversies themselves – about ancients and moderns or about the mingling of tragedy and comedy – are aptly suited to the country-house library or the London coffee-house. The world of Wordsworth's *Prelude*, of Shelley's *Revolt of Islam*, and Holcroft's *Hugh Trevor* is a very different one. Never again will a French royal court provide the image and model for mind and manners in the ultimate state of refinement. The French Revolution, with its incongruous spectacle of fervour for liberty and thirst for blood, heartened and appalled the watching world. It could not but be an issue in the careers of alert contemporaries. It fed two

217

contrary impulses, the demand for political and social reform, and the determination to avoid a blood-bath. The rise of Napoleon and the war with France cast a shadow over many idealistic libertarian movements in England. Yet the intellectual ferment of which the revolution was born infected thinking men and women with disturbing uncertainties, not only about the inherited social fabric of society, but also about the inherited fabrics of belief and morality. The ferment was inspired by powerful literary figures, going back to Jean-Jacques Rousseau (1712–78), the apostle of individual autonomy in the face of corrupting civilisation. At home controversy was fuelled by thinkers such as Tom Paine (1737–1809) with his book *The Rights of Man* (1791), William Godwin (1756–1836) with his *Political Justice* (1793), and Mary Wollstonecraft (1759–97) with her *Vindication of the Rights of Woman* (1792).

A new connotation was given to the concept of truth to nature. Nature is no longer primarily the principle of simplicity which fashionable society offends against with its ornaments and fopperies. It is the force which binds man to mother earth, which surrounds him with hills and covers him with the sky. And what offends against it is the mill chimney and the steam engine, factory-labour and the city slum. Indeed, for some thinkers, what offends against it is also that conjunction of man and wife in holy matrimony which for Sir Thomas Elyot symbolised and epitomised the principle of universal order. We do not expect to find in literary criticism a straight record of the basic controversies that rocked the foundations of social and moral life, but the casting off of mental fetters together with the commercialisation of publishing transformed the critical scene.

I William Wordsworth

When William Wordsworth (1770–1850) prefixed an 'Advertisement' to the first edition of the *Lyrical Ballads* (1798) which he and Coleridge had written, he addressed the reader with some caution.

> The majority of the following poems are to be considered as
> experiments. They were written chiefly with a view to ascertain
> how far the language of conversation in the middle and lower classes
> of society is adapted to the purpose of poetic pleasure.

But the tone quickly changes. It is readers 'accustomed to the
gaudiness and inane phraseology of many modern writers'
who may wonder whether what they are reading is poetry at
all. They would do well to forget the word 'Poetry' and
simply ask themselves whether what they read 'contains a
natural delineation of human passions, human characters,
and human incidents'.

In the second edition of the *Lyrical Ballads* (1800) Wordsworth expanded his observations into a full-blown 'Preface'.
He declares that he has purposely chosen 'incidents and
situations from common life' and endeavoured to deal with
them 'in a selection of language really used by men'. A novel
'colouring of imagination' gives this material distinctiveness.
And the incidents are made 'interesting' because 'the
primary laws of our nature' are traced through them. Poets
confer honour neither on themselves nor on their work by
using a sophisticated diction. In fact it alienates natural
human sympathy. Simple rural people are less restrained and
artificial in their feelings and in their utterance, and those
feelings are more at one with their environment. Wordsworth
is at pains to point out that his is neither a recipe for nor a
justification of 'triviality' or 'meanness': for each of his poems
has a worthy purpose. Indeed, though 'all good poetry is the
spontaneous overflow of powerful feelings', the poet's sensibility, and his long training in deep reflection, cannot but
bear on his subjects in such a way that the reader is
enlightened and emotionally purified. And a distinctive
feature of his poems is 'that the feeling therein developed
gives importance to the action and situation, and not the
action and situation to the feelings'.

In a challenging parenthesis, Wordsworth comments on
the evil effects of contemporary developments, notably the
spread of industrialisation, the over-standardisation of urban
life, and the consequent thirst for stimulation by sensational
news. His poems represent a slight effort to refocus people's

minds on the 'inherent and indestructible qualities of the human mind, and likewise of certain powers in the great and permanent objects that act upon it'.

In expanding the apologia for his rejection of 'poetic diction' in favour of 'the very language of men', Wordsworth asserts that 'there neither is, nor can be, any *essential* difference between the language of prose and metrical composition', and repeats that the language of poetry should as far as possible be 'a selection of the language really spoken by men'. If true taste and feeling are applied to the process of 'selection' then what results will be firmly distinguished from the 'vulgarity and meanness of ordinary life', and if metre is 'superadded', then what other possible distinction can poetry have? Wordsworth insists that if the subject is properly chosen, it will naturally itself lead the poet to feelings whose appropriate expression will have dignity, beauty, and metaphorical vitality. Moreover he speaks of how unfortunate it would be were the poet to 'interweave any foreign splendour of his own with that which the passion naturally suggests'. The words seem to imply that anything deriving directly from the poet's contrivance will vulgarise rather than enrich.

Yet when Wordsworth comes to answer the question, 'What is a Poet?' the claims made are almost awesome.

> He is a man speaking to men; a man, it is true, endowed with more lively sensibility, more enthusiasm and tenderness, who has a greater knowledge of human nature, and a more comprehensive soul, than are supposed to be common among mankind; a man pleased with his own passions and volitions, and who rejoices more than other men in the spirit of life that is in him; delighting to contemplate similar volitions and passions as manifested in the goings-on of the Universe, and habitually compelled to create them, where he does not find them.

The poet also has the ability to conjure up passions in himself which resemble those produced by real events, and has a greater readiness and power in expressing what he feels. Nevertheless, however great the poet, his language will often 'fall short of that which is uttered by men in real life' under the actual pressure of passion. Wordsworth will have nothing to do with the suggestion that the poet should take the same liberties as the translator and, where he cannot match certain excellencies, substitute others, or even try to surpass the original in places to compensate for inadequacies elsewhere. Such policies totally misread the character of poetry. It is not 'a matter of amusement and idle pleasure'. It is 'the most philosophic of all writing': 'its object is truth, not individual and local, but general and operative'. It is 'the image of man and nature'. The poet's only duty is to give 'immediate pleasure to a human Being possessed of that information which may be expected from him, not as a lawyer, a physician, a mariner, an astronomer, or a natural philosopher, but as a Man'. The duty of producing immediate pleasure is no degradation of the poet's art. It is 'an acknowledgement of the beauty of the universe' ... and 'it is a homage paid to the native and naked dignity of man'.

For Wordsworth, the poet's speciality is the interaction between man and his environment, the complexities of pleasure and pain that arise therefrom, and the deep sympathies by which they are interrelated. The poet's special knowledge is of what is inalienably ours by natural inheritance, while the scientist's special knowledge is a slowly gathered individual acquisition involving no sympathetic connection of man with man. The poet thus joyfully makes of truth a constant companion, while the scientist seeks it as a remote benefactor: 'Poetry is the breath and finer spirit of all knowledge ... Poetry is the first and last of all knowledge – it is as immortal as the heart of man.'

It is by virtue of this sublime concept of the poet that Wordsworth decries as utterly unworthy any descent to the manipulation of verbal artifices. There is a sanctity and truth about the poet's descriptions which it would be sacrilege to try to trick out with 'transitory accidental ornaments'. Thus the sense of the poet as craftsman is anathema to Wordsworth. The qualities that make a poet are not different in kind from what other men have. The only difference is a difference of degree.

The sum of what was said is, that the Poet is chiefly distinguished from other men by a greater promptness to think and feel without immediate external excitement, and a greater power in expressing such thoughts and feelings as are produced in him in that manner. But these passions and thoughts and feelings are the general passions and thoughts and feelings of men. And with what are they connected? Undoubtedly with our moral sentiments and animal sensations, and with the causes which excite these; with the operations of the elements, and the appearances of the visible universe; with storm and sunshine, with the revolutions of the seasons, with cold and heat, with loss of friends and kindred, with injuries and resentments, gratitude and hope, with fear and sorrow.

Wordsworth strains every nerve to give the poet a status far removed from that of the craftsman in words who observes and 'imitates' nature, guided by long-established rules. The poet is a human being whose speciality is humanity. He is a man whose focus is upon man, and not man in society but man in nature. And the poet's function is not limited to recording, however faithfully, however sympathetically. In a letter written to the reviewer John Wilson (Christopher North) in 1800, Wordsworth remarks:

> You have given me praise for having reflected faithfully in my Poems the feelings of human nature. I would fain hope that I have done so. But a great Poet ought to do more than this; he ought, to a certain degree, to rectify men's feelings, to give them new compositions of feeling, to render their feelings more sane, pure, and permanent, in short, more consonant to nature, that is, to eternal nature, and the great moving spirit of things. He ought to travel before men occasionally as well as at their sides.

Now the reader may well reflect that this lofty moral duty of the poet to correct and refine human feelings consorts ill with the claim that the poet must not, like the free translator, tamper with the original that is presented to him. And indeed Wordsworth's critical statements do not add up to a logical thesis. His standing as a critic reflects his standing as a poet. It derives from the scattered, often fragmentary, flashes of insight by which he presented mankind in detachment from the sophistications of social class and social artifice, and involved by links of beauty and feeling with the ordered elemental world of nature. The egalitarian implications of his insights drove him at first to sympathy with the French Revolution. The literary implications drove him to mark out humble rustic life as the subject matter of his poetry and the language of ordinary men as its vehicle.

II Samuel Taylor Coleridge

There is a good deal in the *Biographia Literaria* (1817), the major critical work of Samuel Taylor Coleridge (1772–1834), that arises from the collaborative friendship with Wordsworth. It is, however, a frankly formless book. It directly reflects Coleridge's tendency to make great designs which his temperament never allowed him to fulfil. Yet it is a most fascinating book. Like Johnson, Coleridge was a great talker. What flows from his pen in this book is a mixture of autobiography, literary theory, and metaphysical speculation. The literary criticism, when disentangled from its context, constitutes a healthy menu of logic and sensibility. In speaking of his early years Coleridge tells how the sonnets of William Lisle Bowles captivated his adolescent mind. He was quick to react against the poetry of the school of Pope. He recognised that its quality lay in 'just and acute observations on men and manners in an artificial state of society', and in the logic of wit and smooth epigram. However it seemed to consist not of 'poetic thoughts' but of 'thoughts translated into the language of poetry'. Like Wordsworth too he disliked the prevalence of 'dead' personification such as is found in Gray ('Youth' and 'Pleasure' capitalised but not effectively conceptualised). Lines that can be paraphrased without loss of meaning are to that extent 'vicious in their diction'. You cannot interfere with a single word in Shakespeare or Milton without changing the meaning. The characteristic faults of former and more recent poets are contrasted.

> In the former, from Donne to Cowley, we find the most fantastic out-of-the-way thoughts, but in the most pure and genuine mother English, in the latter the most obvious thoughts, in language the most fantastic and arbitrary.

The older poets, at their worst, may have sacrificed the heart to the head; the moderns sacrifice 'both heart and head to point and drapery'. Coleridge praises Cowper and Bowles for effecting a reconciliation between heart and head, and combining natural thoughts with natural diction.

It is characteristic of Coleridge's method that, having reached this point at the end of his first chapter, he inserts a chapter on a scarcely relevant subject. Supposedly tackling the question, Are men of genius irritable? it is in fact an onslaught on critics. For Coleridge argues that in matters pertaining to themselves (as opposed to, say, issues of principle or of public weal), geniuses tend to be men of 'calm and tranquil temper'. Even Milton 'reserved his anger for the enemies of religion, freedom, and his country'. It is not genius that produces irritability, but the lack of it in men who want it. The mediocre and worse, who long for poetic reputation and are devoid sometimes of even the modestest talents, awake from their 'dream of vanity to disappointment and neglect with embittered and envenomed feelings'. They turn critic to work off their envy and malevolence.

Coleridge now pays an ironic tribute to contemporary critics who have so persistently attacked him, thereby keeping his name before the public, for 'the reader will be apt to suspect that there must be something more than usually strong and extensive in a reputation, that could either require or stand so merciless and long-continued a cannonading'. Looking at his personal relationships and achievements, he is at a loss to account for the degree of hostility. There can be but one explanation of it. '*I was in habits of intimacy with Mr. Wordsworth and Mr. Southey!*' The argument turns into a substantial defence of Southey's achievements, talents, and personality.

Coleridge argues that neither Southey's output nor his own justifies the 'fiction of a new school of poetry'. Nor do Wordsworth's *Lyrical Ballads* in themselves. It was Wordsworth's preface which sparked off the unprecedented opposition. Critics seized on the 'humbler passages' in his poems in order to ridicule the theory. Indeed simplicities which could have been overlooked as lapses provoked hostility when they were defended as deliberate and intentional. Coleridge turns with withering scorn on the critics' untenable assumption that what they saw as sheer childishness and silliness in style and trivial and degrading in substance should succeed in forming a 'school' of ardent, educated young men. Can it indeed be bogus and worthless poetry that has obsessed critical reviewers for nearly twenty years? Looking more closely at Wordsworth's earliest work, Coleridge explains that 'the language is not only peculiar and strong, but at times knotty and contorted, as by its own impatient strength'. It was not just Wordsworth's freedom from false taste that won Coleridge's admiration:

> It was the union of deep feeling with profound thought; the fine balance of truth in observing, with the imaginative faculty in modifying, the objects observed; and above all the original gift of spreading the tone, the atmosphere, and with it the depth and height of the ideal world around forms, incidents, and situations, of which, for the common view, custom had bedimmed all the lustre, had dried up the sparkle and the dew drops.

Determined to plumb the nature of Wordsworth's gifts, Coleridge concluded 'that Fancy and Imagination were two distinct and wildly different faculties'. Milton, for instance, 'had a highly *imaginative*, Cowley a very *fanciful* mind'. Anxious to pursue this issue to its roots, Coleridge plunges into six chapters of philosophical enquiry. Where earlier, eighteenth-century critics might have dug down into the works of the ancients in order to discover the origins of literary forms, Coleridge explores the works of the philosophers in order to shed light on the vital driving force in the mind which begets a work of art.

It is not until he gets to chapter XIII that Coleridge launches into the main thesis for which all that has gone before has but laid the foundations. He defines 'Imagination' as the 'Esemplastic' power, coining the word to mean 'unifying' or 'building into one'. The imagination is primary or secondary. The primary imagination is the 'living power and prime agent of all human perception'. It is 'a repetition in the finite mind of the eternal act of creation in the infinite I AM'. The secondary imagination is its echo, alike in kind with the primary but different in degree and in mode of operation. It dissolves and diffuses in order to recreate. It 'struggles to idealize and to unify'. It is essentially vital. 'Fancy, on the contrary, has no other counters to play with, but fixities and definitions.' It is just 'a mode of memory emancipated from the order of time and space'. Like the memory, it receives 'all its materials ready made from the law of association'.

Armed with this definition, Coleridge turns to describe how he and Wordsworth conceived the *Lyrical Ballads*. The two of them had discussed the 'two cardinal points of poetry'. These were 'the power of exciting the sympathy of the reader by a faithful adherence to the truth of nature', and 'the power of giving the interest of novelty by the modifying colours of imagination'. They decided on a series of poems of two sorts, one involving the supernatural, the other on subjects drawn from ordinary life. Coleridge was to handle the supernatural with sufficient semblance of truth to produce 'that willing suspension of disbelief ... which constitutes poetic faith'; while Wordsworth was to 'give the charm of novelty to things of every day'. Such was the genesis of *Lyrical Ballads*. Wordsworth however added his lengthy preface to the second edition in which the defence of experimentation with poems in the language of ordinary life was blown up into a doctrine for poetry in general. With this Coleridge could not concur. And in order to clarify his position he once more dives back into laying philosophical foundations. What is a Poem? And what is Poetry?

Since a poem contains the same elements as a prose composition, the distinction must lie in a difference in their combination and in the objective. The communication of pleasure is one object of poetry, but it might also be the object of a piece of prose. Coleridge thrashes his way through to this conclusion:

> A poem is that species of composition, which is opposed to works of science, by proposing for its *immediate* object pleasure, not truth; and from all other species – (having *this* object in common with it) – it is discriminated by proposing to itself such delight from the *whole*, as is compatible with a strict gratification from each component *part*.

The parts must mutually support and explain each other, and the reader should be carried forward not just by curiosity but by the 'pleasurable activity of mind' aroused by its journey. Having so defined a poem, Coleridge decides that the question What is *Poetry*? is virtually synonymous with the question What is a *poet*?

> The poet, described in ideal perfection, brings the whole soul of man into activity, with the subordination of its faculties to each other according to their relative worth and dignity. He diffuses a tone and spirit of unity, that blends and (as it were) *fuses*, each into each, by that synthetic and magical power, to which I would exclusively appropriate the name of Imagination ...
>
> Finally, Good Sense is the Body of poetic genius, Fancy its Drapery, Motion its Life, and Imagination the Soul that is everywhere and in each; and forms all into one graceful and intelligent whole.

Coleridge now turns his attention to practical criticism, making a critical analysis of Shakespeare's *Venus and Adonis* and the *Rape of Lucrece* in order to pinpoint 'promises and specific symptoms of poetic power' as opposed to mere talent for versifying. The first indication is 'sweetness of versification'. There must be music in the soul of the poet. The sense of musical delight is one of the gifts of imagination. The second indication is the ability to deal with a subject remote from 'the private interests and circumstances of the writer himself'. The poet stands back and what reaches the reader directly is the characters and incidents. The third indication is the handling of imagery. Images in themselves do not characterise the poet. It is the way they are 'modified by a predominant passion', the way they are moulded and coloured to match the circumstances and feeling foremost in the mind. And the fourth indication is 'depth and energy of thought'. 'In Shakespeare's poems the creative power and the intellectual energy wrestle as in a warm embrace.'

There is one more interlude before Coleridge tackles Wordsworth in detail. It is a chapter commenting on the differences between recent poets and poets of the fifteenth and sixteenth centuries. In particular Coleridge remarks how formerly 'novelty of subject' was avoided. 'Superior excellence in the manner of treating the same subjects was the trial and test of the artist's merit.' The essence of poetry lay 'in the art', in polished phrases, in melodious cadences, and in gentlemanly vocabulary. And so to Wordsworth. In so far as he contended for a reformation of poetic diction, he undertook a useful task. Moreover he has had an influence on other poets, even on some who professed hostility to his theories. But Coleridge cannot accept the doctrine that the proper diction for poetry in general is what comes from the mouths of men in real life. In the first place, the rule could apply only to a certain kind of poetry. In the second place, even there it applies only in a sense which has always been recognised. And in the third place, it is a useless rule.

Coleridge looks at such 'dramatic' poems as 'The Brothers', 'Michael', 'Ruth', and 'The Mad Mother'. The characters there are not taken from low or rustic life. They are distinguished by the independence of the Cumberland and Westmorland shepherd-farmers and by familiarity with the language of the Bible and the Book of Common Prayer. Nature alone cannot influence an unschooled yokel. Some degree of education and native sensibility is necessary. Poetry is essentially ideal. Characters must be representative of a class, as Wordsworth's Michael is, or explore 'human feelings in general', as Wordsworth does in 'Harry Gill' and 'The Idiot Boy'. In the case of the latter, Coleridge feels that Wordsworth did not take adequate steps to eliminate in advance the prevalent 'disgusting' associations of idiocy. In 'The Thorn', Wordsworth made the mistake of thinking that a boring, garrulous narrator could be given his head without becoming boring. On the general question of the language of rustics; if it is purified and grammatically corrected, it will not differ from the language of other men, however learned or refined, except in so far as it covers a smaller range of ideas. Nor can communication with nature be said to furnish a rustic with anything but a scanty vocabulary. Uncivilised tribes, surrounded by magnificent scenery, have the utmost difficulty in receiving the simplest moral and intellectual concepts. Indeed the language which Wordsworth has in mind is certainly not the real language of rustics. As for Wordsworth's reference to the language used by rustics 'in a state of excitement', Coleridge insists that the heat of passion can bring only a known vocabulary into play.

Coleridge now turns (chapter XVIII) to deny Wordsworth's claim that there can be no 'essential difference between the language of prose and metrical composition'. Here Coleridge clears the ground. The question in not whether poetry might not contain prosaic passages (such as Wordsworth illustrated from Gray), but whether there may not be modes of expression acceptable in prose which would be inappropriate in poetry. Metre, 'the language of excitement', frequency and intensity of imagery, vivacity, vividness of description, and wholeness of organisation are characteristics of poetry. It is when poetry lapses into the verbal triteness of prose that we declare it 'unpoetic'. Coleridge surmises, however (chapter xix), that what Wordsworth was really after was that quality in which conversational naturalness is sustained in rhymed verse that is dignified, attractive and metrically correct. Such is the charm to be found in Spenser, Chaucer, and George Herbert. But in fact (chapter xx) this is *not* the characteristic excellence of Wordsworth's style. And it is remarkable that a defence of *'lingua communis'* should have come from a poet whose diction, after Shakespeare's and Milton's, is 'of all others the most *individualised* and characteristic'. Indeed literal adherence by Wordsworth to the principles of his own 'Preface' would exclude at least two thirds of the marked beauties of his work.

Coleridge ends his work on Wordsworth with a substantial chapter (XXII) examining in turn the defects and beauties of his poetry. And first defect is that *'inconstancy* of style' whereby Wordsworth's poetry suddenly lapses from what is felicitous into what is quite 'undistinguished'. The second defect is a *'matter-of-factness'* in certain poems, which involves too much 'minuteness and fidelity' in description of objects and also the insertion of excessive detail in the characterisation. In this respect Wordsworth does not leave enough to the imagination. And he particularises in a way proper to the historian rather than to the poet. The treatment of pedlars and leech-gatherers is such that *'truth'* rather than *'pleasure'* becomes the immediate object, and this is more proper to a sermon than to poetry. The world does not abound in ploughmen-poets like Burns. Biography is acceptable in fictions like Defoe's, but not in Fielding's *Tom Jones* where characters remain representative. Excessive verisimilitude can be an obstacle to that poetic faith which transcends historic belief. And anyway, is there, for instance, one word attributed to the pedlar in *The Excursion* characteristic of a *pedlar?* The third defect is 'an undue predilection for the *dramatic* form in certain poems'. It produces incongruity of style where the thoughts and diction differ from the poet's own. And where they are indistinguishable from the poet's, 'then it presents a species of ventriloquism'. The fourth defect is 'an intensity of feeling disproportionate' to the knowledge and value of objects described. And the fifth defect lies in the 'thoughts and images too great for the subject'. It is 'mental bombast' as opposed to verbal bombast, and it is a 'fault of which none but a man of genius is capable'.

The characteristic excellencies of Wordsworth's poetry are listed with repeated emphasis that they far outweigh the defects. The first is 'an austere purity of language' and 'a perfect appropriateness of the words to the meaning'. The second is the 'correspondent weight and sanity of the Thought and the Sentiments' which spring not from books but from the poet's own meditative observation. 'They are *fresh* and have the dew upon them.' The third beauty lies in 'the sinewy strength and originality of single lines and paragraphs'. The fourth is 'the perfect truth of nature in his images and descriptions'. The fifth is 'a meditative pathos, a union of deep and subtle thought with sensibility; a sympathy with man as man'. Wordsworth can detect the image and superscription of the Creator 'under the dark lines with which guilt or calamity has cancelled or cross-barred it'. And finally, Wordsworth has 'the gift of Imagination in the highest and strictest sense of the word'. Coleridge illustrates his points with reference and quotation which reveal how deeply and thoroughly Wordsworth's poems have permeated his thinking. The acumen he brings to bear and the illumination he sheds give this study its rank beside the finest criticism of Dryden and Johnson.

III Romanticism at bay

The other major Romantic poet to issue a manifesto on the nature of poetry was Percy Bysshe Shelley (1792–1822). Shelley's *Defence of Poetry*, written in 1821 but not published until 1840, was a direct reply to 'The Four Ages of Poetry', an essay by Thomas Love Peacock (1785–1866) which was published in *Ollier's Literary Miscellany* in 1820. Nowhere is the collision between neoclassical detachment and Romantic fervour more acutely represented than in these two essays. Peacock's is essentially comic, yet it conveys a penetrating critique of many fashionable Romantic assumptions. The 'four ages' are those of Iron, Gold, Silver, and Brass. The iron age is the age of primitive panegyric supplied by bards under pressure from royal warriors and in exchange for liquor, itself an inspiration. The golden age is the age in which poetry becomes retrospective. Something like a civil polity has been established, individual heroism has given place to institutionalism. So poets acclaim an early founder whose courage and glory in the misty past can be celebrated as represented in his current successor. 'This is the age of Homer, the golden age of poetry.' In the silver age there are two kinds of poetry; the imitative which recasts the poetry of the age of gold as Virgil recast Homer, and the original, chiefly comic, didactic, and satiric, in which there is fastidiousness of style and a choice harmony of expression that bores by its repetitiveness. It is only obvious moral truisms that lend themselves to poetic expression, and as the sciences of morals and of mind mature, they move beyond the reach of imaginative and emotional treatment. Since there is a limited scope for polished versification of good sense and elegant learning, poetry declines towards extinction. In conclusion comes the age of brass. It rejects the 'polish and learning of the age of silver' and regresses to the crude barbarisms of the age of iron, which pretending 'to return to nature and revive the age of gold'.

So far as modern literature is concerned, Peacock identifies the mediaeval age of romance, chivalry and knightly honour as the age of iron. The golden age was the Renaissance when the riches of all ages and nations were compounded in such

writers as Ariosto and Shakespeare. The silver age was the
reign of authority, the age of Dryden and Pope. But soon the
influence of Hume and Gibbon, Rousseau and Voltaire
brought every authority into question. The changes had
been rung on conventional pastoralism. Even poets began
to think it necessary to know something of what they talked
about. Thomson and Cowper actually *looked* at trees and hills
instead of just being content to write about them. The effect
of this change was revolutionary. Poetical genius began to be
reckoned the finest of all things, and only poetical impressions could nourish it.

> Poetical impressions can be received only among natural scenes: for
> all that is artificial is anti-poetical. Society is artificial; therefore we
> will live out of society. The mountains are natural, therefore we will
> be in the mountains. There we shall be shining models of purity and
> virtue, passing the whole day in the innocent and amiable accupation
> of going up and down hill, receiving poetical impressions, and
> communicating them in immortal verse to admiring generations.

Peacock's attack is wholesale yet good-natured. He ridicules
the notion of a poetic return to nature in nineteenth-century
England. Historians and philosophers are making progress
while poets are 'wallowing in the rubbish of departed
ignorance'.

> Mr Scott digs up the poachers and cattle-stealers of the ancient
> border. Lord Byron cruizes for thieves and pirates on the shores of the
> Morea and among the Greek islands. Mr Southey wades through
> ponderous volumes of travels and old chronicles, from which he selects
> all that is false, useless, and absurd ... Mr Wordsworth picks up
> village legends from old women and sextons ...

Coleridge, Moore and Campbell all come in for scathing
ridicule. 'A poet in our time is a semi-barbarian in a civilised
community', obsessed with the barbaric and superstitious
past. The true philosophic poise which surveys the world
coolly and justly, gathers and analyses data, and thus
develops new and useful thinking is the direct opposite of
the poetic mind. For the inspiration of poetry lies in 'the rant
of unregulated passion, the whining of exaggerated feeling,

and the cant of factitious sentiment'. Poetic composition is simply a waste of time that might be given to useful work.

'Your anathemas against poetry itself excited me to a sacred rage,' Shelley wrote to Peacock, recommending him to read Plato's *Ion*; and the Platonic influence on Shelley's *Defence is* evident. He contrasts the synthetic principle of imagination with the analytical principle of reason. 'Reason is to imagination as the instrument to the agent, as the body to the spirit, as the shadow to the substance.' Poetry is 'the expression of the imagination'. In the widest sense of the word, not only artistic creators but the founders of laws and civilisation, as well as other inventors, are all poets. For the poet 'participates in the eternal, the infinite, and the one', and he seeks to express the order and beauty he discerns. The poet in the more restricted sense uses language as his medium. 'A poem is the very image of life expressed in its eternal truth.' It is creating 'actions according to the unchangeable forms of human nature, as existing in the mind of the Creator', that distinguishes a 'poem' from that 'dialogue of detached facts' which constitutes a 'story'. A 'story of particular facts' obscures and distorts what should be beautiful: poetry makes what is distorted beautiful. Shelley's definitions preclude the distinction between poets and prose writers as 'a vulgar error'. Great philosophers and historians have been poets. Shelley's idealism is such that he speaks as though the poet is generally reduced to making do with inadequate contemporary morals and fashions as his material. Few poets have 'chosen to exhibit the beauty of their conceptions in its naked truth and splendour'. Indeed 'the alloy of costume, habit, &c' is probably 'necessary, to temper this planetary music for mortal ears'. So the mystic's sense that, as T. S. Eliot puts it, 'humankind / Cannot bear very much reality' is appropriated by Shelley as an equivalent limitation on the poet. He seems obsessed by the sheer potency of poetry. Ethical science can provide us with schemes and models, but poetry acts in a 'diviner manner', awakening and enlarging the mind, and lifting the 'veil from the hidden beauty of the world'. Shelley's prose is nothing if not inspired and inspiring. The imagination is 'the great instrument of moral good' which strengthens man morally as

exercise strengthens him physically. Shelley seems to be close
to Wordsworth here: but he makes clear that direct moral
instruction demeans poetry and diminishes the poet.

As Peacock made a comic survey of the history of poetry,
Shelley now makes a serious one. He gives due praise to
Greek poetry, but insists that *King Lear* is 'the most perfect
specimen of the dramatic art existing in the world'. Tracing
the connection between great drama and the moral health of
society, he notes that in our own age 'the greatest degradation of the drama is the reign of Charles II' in which only
Milton stood aloof from acclaiming the defeat of liberty and
virtue by monarchy. But the peculiar stamp of Shelley's
theorising about poetry emerges most clearly when, comparing the Romans with the Greeks, he argues that 'the true
poetry of Rome lived in its institutions'. The disinterested
achievements which built the empire amounted to poetry.
'They are the episodes of that cyclic poem written by Time
upon the memories of men.' Likewise whatever evil there was
in the darkness of the dark ages 'sprang from the extinction
of the poetic principle'. It seems that Shelley's concept of
what constitutes poetry embraces everything that is good.

Small wonder, then, that he rejects Peacock's challenge to
poets 'to resign the civic crown to reasoners and mechanists',
and the argument that denies poetry its usefulness. On the
contrary, 'whatever strengthens and purifies the affections,
enlarges the imagination, and adds spirit to sense, is useful'.
Those who serve society in seemingly more practical ways
merely follow in the footsteps of poets. In fact we have more
moral, political and historical knowledge than we can
handle. It is for lack of the creative faculty and imaginative
power that our civilisation remains enslaved to materialism.
It is precisely at such periods as the present that the
cultivation of poetry is most desperately necessary.

Shelley's rhetoric takes wing as he proclaims his gospel:

> Poetry is indeed something divine. It is at once the centre and
> circumference of knowledge; it is that which comprehends all science,
> and that to which all science must be referred.

Even so, the most glorious poetry is probably but a 'feeble
shadow' of the poet's original conceptions. 'Poetry is the record

of the best and happiest moments of the happiest and best minds.' It represents 'the interpenetration of a diviner nature through our own'. It immortalises all that is best and most beautiful in the world. The poet therefore must be incontrovertibly 'the wisest, the happiest, and the best' of men. Indeed poets are 'the hierophants of an unapprehended inspiration'. 'Poets are the unacknowledged legislators of the world.'

There was a Shelleyan hot-headedness about some of the critical aphorisms of William Blake (1787–1827). He declared Reynold's *Discourses* to the Royal Academy to be the 'Simulations of the Hypocrite' because Reynolds thought that 'Genius May be Taught & that all Pretence to Inspiration is a Lie & a Deceit'. Reynold's *Discourses* derived from Burke's treatise *On the Sublime*, and Burke's treatise from Newton and Locke. All such books are abhorrent because 'they mock Inspiration & Vision'. Like Shelley, Blake defines imagination in Platonic terms. 'This world of Imagination is the World of Eternity ...' The realities of Eternity are reflected in the mirror of Nature. But for Blake, eternity is 'the divine bosom into which we shall go after the death of the Vegetated body', and 'all things are comprehended in their Eternal Forms in the divine body of the Saviour'. Though all forms of art are 'visions of eternity', the reflection of the eternal in the natural is such that the imagination reaches outside the world apprehended by the senses into the spiritual sphere. Blake, therefore, is unhappy with the way Wordsworth pins down the operation of the imagination in natural objects. 'Natural Objects always did & now do weaken, deaden & obliterate Imagination in Me.' Wordsworth ought to be aware that what he has to reveal is not something that can be found in Nature. 'I see in Wordsworth the Natural Man rising up against the Spiritual Man Continually, & then he is No Poet but a Heathen philosopher at Enmity against all true Poetry or Inspiration.'

Thus, in 1826, Blake annotated his copy of Wordsworth's *Poems* volume I (1815). In particular he could not abide Wordsworth's prayer

And I could wish my days to be
Bound each to each by natural piety

declaring, 'There is no such thing as Natural Piety because The Natural Man is at Enmity with God.' Blake had early come across the work of Thomas Taylor (1768–1835), the mathematician and philosopher who translated Plato and Plotinus and has been credited with playing an influential part in bringing about the revival of mythology in the poetry of Shelley, Coleridge, and Blake himself. Nearly a century later, the poet W. B. Yeats was to find Plotinus's thought inadequate to his needs because the philosopher postulated a real existence to which there was no substantial antagonism. Yeats's own religious thought was antithetical and demanded antagonism. In the same way Blake's vision of human wholeness involved accepting antinomies without diluting them. The contradictory potencies of the spiritual and the physical could not be reconciled by recourse to easy evasions such as the notion of 'natural piety'.

Blake's emphasis on imagination and inspiration, and Wordsworth's emphasis on the primacy of feeling ('the spontaneous overflow of powerful feeling') acquired in the one case a mystical dimension and in the other case a moral dimension which introduced an element of self-discipline. The exaltation of emotion and intuition above logical reasoning can readily disentangle them from any such disciplinary anchorage. John Keats (1795–1821) committed himself in letters to generalisations which seem to show this process at work: 'I am certain of nothing but of the holiness of the heart's affections and the truth of Imagination.' So Keats wrote to Benjamin Bailey on 22 November, 1817. Our passions are 'all in their sublime creative of essential Beauty', and it is in beauty that truth is to be found. 'O for a Life of Sensation rather than of Thoughts,' Keats declared, hammering home his suspicion of the intellect. And he defined the essential quality of Shakespeare as *negative capability*, that is when a man is capable of being in uncertainties, mysteries, doubts, without any irritable reaching after fact and reason ...' Thus Keats distinguished his own poetic character from what he called 'the Wordsworthian or egotistical sublime' as that of a characterless, identityless being to whom true poetry will come effortlessly as he submits his imaginative sensitivities to the sphere of sensation. 'The Genius of Poetry must work out its own salvation in a man ...' Keats felt no obligation to accommodate himself, this way or that, to Christianity. The frameworks of belief which Blake, Wordsworth, and even (though perversely) Shelley grappled with, meant nothing to him. There is a curious air of modernity about his willingness to theorise directly from self, as poet and man of feeling, in a kind of philosophical vacuum.

IV Hazlitt and De Quincey

We turn from poets, for whom criticism was in most cases an offshoot of poetic endeavour, to prose writers who made their names as essayists, critics and journalists. William Hazlitt (1778–1830) was a radical with a social conscience who fervently supported the French Revolution and Napoleon, and continued to do so when fellow-enthusiasts all around him were repelled by the excesses of both. The edgy, rebellious streak in his character could only be intensified by his somewhat beleaguered isolation in this respect. But his combativeness, like his positive enthusiasms, often served him well as a writer. Vitality, enthusiasm, ardour, gusto – such terms spring to mind in characterising Hazlitt's work. He is not the kind of critic to examine basic principles. He is no theoretician. Indeed he can be careless, slapdash, and prejudiced. He is essentially a *descriptive* critic, who fastens on the beauties and defects of literary works with fluent outpourings of praise or blame, and above all with flashes of acumen, of inspired aphoristic brilliance which can illuminate aspects of a writer's work unforgettably. It is easy to pick holes in Hazlitt's critical reputation by pointing to his lack of philosophical discrimination and his tendency to let his rhetoric run away with him, but his work remains obstinately readable.

There is no question in Hazlitt of appealing to rules or models, theories or systems. His critical works are the record of his own personal response to what he has read. In his *Characters of Shakespeare's Plays* (1817) he takes his starting-point from a statement by Pope that 'every single character in Shakespeare is as much an individual as those in life itself' and proceeds through the plays in turn, illustrating the depth of Shakespeare's penetration of the human heart and the subtlety of his exploration of the human mind. Admittedly the descriptive technique is a matter of exploiting a ready-made emotive vocabulary. We read about the 'uncontrollable anguish in the swollen heart of Lear' and 'the petrifying indifference, the cold, calculating, obdurate selfishness of his daughters', not to mention their 'stony hearts'. The commentary on behaviour, of course, too readily assumes a tendency to distribute praise and dispraise, moral approval and disapproval, in a vein which blurs the distinction between literature and real life. But this kind of excited appreciation of naturalism in characterisation was not yet hackneyed. We ought not to blame Hazlitt for the fact that the brand of criticism he launched was to become the stock-in-trade for candidates in public examinations a century after this death.

There are sections of Hazlitt's critical work which fasten on more general issues. Sometimes a sub-heading will seem to forecast a more abstract and theoretical examination of a literary quality. For instance, in *Lectures on the English Comic Writers* (1819) there is a chapter 'On Wit and Humour'. Yet what gives the piece its vitality is, not the thoroughness of the enquiry into the question, but the sheer charm and abundance of the anecdotes and illustrations which flow from Hazlitt's pen. Hazlitt was sufficiently well-read to be able to cite examples from a wide range of literature, and he was also sufficiently sensitive and responsive to the quirks and oddities encountered in daily life to be able to rustle up an apt analogy to press home a point vividly and memorably. In illustrating the relationship of tears to laughter he produces lively examples of the way children respond to different kinds of surprises in games of hide-and-seek or blindman's buff, or when a masked face is pressed to theirs. The effect of contrast and seeming absurdity is revealed in vivid examples.

> We laugh at the dress of foreigners, and they at ours. Three chimney-sweepers meeting three Chinese in Lincoln's-inn Fields, they laughed at one another until they were ready to drop down.

Thus Hazlitt piles up instances of how humour results from surprise, incongruity, absurdity and misunderstanding.

He does not shirk abstract definition and clarification when it is needed.

> Humour is the describing the ludicrous as it is in itself; wit is the exposing it, by comparing or contrasting it with something else. Humour is, as it were, the growth of nature and accident; wit is the product of art and fancy.

He accepts that wit most often produces its effect by comparison. But he rejects as too wholesale the definition of wit emanating from Locke and Hobbes – a business of 'finding out striking and unexpected resemblances in things', which contrasts with the business of judgment and reason in separating things and distinguishing differences. On this principle 'demonstrating the equality of the three angles of a right-angled triangle to two right ones' would be a piece of wit. Hazlitt reveals himself a true romantic when he stresses 'the intrinsic superiority of poetry or imagination to wit'. Wit operates on a more superficial level than imagination. It tends to deflate rather than to exalt, 'to disconnect our sympathy from passion and power' rather than 'to attach and rivet it to any object of grandeur and interest'.

Hazlitt's finest criticism is to be found in his *Lectures on the English Poets* (1818) and in *The Spirit of the Age* (1825), two books which overlap in that the former ends with a chapter 'On the Living Poets'. The *English Poets* opens with a chapter 'On Poetry in General' in which Hazlitt piles up testimony to his enthusiasm:

> Poetry is the language of the imagination and the passions ... Poetry is the universal language which the heart holds with nature and itself.

History treats of 'the empty cases' into which the world's affairs are packed, but poetry is 'the stuff of which our life is made'. It represents 'the excess of the imagination beyond the actual or ordinary impressions of any object or feeling'. The imagination represents things 'not as they are in themselves, but as they are moulded by other thoughts and feelings'. Though poetry is 'the highest eloquence of passion', yet impassioned poetry emanates from the moral and intellectual as well as the sensitive part of our nature. That is why the tragedy of Lillo weighs so heavily on the mind while Shakespeare stirs 'our inmost affections'. In considering whether verse is essential to poetry, Hazlitt insists that the prose works that come nearest to being poetry are the *Pilgrim's Progress*, *Robinson Crusoe* and Boccaccio's *Tales*. By contrast Richardson comes under censure. And we see Hazlitt at his liveliest when he turns to characterise something he does not like. The repetitious blows rained on Clarissa 'have no rebound'. The sympathy they excite 'is not a voluntary contribution but a tax'.

> Clarissa, the divine Clarissa, is too interesting by half. She is interesting in her ruffles, in her gloves, her samplers, her aunts, and uncles – she is interesting in all that is uninteresting.

In the subsequent lectures, Hazlitt works through from Chaucer and Spenser to the present day. He praises not only Chaucer's 'downright reality', but also the 'depth and pathos and intensity of conception' in which none, not even the Greek tragedians, come near him. Spenser, by contrast, takes us into an 'ideal world', and it is a revealing commentary on the Romantic mind that the allegory is undervalued. Readers should not worry about it. 'If they do not meddle with the allegory, the allegory will not meddle with them.' This was to be a nineteenth-century estimate of grave moral Spenser. In the same way Hazlitt's claim for *Paradise Lost* that 'Satan is the most heroic subject that ever was chosen for a poem' was to supply his successors with the ideal excuse for not taking Milton's theological scheme too seriously. Moreover, the lectures on Dryden and Pope, and on Thomson and Cowper, set the guide-lines for distinguishing the qualities of successive ages which have become clichés of the history of literature.

It is when he comes to his last lecture 'On the Living Poets' that Hazlitt's persona shines through at its freshest and sharpest. Judgments tend to be simplistic, but there are neat thumb-nail sketches of Tom Moore ('Everything lives, moves, and sparkles in his poetry', but his facility, his 'graceful ease', and his fluency preclude 'momentum and passion'), of Byron (he has 'more depth of passion, more force and impetuosity, but the passion is always of the same unaccountable quality'), and of Scott and Southey. There is also a sly summary of what the 'Lake school of poetry' represents which has a positively Peacockian flavour. But there is more subtlety and penetration in Hazlitt's full-scale survey of his contemporaries in *The Spirit of the Age* (1825). Here, in terms more measured and mature, Hazlitt gives us a gallery of portraits of astonishing clarity and firmness. He makes a just estimate of Scott's poetry and then acclaims the novels. They are 'like the betrothed of our hearts, bone of our bone, and flesh of our flesh, and we are jealous that anyone should be as much delighted or as thoroughly acquainted with their beauties as ourselves'. After working up to a climax of praise – 'His works (taken together) are almost like a new edition of human nature' – he turns to rend Scott the man to pieces as a person utterly degraded by fanatical Toryism. In a succeeding contrast with Byron, Scott the writer comes off unquestionably the better for the sheer range of his interests.

> Lord Byron makes man after his own image, woman after his own heart; the one is a capricious tyrant, the other a yielding slave; he gives us the misanthrope and the voluptuary by turns; and with these two characters, burning or melting in their own fires, he makes out everlasting cantos of himself.

Hazlitt cries out for quotation. On page after page of his work sentences leap out at the eye to be noted and remembered. Of Wordsworth he wrote, 'Remote from the passions and events of the great world, he has communicated interest and dignity to the primal movements of the heart of man ...' Rogers's *Pleasures of Memory* is 'a tortuous, tottering, wriggling, fidgetty translation of everything from the vulgar tongue, into all the tantalising, teasing, tripping, lisping *nimminee-pimminee* of the highest brilliancy and fashion of poetical diction'. We can forgive Hazlitt for being prejudiced and for making severe misjudgments. He launched on its course a species of criticism in which the writer romps across the literary scene shouting to the world at large about the fervent delight he takes in what he reads, and scattering gems of imaginative insight.

> If Bloomfield is too much the Farmer's Boy, Crabbe is too much the parish beadle, an overseer of the country poor. He has no delight beyond the walls of a workhouse, and his officious zeal would convert the world into a vast infirmary.

While his work testifies chiefly to his zest, those who knew Hazlitt personally made much of his gloomy irritability. He figured in George Gilfillan's 'A Gallery of Literary Portraits' in *Tait's Edinburgh Magazine* in 1845. In reviewing the portrait, De Quincey insisted that for Hazlitt 'Whatever *is* – *is wrong*'. He compared Hazlitt with Rousseau in this respect, but to Hazlitt's advantage. Where Rousseau interpreted his acquaintances' acts and motives as designed to damage him personally, Hazlitt saw 'all personal affronts or casual slights towards himself' as covers for deep antagonism to the social causes he advocated. 'It was not Hazlitt whom the wretches struck at; no, no; it was democracy, or it was freedom, or it was Napoleon ...'

Thomas De Quincey (1785–1859) tended thus to encapsulate psychological aspects of the writers he judged. His own experience as an opium-addict led him to focus on states of mind, and explore what the feelings and the imagination could effect in defiance of reason. Hazlitt's studies of Scott and Southey in the one case showered praise on the work and scorn on the man, in the other case praise on the man and scorn on his work. No unity of interpretation threads the judgments together. While it would be idle to deny that De Quincey's studies of contemporaries abound in entertaining personal anecdotes that are irrelevant to any commentary on their work, nevertheless De Quincey often revealed the itch to define the writer's mind as operative in his work.

Alongside this psychological interest, De Quincey shared in the romantic reappraisal of the relationship between reason and imagination: 'Here I pause for one moment, to exhort the reader never to pay any attention to his understanding, when it stands in opposition to any other faculty of his mind.'

So he remarks at the beginning of his celebrated essay 'On the Knocking at the Gate in *Macbeth*' (*London Magazine*, October 1823), where he argues that Shakespeare's poetry takes us into the company of two murderers bereft of human feelings, transfigured by fiendish evil. It was necessary to insulate this horror from the ordinary current of human life. The knocking at the gate recalls us by force of contrast to the world of daily affairs, making us 'profoundly sensible of the awful parenthesis that had suspended them'.

De Quincey evolved a definition of what is and what is not 'literature'. In 'Letters to a Young Man whose Education has been neglected' in the *London Magazine*, March 1823, he declares that the 'antithesis of literature is books of knowledge' – all books in which the matter to be communicated is paramount to the manner or form of its communication'. The old formula distinguishing the motive to instruct or to amuse is of no service. 'The true antithesis to knowledge, in this case, is not *pleasure*, but *power*. All that is literature seeks to communicate power; all that is not literature, to communicate knowledge.' Thus in an essay in *Blackwood's Magazine* in December 1839, he declares that Milton is 'not a poet amongst poets, but a power amongst powers' and *Paradise Lost* 'not a poem amongst poems, but a central force amongst forces'. And, in reviewing a new edition of Pope's works in the *North British Review* in August 1848, he develops the thesis:

> What you owe to Milton is not any knowledge ... what you owe is *power*, that is, exercise and extension to you own latent capacity of sympathy with the infinite, where every pulse and each separate influx is a step upwards – a step ascending as upon a Jacob's ladder from earth to mysterious altitudes above the earth.

Where the literature of knowledge speaks to the '*mere* discursive understanding', the literature of power speaks ultimately, perhaps, 'to the higher understanding, but *always* through affections of pleasure and sympathy'.

De Quincey became deeply attached to a principle of literary power which he called 'antagonism'. It is present, in his view, in the reaction represented by the knocking on the gate in *Macbeth*, when the human makes 'its reflux upon the fiendish'. It is present in those rich descriptive passages in *Paradise Lost* where 'images of elaborate architecture and of human workmanship' impinge on the scene of mere natural beauty in the Garden of Eden. This represents no display of pedantry and erudition, as critics such as Addison and Johnson suggested. It was a conscious determination that imagery of cities, crowds, and artistry should collide with the imagery of rest, solitude, and primal innocence. De Quincey illustrates this point by citing a current fashion for using phrases like 'amphitheatre of hills'. Its piquancy lies in the 'evanescent image of a great audience' half flashed upon the eye in powerful collision with the silence of the hills.

De Quincey was no master of keeping to the point. He enters upon long digressions, and his illustrative anecdotes expand into separate episodes. So lively they generally are, however, that the reader would not sacrifice them. The rich jumble of autobiography, character studies, accounts of social life, anecdote, gossip, and literary comment found in the *Recollections of the Lake Poets* gathered into a volume by E. Sackville-West in 1948, makes it one of the most fascinating books in our literature. But generally speaking, with De Quincey the choice pieces of literary criticism are scattered nuggets. This applies often to even the most substantial essays on literary personalities or topics. They were the product of his long years as a contributor to magazines such as the *London Magazine*, *Blackwood's*, and *Tait's*. And they frequently took the form of reviews of recent books, so that the weightier critical comment is incidental to the main argument.

One such review, of Richard Whately's *Elements of Rhetoric* (1828), published in *Blackwood's* (December 1828), amounted to a substantial treatise, 'Rhetoric'. The distinctiveness of De Quincey's concept of rhetoric emerges when he argues that Milton's prose is sometimes so sublime in its colouring that it rises to the raptures of poetry; conversely, that Milton's poetry lapses into rhetoric in the debates in hell and the councils in heaven. For what should be *intuitive* – that is knowledge apprehended *immediately* – becomes *discursive* – that is knowledge apprehended *mediately*. What is meant here becomes clearer when De Quincey turns to praise

Edmund Burke for the largeness of his understanding. He derides those who laud Burke's 'fancy', as though he were the kind of man 'to play with his fancy for the purpose of separable ornament'. The notion of 'separable ornament' is anathema to De Quincey. Burke's distinction was that he 'viewed all objects of the understanding under more relations than other men'. He had a 'schematizing' or 'figurative' understanding. He did not deliberately lay figures on by way of enamel or ornament. He thought in and by his figures. Imagery did not *dress* his thoughts but *incarnate* them.

By comparison with Burke, even as a conversationalist, De Quincey disparages Dr Johnson. He cites a biographic obituary which set out to expose Johnson's tautologies, quoting, 'Let observation, with extensive view,/ Survey mankind from China to Peru;' and arguing that this in effect says: 'Let observation with extensive observation observe mankind extensively.' Elsewhere, in a piece comparing the conversation of Burke and Johnson in *Tait's Edinburgh Magazine*, October 1847, De Quincey sees Burke's style as moving forward, 'governed by the very necessity of growth', whilst Dr Johnson's 'never, in any instance, GROWS a truth before your eyes'. Johnson's *memorabilia* represent the briefest of flights. There is 'no process, no evolution, no movement':

> He dissipated some casual perplexity that had gathered in the eddies of conversation, but he contributed nothing to any weightier interest; he unchoked a strangulated sewer in some blind alley, but what river is there that felt his cleansing power?

When he presses his favourite or unfavourable judgment to a conclusion that image or anecdote can illuminate, De Quincey's touch has vitality and conviction. Whether right or wrong, the flavour of personal experience carries his judgment on the current of that 'power' he so valued in others.

V Journalists and reviewers

De Quincey toiled laboriously for many years in the world of journals and reviews. The Romantic age was a period in which periodical magazines flourished. The Scottish journals in particular had great influence on the fortunes of contemporary writers. But in addition to the Scottish reviewers, there was one English journalist who was a lively participant in the literary controversies of the day and he had the perspicacity to champion both Shelley and Keats in resistance to the prevailing tide of critical opinion. Leigh Hunt (1784–1859) started the *Examiner* in 1808, and later edited the *Reflector* (1810–11), the *Indicator* (1819–20), and the *Liberal* (1822–3). The literary controversies involving the Romantic writers cannot be wholly disentangled from the political dissensions of the day. Leigh Hunt was a radical. He and his brother got themselves imprisoned for two years for an attack on the character of the Prince Regent in 1813. Nothing could more surely exalt a man to the status of heroic martyr in the eyes of Shelley. Nothing could have been more abhorrent to the Tory journalists. The curious fact is that the championing of Keats by Leigh Hunt was enough to bring down coals of fire on Keats's head. The *Quarterly Review* wrote of Keats as Hunt's 'simple neophyte'.

Hunt's role in the history of literary criticism is not that of a profound illuminator of what he read. It is rather that he showed taste and commonsense in acclaiming the great poets among his contemporaries, often in the face of ridicule. In a piece on Byron in the *Examiner* (July 29, 1821) he reversed the current view of what mattered in the poet's output, and was right. He likes the last canto of *Childe Harold* but thinks little of the romantic narratives with their 'over-easy eight-syllable measure'. They are 'like their heroes, too melodramatic, hasty, and vague'. As for Byron's dramas, though they contain such good passages as a good poet will naturally write, they are not the work of a true dramatist. 'His *Don Juan* is perhaps his best work, and the one by which he will stand or fall with readers who see beyond their times and toilets.' In an earlier *Examiner* (October 31, 1819) Hunt had reviewed the first two cantos of *Don Juan* and cited instances of excessive suddenness in the transitions from 'loveliness and grandeur to ridicule or the mock-heroic'. In his sensitivity to the various aspects of Byron's 'heterogeneous mixture', Hunt detected a struggle in the poet's feelings between the man of compassion and the satirist. He pictured Byron as a man whose early hopes were blighted. In veins of passion the poet works himself up to a point of emotional tension too powerful to be tolerable in the recollections aroused. So he dashes aside into some totally incongruous train of thought. This attempt to psychologise Byron as a deeply vulnerable soul at loggerheads with himself and his past hints at Hunt's potential as a critic. In the same piece he rounds on those who would label the first two cantos of *Don Juan* immoral:

> There are a set of prudish and very suspicious moralists who endeavour to make vice appear to inexperienced eyes more hateful than it really is. They would correct Nature – and they always over-reach themselves.

'They' of course include Southey, for whom Hunt nourished a withering contempt. That is, once the revolutionary radical had become the Tory Laureate. In the *Examiner* of April 13, 1817, a quarter of a century before Southey's life ended, Hunt published an account of the 'Death and Funeral of the Late Mr. Southey'. The funeral procession figures 'Jacobins with their coats turned' as well as a deputation of papists dragging the effigy of Voltaire through the mud, and 'Dr Paracelsus Broadhum Coleridge, holding an enormous white handkerchief to his eyes, and supported by two Bottle-holders'.

As for Shelley, Hunt was already proclaiming him 'a very striking and original thinker' shortly after the publication of *Alastor* (1816). And in February and March, 1818, Hunt devoted spaces in three issues of the *Examiner* to an apprecia-tive account of *The Revolt of Islam*, illustrated with extracts. Plainly Shelley's dissatisfaction with the social and political status quo and his towering revolutionary fervour were what most surely won Hunt's sympathy. But he has high praise too for the 'grandeur of imagery' and the musical appeal of the versification. Shelley is declared to be like Lucretius in 'the boldness of his speculations', like Dante in his 'gloomier and more imaginative passages'. But in one respect he has Dante beaten.

> The sort of supernatural architecture in which he delights has in particular the grandeur as well as the obscurity of that great genius, to whom however he presents this remarkable and constructive contrast, that superstition and pain and injustice go hand in hand even in the pleasantest parts of Dante, like the three Furies, while philosophy, pleasure, and justice, smile through the most painful passages of our author, like the three Graces.

Of the Scottish reviewers the most eminent was Francis Jeffrey (1773–1850) who rose to be a judge and a Member of Parliament. Jeffrey founded the *Edinburgh Review* in 1802 with the aid of Sidney Smith (1771–1845). The *Edinburgh Review*, published by Archibald Constable (1774–1827) was a Whig journal. Its great rival was the *Quarterly Review* founded by the publisher John Murray (1778–1843) in 1809, and firmly Tory. The *Edinburgh* acquired a second Tory rival in 1817, *Blackwood's Edinburgh Magazine*. Where Leigh Hunt's *Examiner* lasted until 1881, the three Scots journals survived into the twentieth century, the *Edinburgh* until 1929, the *Quarterly* until 1967, and *Blackwood's* until 1980. These journals, flourishing at a time of literary rebellion and innovation, inevitably became involved in heated controversy over the reputation of new writers. Never before or since, it would appear, have the fortunes of major writers been so intertwined with the careers of critics.

In *English Bards and Scotch Reviewers* (1809) Byron hailed Jeffrey as the inheritor of 'bloody' Judge Jeffreys, sentencing letters as the former once sentenced men 'With hand less mighty, but with heart as black,/ With voice as willing to decree the rack ...'

It is true that the motto of the *Edinburgh Review*, *judex damnatur cum nocens absolvitur* ('the judge condemns himself when the guilty man is acquitted') advertised a principle of critical rigour, and some scathing reviews, of Wordsworth especially, made it tempting to picture Jeffrey as Byron pictured him. But Jeffrey was a discerning and judicious reviewer who studied what he passed judgment on with great care. His highly sympathetic review of Keats's *Poems* of 1820 (August 24, 1820) followed hard on the celebrated assault on Keats in the *Quarterly*. Jeffrey concedes that the 'imitation of our older writers' has produced 'a second spring in our poetry' and few of its blossoms are 'either more profuse in sweetness, or richer in promise' than what is contained in Keats's volume. Defects are pointed out, but Jeffrey speaks lyrically of the 'intoxication' of the sweetness of the poems, and 'the enchantments they so lavishly present'. There are plenty of learned people, Jeffrey argues, who are insensitive to the 'true genius of English poetry' and its 'most exquisite beauties'; but Keats is 'deeply imbued with that spirit':

> We are very much inclined indeed to add, that we do not know any book which we would sooner employ as a test to ascertain whether any one had in him a native relish for poetry, and a genuine sensibility to its intrinsic charm.

Jeffrey's appreciative range was not narrow. He repeatedly reviewed Crabbe favourably. He was genuinely appreciative of Crabbe's realistic portraiture, and he made his tribute in April, 1808 an opportunity to lambaste Wordsworth. From his 'childish and absurd affectations we turn with pleasure to the manly sense and correct picturing of Mr. Crabbe'. He was sensitive to Byron's qualities, and prepared to subject to thorough analysis, balanced and penetrating, the charge that Byron's poetry might corrupt by its immorality. He wrote a review of Scott's *Marmion* which combines due praise of the powerful poetry in 'the picturesque representation of visible objects, in the delineation of manners and characters, and in the description of great and striking events' with a rigorous enumeration of defects such as a modern critic might point out. What is most perceptive here is Jeffrey's insistence that Scott is misapplying the extraordinary talents. And when he reviewed *Waverley* in 1814 he immediately recognised it as a work which 'cast the whole tribe of ordinary novels into the shade'.

Jeffrey had a blind spot so far as Wordsworth was concerned. He identified Wordsworth and his followers as the 'Lake School of Poetry' in a review of Southey's *Thalaba* in October, 1802. With much that Jeffrey says of *Thalaba* the modern reader would be sympathetic. But Jeffrey takes the opportunity to question the 'peculiar doctrines' of the sect of which Southey is regarded as 'one of the chief champions'. Jeffrey's starting-point is a dogmatic one:

> Poetry has this much, at least, in common with religion, that its standards were fixed long ago, by certain inspired writers, whose authority it is no longer lawful to call in question ...

For Jeffrey, the Lake poets have broken from authority and 're-asserted the independence of genius' without creating any new models. They voice the 'antisocial principles and distempered sensibility of Rousseau', they affect simplicity and familiarity of language and then lapse into 'mere slovenliness and vulgarity'. Their simplicity is not just a rejection of excessive ornament, it is a rejection of *art* altogether. And not only is language depraved, but the distinction between refined and low-bred people is obliterated in the choice of 'low-bred heroes and interesting rustics'.

Jeffrey took up the case against Wordsworth in a review of his *Poems in Two Volumes* in October, 1807. Wordsworth, he protests, seems determined on a kind of wilful 'literary martyrdom' by 'connecting his most lofty, tender, or impassioned conceptions, with objects and incidents, which the greater part of his readers will probably persist in thinking low, silly, or uninteresting'. By the time he came to review Wordsworth's *The Excursion* in November, 1814, Jeffrey had concluded that it was a waste of time to argue with one so irredeemable. 'This will never do!' he began. Wordsworth's case was 'hopeless', 'incurable'. 'Why should Mr. Wordsworth have made his hero a superannuated Pedlar?' There is of course some sense in Jeffrey's objection: 'A man who went about selling flannel and pocket-handkerchiefs in this lofty diction, would soon frighten away all his customers.'

Hazlitt paid tribute to Jeffrey's qualities in *The Spirit of the Age*: 'His strength consists in great range of knowledge, an equal familiarity with the principles and details of a subject, and in a glancing brilliancy and rapidity of style.' By contrast, he poured scorn on the pretensions of William Gifford (1756–1826), the first editor of the *Quarterly Review*:

> 'Mr. Gifford has no pretensions to be thought a man of genius, of taste, or even of general knowledge.'

It is now generally accepted that the editorship was a post for which Gifford was quite unfitted by his hostility to what was new or experimental. Yet he was capable of appreciating Byron. When, in September 1816, John Murray wrote to tell Byron about his reader's reception of the manuscript of *Childe Harold* canto III, he said:

> Never, since my intimacy with Mr Gifford, did I see him so heartily pleased, or give one-fiftieth part of the praise, with one-thousandth part of the warmth ... When he called upon me some time ago, and I told him that you were gone, he instantly exclaimed in a full room, 'Well! he has not left his equal behind him – that I will say!'

But *Don Juan* disillusioned Gifford. 'I read the second canto this morning,' he wrote to Murray in 1819, 'and I lost all patience at seeing so much beauty wantonly and perversely disfigured.'

One of the regular contributors to the *Quarterly* was John Wilson Croker (1780–1857). A Member of Parliament, and a scholar with a special interest in eighteenth-century litera-ture, he left valuable personal records behind him which were published as *The Croker Papers* (1884). He seems to have seen his work for the *Quarterly* as an extension of his political activities in staunch Tory defence of established institutions and traditional morality, at a time when they were much under threat from contemporary developments in Europe. His Anglicanism gave a religious dimension to his assaults on what he saw as subversive and corrupting tendencies in contemporary literature. His name has come down to posterity linked with the notorious attack on Keats's *Endymion* in 1818, which Byron and Shelley saw as fatally wounding. His antagonism to Leigh Hunt is explicable enough, and he saw Keats as one of his camp. Croker's defensiveness on behalf of English political moderation linked itself with a dread of excess, libertarianism, and anti-traditionalism in literature. He saw the increasing concern of contemporary novels with themes of adultery, incest, and sexual licence as a grave threat to public morality and especially to female chastity. Thus, while he could give generous approval to novelists such as Scott and Maria

Edgeworth, he poured abuse on such writers as Charles Maturin and Lady Morgan. (In *Melmoth the Wanderer* 'the new ravings of the unhappy patient exceed the old folly and indelicacy', and Lady Morgan is guilty of 'Bad taste – Bombast and Nonsense – General Ignorance – Jacobinism – Falsehood – Licentiousness, and Impiety'.) But Croker was a lively and valued reviewer, and his very venom testifies to his comprehensive awareness of the binding links between the tremendous political and social upheavals of his day and the outburst of innovation in literature and philosophy.

Croker, of course, does not fairly represent the attitude of the *Quarterly* over the whole field of literature. Its most distinguished contributor was Sir Walter Scott (1771–1832). A Tory, like Croker, Scott nevertheless managed to display a magnanimity in ideological matters and in literary judgments which together mark his critical works with good temper and persuasiveness. His critical output was considerable. It included the various introductions he wrote to his novels and poems, the learned editions of Dryden and Swift, and the numerous biographical and critical sketches he wrote for Ballantyne's *Novelists' Library*, as well as the reviews and the scattered comments on writers found in his *Letters* and his *Journal*. Scott belonged to the Romantics in his conviction that poetry springs from impulse and emotion, and that the poet cannot be fettered by the hackneyed regulations of the critics. His own writing was rapid and unpremeditated. He valued what he called the 'hurried frankness' of his composition which was calculated to please youthful, active and vigorous personalities. He recognised that the writer might have to pay a price in mental and nervous strain for his commitment to the 'feverish trade of poetry'. He observed this phenomenon in the case of Burns, Monk Lewis, and Byron. For Scott, what disciplines the spontaneous outflow from the restless emotional deeps and the powerful imagination of the artist is his sure contact with the outer world. This involves observant appreciation of the natural world, sympathetic entry into the minds and hearts of his fellow beings, and a sense of the influence of historic background and local environment. The good taste of the artist and the gentleman will ensure that he subjects the liberty of the writer to the dictates of prudence and morality. In Scott's judicious blend of the man of feeling, the conscious artist, and the gentlemanly citizen, one modern critic has seen him as balancing the views of Wordsworth with those of Jeffrey.[1]

Scott's *Lives of the Novelists* represents a worthy successor to Johnson's *Lives of the Poets*, not in exuding the same aphoristic brilliance, but in showing a comparable weight of good sense and literary sympathy brought to bear on a variety of writers. Scott does justice to Richardson, Fielding, Smollett, and Sterne with touching objectivity. Richardson's power in scenes of tragedy is accepted, but a sly note sometimes intrudes into the account of *Sir Charles Grandison*, especially of the hero, 'the twenty-thousand prize, which was to be drawn by either of the ladies who might be so lucky as to win it'. And Scott's observation on the 'numerous and long conversations upon religious and moral topics' is to recall the case of an old lady for whom *Sir Charles Grandison* was her favourite book, because if she fell asleep while it was being read, she found on waking that the story remained where it was when she dropped off. Fielding gets his due of praise as 'the father of the English novel' and Scott makes short work of the complaint by Richardson's admirers that Fielding encouraged licentiousness. He quotes Dr Johnson. "Men ... will not become highwaymen because Macheath is acquitted on stage" and they will not become 'licentious debauchees because they read *Tom Jones*'. If there is prejudice in Scott, it emerges in his readiness to put his compatriot Tobias Smollett on a level with Fielding. It is the sheer range and fertility of Smollett's inventiveness which in Scott's eyes counterbalances 'Fielding's superiority of taste and expression'. As for Sterne, Scott believes that the characters of 'Uncle Toby and his faithful squire' are so delightful as to far outweigh anything negative in Sterne's 'literary peculations, his indecorum, and his affectation'.

> The Gothic order of architecture is now so generally, and, indeed indiscriminately used, that we are rather surprised if the country-house of a tradesman retired from business does not exhibit lanceolated windows, divided by stone shafts, and garnished by painted glass, a cupboard in the form of a cathedral stall, and a pig-house with a front borrowed from the facade of an ancient chapel.

So Scott wrote in his study of Horace Walpole, but it did not prevent him either from designing Abbotsford or from relishing the powerful preternatural element in Gothic novels. In his study of Ann Radcliffe, he attacks those who rail against her novels, stressing the sheer pleasure they gave the reader. He praises her skill in working on her reader's feelings. He acclaims her as 'the first poetess of romantic fiction'; but, in comparing her with Walpole, he condemns her practice of finally explaining mysteries away in naturalistic terms. The 'reader feels indignant at discovering that he has been cheated into sympathy with terrors' now disinfected. Moreover 'these substitutes for supernatural agency are frequently to the full as improbable as the machinery which they are introduced to explain away and to supplant'.

Scott has been accused of being too nice a man to be a good critic of his contemporaries. It is true that his public judgments were dexterously arranged to give as little offence as possible. 'The last part of *Childe Harold* [meaning canto III] intimates a terrible state of mind' he wrote to Joanna Baillie on November 26, 1816. His review in the *Quarterly* of February 1817 does justice to Byron's poetic genius, to 'the deep and powerful strain of passion' and to 'the original tone and colouring of description', before going on to lament Byron's political prejudice and, with great delicacy, to suggest that he ought to moderate his darkness of spirit and his scepticism, to tame the fire of his fancy, and to narrow his desires within practicable compass. It is an urgent moral exhortation, but so deftly presented that Byron liked it and was gracious enough to tell Tom Moore that the article was more honourable to Scott than to himself. Scott returned to the velvet-gloved fray in reviewing canto IV of *Childe Harold* in September, 1818. He notes that, since Cowper, Byron is the first poet who has 'directly appeared before the public, an actual living man expressing his own sentiments, thoughts, hopes, and fears'. He willingly renders 'to this extraordinary poem the full praise that genius in its happiest efforts can demand from us', yet he gently registers his protest, questioning 'the justice and moral tendency of that strain of dissatisfaction and despondency, that cold and sceptical philosophy which clouds our prospects on earth, and closes them beyond it'.

Scott's son-in-law, John Gibson Lockhart (1794–1854) was editor of the *Quarterly* from 1825 to 1853. He had already distinguished himself as a prominent reviewer for *Blackwood's* from the time of its foundation in 1817, and it was there that the 'Cockney School of Poetry' was ridiculed, and Hazlitt, Leigh Hunt, and Keats were pilloried as its representatives. Lockhart's principles as an Anglican and a conservative were combined with a high degree of sensitivity to the emotional and imaginative content of literature. Hence we find him beginning his review of Shelley's *Revolt of Islam* in *Blackwood's* (January 1819) with firm condemnation of the poet's pernicious opinions, 'superficial audacity of unbelief' and general 'uncharitableness'. Yet he then turns to the poem:

> As a philosopher, our author is weak and worthless; our business is with him as a poet, and, as such, he is strong, nervous, original; well entitled to take his place near to the great creative masters, whose works have shed its truest glory around the age wherein we live.

As evidence of Shelley's greatness Lockhart cites his portrayal of the 'intense, overmastering, unfearing, unfading love' of Laon and Cythna. He appreciates how 'in the midst of all their fervours' Shelley has shed around the lovers 'an air of calm gracefulness, a certain majestic, monumental stillness, which blends them with the scene of their earthly existence'. His final advice to Shelley, however, is to cease to pervert his talents.

> Mr Shelley, whatever his errors may have been, is a scholar, a gentleman, and a poet; and he must therefore despise from his soul the only eulogies to which he has hitherto been accustomed – paragraphs from the *Examiner*, and sonnets from Johnny Keats.

Lockhart was a well-read, lively-minded writer of diverse talents. His novel *Adam Blair* (1822) is a story of adultery with passages of intense emotional profundity, and his massive *Life of Sir Walter Scott* (1837–8) brought powers of thoroughness, organisation and personal sensitivity into play which permanently institutionalised the impressive public image of the Wizard of the North and Laird of Abbotsford.

There was too in Lockhart a vein of satiric insight and
psychological subtlety which, when combined with his play-
fulness and not marred by antipathy, could produce gems
such as his anonymously issued *Letter to the Right Hon. Lord
Byron. By John Bull* (1821). Adopting an intimate, man-to-
man, word-in-your-ear, elbow-in-your-side tone to begin
with, it manages to be utterly inoffensive in declaring: Come
off it! Drop the pose! Lockhart moves from direct address to
dramatised fantasy like a twentieth-century novelist:

> How melancholy you look in the prints! Oh! yes, that is the true cast
> of face. How tell me, Mrs Goddard, now tell me, Miss Price, now tell
> me, dear Harriett Smith, and dear, dear Mrs Elton, do tell me, is not
> this just the very look, that one would have fancied for Childe
> Harold? Oh what eyes and eyebrows ... Perhaps her *Ladyship* was in
> the wrong after all. – I am sure if I had married such a man, I would
> have borne with all his little eccentricities ...

So Lockhart 'rags' the moody Lord for laughing up his sleeve
while picturing such scenes as this, for the 'triumphs of
humbug' ... 'you ought to be ashamed of them'. Lockhart's advice is 'Stick to *Don Juan*: it is the only sincere
thing you have ever written'. Indeed, in Lockhart's opinion,
there is not much in present day literature that will 'stand
the test of half a century' except the Waverley Novels and
Don Juan. Byron understood the 'spirit of England', its
society, its ladies and gentlemen. So, after ribbing Byron
for pretending to admire Rogers and disparaging Wordsworth, he ridicules those who would denigrate Byron now for
sticking to what is 'coarse, comic, obvious' and having
'neither heart nor soul for the grand, the sublime, the
pathetic, the truly imaginative'. And here he makes his
firmest claim on Byron's behalf. Longinus's idea of 'the
sublime' is essentially 'the *energetic*'; and this Byron well
knows himself.

In giving its lively, contentious flavour to *Blackwood's* in its
early days, Lockhart was aided by James Hogg (1770–1835)
and John Wilson (1785–1854). Wilson used the pseudonym
'Christopher North'. The two collaborated over 'The Chal-
dee MS', a spoof which appeared in *Blackwood's* in 1817 over

the conflict with the *Edinburgh Review*, and made well-known Edinburgh personalities look ridiculous. Wilson was also responsible for a large part of the series of dialogues, 'Noctes Ambrosianae', which appeared in *Blackwood's* between 1822 and 1835. These are conversations in a tavern which feature Wilson as 'North' and James Hogg as the 'Shepherd' among the speakers. Wilson's critical reviews were somewhat unpredictable. He was an early enthusiast for Wordsworth whom he revered as a potential guide for the young at a time of moral and social decomposition. Yet some articles of his in 1817 so offended Wordsworth that *Blackwood's* was banned from Rydal Mount. In July 1819 we find him writing an appreciative review of Crabbe's *Tales of the Hall*. Crabbe 'has evidently an intense satisfaction in moral anatomy; and in the course of his dissections, he lays bare, with an unshrinking hand, the very arteries of the heart'. Wilson recognises the intimacy and thoroughness of Crabbe's portraiture ('He seems to have known them all personally') and a note of surprise seems to be audible as he marvels at the revelation of passions that cut across class barriers in 'scenes and characters from which in real life we would turn our eyes with intolerant disgust'.

Wilson has much to his credit. It was he who persuaded De Quincey to come to Edinburgh and contribute to *Blackwood's*. De Quincey, speaking later of *Blackwood's*, said that Wilson had been 'its intellectual Atlas'. He was the authority responsible for a shift of attitude by *Blackwood's* after 1830. The long record of abusing the 'Cockneys' came to an end. By 1834 (*Blackwood's* XXXVI, 273) Wilson was replying angrily to someone wanting to abuse Leigh Hunt. 'Hunt has more talent in his little finger than the puling prig ...'

It is not easy to decide how to place in the history of criticism a man whose commentaries on literary figures of his age came publicly to light only after the age had passed away. Henry Crabb Robinson (1775–1867), a lawyer, kept diaries in which he recorded impressions of contemporary writers and their works. The *Diaries and Journals*, edited by Thomas Sadler, were first published in 1869. Robinson is a man whose friendly personality intrudes repeatedly into the story of Wordsworth and his circle. He seems to know

everybody. He visits Blake and reads Wordsworth's 'Intimations of Immortality Ode' to him. He is Coleridge's good
friend. He turns up at Charles Lamb's. He calls upon Keats.
He is dining at William Godwin's when Shelley is letting off
political steam. He is visiting the Isle of Man, Staffa and
Iona or Italy with Wordsworth, and he is comforting
Wordsworth at Rydal Mount after Dora's death. His
jottings abound in fresh reactions to first readings. 'With a
few energetic lines expressing a diseased state of feeling, the
thing is as worthless and unmeaning as I should have
expected.' That is the reaction to Byron's *The Giaour* in
1813. As for *Cain*, in 1822, 'It is certainly a mischievous
work calculated to do nothing but harm'. In Shelley he finds
much that is delightful. Even in *The Cenci* he finds 'all is well-
conceived and the tragedy is a perfect whole'. When first
reading *Prometheus Unbound* he cannot get on with it, and
throws it aside, encouraged to do so by the review in the
Quarterly ('It is good to be now and then withheld from
reading bad books'), but three years later, in 1824, he is
enjoying 'Lines Written among the Euganean Hills' and 'The
Sensitive Plant' and deciding that Shelley is 'worth studying
and understanding if possible'.

9
The Victorian Age

The Victorian age was a period of immense consolidation in
terms of peace and prosperity, in terms of wealth and power,
and in terms of artistic productivity. When Queen Victoria
celebrated her Diamond Jubilee in 1897, her imperial sway
extended over a fifth of the habitable world. Her capital city
and her Houses of Parliament represented the apex of
international dominion. The reign which began in the age
of the stage coach ended with the British Isles netted from
corner to corner with railways linking manufacturing city
with country town, pit-head with dock, rural estate with the
metropolis. And the reign was accounted an era of peace.
The Crimean War (1853–56) and the Indian Mutiny (1857–
58) were significant enough to stir patriotic fervour, but too
far away to disturb public complacency. Irish political unrest
and even the suffering endured during the potato famine of
the 1840s seem scarcely to have ruffled the nation's peace of
mind. Agitations of a more intellectual kind preoccupied
many thinking people. The debate opened up by the
publication of Charles Darwin's *On the Origin of Species*
(1859) flung fundamentalist Christians into bitter conflict
with scientific proponents of evolutionism. The Oxford
Movement, led by Pusey, Newman, and Keble, flung the
old high church and low church wings of the Church of
England into collision as Anglo-Catholics and Evangelicals.
But the public imagination of the more gravely disturbed
twentieth century tends to look back to the Victorian age as
the stable era of the Great Exhibition and the spread of
universal education.

In literature the age was certainly an age of consolidation. It
built on the innovations of the Romantic movement. What
Wordsworth and Byron, Shelley and Keats had done to

intensify the focus of the poetic imagination and to enrich the range of poetic utterance was there to hand, for the practitioners of the new age to imitate or modify. Scott had so thoroughly subsumed into his fictional presentation what the writers between Fielding and himself had done to enrich the novel form that there was a genre waiting to have its varied potentialities exploited, given the writers and given the society to be brought under survey. The Victorians supplied both.

What made Victorian society such a fruitful field for fiction was its peculiar combination of virtues and defects – the extremes of wealth and poverty, the rigid stratification of social class, the inflexible ideal of the family structure, and the competitiveness for place and cash in a sharply individualistic environment. Collisions between passion and convention, idealism and materialism were built into the fabric of the society that the Victorian novelists surveyed. It is perhaps small wonder that a handful of them created a monumental inheritance, the Victorian Novel, whose status remains unassailable.

The Victorian Novel is richly informative about its own age – the landed gentry and the mill-owners, the politicians and the city men, gaols and work-houses, schools and law-courts, country houses and slums. The thinking that passed judgment on what man was doing to man in the hey-day of industrial splendour could not be excluded. And when critics turned their attention to the novels that presented their age, a further layer of principle or prejudice, insight or obtuseness was often imposed on the picture to add to our understanding of the age.

I Aftermath of Romanticism

In 1829 in the 'Noctes Ambrosianae', Christopher North and the Ettrick Shepherd celebrated the great age of reviewing.

> *NORTH*: Our current periodical literature teems with thought
> and feeling, James, – with passion and imagination.

The great names of contemporary contributors are rehearsed, and they are praised for the 'tender, and true, and deep things' they say, not in dully heavy, formal theorising – 'but flung off-hand, out of the glowing mint – a coinage of the purest ore – and stamped with the ineffaceable impress of genius'. Among the great names listed is that of Thomas Carlyle (1795–1881). But two years later, in his essay 'Characteristics' (1831), Carlyle was lamenting the rise of the reviewer.

> By and by it will be found that all literature has become one boundless self-devouring Review; and, as in London routs, we have to *do* nothing, but only to *see* others do nothing – Thus does Literature also, like a sick thing, superabundantly "listen to itself".

Carlyle studied German literature and philosophy early in his career and was influenced especially by the critical thinking of Karl W. F. von Schlegel (1772–1829), one of the originators of the German Romantic movement, who asserted the paramount function of the individual subjective mind in the pursuit of knowledge. For Carlyle it is not the conscious mind, 'the mind as acquainted with its strength' that is the spring of health and vitality, for its concern is with the mechanical and the overt. The unconscious is the source of dynamism, for it is in touch with the region of meditation, those mysterious depths that lie below the level of conscious argument and discourse.

'Manufacture is intelligible, but trivial; Creation is great, and cannot be understood.' The debater and demonstrator is ranked by Carlyle as 'the lowest of true thinkers', and the Artist as the highest. The former 'knows what he has done, and how he did it'. The latter 'knows not': he must speak of Inspiration and the 'gift of a divinity'. Carlyle has been seen to foreshadow the thought of twentieth-century critics in locating in the unconscious a positively creative function. If this attribution and the emphasis upon the artist's supremacy as an inspired being link him firmly with the Romantics, there is another vein of thought, illustrated to some extent in his remarks about reviewing, which makes him deeply critical of the self-indulgent postures of Byron and the early Goethe. These postures are the product of a diseased self-consciousness. For Carlyle, literature is 'but a branch of

Religion' and partakes of the prevailing malady which ousts 'spontaneous devotion to the object, being wholly possessed by the object', in favour of introspective awareness of the self. He contrasts the way 'view-hunting' has superseded unself-conscious painting of scenery for its own sake. Worshipping Nature with the self-conscious awareness that it is a credit-able thing to do is a malady comparable to the malady of perpetual literature-tasting that reviewers indulge in. The development is also comparable to the way in which religion has been cerebralised, so that 'the most enthusiastic Evange-licals do not preach a gospel, but keep describing how it should and might be preached'.

Carlyle reviewed Lockhart's *Life of Scott* in the *London and Westminster Review* in 1838. It is an extensive essay, making a careful analysis of Scott's character and achievement. It reads like the work of a restless mind struggling to reconcile seemingly contradictory evidence. When Carlyle gets the bit between his teeth on the subject of Scott's deficiencies, the accusations accumulate. Scott was worldly and ambitious, he conveyed no elevating message, his words are addressed 'to the everyday mind' and 'for any other mind there is next to no nourishment in them'. There are no opinions, emotions, principles, doubts or beliefs 'beyond what the intelligent country gentleman can carry along with him'. There is nothing in them to heal the sick heart or guide the struggling heart. Where Shakespeare 'fashions his characters from the heart outwards', Scott 'fashions them from the skin inwards, never getting near the heart of them'. There was nothing spiritual about Scott. He neither believed nor disbelieved with conviction: he acquiesced. He rarely rose above the commonplace. He never scaled the heights.

On such grounds Carlyle denies to Scott the title of 'great'. But when he dwells on the positive aspects of the man, Carlyle's pen runs to superlatives of a different kind. Scott was essentially a healthy soul, discerning what is good and adhering to it. He would have nothing to do with the bogus and the alien, with cant and pretentiousness. 'Blessed is the healthy nature; it is the coherent, sweetly cooperative, not incoherent, self-distracting, self-destructive one.' Scott inheri-ted the Scottish conscience, the 'sense that man is denizen of the Universe, creature of an Eternity'. And Scott's inward spiritual health rendered him ultimately independent on outward circumstances. Moreover his novels reveal what historians had failed to reveal, 'that the bygone ages of the world were actually filled by living men, not by protocols, state-papers, controversies and abstractions of men'.

The modern reader has to concede that this study, which was influential in establishing what can only be called the half-hearted, half-grudging estimate of Scott in the literary world, is itself a disturbing utterance from a disturbed mind. On the one hand: 'Scott, with all his health, was *infected*; sick of the fearfulest malady, that of Ambition' – and Carlyle mocks the absurdity of 'a Walter Scott writing daily with the ardour of a steam-engine, that he might make 15,000*l* a-year, and buying upholstery with it'. On the other hand: 'It can be said of him, When he departed he took a Man's life along with him. No sounder piece of British manhood was put together in that eighteenth-century of Time.'

The sense we get today from reading Carlyle in this vein is of a man reeling under the impact of a recent writer's virtual literary apotheosis. Somehow the Romantic movement had ensured that literature *mattered*. If further evidence of this fact is required, it can be found in the remarkable case of the philosopher and economist John Stuart Mill (1806–73) who founded the Utilitarian Society in 1823. Mill's early studies led to a mental crisis in 1826, when he was plunged in despair. His *Autobiography* (1873) tells how he found restoration in the poetry of Wordsworth. He was moved to write an essay, 'What is Poetry?' (1833), where he took as his starting-point Wordsworth's claim that the opposite of poetry is not prose 'but matter of fact, or science'. It speaks to the feelings as opposed to the belief, and it works by moving rather than by convincing. Mill insists that the delight in external incident which a story arouses is a delight especially appropriate to the childhood of the race and of the individual. But the delight aroused by poetry from the representation of feeling is something felt rather by maturer people who are conversant with the states of human sensibility described. Enjoying what Mill calls 'novels in verse' is not test of true poetic sensibility such as is appealed to by 'the delineation of the deeper and more secret workings of human emotion'.

Where the truth of fiction is 'to give a true picture of life', the truth of poetry is 'to paint the human soul truly'. The great poet may be ignorant of life, but he has explored his own nature as a human specimen in whom the 'laws of emotion' are boldly inscribed. The novelist's external knowledge of mankind at large is not indispensable to the poet. But the comprehensive appeal of Shakespeare, for instance, is due to his possession of both the poet's and the novelist's gifts in this respect. Mill insists that descriptive writing is not necessarily poetic. 'The poetry is not in the object itself, nor in the scientific truth itself, but in the state of mind in which the one and the other may be contemplated.' He contrasts the way a naturalist or traveller would describe a lion with the way a poet would convey by imagery what it means to contemplate a lion 'in the state of awe, wonder, or terror'. In seemingly describing the lion, the poet is actually describing the spectator's feelings. Indeed 'if the human emotion be not painted with scrupulous truth, the poetry is ... not poetry at all'. In a celebrated aphorism, Mill distinguished two forms of 'impassioned truth', eloquence and poetry: 'eloquence is *heard*; poetry is *over*heard'. The one presupposes an audience, where the other is the fruit of solitude and meditation in utter unconsciousness of a listener.

Mill pushed his subjectivist theory of poetry to a point at which questions bristle. He took up some of them in a subsequent essay, 'Two Kinds of Poetry', published some months later in the same journal as the first essay (*The Monthly Repository*). It distinguishes the poetry of the poet who has cultivated the poetic mind from the poetry of the naturally poetic mind. The one has something to say and 'his feeling waits upon thought', while the other merely 'pours forth the overflowing of his feelings'. Wordsworth is cited as one for whom 'the poetry is almost always the mere setting of a thought' and is therefore less ebullient, less spontaneous than the poetry of Shelley, whose fancy teems naturally with exuberant imagery. Thus ultimately Mill's emphasis leads him to a curious conclusion. Wordsworth has 'a calm deliberateness' which is not characteristic of the poetic temperament: 'his poetry seems one thing, himself another'. And a man is a poet 'not because he has ideas of any particular kind, but because the succession of his ideas is subordinate to the course of his emotions'.

The inquiry into the nature of poetry was pursued in a series of *Lectures on Poetry* which were delivered by John Keble (1792–1866) as Professor of Poetry at Oxford between 1832 and 1841. Originally published in Latin as *Praelectiones Poeticae* (1844), they were translated into English by E. K. Francis in 1912. J. S. Mill had argued that 'all persons, even the most unimaginative, in moments of strong emotion, speak poetry'. This was too simplistic for Keble. He recognised the element of shame which naturally inhibits people from passionate utterance that might relieve a burden of grief or shock. The tension arising between the need for relief and solace, and the demands of modest reserve, is best resolved by 'those indirect methods best known to poets'. The glorious art of Poetry, then, is 'a kind of medicine divinely bestowed upon man: which gives healing relief to secret mental emotion, yet without detriment to modest reserve: and, while giving scope to enthusiasm, yet rules it with order and due control'.

Theorising more akin to Mill's appeared in an essay in *Blackwood's Magazine* for December, 1835, which has been attributed to Alexander Smith (*d.*1851), Postmaster of Banff. The essay, 'The Philosophy of Poetry', rehearses the distinction between prose, which conveys information, and poetry, in which emotion is directly vented. Poetry is the transmission of feeling rather than of information. Smith goes on to examine the language appropriate to this purpose, in particular its figurative and imaginative character. Here he seems to tread new ground. He examines the vivid expression 'dusty splendour' used by Washington Irving of Westminster Abbey. As information, the expression makes nonsense. '*Splendour* is not a subject of which *dusty* could be an attribute.' The expression is one 'not of truth *perceived*, but of an association that is *felt*'. In examining specific imagery of this kind Smith seems to anticipate investigations into the nature and function of metaphor which were to be undertaken in our own century.

This interest in the nature of metaphor received a new impetus when John Ruskin (1819–1900) turned aside in volume III, Part IV (1856) of *Modern Painters* from a discussion of current metaphysical controversy about the use of the terms 'objective' and 'subjective' in reference to the colours and qualities of things, and tackled the subject of poetic diction. Ruskin shared Carlyle's horror of the damaging effects of Victorian materialism. It led him into demands for social reform. It also led him to concern with the relationship between art and morality, and to dissatisfaction with purely aesthetic ideals.

In investigating the difference between the 'true appearance of things to us, and the extraordinary, or false appearances, when we are under the influence of emotion, or contemplative fancy', Ruskin coined the expression 'pathetic fallacy' to define what poets do when they attribute human characteristics to other objects. He quotes from Kingsley's *Alton Locke*:

> They rowed her in across the rolling foam –
> The cruel, crawling foam.

The foam is not cruel and does not crawl. 'The state of mind which attributes to it these characters of a living creature is one in which the reason is unhinged by grief.' Ruskin also quotes from Coleridge's 'Christabel':

> The one red leaf, the last of its clan,
> That dances as often as dance it can,

and complains that Coleridge nourishes a 'false idea about the leaf'. He 'fancies a life in it, and will'; he 'confuses its powerlessness with choice, its fading death with merriment, and the wind that shakes it with music'. Ruskin argues that the greatest poets have rarely misrepresented nature. Yet he accepts that such misrepresentations can be beautiful. Indeed they can be condoned when they are in harmony with the *feeling* of the context. He cites an instance from Pope's Homer in which Ulysses greets with surprise the shade of his youngest follower, Elpenor, who fell to his death from an upper room in Circe's palace.

> How could thy soul, by realms and seas disjoined,
> Outfly the nimble sail, and leave the lagging wind?

The references to the nimbleness of the sail and the laziness of the wind are totally inappropriate to Ulysses's mood and situation. Ulysses is curious; he urgently wants to learn the facts; he is certainly in no mood to toy with pretty images. The conceits jar discordantly. 'Coleridge's fallacy has no discord in it, but Pope's has set our teeth on edge.' Ruskin was particularly hard on the manufacture of figures of speech as a contrived poetic currency. His concern was with 'truth'. In so far as the attribution of human feelings to other objects was false it was questionable. In so far as the attribution involved feelings inappropriate to the given context it was doubly questionable.

Ruskin's love of 'truth' stopped short of approving the realism of George Eliot. In a series of articles in *The Nineteenth Century* in 1880–1, called 'Fiction, Fair and Foul', he poured withering vituperation on the 'railway novel' which presents the vilest characters with all their blotches and pimples.

> *The Mill on the Floss* is perhaps the most striking instance extant of this study of cutaneous disease. There is not a single person in the book of the smallest importance to anybody in the world but themselves...

The book is a waste of printer's ink on 'the sweepings out of a Pentonville omnibus'. The 'English Cockney school' is consummated in George Eliot, in whose work 'the personages are picked up from behind the counter and out of the gutter'.

Ruskin's peculiar passion for 'truth' emerges in scattered comments about the work of Dickens. There is ambiguity of response largely due to Ruskin's worries about the element of caricature. He thought the technique of exaggeration detracted from Dickens's usefulness as a social propagandist, because it turned material into entertainment which might have been educative. He pressed this point in a footnote to *Unto this Last* (1860). Dickens's caricature is gross but, 'allowing for his manner of telling them, the things he tells us are always true'. The fact that Mr Bounderby in *Hard*

Times is 'a dramatic monster' and Stephen Blackpool 'a dramatic perfection' instead of justly representing their prototypes, dilutes the book's message.

II Matthew Arnold

We shall have to return to the debate about the alleged falsity of Dickensian caricature. It is one theme in the running commentary on contemporary literature which was sustained in periodical reviewing throughout the century and which engaged several lively-minded critics. But the very greatest critics have always judged the output of their own age against a wider background of cultural history and literary tradition. Matthew Arnold (1822–88) stands apart from and above all other Victorian critics in this respect. Like Carlyle and Ruskin, he was a harsh critic of contemporary materialism and philistinism. The son of Thomas Arnold, the great headmaster of Rugby who reformed the public school ethos, he inherited his father's moral fervour without his firm religious conviction as a Protestant Anglican. Arnold's critical output was, much of it, published in journals in the form of essays, before being collected into volumes. Crucial volumes include *Essays in Criticism* (1865 and 1888), *Culture and Anarchy* (1869), and *Literature and Dogma* (1863).

An early exposure of his critical stance is found in the 'Preface' to *Poems* (1853), a book which gathered together material from two volumes he had published anonymously in 1849 and 1852. The new collection omitted his 'Empedocles on Etna', the dramatic poem in which the Greek philosopher Empedocles, disillusioned of the hope that peace and joy and understanding can ever be found to appease man's desperate longings, hurls himself into the crater of Etna. The 'Preface' carefully explains its omission. A poetical work requires for its justification, firstly, that it should be an 'accurate and therefore interesting representation', and secondly, that enjoyment can be derived from it. Tragic circumstances can be so represented as to be enjoyable, but not circumstances 'in which the suffering finds no vent in action'.

Prolonged mental distress unrelieved by hope and unresolv-
able in action cannot be a proper subject for poetry.

Arnold goes on in his 'Preface' to dispute a current critical
view that subjects from the far past should be superseded in
poetry by material 'of present import'. The 'eternal objects of
poetry' are human actions having an inherent interest. It is a
fallacy to believe that the poet, by his treatment of a subject,
can compensate for lack of such interest. The Greeks understood this. The modern heresy, by which the expression
predominates over the action, lays an emphasis on separate
parts which ought to be laid on the whole. Critics concentrate attention on 'detached expressions', on the 'language
about the action' and not the action itself. Moreover the false
ideal recommended is 'a true allegory of the state of one's
own mind in a representative history'. No great poetical
work could ever be produced on that principle. Arnold is
especially interesting on doubtful aspects of Shakespeare's
influence. Shakespeare had all that Arnold recommends in
the way of knowing what constitutes a poetical action and
having supreme powers of creation and construction. With
these gifts he combined an abundance of thought and
imagery; and it is these 'attractive accessories of a practical
work', rather than his fundamental gifts, that have mesmer-
ised would-be imitators, to the neglect of his more basic
qualities. Indeed, in Arnold's eyes, Shakespeare's gift of
expression is something which sometimes 'leads him astray',
making it impossible for him to say a thing plainly. On the
same basis Arnold finds Keats's 'Isabella' 'a perfect treasure-
house of graceful and felicitous words and images', yet so
feeble and loosely constructed in its action that the total
effect is nil.

Arnold's views represented a reaction against much that
the Romantics had stood for. In 'The Function of Criticism
at the Present Time' he asserted the value of the critical
function in relation to the creative. He argued that for the
proper functioning of the creative genius there were two
necessities; the genius itself, and the conditions under which
it could flourish. The creative power works with *ideas*, and
appropriate ideas must be current if the creative power is to
work fruitfully. The intellectual atmosphere is not within the

control of the creative power but of the critical power, whose function is 'in all branches of knowledge ... to see the object as in itself it really is'. Arnold argues that the Romantic movement in England was premature because the poets 'did not know enough'. This made 'Byron so empty of matter' and 'Shelley so incoherent'. Even Wordsworth, profound as he was, would have been greater still had he read more books. Not that books are what conduce to 'a current of ideas' that animates and nourishes the creative power in an environment such as Shakespeare's England, for instance. But reading can enable the environment to be mentally constructed when it is lacking. The England of the Romantics had neither the 'national glow of life and thought' that the Elizabethans enjoyed, nor yet 'a culture and a force of learning and criticism' such as the Germans had and Goethe benefited from. The French Revolution may have been 'the greatest, the most animating event in history', but though basically inspired by enthusiasm for reason, it was transformed into a practical political programme, and the English are all too prone to treat all fine ideas like that. Yet real criticism is essentially the exercise of a *disinterested* curiosity which 'seeks to know the best that is known and thought in the world, irrespectively of practice, politics, and everything of the kind'.

Arnold, however, holds out hope that the 'epoch of concentration' that has followed the French Revolution may now bring in an 'epoch of expansion', for the crude pursuit of material progress may possibly lead to 'an apparition of intellectual life'. In short, when man has finally made himself perfectly comfortable and is wondering what to do next, he 'may begin to remember that he has a mind'. This would leave room for the critical activity which is essentially *disinterested* – aloof from the practical view of things. At present criticism in England is stifled by the subservience of the organs of criticism to ulterior practical ends. Arnold insists finally that the English critic needs to dwell much on foreign thought, for current English literature cannot be said to contribute much to 'the best that is known and thought in the world'. The criticism now needed must regard 'Europe as being, for intellectual and spiritual purposes, one great confederation'.

A most forthright declaration of Arnold's position is given in the essay 'Sweetness and Light' which became the first chapter of his book *Culture and Anarchy* (1869). While healthy curiosity is regarded as a just intellectual motive for the pursuit of culture, there is also a moral motive in that the pursuit has its origin in the 'love of perfection'. The 'scientific passion for pure knowledge' is accompanied by 'the moral and social passion for doing good'. We seem to hear Arnold arguing with his father as he proclaims that the latter passion, without the former, tends to be 'overhasty in determining what reason and the will of God say', for it is predisposed to action rather than thought. But the latter passion is essential. For culture is not only an endeavour to see and learn what the will of God is, but also the endeavour 'to make it *prevail*'. This is what justifies culture morally and socially.

For Arnold seeing and learning 'what the will of God is' is synonymous with acquiring a 'knowledge of the universal order which seems to be intended and aimed at in the world'. And thus religion and culture have a common aim. Both religion and culture place human perfection 'in an *internal* condition' (The kingdom of God is within you), in the growth and predominance of our humanity over our animality. Yet contemporary thinking in England is hostile to the ideals of culture: 'The idea of perfection as a *general* expansion of the human family is at variance with our strong individualism ... our maxim of "every man for himself".' And finally the 'ideal of perfection as a *harmonious* expansion of human nature is at variance with our want of *flexibility*'. Thus Arnold attacks the current reliance upon machinery as an end in itself. He ridicules the boast that every man in England 'can say what he likes' when it is made irrespectively of whether what is said is worth saying. He mocks a current claim that our coal is 'the real basis of our national greatness', for its fallacious notion of 'greatness' – which in truth is 'a spiritual condition worthy to excite love, interest, and admiration'. The greatness of a country cannot be measured by its wealth. And culture provides the only brake on contemporary worship of wealth. In Arnold's eyes not only railways and wealth, but also 'freedom', 'population', 'bodily health and vigour' become mere 'machinery' if they are disjointed from any idea of the spiritual. The cultivation of physical well-being must be subordinate to higher ends. The perfection sought by culture can be summed up in the felicitous words of Swift in *The Battle of the Books*, 'the two noblest of things, *sweetness and light*'.

Arnold cites the Greek fusion of aesthetic and moral ideals, the blend of poetry with religion, in order to show up the inadequacy of the current English ideal of perfection. It is unsatisfactory merely to brace the moral fibre if there is no ideal of beauty and harmony too. In this respect English Protestantism has distorted our ideals. Poets and men of culture may have failed morally, and puritans may have succeeded morally, but the former have cultivated a true ideal of perfection, 'sweetness and light, and a human culture complete on all its sides', where the latter have had a 'narrow and inadequate' ideal of perfection. How, Arnold asks with some heat, can the contemporary organised religion of English Protestantism ever bring humanity to its true goal? The ideal its practice represents is 'so unlovely, so unattractive, so incomplete'. If our religious organisations are to be judged by their results, then consider the 'unutterable external hideousness' of our capital city, London, its internal canker of public need and private opulence, its weightiest vocal organ the *Daily Telegraph*! It is the failure of religion, in Arnold's eyes, that leaves culture as the only remedy against philistinism. In so far as the great movement towards industrial wealth demands a concentration on laying sound foundations for future material well-being, it demands a consequent sacrifice of passing generations to this end.

A century later Arnold's claims ring ironically in the ear. For he differentiates all attempts to indoctrinate the masses by popular literature, by religious and political organisations, from the true aim of culture, which does not 'try to reach down' to win people with 'ready-made judgments and watchwords', but 'seeks to do away with classes; to make the best that has been thought and known in the world current everywhere; to make all men live in an atmosphere of sweetness and light'.

Arnold came to the conclusion that, as the dogmatic foundations of religion were shaken and received traditions were threatened with dissolution, poetry provided the only sure bulwark of confidence: 'More and more mankind will discover that we have to turn to poetry to interpret life for us, to console us, to sustain us.' ('The Study of Poetry', 1880). The current concerns of religion and philosophy, by comparison with what poetry has to offer, are 'but the shadows and dreams and false shows of knowledge'. By contrast Arnold finds in poetry a sphere where the distinction between what is excellent and inferior, sound and unsound, true and untrue or only half-true, can be maintained against the charlatanism which invades so much practical life. For poetry is 'a criticism of life under the conditions fixed for such a criticism by the laws of poetic truth and poetic beauty'. In this respect we must be wary lest our sense for the best in poetry is superseded by one of two fallacious estimates: the estimate which overvalues a poem because of its adventitious historic significance, and the estimate which overvalues a poem because of an adventitious personal predilection. Perhaps no influence that Arnold exerted was healthier than what G. K. Chesterton called his emphasis on the 'purely intellectual importance of humility' in the determination to see things as they really are and get the self 'out of the way'. When he comes to define 'the best' in poetry, he insists that the great masters provide the only touchstone, and falls back on quotation of lines possessing 'the very highest poetical quality'.

> If we are thoroughly penetrated by their power, we shall find that we have acquired a sense enabling us, whatever poetry may be laid before us, to feel the degree in which a high poetical quality is present or wanting there.

The best will have a 'superior character of truth and seriousness in the matter and substance' combined with 'superiority of diction and movement'.

Arnold's tastes are, of course, more fully spelt out in his judgments on individual poets. Milton best meets our need in England of 'the discipline of respect for a high and flawless excellence'. In the 'sure and flawless perfection of his rhythm and diction' he is in the same class as Virgil and Dante.

274 A HISTORY OF LITERARY CRITICISM

Where Shakespeare can fall into 'fantastic and false diction', Milton never lapses. He can be recommended as a substitute for the classics of Greece and Rome for the millions ignorant of Greek and Latin. Indeed, 'All the Anglo-Saxon contagion, all the flood of Anglo-Saxon commonness, beats vainly against the great style but cannot shake it, and has to accept its triumph.'

Writing on Keats, Arnold used him as a means of distinguishing the two great modes of interpretation at the disposal of poetry. There is the 'faculty of naturalistic interpretation': and here Keats has a felicity of expression and a 'perfection of loveliness' that matches Shakespeare's. But he lacks the 'faculty of moral interpretation', the power over the *architectonics* of poetry which is necessary to the production of great works like *King Lear* and the *Agamemnon*. Of the Romantics, it is Wordsworth who most excites Arnold's enthusiasm, but it is a warily modified enthusiasm. He quotes Voltaire's view that English poetry is distinguished by 'the energetic and profound treatment of moral ideas'. Because poetry is 'at bottom a criticism of life' the greatness of a poet 'lies in his powerful and beautiful application of ideas to life, – to the question: How to live'. Arnold is at pains to point out that he parts company with 'the Wordsworthians' who praise Wordsworth for the wrong things and 'lay far too much stress upon what they call his philosophy'. *The Excursion* abounds with philosophy, and Arnold cites specimen passages which are 'a tissue of elevated but abstract verbiage, alien to the very nature of poetry'. This is not 'poetic truth'. Indeed even the philosophical message of the 'Intimations' Ode lacks 'solidity' and is of doubtful validity.

> Wordsworth's poetry is great because of the extraordinary power with which Wordsworth feels the joy offered to us in Nature, the joy offered to us in the simple primary affections and duties; and because of the extraordinary power with which in case after case, he shows us this joy, and renders it so as to make us share it.

At its best Wordsworth's poetry has the inevitability of Nature herself. 'Nature herself seems, I say, to take the pen out of his hand, and to write for him with her own bare, sheer, penetrating power.'

Arnold's greatness lies partly in his rejection of the biases of the individual and of the age. Criticism must unshackle itself from personal predilection, and it must never truckle to the *Zeitgeist*. Indeed the test of great literature itself lies in the permanence of its acceptability. Arnold distinguishes the 'famous men of genius' in literature from the 'famous men of ability'. The 'criticism which the men of genius pass upon human life is permanently acceptable to mankind; the criticism which the men of ability pass upon human life is transitorily acceptable'.

III Victorian reviewers

One of the more philosophically-minded of Victorian critics and reviewers was George Henry Lewes (1817–79), who contributed thoughtful essays to periodicals such as the *Quarterly*, the *Edinburgh*, and the *Fortnightly* over many years. He was one of those who found Dickens's cartoonery a serious defect in his work. Lewes's long-standing liaison with George Eliot made it possible for champions of Dickens to insinuate that he had an ulterior motive for denigration of Dickens. But Lewes was a consistent critic of 'unnaturalness', not only in fiction but on the stage. For he was a seasoned dramatic critic and in his study *On Actors and the Art of Acting* (1875) he wrote, 'The striving to be effective easily leads into the error of exaggeration,' applying this judgment to actors and authors alike, and he added, as Ruskin might have added, 'Exaggeration is a fault because it is an untruth.'

It was in reviewing volume I of Forster's *Life of Dickens* in the *Fortnightly Review* for February, 1872 that Lewes made his most general assault upon Dickens, and irritated the faithful by presenting his case as a reasoned investigation of a teasing mystery: Why are fastidious critics so loath to admit Dickens's greatness? 'How are we to reconcile this immense popularity with this critical contempt?' To be fair to Lewes, he strains hard to applaud the immense powers that have delighted young and old: the humour, the vividness, the emotional sympathy, the potent imaginative power. But the gifts amount to a kind of wizardry by which his human figures blaze so vividly that 'their falsity' passes unnoticed. It requires critical reflection to detect that Dickens's figures are merely masks – 'not characters, but personified characteristics, caricatures and distortions of human nature'. Dickens exploited the general reader's incapacity for reflection. A child can believe more firmly in his wooden horse than in an accurately pictured horse; 'It may be said of Dickens's human figures that they too are wooden, and run on wheels ...' Lewes keeps reverting to Dickens's astonishing qualities, but it is his strictures which shout out from his paragraphs where praise and condemnation are juxtaposed. They convey the conviction of a man who scarcely trusts his own words of approval:

> He set in motion the secret springs of sympathy by touching the domestic affections. He painted nothing ideal, heroic; but all the resources of the bourgeois epic were in his grasp. The world of thought and passion lay beyond his horizon.

Indeed Lewes affects to tussle with the insoluble mystery that 'an observer so remarkably keen could make observations so remarkably false'. There is a 'pervading commonness' in the works. 'Thought is strangely absent from his works. I do not suppose a single thoughtful remark on life or character could be found throughout the twenty volumes.' There is no sense of the past, no capacity for philosophical generalisation. 'Compared to Fielding or Thackeray, his was merely an *animal* intelligence, *i.e.*, restricted to perceptions.'

By contrast, Lewes praises Thackeray for 'the strong sense of reality pervading his writing'. He is a man of experience who reflects on that experience: 'Life, not the phantasmagoria of the stage and circulating library, is the store house from whence he draws.' Nevertheless Lewes the moralist takes issue with Thackeray for erring against both art and nature in making sincerity and affection the exception rather than the rule in life. In this limited respect, indeed, Dickens is granted the edge on Thackeray. The jester always needs to be watched. 'He throws us off our guard, and storms conviction by enveloping it in laughter.' Even so Thackeray tries to palm off upon us an unworthy scepticism about human nature under cover of humour.

Doubts about the reality of Dickens's created beings became an issue among the critics. In her *Autobiography* (1877), Harriet Martineau (1802–76) took Dickens's failure in this respect for granted. 'While he tells us a world of things that are natural and even true, his personages are generally, as I suppose is undeniable, profoundly unreal.' She had earlier spoken warmly of Dickens's sympathies for the suffering and the frail, praising his powers of observation, his pathos and his humour; but she had reservations about the soundness of Dickens's social philosophy. She wished his 'fervent and inexhaustible' kindliness could have been equally 'well-informed and well-directed'. Years earlier Harriet Martineau had written an article in *Tait's Magazine* (January, 1833) enthusiastically proclaiming Scott as a great moral teacher who had shown what fiction could do 'as an agent of morals and philosophy'. There were lots of areas of experience waiting to be dealt with comparably – the life of the poor, for instance. This, no doubt, was what Harriet Martineau would have liked to have had from Dickens – an embodiment of the truth about the social scene he recorded. But, alas, she found the 'characters, conversations, and incidents' of *Hard Times* totally unlike real life in Lancashire and England, and they deprived the book of practical influence.

Another critic with a distinctive approach to Dickens's social message was Walter Bagehot (1826–77). He and R. H. Hutton (1826–97) became joint editors of the *National Review* in 1855. (It was in an article in this journal in 1864, on the subject of the French thinker, Joseph Joubert, that Matthew Arnold made the distinction we cited above between men of genius and men of ability.) Bagehot's connection with his family's shipping and banking business and his training in law were turned to fruitful account in his study *The English Constitution* (1867) and in his political and economic writings. These interests also emerged sometimes in his literary criticism. Writing on Dickens in the *National Review* in October 1858 – an essay later re-issued in *Literary Studies* (1879) – Bagehot finds a deficiency of reasoning, reflection, and that sagacity which 'gives a unity to all which it touches'. On the other hand Dickens is 'full of acute remarks on petty doings', and he never forgets 'the pecuniary part of life'.

> In most novels money *grows*. You have no idea of the toil, the patience, and the weary anxiety by which men of action provide for the day, and lay up for the future ...

Dickens's characters have definite occupations; they talk about their occupation and 'you cannot separate them from it'. But it is in describing the toiling classes, not the middle classes, that Dickens's delineations are vivified by familiar detail.

In turning to Dickens's social message, Bagehot looks back over the growth of political radicalism between 1825 and 1845. He differentiates Dickens's 'sentimental radicalism' from the philosophical radicalism of the Benthamites and the Manchester 'definite-grievance' radicalism. It was provoked by the harshly unfeeling legislation and administration during the first twenty years of the century. Bagehot argues that Dickens's perfectly justifiable sentimental radicalism, which focused on the need to ameliorate harsh customs and remove dreadful penalties, became eventually something quite improper. He moved from describing 'really removable evils' to describing 'the natural evils and inevitable pains of the present state', implying that they too are removable, but not explaining how.

Bagehot's resistance to what seemed like unnecessary dissemination of discontent emerges again when he writes on Thackeray in the *National Review* for April 1864 (an essay also reprinted in *Literary Studies*). He praises Thackeray for his 'instinctive sympathy with humble persons' such as grooms and footmen. But Thackeray became obsessed with lacerating 'snobs' and 'thought too much of social inequalities'. Bagehot's position is made clear when he distinguished three methods of constituting society. The first is the 'equal system' prevailing in France and the United States 'where everyone is on a level with everyone else'; a democratic system fatal to the development of individual originality and greatness. The second is its opposite, the system of rigid caste-structure and 'irremoveable inequalities' found in the East. The third system is our own, the happy medium between extremes, the system of *'removeable inequalities'*, where all those who are inferior to and worse off than others may in theory at least *hope* to climb.

Bagehot was in minor respects a clear and stimulating thinker. In reviewing Tennyson's *Idylls of the King* in the *National Review* in October 1859, he distinguishes between the coteries of early enthusiasts for a poet's work – the 'Wordsworthians' and the 'Tennysonians' – and the general public which is slower to acclaim it. And he has the shrewdness to suggest that the 'Tennysonians', who were excited by *Maud*, will not be so keen on the *Idylls*. For himself the difference between *Maud* and the *Idylls* is the difference between feverish youth and maturity. For the poet of *Maud* seemed to share the 'irritable confusion of fancy' and the 'diseased moodiness of feeling' attributed to his hero. Nevertheless Bagehot's approval of the *Idylls* is qualified. He believes that the preference for an ancient subject and setting is an easy option because selectivity is permissible in representing the remote past. No doubt in King Arthur's time there were peasants with wives and children who caught measles, but the poet is excused from attending to such matters. The expectations in the traditional imagination will be fully satisfied with the usual recipe of chivalrous fighting and falling in love. And Bagehot is alive to some of the poem's defects:

> The imagination cannot rest with satisfaction either on Guinevere's relation to Arthur or on her relation to Lancelot. In each there is a disagreeable and disenchanting something.

Bagehot returned to Tennyson in a celebrated essay on 'Wordsworth, Tennyson, and Browning; or Pure, Ornate, and Grotesque Art in English Poetry' (*National Review*, November 1864). Wordsworth's style is a nearly perfect specimen of the 'pure' art which does not mutilate its object but 'represents it as fully as possible with the slightest effort which is possible'. The extreme opposite to this is the 'ornate' style which surrounds the typical idea 'with the greatest number of circumstances which it will *bear*'. Tennyson's 'Enoch Arden' is the poem at issue, and Bagehot shows how a simple story is enhanced by a 'rich and splendid composite of imagery and illustration'. The main defect of the ornate style is that 'nothing is described as it is, everything has about it an atmosphere of *something else*'. Where the pure style 'calms by conciseness', the ornate style 'leaves on the mind a mist of beauty'.

> That which is chaste chastens; there is a poised energy – a state of half thrill and half tranquillity – which pure art gives; which no other can give ...

It takes a sensitive critic to write like that. It takes a Victorian critic to complete the sentence as Bagehot completed it:

> a pleasure justified as well as felt; an ennobled satisfaction at what ought to satisfy us and must ennoble us.

Bagehot's fellow co-editor, R. H. Hutton, who in 1861 became joint editor of the *Spectator*, was a critic with strong theological interests who reviewed some of the major works of the age as they came out. He did so with a degree of penetration which gave many of his essays durability. In a full-length study of Tennyson's work to date, 'Tennyson', included in his *Literary Essays* (1888), he explored the combination in Tennyson of a sometimes 'too lavish fancy' and the love of 'measure and order'. In a finely phrased analysis of the lyric 'Break, break, break' he illustrates Tennyson's 'wonderful power of putting Nature under contribution to help him in delineating moods of feeling', so that the ordinary sea-shore landscape becomes a means of finding 'a voice indescribably sweet for the dumb spirit of human loss'. Hutton combs *In Memoriam* for telling instances of Tennyson's use of the magnifying glass on secret feelings, his way of putting 'brooding reverie under a microscope'. Hutton has been called a 'moralistic critic', and indeed he replies cogently in this essay to Swinburne's contention that 'the worth of a poem has properly nothing to do with its moral meaning or design', and that 'the only absolute duty of Art is the duty she owes herself'; but what strikes the reader today is the felicity of Hutton's vocabulary in doing justice to the subtleties and refinements of Tennyson's imagery and expression. And Edmund Gosse tells us that Hutton, 'dazzled' by Swinburne, had invited him to contribute to the *Spectator* in his first year as editor.

When Hutton wrote on 'Mr Dickens's Services to Literature' in the *Spectator* for 17 April 1869, he allowed that Dickens's influence on the whole had been 'healthy and good' and certainly 'profoundly humane', but he insisted that one would look in vain in Dickens for 'the diffusion of a genuine reverence for absolute sincerity and realism'. Dickens is a master of melodrama, and he often falls 'into the most mawkish and unreal sentimentalism'. The 'geniality' which is supposed to be Dickens's great merit is mostly 'vulgar good-humour of temperament – a strong disposition to approve the distribution of punch and plum-pudding, slap men heartily on the back, and kiss pretty women behind doors'. In short his great service lies not in his 'high morality, which is altogether wanting in delicacy of insight, but in the complete harmlessness and purity of the immeasurable humour into which he moulds his enormous stores of acute observation'.

R. H. Hutton was rarely out of his depth, but he seems to have been uncomfortably lost in reviewing Meredith's *Modern Love and Other Poems* in the *Spectator* for May 20 1862. However, he struggled to be fair to Meredith's *Harry Richmond* (*Spectator*, January 20 1872) and to *The Egoist* (*Spectator*, November 1 1879). Clearly he appreciated much that he found in Meredith.

> He makes us think of him a great deal, not by directly introducing himself to us, as Thackeray does, but after the same fashion that we are led to think of Carlyle while reading his *French Revolution*. In fact, Mr Meredith often calls up an image of a handsome, witty, juvenile cousin of Carlyle, in eighteenth-century costume, with neat, powdered wig, lace ruffles, knee-breeches, and silk-stockings, of keen and curious vision, but too courteous to be profound or stirring, who regards the

world as a foolish piece of protoplasm, chiefly valuable as stuff out of which to cut epigrams and apt similes.

Of George Eliot, Hutton was deeply appreciative from the start. He acclaimed *Silas Marner* in superlatives in the *Economist* for April 27 1861. His perception of the underlying philosophical dimensions of George Eliot's work and the significance of the moral patterns she wove into the fabric of her plots was balanced by an acute awareness of her psychological insight. His enthusiasm led him to overpraise *Romola*, but he was not insensitive to George Eliot's defects. While praising the 'overflowing affluence of lively and striking detail' in *Felix Holt* (*Spectator*, June 23 1866) he put his finger on the fact that Felix Holt's struggle between political and moral radicalism 'is almost past away before the story opens'. 'Felix Holt seems a grand *stump* of a character in an impressive but fixed attitude.'

When *Middlemarch* was published in separate instalments in 1871–2 Hutton reviewed the successive books as they came out. Considering the difficulty of passing judgment on a book section by section without knowledge of what is to follow, Hutton's critical running commentary is continuously perceptive. Where he pinpoints weaknesses or qualities, they are weaknesses and qualities which subsequent criticism has recognised. He is doubtful about the likelihood of a Dorothea's being swept into marriage by a Casaubon. And he pounces on a central defect in the connection between the supposed thesis and what actually happens. Rosamond Vincy is 'too unique' to represent a serious contribution to the "woman" question. 'It is her disguised selfishness, not her ignorance, which ruins Lydgate's life.' Had Rosamond been just as totally out of touch as she is with Lydgate's intellectual aims, and 'yet been what Lydgate thought her, a tender, devoted woman, his life would not have been wrecked as it is'. *Middlemarch* so stupendously achieved the aim of registering provincial life in authentic detail that controversies proper to real life were provoked by its engineered love-affairs and marriages, and where so much is put in, the character of what is left out becomes prominent. Awkward lacunae are created by inadequate specification of the struggle between human freedom and human destiny, human will and human temperament. Hutton defines one aspect of this in his own theological idiom. In the case of the supposedly religious characters, Dorothea and Caleb Garth, the 'province chosen for the religious temperament is solely the discharge of moral duty, and the side of these minds turned towards the divine centre of life, is conspicuous only by its absence'.

George Eliot's portraits of the pedant Casaubon and his fervent young wife Dorothea were said to have been based on Mark Pattison (1813–84) and his wife. Pattison, a graduate of Oriel College, Oxford, was in his early manhood associated with Pusey and Newman as a keen Tractarian, but later lost his faith. He became a fellow of Lincoln College, Oxford, and was deeply soured when, in spite of his outstanding fitness for the post, he was not made Rector of the college in 1851. Jealous intrigue lay behind this decision, but Pattison was in fact elected to the rectorship when it became vacant again ten years later. This was the year, 1861, in which Pattison married Emilia Frances Strong. She was 21 while he was 48, and the way the two of them consorted might well have given George Eliot her cue for the marital situation between Casaubon and Dorothea. Pattison's interest to us here is as a critic, if a minor one, who worked on a massive study of European learning based on the life of Scaliger, and never finished it. He did complete his masterwork *Isaac Casaubon* (1875), a study of the Swiss scholar (1559–1614), a classicist and theologian who moved to Paris, then to England to become a canon of Canterbury under the patronage of James I. Pattison's work as a critic included a life of Milton in the *English Men of Letters* series, contributions to the *Encyclopaedia Britannica* (ninth edition), and articles in the *Quarterly* and other reviews. It is intelligent without being distinctive. Passing judgment on Meredith's poetry provided perhaps as good a test of a contemporary's alertness as any other commission, and here he seems to have the edge on R. H. Hutton. Reviewing *Poems and Lyrics of the Joy of Earth* (1883) in the *Academy* for July 21 1883, he recognised that Meredith's obscurities arose from a better motive than that of making 'platitudes into verbal puzzles', but protested against the profusion of stop-gap compounds such as 'poppy-droop', 'swan-wave', 'shore-bubble', 'dew-delighted' and the like. He insisted, however, that Meredith was 'a poet in prose'. And, by the way, he voiced a view of Wordsworth that was becoming commonplace, that 'all that is instinct with vital power in Wordsworth might be contained in a volume of much less compass than Matthew Arnold's *Selections*'. Indeed 'we may strike out everything written after 1809'.

It seems an ironic fate for a critic to go down to posterity in literary circles as the model for satiric fictional portraiture. In this respect a fellow-victim, Leslie Stephen (1832–1904) fared better than Pattison when Meredith portrayed him in *The Egoist* (1879) as Vernon Whitford ('Phoebus Apollo turned fasting friar'), the serious scholar and polemicist whom Sir Willoughby Patterne keeps in dependence. Stephen was to be fictionalised again in a later generation by his daughter Virginia Woolf as Mr Ramsay in *To the Lighthouse* (1927). He progressed from early Evangelicalism to agnosticism. He contributed to the *Saturday Review* (founded 1855) and *Fraser's Magazine* (founded 1830), and in 1871 became editor of the *Cornhill Magazine*. The *Cornhill*, which was started in 1860 and of which Thackeray was the first editor, published poems and serialised novels, and indeed Matthew Arnold had written substantial critical essays for it in its early days.

In the *Cornhill* for September 1871, Stephen wrote 'Some Words About Walter Scott', one of the essays which were later re-issued in his collections, *Hours in a Library* (1874; 1876; 1879). It is characteristic of Stephen in trying to track down the larger movements of taste from generation to generation. He tackles the question raised by the contemporary complaint that Scott is 'dull' and the Waverley Novels are passé. It is likewise characteristic of Stephen that he should build the first part of his answer around Carlyle's analysis of Scott's personal and literary qualities. He deals cogently with the charges that Scott had no gospel to deliver and wrote for cash, observing that both charges could apply equally to Shakespeare. He replies to the charge of over-hasty composition, noting that there had been long years of gestation before Scott began to harvest his produce in the

Waverley Novels at the age of 43. But beyond this Stephen's thinking is uninspired. We hear the usual complaints about mediaeval upholstery, 'wooden' heroes, lack of passion, and the usual concessions in favour of vividly portrayed Covenanters and countrymen. For the rest, though fine things are said about Scott's 'sound healthy love of wild scenery', the contrast now seems to be too sharply drawn between the qualities of the sturdy dalesmen, the indomitable puritans, and the open-air delight in scenery on the one hand, and on the other hand, the 'romantic nonsense', the 'exploded feudalism', and the 'faded romance'. Stephen seems to be fixing the sign-posts for the misjudgment and underestimate of Scott that was to obtain for sixty or seventy years to come.

It is perhaps unwise to look for ruthless objectivity in Stephen's pieces on 'The Writings of W. M. Thackeray' (1878–9), for Stephen's first wife was Thackeray's younger daughter, but it provides another instance of Stephen's determination to place a writer in his literary context in a way that only a critic well-read in previous literature could adopt. The same determination is evident in his treatment of George Eliot. He wrote an article for the *Cornhill* (February 1881) shortly after her death in 1880. Full of praise as it is for George Eliot's status, it is wrong-headed enough to underestimate *Middlemarch* as representing declining powers. The modern reader may well feel that if Meredith's poetry provided a sound gauge for measuring a critic's poetic insight, then *Middlemarch* provided a comparable touchstone of taste in the world of prose fiction. In this respect Stephen seemed not to mature with the years. When he wrote his study *George Eliot* (1901) for the *English Men of Letters* series, he was still arguing that the 'immediate success of *Middlemarch* may have been proportioned rather to the author's reputation than to its intrinsic merits'. He complains that the book 'is prompted by a sympathy for the enthusiast, but turns out virtually to be a satire upon the modern world'.

By this time, however, Stephen is looking back to *Adam Bede* (1858) as the book which put George Eliot in the first rank of the new 'Victorian' novelists. He casts his eyes over what was happening in the late 1840s and the 1850s with publications appearing from Thackeray, Dickens, Charlotte Brontë, Trollope, Mrs Gaskell, Charles Reade, George Meredith, Charles Kingsley and Bulwer Lytton, and he considers the temper of the time.

> The generation which had been in its ardent youth during the Reform of 1832 believed in progress and expected the millennium rather too confidently. It liked plain commonsense. Scott's romanticism and Byron's sentimentalism represented obsolete phrases of feeling, and suggested only burlesque or ridicule. The novelists were occupied in constructing a most elaborate panorama of the manners and customs of their own times with a minuteness and psychological analysis not known to their predecessors. Their work is, of course, an implicit 'criticism of life'.

IV Laughter and glory

Oddly enough, if early recognition of Meredith's quality is taken as some sort of critical touchstone, then a man who shows up quite well is Charles Kingsley (1819–75). Reviewing a group of new poets in *Fraser's Magazine* in 1851, three years after his own novel *Yeast* had been serialised there, Kingsley gave a warm welcome to Meredith's *Poems* (1851).

> It is something to have written already some of the most delicious little love-poems which we have seen born in England in the last few years, reminding us by their richness and quaintness of tone of Herrick; yet with a depth of thought and feeling which Herrick never reached.

Kingsley concedes that the poems are often 'over-loaded', even 'clumsy', and wishes that Meredith 'had been thinking now and then of Moore instead of Keats', but recognises that the poems have 'evidently not been put together, but have grown of themselves'. His advice to Meredith is that he should visit the National Gallery and see how Correggio can indulge 'exquisite lusciousness of form, colour, and chiaroscuro, without his pictures ever becoming tawdry or over-wrought', because he so carefully preserves unity and 'harmonious gradation of parts'.

George Meredith (1828–1909) himself entered the critical arena when in February 1877 he delivered a lecture 'On the Idea of Comedy and the Uses of the Comic Spirit' at the London Institution. Meredith was then at the peak of his powers. His novel *The Egoist* was to be published two years later. The lecture itself was first published as *An Essay on Comedy* in 1897. It is a stimulating exercise, remarkable for the sheer concentration of the exposition and the energy of the thinking behind it. And the whole is given a special piquancy by the fact that it is itself something of an exercise in the comic. Meredith's definitions can certainly be pensively weighed, but sometimes they roll off the tongue with the aphoristic glitter of a sustained leg-pull. For Meredith, the true comic spirit is intellectual rather than sentimental. Comedy has a corrective purpose revealing what is offensive to reason, but does so without the element of ridicule that provokes resentment. Fielding, Goldsmith, Jane Austen, and Galt are cited as 'delightful Comic writers'. Capacity for Comic perception can be measured by how far ridicule can be given or taken without any diminution of love. Satire lays about people with a rod to make them writhe and shriek. Irony stings under a semi-caress. Humour laughs all round its object, tumbles him, rolls him about, smacks him and drops a tear of fellow-feeling on him. The Comic is the governing spirit behind all this, but differs from satire 'in not sharply driving into the quivering sensibilities, and from humour in not comforting them and tucking them up'.

> Byron had splendid powers of humour, and the most poetic satire that we have example of, fusing at times to hard irony. He had no strong comic sense, or he would not have taken an anti-social position, which is directly opposed to the Comic; and in his philosophy, judged by philosophers, he is a comic figure by reason of his deficiency.

The Comic poet requires a 'society of cultivated men and women ... wherein ideas are correct, and the perceptions quick'. He must exercise subtlety. 'People are ready to surrender themselves to witty thumps on the back, breast, and sides; all except that head: and it is there that he aims.' The great humourist embraces 'contrasts beyond the scope of the Comic poet'. Cervantes was master of both. 'The juxta-position of the knight and the squire is a Comic conception, the opposition of their natures most humorous.' The contrasts between high aim and futile mishap, chivalrous valour and absurdity, the mingling of compassion with ridicule, of good sense with craziness, represent 'the loftiest moods of humour, fusing the Tragic sentiment with the Comic narrative'. For humourists the feelings are primary, and they can, like Sterne, turn sentimental. But Comedy is 'an interpretation of the general mind, and is for that reason of necessity kept in restraint'.

> The laughter of satire is a blow in the back or the face. The laughter of Comedy is impersonal and of unrivalled politeness, nearer a smile and often no more than a smile. It laughs through the mind, for the mind directs it; and it might be called the humour of the mind.

In Meredith's eyes, an excellent test of a country's civilisation is 'the flourishing of the Comic idea and Comedy', while the test of true Comedy 'is that it shall awaken thoughtful laughter'. His lecture neatly passes the test.

Criticism from an artist, such as Meredith's, is thrown off in the sheer high spirits of creativity taking a busman's holiday. It is very different from the criticism of an artist such as Wordsworth who took up the critical pen to justify his own practice. So doing, Wordsworth coined a few phrases which enriched the verbal currency of criticism. What is innovative may call for explanatory comment from the innovator. The poet Gerard Manley Hopkins (1844–89), in explaining his own innovations in various letters and notes, added to the concepts and terminology of criticism. His experiments with metre led him to formulate the distinction between traditional 'Running Rhythm' and what he called 'Sprung Rhythm'. In Sprung Rhythm there is one stressed syllable in each foot, but the foot may contain anything from one to four syllables, for the number of 'slack' or unstressed syllables is variable and may even on occasions exceed three. Thus the system allows for two stressed syllables in succes-sion, or two stressed syllables may be separated by one, two, or three unaccented ones. It also permits the scansion to be carried over from one line to the next. Unaccented syllables at the end of a line may be 'compensated for' at the beginning of the next line. In short, the system allows for scansion by stanza rather than by individual lines. Hopkins argued that the limits of flexibility in traditional Running Rhythm were reached when, say, feet were inverted in blank verse, trochees being imposed on what is basically an iambic pattern. (Thus the first foot of the five breaks the sequence of iambs in 'England,/ with all/ thy faults,/ I love/ thee still'.) The 'mounting' of a new rhythm on a different base produces the effect of 'counterpoint' in that the ear takes in the imposed rhythm while the mind naturally supplies the base which it temporarily overlays. Hopkins avers that Milton is the great master of Counterpoint Rhythm. It is notably exploited in the choruses of *Samson Agonistes*. Sprung rhythm does not allow of counterpoint, and does not need it, for its flexibility is basic. Hopkins argues that it is the rhythm of common speech and of written prose, and in so doing gives a handle to those who would regard his theory as an attempt to provide a system for scanning the unscannable.

The other terms which Hopkins added to critical vocabulary derive from his theological position and his way of reading God's world. In a letter to Robert Bridges he wrote 'as air, melody, is what strikes us most of all in music and design in painting, so design, pattern or what I am in the habit of calling "inscape" is what I above all aim at in poetry'. As a picture that makes a single whole thing out of a stretch of country is called a 'landscape', so the distinctive individual structure of a thing, revealed through the senses in a moment of illumination is its 'inscape'. There is a force which preserves inscape, enabling a thing to cohere in its individualness, and this is 'instress'. Instress both makes a thing what it is and gives it its power to affect the beholder. In this respect Hopkins's thinking derives from the philosopher Duns Scotus (c.1266–1308) who developed a theory of 'individuation'. He superimposed on the scholastic distinction between 'matter' and 'form' a third principle, *haecceitas* or 'thisness', the individuality of a thing. Hopkins seized on this notion of what gives its special individual unity of being to a thing. In grasping what he considered to be the essence of its nature, he referred to its 'inscape', thereby pinning down mentally the unified pattern of its attributes. The energy which holds the inscape together in being is the 'instress'. This same energy carries its wholeness into the grasp of the observer. The uniqueness of any perceived object or scene, its distinctive character, is given to it by God, and reveals some fractional aspect of his perfection. The divine instress turns creation into a chorus of voices at once revealing and glorifying God.

V Aestheticism

A new direction was given to Victorian thinking by Walter Horatio Pater (1839–94). He had come into contact with John Keble while still a schoolboy, and had decided to become a priest and a poet. His tractarian piety gave way to scepticism when he went up to Queen's College, Oxford, but the experience of the Oxford Movement left its mark on him in his alertness to the sensuous aspects of worship and ritual. He made his novel position clear in the Preface to his *Studies in the History of the Renaissance* (1873). It is basically a revolt against any recognition of absolutes. Beauty must be defined, not in the abstract, but through its concrete manifestations. Arnold's dictum that the aim of true criticism is 'to see the object as in itself it really is' is commended, and then turned upside down. In Pater's eyes seeing the object as in itself it really is can only mean knowing 'one's own impression as it really is'. The impressions made by works of art on the experiencing subject are the primary data for aesthetic criticism. In this respect songs, pictures, personalities and natural objects are all forces which can produce pleasurable sensations. To discriminate and analyse them, each in its own peculiar or unique kind, is the business of the aesthetic critic, and moral or metaphysical questions are of no concern to him. Pinning down the 'virtue' by which the object produces the 'special impression of beauty or pleasure' is the critic's task, and for this the necessary qualification is a 'certain kind of temperament, the power of being deeply moved by the presence of beautiful objects'.

Pater pursues his argument in the 'Conclusion' to the book. The location of significance in the impressions of outer things that strike the individual isolates him, 'each mind keeping as a solitary prisoner its own dream of a world'. But at every moment some beauty of a person or a scene, some emotional or intellectual excitement, is realised. The moment of such realisation is an end in itself.

> To burn always with this hard gem-like flame, to maintain this ecstasy, is success in life. Failure is to form habits; for habit is relative to a stereotyped world.

Making the most of the intense moments in the face of life's 'awful brevity' will leave no time for fashioning 'theories about the things we see and touch'. There can be no justifiable claim to sacrifice any part of this pleasurable experience to 'abstract morality' that is only conventional.

Pater's argument and his very vocabulary set him in sharp opposition to the high priests of Victorian moralism. There is no mention of truth. The Arnoldian sense of a great continuing tradition of the best that has been thought and said, which can shed its illumination and nourish the good life, gives way to a picture of a world in flux in which the individual can but snatch at fleeting impressions thrown off by a flickering, unstable, disintegrating environment. Making direct sensation the only mode of critical awareness devalues the traditional objective criteria of historical criticism. Ultimately there seems to be no place left for evaluating works of art except in terms of what is subjective. Indeed in an article on 'Coleridge's Writings' published in the *Westminster Review* in 1866, Pater sees Coleridge as one whose literary career was marred by his restless pursuit of the absolute and his rejection of that relativism on which the growing life of the mind depends. As Pater sees it, Coleridge's was a more intellectual talent than Wordsworth's, and some kind of dramatic poetry with a proportionate intellectual content might have given him a path to artistic success. 'But in order to follow that path one must hold ideas loosely in a relative spirit', for none of the modes of the inward life must be stereotyped. Ideas must be devoted to the service of art.

Pater wrote an appreciative essay on 'Wordsworth' in the *Fortnightly Review* for April 1874 (reprinted in *Appreciations*, 1889). The poet's function is not that of the moralist and his first aim is 'to give the reader a peculiar kind of pleasure'. Nevertheless, the pleasure becomes the means of conveying an 'extraordinary wisdom' – and one lesson above all, 'the supreme importance of contemplation in the conduct of life'. Most people are preoccupied with pursuing unattainable ends, often by the wrong means, and saddening themselves in the frustrating process. 'Contemplation – impassioned contemplation – that is, with Wordsworth, the end-in-itself, the perfect end.' For most of us, thinking in terms of ends and means reduces life to machinery, and Wordsworth's poetry, like all great art, represents a protest against this habit. It would rather justify the end by the means.

> That the end of life is not action but contemplation – *being* as distinct from *doing* – a certain disposition of the mind: is, in some shape or other, the principle of all higher morality.

Pater's doctrine, for all its relativism, had about it a sense of the need for a kind of discipline – even if only a discipline of pleasure – which was to be totally lost as the 'art for art's sake' movement degenerated in the postures of many who claimed to be his disciples. In his novel *Marius the Epicurean* (1885), the hero's religious idealism eventually leads him to sacrifice his life to save a Christian friend. But the martyrdom is the culminating experience of one drawn to Christianity for satisfaction of a cultural need. The spiritual concerns central to valid Christian self-surrender are scarcely at issue. Pater had argued that ideas must be devoted to the service of art, and Christianity is one more 'idea'. It is subsumed into the artistic pattern. This in itself seems to constitute a 'point' made about life.

An early admirer of Pater's work was the poet Algernon Charles Swinburne (1837-1909). When he told Pater as much, Pater returned the compliment. His first papers in the *Fortnightly* owed their inspiration to Swinburne's work in the same line. But there is nothing in Swinburne to compare with Pater's blueprint for a new aesthetic. Swinburne was not a critical theorist. He was an enthusiastic reader whose enthusiasm flowed over into appreciative commentary on what he read. T. S. Eliot observed that 'the notes upon poets by a poet of Swinburne's dimension must be read with attention and respect'.[1] His historical importance is that he helped to form opinion on the writers of his own century and did much to revive interest in Elizabethan and Jacobean drama. He was quick to write in defence of Meredith's *Modern Love* (1862) against R. H. Hutton's dismissive review in the *Spectator*. His affinities with Pater emerge in the way he refutes Hutton's charge that Meredith has dealt with a painful subject on which he has no convictions to express.

> There are pulpits enough for all preachers in prose; the business of verse-writing is hardly to express convictions ... and if some poetry, not without merit of its kind, has at times dealt in dogmatic morality, it is all the worse and all the weaker for that.

In an essay on 'Heinrich Heine' in the *Cornhill* (August 1863) Matthew Arnold had written:

> Look at Byron, that Byron whom the present generation of Englishmen are forgetting; Byron, the greatest natural force, the greatest elementary power ... which has appeared in our literature since Shakespeare. And what became of this wonderful production of nature? He shattered himself to pieces against the huge, black, cloud-topped, interminable precipice of British Philistinism.

Swinburne took up this suggestion that Byron was neglected in a Preface he wrote for an edition of Byron's *Poems* (1866) and re-issued it in *Essays and Studies* (1875). He argues that the generation brought up on Tennyson have got used to 'better verse and carefuller workmen' than Byron, and have failed to recognise the 'splendid and imperishable excellence' of Byron which outweighs all his defects, namely 'the excellence of sincerity and strength'. Byron, he claims, made his way in spite of those major impediments to success, his youth, his genius and his ancient name. He accepts that Byron's serious poetry is often 'rough and loose', 'weak in the screws and joints', but *Don Juan* is a 'magnificent masterpiece', and Swinburne speaks enthusiastically, not only of its

vitality but also of its 'exquisite balance' as a whole.
Swinburne moves with curious swiftness between an encomium on Byron and a sharp commentary on his defects. The
reader senses that what he says at any given moment is
inspired by a desire to reply to some unmerited praise or
blame, to readjust a disturbed critical balance, and to do so
with fervour. Thus corrective exaggerations designed to
shake easy misconceptions flow from his pen.

> Coleridge and Keats used nature mainly as a stimulant or a sedative;
> Wordsworth as a vegetable fit to shred into his pot and pare down like
> the outer leaves of a lettuce for didactic and culinary purposes ...
> Turn now to Byron or to Shelley. These two at least were not content
> to play with her skirts and paddle in her shallows ... They feed upon
> nature with a holy hunger ...

A moment later we are being told of Byron's 'bad' ear. 'His
verse stumbles and jingles, stammers and halts ...'
  Swinburne's poetic talent reveals itself in the rolling
rhetoric which surges to its climaxes as his enthusiasms feed
themselves with ever new phrases of excited appreciation. It
also reveals itself in the imagery in which sensitive critical
insights are encapsulated:

> The supreme charm of Mr Arnold's work is a sense of right resulting
> in a spontaneous temperance which bears no mark of curb or snaffle,
> but obeys the hand with imperceptible submission and gracious
> reserve.

So he writes in an article 'Matthew Arnold's New Poems'
contributed to the *Fortnightly Review* (October 1867) and
revised for *Essays and Studies* (1875). Yet Swinburne the poet
cannot let it go at that, and the point about stylistic
'temperance' becomes a theme for mounting verbal variations ('that tender and final quality of touch which tempers
the excessive light and suffuses the refluent shade ...' etc.
etc.). It is notable too that the question of theological or
philosophical content in poetry is one which Swinburne
treats with scornful dismissiveness. Whether a poet is a
devout Christian or a frightful pagan is a purely domestic
matter irrelevant to the critic. As for poetry, 'all emotion is

serviceable to it, that of the anchorite neither more nor less than that of the blasphemer'. As a critic Arnold earns high praise from Swinburne for his attempt to strip his countrymen of their errors. And this theme too is diversified as Swinburne pictures the great dumb Briton ahead of all men in sheer stolid, mute self-esteem.

Swinburne also paid tribute to Browning, rising as usual against a negative judgment, that Browning was 'obscure'. He wrote a study *George Chapman* (1875), and took the opportunity while dealing with 'obscurity' in Chapman to digress on the subject of the charge brought against Browning. It is 'random thinking' and 'random writing' that produce obscurity, and there is plenty of that in Chapman. In Browning there is no such randomness. His thinking is decisive and incisive. He is sure in his perception and in his aim. Indeed he is the very reverse of obscure. He is 'too brilliant and subtle' for the ready reader to keep track of him as his intelligence leaps on with such rapidity. He thinks at full speed and demands a comparable alertness in the reader.

Swinburne is continuously arresting. He may not teach the intelligent reader much that is new. But the flowing observations clarify the reader's own personal responses vividly and renew his sense of intimacy with the works in question. And the reader rarely wants to quarrel with him once he has chased all round his subject. If he served Byron's reputation well in his day, he also served well the reputation of the Brontë sisters. His book *A Note on Charlotte Brontë* (1877) did much to restore the balance of critical opinion in her favour at a time when George Eliot's reputation was in the ascendant. He formulated a bold classification of three classes of imaginative work. The lowest class demands of the reader nothing more than complacent acquiescence. The second challenges us to assent or dissent. The third compels us to acceptance. George Eliot and Meredith are in the second category and Charlotte Brontë in the third. Swinburne sees the greatest proof of her genius in 'the handling of human characters in mutual relation and reaction'. Her supreme gift lies in making the reader feel the sheer inevitability of what her characters do and suffer. He accepts that in knowledge and culture 'Charlotte Brontë was no more comparable to George Eliot than George Eliot is comparable to Charlotte Brontë in purity of passion, in depth and ardour of feeling, in spiritual force and fervour of forthright inspiration'. George Eliot represents intelligence vivified by a touch of genius, where Charlotte Brontë represents genius directed by the truth of intelligence.

The revival of interest in Elizabethan and Jacobean drama which the Romantic movement initiated and which Charles Lamb fed by his *Specimens of English Dramatic Poets* (1808) was further encouraged by Swinburne in articles and books. T. S. Eliot has said of Swinburne's criticism in this field that he was 'sufficiently interested in his subject-matter and knew quite enough about it' and that his judgments between poets is sound, but that he does not penetrate to the heart of his subjects and one misses the sense of a mind groping towards important conclusions. 'As it is, there are to be no conclusions, except that Elizabethan literature is very great ... the drum is beaten, but the procession does not advance.'[2]

The kind of aesthetic doctrine which Pater promulgated was taken up by Oscar Wilde (1854–1900), embellished, exaggerated, and turned into paradoxical epigrams calculated to infuriate the Victorian public. It would scarcely be proper to speak of the 'serious' critical output in the case of a writer whose appetite for turning the tables on all seeming truisms interfered with logical exposition. The witty paradox was for him the 'fatal Cleopatra'. Nevertheless, the collection of essays, *Intentions* (1891), contained two dialogues between clever, leisured young men which focus on the relationship of art to life. In 'The Decay of Lying' Vivian's initial thesis, lamenting the decay of lying, plainly suggests a tongue-in-cheek approach. Art does not make us love Nature, but reveals her crudities. 'Art is our spirited protest, our gallant attempt to teach Nature her proper place.' Truth to Nature is the death of Art. Even Elizabethan drama contained the seeds of corruption by using life as an artistic method and substituting an imitative for a creative medium. Facts must not be allowed to usurp the domain of Fancy. Far from Art imitating Life, it is Life that imitates Art. Life is the mirror, and Art the reality. (At a time when the connection between television and lawlessness is at issue, Wilde's example of how

boy-burglars take their cue from reading the adventures of
Dick Turpin and the like, cuts near the bone.) 'Art never
expresses anything but itself. It has an independent life, just
as Thought has ...' In no case does it reproduce its age. Bad
art comes from 'returning to Life and Nature and elevating
them into ideals'. Life and Nature can be used by Art, but
they must be translated into artistic conventions. 'As a
method Realism is a complete failure.' 'Lying, the telling of
beautiful untrue things, is the proper aim of art.'

There is far more substance in the fuller dialogue, 'The
Critic as Artist', where the spokesman for Wilde is Gilbert,
and he takes to pieces every conventional utterance of his
friend Ernest. There is not a great deal of specific reference to
individual Victorian writers, but Browning gets commendation as a man who was 'always thinking, and always thinking
aloud', but fascinated not so much by thought as by the
process by which thought moves. 'It was the machine he
loved, not what the machine makes.' As a creator of
character he ranks with Shakespeare: 'The only man who
can touch the hem of his garment is George Meredith.
Meredith is a prose Browning, and so is Browning. He used
poetry as a medium for writing in prose.' The thesis stresses
the interdependence of the critical and creative faculties.
There can be no worthwhile artistic creation without the
critical faculty. An age without criticism will be an age in
which art is immobile or non-existent. 'For it is the critical
faculty that invents fresh forms. The tendency of creation is
to repeat itself.' Criticism 'demands infinitely more cultivation than creation does'. Anybody can write a novel. When
Ernest suggest that it is more difficult to do a thing than to
talk about it, Gilbert upends another conventionality. 'It is
very much more difficult to talk about a thing than to do it
... Anybody can make history. Only a great man can write
it.' Action is 'the last resource of those who know not how to
dream ... When man acts he is a puppet. When he describes
he is a poet.'

In the course of his canter from paradox to paradox,
Gilbert declares en route that 'what is called Sin is an
essential element of progress', and that the survival of
conscience is a 'sign of imperfect development'. The serious

core of his case seems to be that criticism is creative. Indeed 'the highest Criticism, being the purest form of personal impression, is in its way more creative than creation'. Arnold's view that 'the proper aim of Criticism is to see the object in itself as it really is' is a serious error. 'For the highest Criticism deals with art not as expressive but as impressive purely.' Who cares whether Ruskin's views on Turner are sound or not? His majestic eloquence is at least as great a work of art as those wonderful sunsets. Who cares whether Pater sees in the Mona Lisa something Leonardo never dreamed of? His criticism is of the highest kind in treating a work of art 'simply as a starting-point for a new creation'. Good criticism can no more be imitative of the work it deals with than decorative art can be purely imitative of Nature.

In so far as the critic is an interpreter he may well deepen the mystery of a work of art rather than explain it. This is because the highest criticism deals with art not as expressive but as impressive. It follows that the critic can only interpret the work and personality of the artist by intensifying his own personality. (Clearly we have here reached the stark opposite of what Chesterton called Arnold's view, that the critic must get himself out of the way.) And as civilisation progresses 'the critical and cultural spirits will grow less and less interested in actual life, and *will seek to gain their impressions almost entirely from what Art has touched*'. For from the artistic point of view, life is a failure. 'There is no mood of passion that Art cannot give us', and we can be selective in choosing our moment for experiencing them. And since 'emotion for the sake of emotion is the aim of art, and emotion for the sake of action is the aim of life', it follows that all art is immoral. Action belongs to the sphere of ethics. The calm, self-centred contemplation of life by the aesthetic critic is the true ideal. 'With us, Thought is degraded by its constant association with practice.' Confusing the spheres of art and ethics is a recipe for chaos.

When he comes to define the qualifications of the true critic Gilbert draws on Pater. 'Temperament is the primary requisite for the critic – a temperament exquisitely suscept-ible to beauty, and to the various impressions that beauty gives us.' To protest because a poet 'has nothing to say' is absurd. If he had something to say, 'he would probably say it, and the result would be tedious'. It is Form that creates both the critical temperament and the aesthetic instinct. A great artist will not fully appreciate the beauty of work different from his own. Because 'creation limits, while contemplation widens, the vision', it follows that the proper judge of a thing will be the man who could not do it himself. Wilde's Gilbert claims finally to be with Arnold in recognising that criticism creates the intellectual atmosphere of an age, and that it was never more needed than now.

VI Le fin de siècle

The last decade of the nineteenth century saw the emergence of critical thinking which was to influence the character of the literature of the new century. Arthur Symons (1865–1945), poet and critic, who knew Wilde as well as Yeats, encouraged the recognition in England of the work of the French Symbolist poets, Baudelaire, Verlaine and Mallarmé. Both Yeats and Eliot were to acknowledge their indebtedness to him in this respect. A disciple of Pater, Symons warmed to the literary movement in France which saw the autonomous artist as the foe of bourgeois society, and encouraged the pursuit of new sensations. In his essay 'The Decadent Movement in Literature' (1893), Symons defines the representative literature of the day as possessing the qualities that belong to the 'end of great periods ... an intense self-consciousness, a restless curiosity in research, an over-subtilizing refinement upon refinement, a spiritual and moral perversity'. Contrasted with the classic qualities of simplicity, sanity, and proportion, this new literature is a 'beautiful and interesting disease'. It is a *maladie fin de siècle*, typical of a civilisation grown over-luxurious, over-inquiring, too languid for the relief of action, too uncertain for any emphasis in opinion or in conduct'. 'Decadence' is the fit umbrella term covering 'Impressionism' and 'Symbolism', which convey the truth of appearances to the senses and the truth of spiritual things to the spiritual vision. There is no attempt [in Arnold's words] 'to see life steadily and to see it whole', no search for harmony of phrase: rather allowance is made for the feverish vision and the over-excited nerves. The aim is 'to flash the impression of the moment, to preserve the very heat and motion of life'. Symons commends especially as a unique masterpiece Huysmans's novel *A Rebours* (1884), whose hero, Des Esseintes, is the prototype of decadence, for the way in which it concentrates 'all that is delicately depraved, all that is beautifully, curiously poisonous, in modern art'. Des Esseintes is 'the last product of our society', creating an 'artificial paradise' in the 'wilderness of a barren and profoundly uncomfortable world'. In Symons's eyes this work, 'so fascinating, so repellent, so instinctively artificial', expresses an epoch.

In *The Symbolist Movement in Literature* (1899) Symons speaks of 'Decadence' as 'an interlude, half a mock interlude' ... diverting the attention of critics 'while something more serious was in preparation'. That something was Symbolism. And the Symbolist movement is 'all an attempt to spiritualise literature, to evade the old bondage of rhetoric, the old bondage of exteriority'. It is one more revolt against 'a materialistic tradition' in its endeavour to 'disengage the ultimate essence, the soul, of whatever exists'. In this task literature attains liberty, paradoxically by burdening itself anew with what has previously been the duties and responsibilities of religion.

More than once Symons draws the parallel between the saint, the lover, and the artist, each giving himself with 'a kind of sublime selfishness' to religion, passion, and art. Each experiences an 'incommunicable ecstasy' which is his ultimate attainment. But it is an escape in which he flees from the realisation of our mortality.

Perhaps the most prophetic and productive aspect of Symons's critical thinking was the way in which, as a poet himself, he recognised the need of poets to adapt to the new scientific, urban culture.

> To be modern in poetry, to represent really oneself and one's surroundings, the world as it is today, to be modern and yet poetical, is perhaps, the most difficult, as it is certainly the most interesting, of all artistic achievements.

So Symons wrote in a piece on 'Modernity in Verse' in 1892.[3] Half a century later, in a radio programme in 1957, T. S. Eliot told how reading the poetry of Symons, Dowson, and Davidson impressed him. 'From these men I got the idea that one could write poetry in an English such as one would speak oneself. A colloquial idiom.'[4]

A legacy of a very different kind from this was also handed on from the one century to the next. The Victorian age launched on its course the output of books about writers which blended biography with descriptive criticism. It was the initiation of what was to become a vast industry. John Morley (1838–1923), journalist and historian, who became a Liberal MP and eventually rose to be Lord President of the Council, edited Macmillan's 'English Men of Letters' series to which a wide range of distinguished writers contributed. Trollope wrote on Thackeray, Henry James on Hawthorne, Leslie Stephen on Pope and Johnson, Mark Pattison on Milton, and R. H. Hutton on Scott. George Saintsbury (1845–1933), voluminous critic and literary historian, whose works include *A Short History of English Literature* (1898) and *The History of Criticism and Literary Taste in Europe* (1900–4), wrote on Dryden. The poet Austin Dobson (1840–1921) added *Samuel Richardson* (1902) to his biographies of Steele, Goldsmith, and Frances Burney. A. C. Benson (1862–1925) contributed *Rossetti* (1906) and G. K. Chesterton (1874–1936) contributed *Browning* (1903). Perhaps Chesterton's lively study is one of the few which has the added distinction of a rich flow of imaginative commentary that turns the author rather than his subject into the focus of literary fascination.

If the 'English Men of Letters' series is to be described as 'run-of-the-mill' criticism, then the mill is a valuably efficient one and the millers tend to be prestigious suppliers. The poet and art critic John Addington Symonds (1840–93) wrote the volume *Sir Philip Sidney* (1889) which might stand as representative of a kind of study which readably sweeps through the hero's life and works, but in style and approach the Victorian formality can escalate into a declamatory idiom that now rings hollowly. Sidney's career bequeathed a noble lesson to Victorian England, we are told.

It is a lesson which can never lose its value for Greater Britain also, and for that confederated empire which shall, if fate defeat not the high aspirations of the Anglo-Saxon race, arise to be the grandest birth of future time.

A more scholarly, and still very useful critic, Edmund Gosse (1849-1928) contributed *Gray* (1882), *Jeremy Taylor* (1904), and *Sir Thomas Browne* (1905) to the series. He has some historical significance for his work as a critic and translator in bringing Ibsen to the attention of the English public, and also for his *Life and Letters of John Donne* (1899), which heralded the later rehabilitation of the Metaphysical poets. His personal connection with Swinburne and the Pre-Raphaelites stood him in good stead when he published his full-length biographical study *The Life of Algernon Charles Swinburne* (1917). The study of *Southey* (1880) in the 'English Men of Letters' series was contributed by Edward Dowden (1843-1914), for over forty years Professor of English at Trinity College, Dublin. Dowden was long remembered for his work on Shakespeare, in particular for his *Shakespere: his Mind and Art* (1875) which proved a highly influential specimen of the blend of biography with critical exploration of the works. Psychological analysis moves between the two, so that the works tend to be treated as biographical records of the poet's inner emotional and intellectual life. As a reviewer, Dowden championed George Eliot with such fervour that his article in the *Contemporary Review* for August 1872 moved Lewes to tears, he said, and touched the lady herself 'very much'. It is characteristic of Dowden that he claimed the 'most valuable critic' to be 'the critic who communicates sympathy by an exquisite record of his own delights, not the critic who attempts to communicate thought'. We can understand how James Joyce's Stephen Dedalus should have reacted in *Ulysses* to what he saw as Dowden's sentimentalisation of Shakespeare the man:

William Shakespeare and company, limited. The people's William. For terms apply: E. Dowden, Highfield house ...[5]

10
The Twentieth Century:
The Early Decades

The early twentieth century was a period of remarkable literary productivity, rich in quantity and quality, in experimentation and innovation. The publishing industry was expanded and modernised, and there was a huge increase in the production and sale of books. Various developments increased the demand for reading material. Elementary education became universal, and higher education was made available on an unprecedented scale. The public library system was developed. The growing trade union movement reacted against the excessive working hours imposed on the masses in the hey-day of Victorian capitalism, and a vast increase in leisure followed. This was happening in a period that was especially rich in major writers of genius who have taken their places alongside the great writers of the past. The age was also rich in writers of lesser rank who produced neither masterpieces nor works of outstanding imaginative power, but served their readers with works of high entertainment value and accomplished crafts-manship. In short, the age of Joyce and Eliot, Lawrence and Yeats, was also the age of Galsworthy and Wells, Wodehouse and Masefield.

It is tempting to the philosophically-minded to try to relate the rare crop of first-rate writers to contemporary historical developments. Certainly the first half of our century was marked by momentous events – the First World War, the Russian Revolution, the rise of dictatorships, and the relentless slide into the Second World War. Moreover, it was not just thrones and social systems that were shaken. The popularisation of notions derived from thinkers such as Freud and Einstein served to undermine confidence in previously accepted fixities, moral and religious. Whether an age of deep inner unsettlements combined with calamitous public conflicts and upheavals is more likely to produce great writers than an age of peace and stability is arguable. But what is not arguable is the evident connection between the shaking of external and internal foundations in the public domain and the seeming compulsion upon great writers to reflect disturbingly on the human condition. Moreover, it looks natural enough to hindsight that great writers so placed should have sought to submit traditional literary forms and conventions to fresh scrutiny, and to go in for radical literary experimentation in the attempt to come to grips with their age.

A good deal of the critical thinking explored in this chapter is concerned either to defend or to attack contemporary experimentation. The earlier controversies of the period show modernist experimenters and apologists at war with 'Georgianism'. It seems ironic now that the 'Georgian' movement saw itself as throwing off the shackles of Victorian artifice and poeticism; for so often it disinfected Victorian forms of grandeur and finery without putting anything in their place. The real contemporary world impinged on literature in new ways in Eliot and Joyce, and modernist apologetic had to deal with this novelty. The contemporary world impinged on literary criticism in a totally different way in the academic influences which emanated from F. R. Leavis at Cambridge. There was a demand to judge literature through approval or disapproval of the ways of living and social values it represented. This produced a secularised version of the old puritanical onslaught on unfettered imaginative vision.

I Henry James

The turn of the century brought one crucial development in English literary criticism which to hindsight has looked long overdue. Up to this point there had been no theorising about the novel as a genre to match the theorising that had accompanied the growth of tragedy and epic. Yet by the end of Victoria's reign the novel had become the predominant literary form. As a form, it had 'grown', free of methodological prescription. It was the expatriate American novelist Henry James (1843-1916) who detected this deficiency and tried to make amends. In articles contributed to *The Times Literary Supplement* in 1914 under the heading 'The Younger Generation' he noted the flood of new novels and observed that 'no equal outpouring of matter into the mould of literature' had ever been allowed to live its life 'in such free and easy independence of critical attention'. Criticism had been perversely unresponsive to a vociferous and incessant appeal. It was a matter of 'responsibility declined in the face of disorder'.

James did not hold that the English novel was necessarily any the worse for the lack of theoretical attention to it as a literary form. But he clearly resented the lack of professionalism with which it had been regarded.

> There was a comfortable, good-humoured feeling around that a novel is a novel, as a pudding is a pudding, and that our only business with it could be to swallow it.

So he had written in his essay 'The Art of Fiction' (1884) thirty years before his pieces on 'The Younger Generation'. It was the formlessness of the novel that offended him. It was a defect he found in Tolstoy's *War and Peace* as well as in Arnold Bennett's *Old Wives' Tale*. They lack a 'centre of interest', and they lack a 'sense of the whole'. They try to compensate by 'saturation in the actual'. There is a disconnection of matter and method due to the novelist's determination to squeeze the factual orange dry.

James's theory of the need for selectivity by the novelist was closely related to his belief that life itself was 'all inclusion and confusion'. Life is a fluid, disorderly, aggregative experience in which relations never stop, and it is the novelist's duty, by 'discrimination and selection' to create the illusion of wholeness, or roundedness. How James himself set about this task is made clear in the series of Prefaces he wrote for the collected edition of his novels published by Charles Scribner's in New York between 1907 and 1909. These

Prefaces represent the cream of James's critical writing. They break new ground by taking the reader behind the scenes into the mind and experience of the novelist as he is at work. 'There is the story of one's hero, and then, thanks to the intimate connection of things, the story of one's story itself.' So James writes in the Preface to *The Ambassadors*. He had already told, in the Preface to the *Portrait of a Lady*, how the artist's conception grew from 'the germ of my idea', in this case 'the character and aspect of a particular engaging young woman'. Such germs are floated into the mind by the current of life; the imagination invests some conceived or encountered individual with 'the germinal property and authority'. James could never work by first seeing a fable and then making out its agents. The intensity of suggestion residing in the young woman was such that he grasped her as a single character, something seen 'in transit', something 'bent upon its fate'.

> The point is, however, that this single small cornerstone, the conception of a certain young woman affronting her destiny, had begun with being all my outfit for the large building of *The Portrait of a Lady*.

The 'house' had to be 'put up round my young woman while she stood there in perfect isolation'.

James argues that the young heroines of Shakespeare and George Eliot are 'never suffered to be sole ministers' of the appeal to the reader, but have their 'inadequacy eked out with comic relief and under-plots'. He determined not to evade the maximum possibilities of importance in the heroine herself. 'Place the centre of the subject in the young woman's own consciousness' he told himself. And then 'press least hard, in short, on the consciousness of your heroine's satellites, especially the male; make it an interest contributive only to the greater one'. Thus James explains, stage by stage, how the 'needful accretion' took place, 'the unordered pieces' of the puzzle fell into place. And he is careful to distinguish those characters created as 'wheels to the coach' from the true agents.

There is a special subtlety in the way in which James repeatedly returns to the question of the author's detachment from his work and his involvement in it. In the Preface to *The Golden Bowl* he speaks of his efforts to shake off 'the muffled majesty of authorship', to get down into the arena and do his best 'to live and breathe and rub shoulders and converse' with his characters. The restraining authorial hand performs its function 'by the manner in which the whole thing remains subject to the register, ever so closely kept, of the consciousness of but two of the characters'. This concern with the particular consciousness in which events are registered shows the artistic sensibility in action in such a way as to add a new dimension to criticism of the novel. It is a matter to which James returns again in his Preface to *The Ambassadors*. He locates the first germ of his novel in remarks made by an older man to a younger man in a Paris garden: ' "Live all you can so long as you have your life. If you haven't had that what *have* you had?" ' From this germ grew the concept of the aging man with enough imagination to be brought to the stage of such regret for missed opportunities. So to consideration of the 'felt predicament' or 'false position' which could engender such a state of mind. Thus again, step by step, James traces how his hero Strether's background and errand were formulated and the 'story' fashioned.

In this case, of course, it is Strether's consciousness in which events are registered, and James has some penetrating things to say about why the 'first person' narrative would not do. 'Suffice it, to be brief, that the first person, in the long piece, is a form foredoomed to looseness ...' In novels like *David Copperfield* the author equips his hero 'with the double privilege of subject and object', and the narrating hero's vague stance in relationship to his readers is at loggerheads with lucidity and discrimination. The situation of James's hero is so firmly conceived that the 'terrible *fluidity* of self-revelation' before a gaping reader would destroy him. Denying himself the autobiographical method, James also denies himself the indigestible practice of inserting blocks of 'merely referential narrative' in the manner of Balzac. He has recourse therefore to the expedient of setting up for his hero 'a confidant or two'. In other words he projects for his hero 'a relation that has nothing to do with the matter', the subject, 'but has everything to do with the manner', the presentation, and yet does his best to treat it at close quarters 'as if it were important and essential'.

We cannot fail to be fascinated by James's achievement in opening up to public view questions of form and technique which have become commonplace issues in subsequent criticism of the novel. He himself accepted that 'the Novel remains still, under the right persuasion, the most independent, most elastic, most prodigious of literary forms', and he did not stint his praise of writers vastly different from himself. Writing to H. G. Wells in 1905, after reading *Kipps*, he said he was left 'prostrate with admiration'. The book is 'not so much a masterpiece as a mere born gem'.[1] The two novelists became friends, but it was a friendship doomed to end in a quarrel. James's references to Wells's work in his articles, 'The Younger Generation', for all their good humour, embody a searching artistic judgment. Wells taps the incessant and extraordinarily various experience of his own mind, and that has to suffice as a basis of interest. The more he knows and learns, and establishes his saturation, 'the greater is our impression of his holding it good enough for us, such as we are, that he shall but turn out his mind and its contents upon us by any free familiar gesture and as from a high window for ever open'.

When Wells turned on James, in his novel *Boon* (1915), it was to mock James's notion that 'a novel is a work of art that must be judged by its oneness'. James has a strong, abundant mind, but is totally devoid of penetration. 'He is the culmination of the Superficial type.' The search for unity, as Wells's spokesman has it in the novel, is a matter of penetration, not of organisation. 'Life is diversity and entertainment' and James tries to eliminate discordances by selection, which means omission.

> He omits everything that demands digressive treatment or collateral statement. For example he omits opinions. In all his novels you will find no people with defined political opinions, no people with religious opinions, none with clear partisanships or with lusts or whims, none definitely up to any specific impersonal thing. There are no poor people dominated by the imperatives of Saturday night and Monday morning ...[2]

It may be argued that Wells touched a raw nerve when he pointed to the limitation of 'living human motives' in James's novels, and declared:

> The thing his novel is *about* is always there. It is like a church lit but without a congregation to distract you, with every light and line focused on the high altar.

It is an emptiness redeemed and made tolerable only by 'the elaborate, copious wit'. Thus, sad as the quarrel was in personal terms, the substance of the critical exchange is certainly worth having. If James's discrimination detected what was lacking in Wells, Wells, however heavy-handedly and indeed vulgarly, pointed to limitations in James's vision.

'Pay no attention to the criticism of men who have never themselves written a notable work,'[3] Ezra Pound once declared. We naturally treat with special respect the critical judgments of creative writers with great achievements behind them. But there is a difference of category between the criticism which arises from objective interest in other writers – such as Johnson's *Lives of the Poets* or Scott's *Lives of the Novelists* – and criticism which arises from a writer's wish to explain to the world what he has himself been about. James's Prefaces, like Scott's Prefaces to the collected edition of his works, belong to this latter category. They exist to explain innovation, to account for a technique or a content which the reader might have found difficult or bewildering. James's extremely thorough and careful exhibition to the reader of the workshop of the writer's mind came at a crucial stage in the development of the novel form. It constitutes a delightful running commentary on what was happening to the genre.

II The modernist movement

Literary innovation was of course widespread and far-reaching in the early years of the century, and many major writers turned aside to comment on what they were about. W. B. Yeats (1865–1939) committed himself to no such analysis of his work as the mature James did, but, as a gifted, energetic poet making his way, he cast about for vocational moorings, and there is a special interest for us in his critical observations in that he, more than any other writer of the age, embodied in his own work the total transformation of poetic expression that occurred between the late Victorian decades and the age of 'modernism'. In a celebrated essay on 'The Symbolism of Poetry' (1900), Yeats developed ideas found in Symons's *The Symbolist Movement* (1899), which Symons had dedicated to him. He presses the link between 'the scientific movement' and the tendency of literature 'to lose itself in externalities of all kinds, in opinion, in declamation, in picturesque writing, in word-painting'. By contrast, writers are now dwelling upon 'the element of evocation, of suggestion', in short upon symbolism. Perhaps we see most clearly what Yeats is getting at when he calls for 'a casting out of descriptions of nature for the sake of nature, of the moral law for the sake of the moral law, a casting out of all anecdotes and of that brooding over scientific opinion that so often extinguished the central flame in Tennyson'. In such declarations Yeats's thinking seems to touch tangentially that of James in his reservations about Wells's subject-matter. It is only the 'laws of art' that can bind the imagination. It is symbolism that makes poetry moving by the way emotions and ideas are embodied, and the consequent evocations have a restorative effect on the human heart.

Yeats's indebtedness to Symons emerges again in an essay 'Ireland and the Arts' published in the *United Irishman*, August 31 1904. He takes up the parallel between the vocation to religion and the vocation to art. There is 'only one perfection and only one search for perfection, and it sometimes has the form of the religious life and sometimes of the artistic life'. He quotes the view that it is 'not the business of a poet to make himself understood, but it is the business of the people to understand him', and then adds 'And certainly if you take from art its martyrdom, you will take from it its glory'. No doubt James Joyce read this essay in that last September in Ireland before finally leaving his homeland. He used the thinking of Arthur Symons and of Yeats himself in projecting the artistic idealism of Stephen the artist-priest and the artist-martyr.

> We were the last romantics – chose for theme
> Traditional sanctity and loveliness.

So Yeats wrote in 'Coole Park and Ballylee 1931', looking back on the years when Lady Gregory's house had been a place where writers found refreshment. T. E. Hulme (1883–1917), a philosopher and man of letters who was killed on the Western Front, left behind him a number of literary remains which were gathered together and published posthumously by Herbert Read as *Speculations* (1924). These pieces, of course, reflect on the pre-war literary scene. One of them, 'Romanticism and Classicism', has assumed the status of sign-post to a literary revolution. Its thesis is that, 'after a hundred years of romanticism, we are in for a classical revival'. Romanticism is a kind of disease. It sees man, the individual as 'an infinite reservoir of possibilities'. Progress depends, it assumes, on allowing man to rearrange society by 'destruction of oppressive order'. Classicism is the very opposite. It sees man as 'an extraordinarily fixed and limited animal', and it is only by 'tradition and organisation that anything decent can be got out of him'.

For Hulme, the religious attitude is classical. Indeed, rationalism suppresses the religious instincts into agnosticism, so that they cannot find their proper outlet. Having lost belief in Heaven, you believe in heaven on earth. Hence flows Romanticism, which is simply 'spilt religion'. The romantic is always 'talking about the infinite', while the classical poet never forgets man's finiteness, his limitedness. Hulme goes on to argue that, though 'romanticism is dead in reality', yet 'the critical attitude appropriate to it still continues to exist'. He decries the 'sloppiness which doesn't consider that a poem is a poem unless it is moaning or whining about something or other'. Romanticism is a kind of drug; it produces 'damp' poetry, whereas the properly classical poem is 'all dry and hard'. It accepts accuracy of description; it does not drag the infinite in but recognises that 'man is always man and never a god'. Romantic thinkers have, like Coleridge, tried to deduce critical opinions from fixed metaphysical principles. This is topsy-turvy. Philosophy

312   A HISTORY OF LITERARY CRITICISM

can provide you only with the 'precise language' in which to explain exactly what you mean. 'The ultimate reality is the hurly-burly, the struggle; the metaphysic is an adjunct to clear-headedness in it.' The fundamental quality of good art depends on seeing things as they really are, and then concentrating the mind in such a grip upon oneself that what emerges is the 'actual expression of what one sees'.

Hulme insists that where prose is a 'counter language', poetry is a 'visual, concrete one'. Worn-out epithets and metaphors 'cease to convey a physical thing and become abstract counters'. Only 'the new bowl of metaphor' can convey visual meanings; 'prose is an old pot that lets them leak out'. Indeed 'plain speech is inaccurate'; it is only new metaphors that can make it precise. As for the subject, it doesn't matter: it can be 'a lady's shoe or the starry heavens'. However we regard Hulme's prophecy of a forthcoming 'period of dry, hard, classical verse', it is relevant that a quarter of a century later, W. B. Yeats, in a talk on 'Modern Poetry' on the BBC, looked back to the impression made by the first book from the most revolutionary poet of his life-time, T. S. Eliot. What struck him was that there was 'no romantic word or sound' and no 'special subject-matter'. Here was a poetry for which 'Tristram and Isoult were not a more suitable theme than Paddington Railway Station'.

The use of the word 'romantic' perhaps scarcely helps in defining what the poetic revolution was revolting against. Ezra Pound (1885–1972) looked back on Victorian poetry as 'blurry' and 'messy', 'sentimentalistic' and 'mannerish'. Like Hulme, he sought a new precision and explicitness in rendering nature or emotion.

> Mr Yeats has once and for all stripped English poetry of its perdamnable rhetoric. He has boiled away all that is not poetic ... He has made our poetic idiom a thing pliable, a speech without inversions.[4]

So Pound wrote in 1917 in *A Retrospect* (1918), repeating what he had first published in *The Poetry Review* in 1913. He had earlier declared:

Poetry is a sort of inspired mathematics, which gives us equations, not for abstract figures, triangles, spheres, and the like, but equations for the human emotions. (*The Spirit of Romance*, 1910)[5]

On this basis Pound collaborated with Richard Aldington (1892–1962) and Hilda Doolittle ('H.D.') (1886–1961) in what was called the 'Imagist' movement. He cited its basic principles thus:

1. Direct treatment of the 'thing' whether subjective or objective.
2. To use absolutely no word that does not contribute to the presentation.
3. As regarding rhythm: to compose in the sequence of the musical phrase, not in sequence of a metronome.[6]

Pound's campaign was directed against prolixity, verbosity, and flaccidity; and against shovelling in words to fill up a metrical pattern. He insisted that the young poet had to practise his craft with the same discipline as the young musician. He must give as much time to the study of metrical and aural technique as the musician gives to the study of harmony and counterpoint. Lots of people should be writing poetry, just as lots of people learn to play a tune or two on the piano: but publication is a different matter, for mastering the art of poetry is the business of a lifetime, and no one ever writes very much poetry that really matters.

Pound's definition of an Image is that it 'presents an intellectual and emotional complex in an instant of time' and its instantaneous presentation gives a 'sense of sudden liberation'.[7] Where symbols are used, the symbolic function must not obtrude. And, like Hulme, Pound foresees a twentieth-century poetry that will be 'harder and saner' and 'nearer the bone'. As for the critic's function, all he can do is to focus the reader's gaze. Criticism cannot circumscribe or prohibit, he declares (in spite of his own proscriptions): it can only provide 'fixed points of departure'.

Writing about the pre-war literary scene in a letter to Michael Roberts in 1937, Pound said:

Hulme wasn't hated and loathed by the ole bastards, because they didn't know he was there. The man who did the *work* for English writing was Ford Madox Hueffer (now Ford). The old crusted lice and advocates of corpse language knew that *The English Review* existed.[8]

Ford Madox Ford (1873–1939), as novelist and critic, is perhaps the most astonishingly neglected major writer in the history of English literature. His tetralogy *Parade's End* is surely after *Ulysses* the finest English fiction of the century. He started the *English Review* in 1908 and edited it for over a year, publishing work by new writers such as D. H. Lawrence and Wyndham Lewis as well as by established contemporaries such as James and Bennett. Ford's critical work includes essays written for the *English Review* and other journals (a collection of them was published as *The Critical Attitude*, 1911) as well as *Henry James A Critical Study* (1913) and *Joseph Conrad: A Personal Remembrance* (1924). It culminated in the massive survey *The March of Literature from Confucius to Modern Times* (1938). But there is also a vast amount of fascinating critical commentary and reflection scattered about his volumes of memoirs:*Ancient Lights* (1911), *Return to Yesterday, Reminiscences 1894–1914* (1931) and *It was the Nightingale* (1933). An attempt to present a representative sample of this output was made in *The Ford Madox Ford Reader* (1986) edited by Sondra J. Stang, with a Foreword by Graham Greene.

Greene, one of the young writers Ford encouraged, has said how, when he met Ford, he 'felt his energy like a shot of vitamin in the veins'.[9] It is the vitality and vividness of Ford's critical writing that is irresistible. In literary portraits which he contributed to the *Daily Mail* in 1907, the *Tribune* in 1907–8, and the *Outlook* between 1913 and 1915, the technique of the novelist is brought to bear in the deft interplay of personal characterisation and literary insight. Touches of exaggeration and irony, imaginative embroidery of fact and conjecture, fanciful exploitation of anecdotal drama, and gems from a mind stocked with past literature – all this makes for a heady diet of enlightenment and entertainment such as the reader derives from De Quincey. Ford goes to town with a will on writers who, like Wells and Arnold Bennett, provide much to praise, much to condemn.

Bennett is 'homo duplex', the writer of quiet genius and the creator of the new novel *The Regent* (1913).

> I don't know why Mr Bennett wrote it – to fulfil a contract? to complete his quarter-million guinea fund? to add, in short, another stamp to his collection? One is *so* tired of these self-made men posing before the head-waiters of Clxxxdge's.

By contrast, reviewing Ezra Pound's *Cathay* in 1915, he finds the poems 'of a supreme beauty'. 'What poetry should be, that they are.' For they back up the theory 'that poetry consists in so rendering concrete objects that the emotions produced by the objects shall arise in the reader – and not in writing about the emotions themselves'.

A crucial event in Ford's career was his meeting with Joseph Conrad in 1898, when a period of collaboration began which produced the novels *The Inheritors* (1901) and *Romance* (1903). The two writers, strongly influenced by Flaubert and Maupassant, and in England by Henry James, hammered out new principles for fictional technique to replace what they regarded as the worn-out conventions that relied on direct authorial narration and progress from one dramatic situation to another. Ford looked back on this period of collaboration in the book he wrote after Conrad died, *Joseph Conrad* (1924), and he surveyed the innovations they argued over together. For instance, the novel must have the kind of effect on the reader that life has. And life does not report to you in organised narration. Thus 'the novel more or less gradually, more or less deviously, lets you into the secrets of the characters of the men with whom it deals'. Of course the novel must be selective in rendering its impressions, and so sometimes narration will be unavoidable; but 'the object of the novelist is to keep the reader entirely oblivious of the fact that the author exists – even of the fact that he is reading a book'. Chunks of direct dialogue are to be avoided in favour of 'the indirect, interrupted method of handling interviews'. Ford's aim was to submerge the reader in a subtly manufactured verisimiltude so contrived that the text carried the story forward with increasing speed and intensity. This device he called the *progression d'effet*. Hints and items of fact were to be off-handedly slipped in so that crucial information came as casually to the reader as it might in real life. This device of using seemingly innocuous conversational throwaways to ring a bell in the mind of the attentive reader could be employed in a context where cross-reference might add further resonance to its revelatory peal, to produce what Ford called the 'unearned increment'. Ford was also a keen experimenter with the 'time-shift' by which the totally unnatural method of strictly chronological presentation is avoided. He goes into detail about the best way to introduce new characters and convey appropriate information about their history; he insists on the need for an unaffected English style and cites W. H. Hudson as a model.

> Carefully examined, a good – an interesting – style will be found to consist in a constant succession of tiny, unobservable surprises.

Insights like this, enriched by Ford's brilliance at extempore illustration, give penetration to his work.

> We agreed that the novel is absolutely the only vehicle for the thought of our day.

You can explore any department of life or thought in it. 'The only thing that you cannot do is to propagandize, as author, for any cause.' If you insist on expressing your views through a character, then you must offset him with characters expressing the opposite views.

III Bloomsbury and Eastwood

Another creative writer with an eye to the need to reassess the direction of literature in the post-Victorian world was Virginia Woolf (1882–1941). Daughter of the critic Leslie Stephen, she lived at the centre of the 'Bloomsbury Group' which included Lytton Strachey and the economist Maynard Keynes. The group exuded a provocative self-importance as an avant-garde in respect of artistic, social and sexual attitudes. Virginia Woolf had published only her first novel, *The Voyage Out* (1915), when the critic Clive Bell, a

member of the group, spoke of 'great writers, like Dostoevs-
ky, Joseph Conrad, and Virginia Woolf'. Her own critical
essays and reviews were posthumously gathered together by
her husband Leonard Woolf in four volumes of *Collected
Essays* (1966–7). An essay 'Modern Fiction' (1919) has
assumed to hindsight the status of a critical milestone. It
prefigures the transformation she was about the effect in her
later novels in the technique of representing human experience. Early in the year of its publication (1919) she had
reviewed the fourth volume of Dorothy Richardson's massive
sequence of thirteen novels (*Pilgrimage*), *The Tunnel* (1919).
Dorothy Richardson (1873–1957) consciously set out to
produce a feminine counterbalance to the organised realism
of the masculine novel. Thus she developed an impressionist
stream-of-consciousness technique anticipating Virginia
Woolf's own mature style. Virginia Woolf applauds Dorothy
Richardson's decision to throw out

> the old deliberate business: the chapters that lead up and the chapters
> that lead down; the characters who are always characteristic; the
> elaborate construction of reality; the conception that shapes and
> surrounds the whole.[10]

In its place we have instead the consciousness of the heroine,
Miriam Henderson, and we are invited to 'embed' ourselves
in it, to register in turn whatever impressions flicker through
it. So far, so good. Dorothy Richardson earns her due praise
from Virginia Woolf. But, alas, this registration of sensation
and thought is too superficial and inchoate to flash with new
illumination.

It is clear that Virginia Woolf became determined to
achieve what Dorothy Richardson failed to achieve, bringing to bear on Richardson's impressionistic technique an
imaginative intensity and economy lacking in her model.
What Virginia Woolf, and for that matter Dorothy Richardson, were rebelling against was represented by the novelists
Arnold Bennett, H. G. Wells, and John Galsworthy. 'Materialistic' she calls them in 'Modern Fiction'. By which she
means that 'they write of unimportant things' and they
'spend immense skill and immense industry making the

trivial and the transitory appear the true and the endur-
ing'.[11] But the essential thing, call it 'life' or 'spirit', eludes
them as they labour to construct their solid representations.
For they fail to register the myriad, multifarious impressions
that shower upon the 'ordinary mind on an ordinary day'.
The novelists thus judged are praised in various degrees for
their craftsmanship, but the praise stings; for what they
neglect is really the 'proper stuff of fiction'. In an effort to
exemplify it, Virginia Woolf points to what James Joyce
achieves in the *Portrait of the Artist as a Young Man* and in the
'Hades' episode of *Ulysses*, already in print, where he reveals
'the flickerings of that innermost flame which flashes its
message through the brain'. (It is a pity that Virginia Woolf
did not leave it at that: for she added that Joyce's work 'fails
because of the comparative poverty of the writer's mind'.)

For the most part Virginia Woolf writes her criticism like
the novelist she is. Metaphors vivify her arguments. She early
recognised the quality latent in D. H. Lawrence, and she took
him to task in a review of his novel *The Lost Girl* (1920) for
not sticking to his last as a writer

> with an extraordinary sense of the physical world, of the colour and
> texture and shape of things, for whom the body was alive and the
> problems of the body insistent and important.[12]

For between the points at which his novel glows with
concentration, he drifts into the method of an Arnold
Bennett:

> And then again the laborious process continues of building up a
> model of life from saying how d'you do, and cutting the loaf, and
> knocking the cigarette ash in the ash tray, and standing the yellow
> bicycle against the wall.

Virginia Woolf persistently denigrated the practice of
heaping up facts. She thought Arnold Bennett's efforts to
'achieve infantile realisms' showed only a concern with
'inessentials'.[13] As for H. G. Wells, she sees some of his
characters as so 'humped and loaded' with the 'most
pernicious or typical views of their decade' that they can
scarcely waddle across the stage. She foresees him paying for

contemporary success by the total neglect of posterity. By temperament and principle she is opposed to the misuse of fiction for propaganda. She praises George Moore for his 'power of maintaining that in art life needs neither condemnation nor justification'.[14] Virginia Woolf has sympathy with those Russian writers who stress life's inconclusiveness, its way of presenting unanswerable questions. In life and in art she makes a feminine protest against the tidying up, docketing and ticketing of reality, its patterning in solid-seeming shapes, its interpretation in glib theories and formulae. In a paper 'The Leaning Tower', read to a WEA meeting in 1940, she attacked the poets of the '30s – Day Lewis, Auden, Spender, Isherwood, and MacNeice – for their inability to 'look any class straight in the face', for their advertised unease, their self-pity, and their anger against society.[15] Words like 'bleat' and 'whimper' flow scathingly from her pen in describing their attitudes. No doubt it was the resurgence in their work of moral pontification from the radical political standpoint which rubbed her up the wrong way.

Not all novelists are impressive when they theorise about their work. E. M. Forster (1879–1970) delivered a series of lectures at Cambridge which were published as *Aspects of the Novel* (1927). They are chatty, unpretentious disquisitions and perhaps ought not to be subjected to scrutiny under any searching critical lens. Forster makes a distinction between 'flat' and 'round' characters which has found its way into school classrooms as a handy tool for examination purposes. The 'flat' characters are those which can be summed up in a sentence. The 'round' ones are more highly organised, they 'function all round', and seem capable of an extended life beyond the bounds of the book in which they appear. But even in the process of illustrating this distinction – from Dickens, Wells, Scott, Meredith, Thackeray, and others – precision evaporates and its usefulness begins to seem questionable. Jane Austen gets top marks from Forster at this date. Many years later, in an article written in 1943, 'Our Second Greatest Novel', Proust's *A la Recherche du Temps Perdu*, is being hailed as second only to Tolstoy's *War and Peace*. Forster praises Proust's skill in using an alter ego as hero-narrator, and fastening – not directly on events and people as Tolstoy does – but on 'memories of events and people'. The brilliantly malicious portrayal of the fading French aristocracy and the galaxy of vital characters are also praised, 'Proust was an artist and a tremendous one; he found in memory the means of interpreting and humanising this chaotic world.'[16]

While Forster chatted amiably about novel technique, D. H. Lawrence (1885–1930) blasted away with hectoring rhetoric in aggressive defence of the novel as a crucial influence on the way we live. His essays on the subject include 'Morality and the Novel' (1925), 'The Novel' (1925), and 'Why the Novel Matters', which was not published until 1936 in the posthumous collection, *Phoenix*. Lawrence harangues the reader. Art is concerned with the relation between man and his world. Van Gogh's painting of a sunflower reveals the relation between man and sunflower, and not the sunflower itself. All life consists in achieving relationships between man and what lies about him, human or natural. Where religion, philosophy and science try to nail us down with propositions and prohibitions, the novel represents 'the highest example of subtle interrelatedness that man has discovered'. The superior morality of the novel lies in its acceptance that 'everything is true in its own time, place, circumstance' and false outside. It is a question of preserving a delicate balance which the pressure of an authorial thumb, on this side or on that, will upset. This kind of pressure alone can make a novel truly 'immoral'. Lawrence seems to be close to Virginia Woolf in his thinking here. He insists that a thing is not life 'just because somebody does it'. If an ordinary bank clerk buys a new straw hat, that is not 'life', it is mere experience. But if 'the bank clerk feels really piquant about his hat, if he establishes a lively relationship with it, and goes out of the shop … a changed man, be-aureoled, then that is life'.

Lawrence deals scathingly with conventional divisions of man into body and soul, or body and mind. It is 'bunk' to regard the body as a 'vessel of clay'. 'Nothing is important but life' and what is alive is the whole being, ending only at the finger tips. Saints, philosophers and scientists are all 'renegades', isolating different bits of themselves. The novelist is superior to them all because he deals with the whole. The Bible, Homer and Shakespeare all pass the test of 'wholeness'. And as those works are given Lawrence's *imprimatur* in 'Why the Novel Matters', books whose authors defy his criteria of moral relativism come in for vituperative condemnation in 'The Novel'. Tolstoy is assailed as a 'Judas' for cringing to a 'mangy bloodless Society' by his treatment of Vronsky in *Anna Karenina*. ('Nobody in the world is anything but delighted when Vronsky gets Anna Karenina.') For purpose and inspiration must be one and indivisible. But 'modern' novelists all share the same 'snivelling purpose' and turn themselves into 'little Jesuses'. Forster does not escape the lash; nor does Conrad; not does Joyce. They are bracketed with the authors of best-sellers, like *The Constant Nymph*. If the sharpest venom is reserved for Tolstoy, abetting his hero in *Resurrection* when he wets 'on the flame of his own manhood', Dante comes in for blame for slurring over the fact that he had a 'cosy bifurcated wife in his bed' at home, as well as lusty youngsters. For the novel must inherently be 'quick', that is wholly alive, organically interrelated in all its parts, and 'honourable'. It is the last criterion on which Dante falls down somewhat in failing to mention the wife and kids.

Lawrence, of course, is stimulating, even when he is wrongheaded; and too many critics are boring, even when they see straight. He presents his strictures as largely emanating from the novel itself in protest against abuse of its own vitality and integrity. When looking on other novelists he subverts Forster's evaluations. In his essay 'A Propos of *Lady Chatterley's Lover*' (1929), not only is Tolstoy condemned, but Jane Austen is declared 'mean'. For whereas Defoe and Fielding hold English classes together in 'curious blood-connection', Jane Austen is an 'old maid' who reveals a 'sharp knowing in apartness instead of knowing in togetherness'. This makes her 'thoroughly unpleasant', English in the bad, snobbish sense as Fielding is in 'the good, generous sense'.

A fellow-writer who fell for a time deeply under Lawrence's influence was the critic John Middleton Murry

(1889–1957). He edited a journal *Rhythm* from 1911 to 1913, a periodical supportive of modernist innovators in literature and art, and then the monthly the *Adelphi* (later the *New Adelphi*) which he started in 1923. He also took over the editorship of the long-standing literary review the *Athenaeum* (later the *Nation and Athenaeum*) in 1919. In an early essay on 'The Condition of English Poetry' in the *Athenaeum* (December 1919) Murry contrasted Wilfred Owen's 'Strange Meeting' with run-of-the-mill Georgian poetry. Owen's poem has 'an awe, an immensity, an adequacy to that which has been most profound in the experience of a generation', and it reminds one of the 'forgotten' fact that 'poetry is rooted in emotion and grows by mastery of emotion'. There are no 'tricks of the trade' that can 'conjure emptiness into meaning'.[17] Murry was not always so far-seeing. In the *Adelphi* in 1926 he prophesied oblivion for *The Waste Land* unless Eliot revolutionised his style.

Murry's critical writings are sprinkled with illuminations. Even when we feel that he is being totally mistaken or even unbearably uneloquent, we find things that startle or delight. In his essay 'The Function of Criticism' he makes plain his allegiance to philosophic criticism. Coleridge's criticism is praised because 'the reference to life pervades the whole of what is permanently valuable' in it.

> In Dryden, however, there was no such organic interpenetration. Dryden, too, had a fine sensibility, though less exquisite, by far, than that of Coleridge; but his theoretical system was not merely alien to him – it was in itself false and mistaken ... He took over from France the sterilised and lifeless Aristotelianism which has been the plague of criticism for centuries.

Murry argues that Dryden found this 'dead mechanical framework' something that consistently chafed him.

> He behaves like a fine horse with a bearing rein: he is continually tossing his head after a minute or two of 'good manners and action', and saying, 'Shakespeare was the best of them, anyhow': 'Chaucer beats Ovid to a standstill'.[18]

In *The Problems of Style* (1922), a series of lectures given at Oxford, there is an exploration of the difference between

Poetry and Prose which is not always happily argued, but it throws up lively trains of thought. The importance of the fashion of the age in the matter of literary genre is interestingly illustrated. Hardy was not 'comfortable' with the novel in the way that Shakespeare was 'comfortable' with drama. If poetic drama could have been restored early in the nineteenth century, we should have been spared unwieldy works like *The Dynasts* and *The Ring and the Book* in which the creative impulse is working 'free from the discipline of an accepted form'.[19]

Murry was an earnest crusader who threw himself passionately into a series of causes inspired by spiritual ideals. Though he was capable of the lighter touch, urgency is a more constant characteristic, nowhere more evident than in his study of D. H. Lawrence, *Son of Woman* (1931). Murry's early devotion to Lawrence had been a deeply felt one. His personal entanglement with Lawrence and his wife, Frieda, had been an intimate and at times a turbulent one. His book does not moderate its praise for Lawrence's genius, but it presents him as a man grossly misled by his own psychosexual abnormality and the doctrines it led him to embrace.

IV T. S. Eliot

There is general agreement that T. S. Eliot (1888–1965) soon established himself as a magisterially influential voice in English literary criticism. There is general agreement that his critical pronouncements stimulated a refreshing reappraisal of various major literary reputations. There is general agreement too that he refined the scope and function of criticism itself. But there is surprisingly little agreement about what this total critical achievement in essence amounted to. This is partly because Eliot's critical output was so diverse, partly because his attitudes changed as his thinking developed, and partly because he never achieved the totally disinterested critical outlook of the writer who focuses in detachment upon the work of others. Much of Eliot's critical output remains an adjunct to and a commentary upon his own purpose and programme as a poet. A further complication in judging Eliot results from his practice of withdrawing from controversy behind a veil of reticence, and sometimes of making it understood that what he said ought not to be taken too seriously.

The bulk of the critical work is impressive. The 20s and 30s saw the publication of *The Sacred Wood: Essays on Poetry and Criticism* (1920), *Homage to John Dryden* (1924), *For Lancelot Andrewes: Essays on Style and Order* (1928), *Selected Essays 1917–1932* (1932), *The Use of Poetry and the Use of Criticism* (1933), and *Elizabethan Essays* (1934). This is not a complete list. During the same period, Eliot edited the quarterly *Criterion*. His later critical works, such as *Notes towards the Definition of Culture* (1948) and *To Criticize the Critic* (1965) show the full expansion of his interest from the early focus on literature to a concern with culture and civilisation in general. In 1941 Eliot's friend John Hayward edited, with the poet's approval, a selection from his critical work to date under the title *Points of View*.

Eliot has been seen as Dryden's successor in the sense that his critical work serves the purpose of introducing and justifying his own practice as a poet, and he has been seen as Arnold's successor in so far as he assumed the role of guardian of cultural élitism. By the time he came to write *For Lancelot Andrewes* he was defining his point of view as 'classicist in literature, royalist in politics, and anglo-catholic in religion'.[20] It is certainly tempting to detect the influence of T. E. Hulme in the reaction against romanticism, but in *After Strange Gods* (1933) he dismissed romanticism and classicism as matters which creative writers need not bother about. However, Eliot's emphasis upon tradition and his denial of the literary significance of the poet's 'personality' represented from the first a determination to rehabilitate objectivity and intellect.

The essay 'Tradition and the Individual Talent' in *The Sacred Wood* is seminal in this respect. It questions the habit of praising a poet especially for those elements in his work which are most 'individual' and differentiate him from others. Eliot argues that the best, even the most 'individual' parts of a poet's work may be those most alive with the influence of his poetic ancestors. No poet, no artist is significant in isolation. The whole of past literature will be 'in the bones' of the poet with the true historic sense which recognises the presence, as well as the 'pastness' of the past. Eliot's sense of the interdependence of present and past (which was later to achieve philosophical and spiritual dimensions in its articulation in *Four Quartets*) is something which he believed the poet must cultivate. He must become aware of the larger mind which transcends his private mind, the continuing current of thought which changes, not by casting off old writers as defunct, but by growing more complex and perhaps more refined with time. The poet must be always surrendering what he is at the moment to something more valuable:

> The progress of an artist is a continual self-sacrifice, a continual extinction of personality.[21]

Eliot's emphasis on the depersonalisation effected in creative work shifts the critical focus from the poet to the poetry. It also shifts the critical focus from the individual poem in isolation to the body of poetry to which it belongs – the poet's work as a whole and the living body of all poetry. Eliot sees the poet's mind as 'a receptable for seizing and storing up numberless feelings, phrases, images, which can remain there until all the particles which can unite to form a new compound are present together'. Concepts such as 'sublimity', 'greatness', or 'intensity' of emotion are irrelevant. The 'intensity' belongs to the pressures at work in the artistic process. Eliot is particularly determined to demolish the idea that the poet has a 'personality' to express. Experiences important for the man may have no place in his poetry and *vice-versa*.

> Poetry is not a turning loose of emotion, but an escape from emotion; it is not the expression of personality, but an escape from personality.[22]

As Eliot was at pains to differentiate poetry from self-expression, so too he insisted that it was no function of the poet to do the work of the thinker. In 'Shakespeare and the Stoicism of Seneca' (1927), an essay reprinted in *Elizabethan Essays* (1934), he decried the notion that Shakespeare was a great philosopher with a profound and coherent view of life. This is an 'illusion' which great poetry can give. He made a celebrated distinction between Dante, who had behind him in the thinking of Aquinas a strong and coherent philosophical system, and Shakespeare who had behind him only the thought of men far inferior to himself. Eliot insists that the relative quality of the poetry is quite independent of this vast and wholly fortuitous discrepancy in intellectual background. The poet's business is 'to express the greatest emotional intensity of his time, based on whatever his time happened to think'.[23] Poetry has its own function which can never be that of philosophy or theology.

At several points in his critical work, Eliot touched on the question of what the proper function of the critic should be. In 'The Function of Criticism' (1923), an essay reprinted in *Points of View* (1941), he seems drastically to confine the help a critic can possibly give to understanding of a work. 'Interpretation', he argues, is 'only legitimate when it is not interpretation at all',[24] but simply a matter of supplying useful facts about the background to a work – the conditions under which it was written and how it was conceived. He regards such facts as disinfectant, whereas giving opinion or fancy free rein in interpretative criticism can corrupt taste instead of educating it. Later, in *The Use of Poetry and the Use of Criticism* (1932), Eliot warned the critic against two converse extremes: that of paying too much attention to the moral, social, or religious implications of a work; and that of sticking so closely to the 'poetry', in neglect of what the poet has to say, that the work is emptied of all significance. Eliot tussles a good deal – and not always consistently – with the question of 'meaning' in poetry. There is one kind of poetry in which the 'meaning' may serve no other purpose than that of keeping the reader's mind diverted 'while the poem does its work on him'. The 'meaning', in fact, is the bit of meat which the burglar provides to keep the house-dog quiet. Some poets prefer not to bother with this rather superfluous element at all, and see 'possibilities of intensity through its elimination'.[25]

Eliot's unresolved reservations about 'meaning' in poetry left him uncomfortable with Shelley and less than fully at home with Wordsworth. Indeed he contributed his share to a major shift in public evaluation of the English poetic past. He wrote with enthusiasm of the Elizabethan and Jacobean dramatists and of the seventeenth-century Metaphysical poets, and thus gave primacy of prestige to a more virile and concentrated strain of poetic practice than that which produced the 'big' poems of the Romantics and the Victorians. In 'The Metaphysical Poets', one of the pieces published in *Homage to John Dryden* (1924), he coined a phrase which was to be taken into the currency of criticism with odd eagerness. He argued that the Metaphysical poets, together with the Elizabethan and Jacobean dramatists, had a 'mechanism of sensibility' that could accommodate any kind of experience, but that between the age of Donne and the Victorian age occurred a 'dissociation of sensibility' separating thought from feeling.[26] Ratiocination gave way to reflection and rumination. Thus, in the accompanying essay, 'Andrew Marvell', Eliot distinguishes the wit of the Caroline poets from the wit of Shakespeare, of Dryden ('the great master of contempt'), of Pope ('the great master of hatred'), or of Swift ('the great master of disgust'). This wit is found in some of the songs of *Comus* and in Marvell's *Horatian Ode*. He defines it tentatively as 'a tough reasonableness beneath the slight lyric grace' and argues that it cannot be matched in Shelley, Keats, or Wordsworth.[27]

There is today a tendency to treat Eliot's criticism as more illuminating in reference to his own poetic development than in reference to the literary history it ostensibly surveys. Certainly it must be accepted that the 'tough reasonableness' he admired cannot be regarded as a requisite of all poetry. But Eliot frequently interrupts himself to insert a parenthesis to the effect that there are kinds of poetry other than that for which he is immediately prescribing. What remains in the mind from perusal of Eliot's critical works is a rich scatter of sharp, illuminating comments that in aggregate constitute rather a shower of stimuli to re-examine settled attitudes than a thought-out critical philosophy. He urges on the poet the necessity for study of his predecessors and for a slogging discipline of self-criticism. Study of predecessors is something very different from easy acceptance of the worn tradition stemming from Wordsworth, Keats and Shelley. The poet must not slavishly limit his admired predecessors; he must work what he derives from them into something new and unique, for the poetic tradition thrives by constant reappraisal of the past. The poets to admire most are those in whose work thought and feeling are at one. Indeed the poet's task is to make new wholes, new amalgamations from the chaotic, disparate and fragmentary experience which is life. As for his own intentions, Eliot concedes that he learned from Baudelaire and Laforgue that poetry could be made from the 'sordid aspects' of modern urbanism. Here were untapped resources – 'the unpoetical' out of which poetry could be made.

Not less important, historically speaking, than Eliot's critical pronouncements was his crucial role in speeding recognition of where talent lay. Yeats, Pound, Joyce, and Wyndham Lewis were all acclaimed by Eliot. He was one of the first to champion *Ulysses* and, as a director of Faber, forwarded the publication of *Finnegans Wake*.

V Academic criticism

The critics we have so far dealt with in our review of the early twentieth century have, for the most part, certain things in common. Most of them (all except Hulme and Murry) were major creative writers. Most of them were innovators in both their creative and their critical work. None of them – except Ford in his very latest few years – held academic posts or were officially involved in the teaching of English literature. While they were at work, however, there was an output of literary criticism from writers who differed in various respects from these figures. They wrote in an environment in which new schools of English were attracting more and more university students to the subject. Meeting the needs of these students, during the first four decades of the century, were important academic critics, some of whom, while continuing in the Victorian tradition, were far more widely – if not more deeply – influential than the great figures we have already dealt with, the figures who tend to dominate surveys of criticism. Even in the 1930s it was not to James or Yeats, Ford or Eliot, that the average English literature student was directed when critical help was needed. He or she was more likely to be directed to those scholars who kept alive the tradition of narrative criticism in which writers were historically placed, their works described and their personalities explored.

A preeminent figure in this field was George Saintsbury (1845–1933) whose output as a critic eventually won him the chair of Rhetoric and English Literature at Edinburgh University. His numerous publications included *A History of Nineteenth-Century Literature* (1896), *The English Novel* (1914) and *The Peace of the Augustans* (1916), as well as works we referred to in the previous chapter. Saintsbury's most readable work was made palatable by the gusto with which he celebrated what delighted him in literature. He was a connoisseur of wine who wrote *Notes on a Cellarbook* (1920), and he brought to his savouring of the stylistic pleasures of literature a way of smacking the lips and scenting the bouquet that earned him the label 'hedonist'. Certainly he played down the significance of the 'subject-matter' of literature. What is the test of a good poet? he asked in *The Peace of the Augustans*:

> Why, the only catholic test-question of poetry – Is this the vivid and consummate expression, in metre, of an impression furnished by object, event, passion, imagination, fancy, or whatsoever humanity can be, do, suffer, or experience?

Saintsbury's successor at Edinburgh, Sir Herbert Grierson (1866-1960) had none of his predecessor's easy charm and fecundity as raconteur and literary *bon viveur*, but his scholarship provided a literary landmark when he edited Donne's poems in 1912 and *Metaphysical Lyrics and Poems of the Seventeenth Century* in 1921. For these works were crucial in inspiring the shift of taste towards the seventeenth-century Metaphysical poets which Eliot so powerfully effected. In his introduction to the Metaphysical collection, Grierson's assertion of Donne's importance is both enthusiastic and well-reasoned. Donne is one of those, like Dante and

Lucretius, whose poetry is 'inspired by a philosophical conception of the universe and the risk assigned to the human spirit in the great drama of existence':

> Whether verse of prose be his medium, Donne is always a poet, a creature of feeling and imagination, seeking expression in vivid phrase and complex harmonies, whose acute and subtle intellect was the servant, if sometimes the unruly servant, of passion and imagination.

How needful and salutary was Grierson's championing of the Metaphysicals might be gathered from the attitude of the poet A. E. Housman (1859–1936) who, as late as 1933, delivered a lecture 'The Name and Nature of Poetry' in which certain late nineteenth-century prejudices against the Metaphysicals seem to have ossified. For Housman, the function of poetry is not to transmit thought but to 'transfuse emotion'. Between *Samson Agonistes* and the *Lyrical Ballads* there was 'a whole age of English in which the place of poetry was usurped by something very different'. The Metaphysicals come under fire for their obsession with simile and metaphor, 'things inessential to poetry'. The eighteenth century was the period which established 'a healthy workmanlike prose to supersede the cumbrous and decorated and self-admiring prose of a Milton or a Jeremy Taylor', but much of its verse was 'sham poetry'. Satirical verse does an efficient job, but satire, controversy and burlesque 'are forms of art in which high poetry is not at home'. When the eighteenth-century poets tried to write 'high and impassioned poetry', they went for something as little like prose as possible, and plastered ornamental diction on anything and everything. Housman makes a good case in analysing the damage Dryden did by sheer empty inflation when he tried to improve Chaucer. Pope's *Iliad*, however, provides an even 'more dazzling and seductive example of the false manner'.

Housman does not deny to Pope the title of 'poet', in a certain 'ambiguous' usage of the term, but he insists that to use the word 'poetry' for what Pope wrote is dangerous. Whole-hearted admiration for poetry of that kind destroys 'the power to appreciate finer poetry or even to recognise it when met'. We get to the centre of Housman's thinking when he declares that 'poems very seldom consist of poetry and nothing else, and pleasure can be derived also from their other ingredients'. Two readers of Keble's *The Christian Year*, the one a devout woman, the other an atheist, might admire totally different ingredients exclusively. It is the atheist, of course, who is admiring the 'poetry' of the poems. And hence Housman argues:

> Good religious poetry, whether in Keble or Dante or Job, is likely to be most justly appreciated and most discriminatingly relished by the undevout.

Housman's differentiations may seem naive to modern readers. He goes so far as to declare, 'Poetry is not the thing said but a way of saying it.' Meaning is of the intellect, and poetry most definitely is not. Indeed, Housman adds, the four poets of the eighteenth century in whose work the true poetic accent can be heard were all mad: Collins, Smart, Cowper and Blake. Blake repeatedly gives us what Housman calls pure poetry 'adulterated with so little meaning that nothing except poetic emotion is perceived and matters'.

> Tho' thou art worship'd by the names divine
> Of Jesus and Jehovah, thou art still
> The Son of Morn in weary Night's decline,
> The lost traveller's dream under the hill.

That is 'pure and self-existent poetry'. Precisely because it seems to make theological nonsense, it leaves room for nothing but poetry. Indeed poetry is 'more physical than intellectual'. It has to be kept out of the mind when you are shaving or the skin might bristle inconveniently. A pint of beer for lunch, a two or three hours' walk with the mind set free from particular cogitation – that Housman found the best recipe for poetic composition. The words 'bubble up' from an abyss in 'the pit of the stomach'.

Housman's thinking represents in epitome an influential collection of notions about poetry which, while they beg all kinds of questions, nevertheless fed into the educational system of our country a still persistent attitude.

In the world of Shakespearean studies, a long vastly-admired work was *Shakespearean Tragedy* (1904) by A. C. Bradley, who held chairs in turn at Liverpool, Glasgow and Oxford. He was acclaimed as Coleridge's successor in the tradition of romantic criticism. He analysed the tragedies in detail with a thoroughness so intense in respect of characterisation that the *dramatis personae* become detached from their setting and are investigated as though they were living human beings under detective scrutiny. It is characteristic of Bradley that, in defining the role of the tragic hero, he can observe that Posthumus (of *Cymbeline*) would not have acted as Othello did in Othello's situation, and Othello would not have acted as Posthumus did in Posthumus's situation. Bradley's analyses are thoughtful and perceptive; they probe details of personal response in Shakespeare's characters with a subtlety and sympathy which gave his work an infectious appeal to generations of students. When he replies to the charge that it was weak of Ophelia to lose her reason, he wrings the reader's heart with a pathetic catalogue of the afflictions which have isolated her.

While Bradley touched the hearts of Shakespeare's readers, their minds could be fed through the scholarship of E. K. Chambers (1866–1954) who, having determined to investigate the conditions under which Shakespeare wrote, found it necessary in the interests of thoroughness to go back to the Middle Ages. Thus *The Mediaeval Stage* (1903), in two volumes, preceded *The Elizabethan Stage* (1923) in four volumes. The fruits of Chambers's immense research have benefited Shakespearean studies ever since. Meanwhile the nineteenth-century tradition of Shakespearean production, with its heavy emphasis on elaborate scenery and extravagant declamation, was being superseded through the efforts of Harley Granville-Barker (1877–1966). He recognised that the grandiose productions of Shakespeare in which actors such as Henry Irving and Herbert Beerbohm Tree starred, submerged the true poetic quality of the plays in a fantastic parade of illusion. His productions of *The Winter's Tale* and *Twelfth Night* in 1912 and of *A Midsummer Night's Dream* in 1914 transformed attitudes to Shakespeare by enormously simplifying stage settings, making use of an apron stage, and judiciously speeding up the delivery of blank verse. Gran-

ville-Barker wrote a series of *Prefaces to Shakespeare*, published
in five issues between 1927 and 1947, using his experience as
a director to shed light on Shakespeare's texts from the point
of view of the actor and the producer.

Among those who exercised a healthy influence on the
development of university English studies in the early
decades of the century was W. P. Ker (1855–1922) who
held a chair at University College, Cardiff, and then at
University College, London. He was a specialist in Norse as
well as in English literature, and he recognised the need for a
firm historical and linguistic discipline in English degree
courses. His chief works were *Epic and Romance* (1897), *The
Dark Ages* (1904) and *English Literature: Mediaeval* (1912).
Ker, who in the words of E. K. Chambers, 'said so many of
the best things about mediaeval literature', wore his learning
lightly and explored the various genres of mediaeval
literature in a way which appeals to the general reader,
while it feeds his understanding of the historical development
of literary forms. *English Literature: Mediaeval* was repeatedly
reprinted. So too, in the succeeding decade, was *The
Wandering Scholars* (1927) by Helen Waddell (1889–1965)
who delivered the eighth W. P. Ker Memorial Lecture at
Glasgow University in 1947 ('Poetry in the Dark Ages'). She
told how she planned a book of translations from mediaeval
Latin lyrics (*Mediaeval Latin Lyrics*, 1929) and her introduction 'outgrew the original intention' and became itself a
book. The two volumes – for biographical notes on the poets
are added – together represent the fruit of scholarship in
which the net is cast widely enough to bring in work from
Petronius of the first century AD to the twelfth century.
'Helen Waddell ... touches nothing which she does not
adorn', C. S. Lewis observed, and the charm of her work
derives from acute poetic sensitivity, felicity of style, and
imaginative vitality in sharing with the reader the emotional
fascination which the lyrics and the lyricists exercise for her.

VI Cambridge influences

No more vivid illustration could be found of the vast range of
approaches to literature which the words 'literary criticism'
can comprehend than to move from the fervent lyrical prose

of Helen Waddell to the cool deliberateness of the theoretician I. A. Richards (1893–1979). The connection between
literature and life, so delicately voiced by Helen Waddell, so
noisily proclaimed by D. H. Lawrence, is explored in
Richards's work by his bringing the new science of psychology to bear upon the criteria and technique for judging
literature. His book *Principles of Literary Criticism* (1924) set
out to establish a theoretical framework for criticism which
would dispense once and for all with the abstractions that
have bemused people in the past. There must be no more
talk of 'Beauty' as though it were a quality inherent in
external objects. We must cease in literary criticism to make
loose use of terms that locate 'rhythm', 'stress', 'character'
and so on in what after all is only print on paper. It soon
becomes clear that Richards's interest in psychology is
leading him, not to any fresh investigation of how the mind
of the poet works in composition (for he dismisses this area of
study as offering no basis for reliable enquiry), but to close
analysis of the relationship of the reader to what he reads.
Nevertheless, he regards the arts as a 'storehouse of recorded
value', supplying us with 'the best data available for deciding
what experiences are more valuable than others'.[28]

Richards ridicules metaphysical thinking that presupposes
qualities attaching to objects which might exist independ-
ently of any such attachments. Ultimates like 'beauty'
introduced into aesthetic criticism are simply devices to put
a stop to rational thinking. Richards sees the methods of
experimental science as the only sure means of attaining
reliability in literary criticism. Thus 'value' is defined as
'capacity for satisfying feeling and desire in various intricate
ways'.[29] Value can be measured by the extent to which
appetencies are satisfied, but there is a hierarchy of appetencies and so the measurement is affected both by the
relative 'importance' of the various appetencies satisfied,
and also by the extent to which other appetencies are
concomitantly thwarted. For Richards the mind is the
nervous system, so that satisfaction is ultimately physical.
In so far as he produces what may be called a 'qualitative'
assessment of mental satisfaction, it is derived from a
quantitative evaluation; but this quantitative evaluation

calculates, not the number of minds satisfied, but the number and weight of impulses satisfied within the individual mind. States of mind are 'valuable' in so far as they involve coordination of activities as opposed to curtailment of them, and in this respect no proper measurement can be made so long as we have recourse to abstractions such as virtues and vices. The delight we take in a tragedy is certainly not either a recognition that 'all's right with the world' or that 'somewhere, somehow, there is Justice'; it is an indication that 'all is right here and now in the nervous system'.[30]

In a chapter on 'The Two Uses of Languages', Richards distinguishes two kinds of causation for 'mental events'. The first kind is represented by the stimuli affecting the mind through the senses immediately, and also combining with what survives from comparable related stimuli in the past. The second kind of causation lies in the mind itself, its particular needs and its degree of relevant receptiveness. The interaction of these two kinds of causation will determine the character of the mental event. In the scientific field, impulse should be exclusively derived from what is external. The scientific use of language thus relies on *reference* undistorted by the receiving mind. By contrast there is an *emotive* use of language which is designed not so much to promote 'references' as to arouse attitudes and emotions associated with them. The kind of 'truth' proper to science resides in the accuracy of references and in the logicality of their interconnections. The kind of 'truth' proper to fiction may reside rather in internal coherence than in correspondence with actual facts.[31]

Richards's later book *Practical Criticism, A Study of Literary Judgment* (1929) had an enormous influence for a time on the study of literature. It represented a record of practical research, and to that extent was in tune with Richards's insistence that literary criticism had to escape from dogmatism and argumentation into inquiry. To this end he distributed copies of unidentified poems to his Cambridge students and required them to pass critical judgments on them in ignorance of who wrote them and when. The result was a somewhat startling display of 'bad taste' in that plenty of students rubbished G. M. Hopkins, for instance, and applauded Studdert Kennedy. Richards gives a detailed account of the work submitted and then analyses the chief difficulties of criticism which it illustrates, namely, failure to understand the sense of a poem; insensitivity to the form and movement of words in sequence; wide deviations in responsiveness to imagery; the intrusion into reading of 'mnemonic irrelevancies' based on purely adventitious personal associations; the reliance upon 'stock responses' which involve already established views and emotions; facile responsiveness which constitutes 'sentimentality', and its converse, an inhibited 'hardness of heart'; susceptibility to 'doctrinal adhesions' actually or seemingly relevant to what a poet is saying; presuppositions about fashions of technique due to past experience which has discredited them; and finally 'general critical preconceptions' which intervene between reader and poem.[32]

The experiment Richards made and the material it produced proved more stimulating than the general critical theory into which he subsumed it. Nevertheless some of his terminology (like the distinction between the 'scientific' and the 'emotive' use of language) proved useful in sharpening responsiveness to literary quality and defining it more reliably. Richards distinguished different kinds of 'meaning', citing four distinct aspects: sense, feeling, tone, and intention. The 'sense' is what we direct our hearer's attention to when we utter. But we generally have certain 'feelings' about the items we point to, and we use language to express those feelings. We colour or flavour the information according to a personal bias of interest. Then we pick our words and arrange them with an eye to the character or stance or understanding of the person we address and his relationship to us. This determines the 'tone' of our utterance. Lastly we speak with a conscious or unconscious 'intention', and this purpose modifies our speech. Richards exemplifies how one or other of these functions may predominate according to whether a scientist is writing a treatise, a populariser is trying to appeal to a large public, or a politician is seeking to be elected to Parliament.

Many have criticised Richards for his tendency to isolate the poem from its background, and the philosophical framework on which his psychology is founded has come under fire from many sides. But he did much to discredit the kind of nebulous sentimentality and lax rhetoric which disfigures minor Georgian poetry and a good deal of the fashionable literary history and biography. His encouragement to students to tussle with subtleties and complexities of style and meaning played its part in the shift from the age of Tennyson to the age of Eliot. Indeed the Appendix on 'The Poetry of T. S. Eliot' which he added at the end of *Principles of Literary Criticism* shows him, as early as 1924, quickly alert to what Eliot was about in his use of allusion for the purpose of compression. '*The Waste Land* is the equivalent in content to an epic.'[33]

We have seen how new critical thinking in the 1910s and 1920s, whether directly or indirectly, often expressed dissatisfaction with Georgian poetry. The Georgians simplified poetic diction by eliminating archaisms fashionable with the Victorians and by cutting down on overworked rhetorical artifices. They also eschewed formal pontification, religious or philosophic, and went instead for homeliness and simplicity. In 1929, in *A Survey of Modernist Poetry*, the poets Robert Graves (1895–1985) and Laura Riding (*b*.1901) complained that the result of Georgian avoidance of what might be clamant or controversial was 'a poetry which could be praised rather for what it was not than for what it was'.[34] The stately 'profundities' of the Victorians and the wickedness of the bohemian 'nineties had given way to harmless musing about the countryside and love, age and childhood, sheep and ducks. Graves reacted as a poet against what he called the 'anodynic tradition of poetry', for he valued concentration and intensity as well as lucidity. The *Survey* includes an analysis of Shakespeare's sonnet 'The expense of spirit in a waste of shame' designed to illustrate how several meanings may be interwoven together within a single line of verse.

This exercise inspired William Empson (1906–84), one of I. A. Richards's pupils at Cambridge, to make a full-scale investigation into multiplicity of meaning in *Seven Types of Ambiguity* (1930). He later acknowledged that 'ambiguity' was not perhaps the best term to have used for the combination of multiple significances that occur in the use of words in poetry. Empson came under fire at the time for the iconoclastic tone evident in some of his dismissive comments on such venerated figures as Wordsworth and Tennyson, but his book was the work of a young enthusiast galvanised into fresh thinking, and it became a classic of critical studies. Empson's method inevitably involved close analysis of poetry with detailed concentration on word-by-word explication, and in this respect it matched what I. A. Richards had done in sending would-be critics back to their desks with a scientific zeal for microscopic dissection. Empson's term 'ambiguity' covers 'any verbal nuance, however slight, which gives room for alternative reactions'. He divides the kinds of ambiguity attended to into seven types, though he accepts that this is a somewhat arbitrary classification and that the types overlap.

Empson prefaces his examination of the 'first type' with an attack upon ill-considered contemporary attitudes such as that which would deny that meaning matters in poetry because it is appreciated as pure sound, and the cultivation of a belief in so-called 'atmosphere' which, he argues, vitiated much nineteenth-century poetry. For Empson, 'atmosphere' can only be a by-product of meaning, and the attempt to manufacture it for its own sake is mistaken. Examples of comparisons containing multiple points of likeness lead him, for instance, into a survey of Nash's image:

> Beauty is but a flower
> Which wrinkles will devour.

He shows how bringing to life the 'subdued' metaphorical content of the word 'devour' may turn the wrinkles into 'Time's tooth-marks' as well as 'rodent ulcers, caterpillars on petals, and the worms that are to gnaw it in the grave'.[35] Proceeding to the kind of ambiguities in which 'two or more alternative meanings are fully resolved into one', he shows how

> But change she earth, or change she sky,
> Yet will I love her till I die

may be read in terms of change from one part of the earth to another, from this planet to another, and from the speaker's social sphere to one out of his reach. This is not all. She may alter my earth and sky by bursting my bubble-dream . . . she may upset the whole cosmic and earthly fabric . . . and so on.[36]

The third type of ambiguity is the simultaneous utterance of unconnected meanings, in other words, puns and allegorical compounds. These of course rely upon the reader's full alertness to the verbal subtlety involved. In the fourth type of ambiguity, however, the duplicities of meaning are, as it were, 'absorbed' into the intense exploration of the situation involved. Empson takes Shakespeare's sonnet,

> I never saw that you did painting need,

and shows how packed it is with interpretative possibilities relative to the extremely complex state of mind revealed.[37] It is not just that an individual word like 'painting' or 'need' is open to various readings, but also that sentence-structure from line to line allows of alternative syntactical and grammatical readings. Empson proceeds to the kind of ambiguity manufactured in the very process of writing, to the kind in which a seeming contradiction or irrelevance invites the reader to interpret, and lastly to the kind in which a frank contradiction expresses a division in the poet's mind. In all these cases it is the imagination brought to bear in the practical exemplification of connotative subtleties and multiplicities which gives the study its quality and which caused it to represent another landmark in the shift to modernism.

Another influential figure in the movement to change the map of literary history, to which writers as diverse as Empson, Richards, and Eliot contributed, was F. R. Leavis (1895–1978). In his teaching career at Downing College, Cambridge, he preached and practised an approach to literature which advocated close attention to the text and encouraged sharp discrimination in evaluating what was read. His approach to literature involved an Arnoldian revulsion against the crude philistinism of an increasingly technological and impersonal civilisation. The literary cause he forwarded thus assumed the character of a crusade, and he gathered round him a band of enthusiastic disciples. The narrowness of some of his judgments – which in varying degrees the disciples supported – and the aggressiveness with which they were propounded, together served eventually to produce a backlash, but not before English faculties in universities throughout the Commonwealth had received a scatter of enthusiasts for an extremely limited diet of literary studies, as well as for non-alcoholic drinks and bicycle trouser-clips.

Leavis's early books of literary criticism, *New Bearings in English Poetry* (1932) and *Revaluation* (1936) assail popular conventions of poetic evaluation by acclaim for the work of Eliot, Pound and Hopkins, and by dismissive depreciation of celebrated Victorian and Georgian poets. Leavis follows Eliot in finding in the Metaphysical poets the qualities which twentieth-century writers desperately needed to recover. Recasting the canon of English poetry involves downgrading Milton and Shelley; it is significant that Leavis's insensitivity to the connotative resonances enriching Milton's blank verse should be later matched by his coolness towards Joyce's verbal acrobatics. Praise of Hopkins focuses on the fact that, by contrast, he displays how small are the resources of the English language that other Victorian poets exploit.

> His words seem to have substance, and to be made of a great variety of stuffs. The intellectual and spiritual anaemia of Victorian poetry is indistinguishable from its lack of body.[38]

In this connection Leavis praises the art of 'concrete realisation' – the poetic energy which enables words not to present something to the reader, but to act upon him. He instances the tactile force and 'sensuous firmness' of the word 'plump' in Keats's 'Ode to Autumn':

> To swell the gourd, and plump the hazel shells
> With a sweet kernel.

Probably Leavis's most influential work, however, was his book *The Great Tradition* (1948) in which he turned from poetry to the novel. The positive thing about this study was the way Leavis, following Henry James, recognised that the novel justified the kind of critical attention in detail which formerly had been given only to poetry and drama. We are apt to take this for granted today, but Leavis was a pioneer in arguing that English poetic energy in the nineteenth century went into prose fiction. Enthusiastic Leavisites have claimed that by virtue of his treatment of novels in this books, *The Great Tradition* has in English literary history a status comparable to that of Johnson's *Lives of the Poets* and Arnold's *Essays in Criticism*. Yet Leavis's praise of George Eliot, Henry James, Joseph Conrad and D. H. Lawrence is rendered partisan by its exclusiveness and provokes negative reactions. Herein lies a curious weakness of the Leavis school. It encouraged the emergence of an 'English specialist' who need not trouble to open the pages of great writers who happened not to be among the master's elect. Thus, while setting out to guide others in his book *What to Read in English Literature* (1975), Denys Thompson tells us why he has not mentioned Sir Walter Scott among the novelists of his age. 'The reason is that I do not happen to have read anything of his except a few poems ...'[39]

As Leavis saw it, the study of literature could perform a key function in rescuing the quality of life in an age of crisis when it was threatened by a civilisation whose technology and media together debase standards and empty daily life of human content. The literature of the past can serve to keep alive an awareness of existence in the past at a time when the individual partook of a rich cultural life. In *The Common Pursuit* (1952) he cited the quality of the language of Bunyan's *Pilgrim's Progress* as exemplifying a blend of traditional art with the raciness of life lived. Historians have queried Leavis's simplistic notion of seventeenth-century man's place in society, but his critique of the contemporary was not thereby invalidated. However, the rapidity with which Leavis jumps between judgment of a writer's language and judgment of his attitude to life is symptomatic of what is perhaps an unresolved inner contradiction. He describes Henry James as a 'poet-novelist' in *The Great Tradition* and explains that he has done so because 'the determining and controlling interests in his art engage what is "deepest in him" and appeal to what is deepest in us'.[40] Leavis is at pains to make clear that it is such profundity of engagement which makes a novelist a 'poet' – and not verbal decoration. Indeed, he urges, it would be ridiculous to call Virginia Woolf a poet. What she gives us is really 'the equivalent of Georgian poeticising'.

Leavis's astringency and bellicosity inevitably bred controversy. The neglect he long suffered as editor of *Scrutiny* and as rebellious Cambridge tutor left a legacy of bitterness. Moreover, with increasingly scathing intensity, he identified as the Enemy to which all integrity and true culture were opposed the academic establishment, the BBC, the British Council, the so-called 'quality' press, and many who simply chose to stay outside the circle of his admirers. His belief that an educated public could only be produced by a minority of people who spread the gospel strengthened the cult-consciousness among his disciples. Ultimately, when C. P. Snow delivered his Rede Lecture *The Two Cultures and the Scientific Revolution* in 1959, Leavis replied with his Richmond Lecture *Two Cultures? The Significance of C. P. Snow* (1961) and his venom exceeded all bounds in repeated denunciation of his opponent's ignorance: it gives the impression of a man whose judgment has been totally distorted by personal obsessions.

VII Symbol and myth

There were one or two books published during the 1920s and 1930s which helped to alert readers to the character and potency of poetic utterance. To a certain extent they represented dissatisfaction with the kind of semantic thinking which lay behind *The Meaning of Meaning* (1923) by I. A. Richards and C. K. Ogden (1884–1957). This book attempted to distinguish between the strict scientific use of words where the word directly stands for its referent, and the emotive use of words in which the process of reference gives place to the more primitive business of expressing or exciting feelings and attitudes. The correct 'referential' use of words involves a relation between symbol and referent which is true. 'The height of the Eiffel Tower is 900 feet' is thus a true statement. But 'Poetry is a spirit' or 'Man is a worm' are not statements at all and cannot therefore be either true or false.

In 1928 Owen Barfield (*b*.1898), a member of the circle of friends that gathered around C. S. Lewis, published *Poetic Diction, A Study in Meaning*. Barfield took Ogden and Richards to task for failing to recognise that the very vocabulary they used (terms such as 'reference' and 'stimulus') is figurative in origin and therefore itself required scrutiny. Barfield argued that it is impossible to build any semantic theory on the contrast between so-called 'scientific' language and metaphorical language because much of the technical vocabulary of science is itself metaphorical. He cites the history of words such as 'focus', 'gravity', 'function', 'concept', and 'intuition' to indicate the strength of metaphorical residue inhering in so-called 'scientific' vocabulary. He decries the false dichotomy between science and poetry as modes of knowing and experiencing life. It leads to the shallow conception of 'art as meaningless emotion – as *personal* emotions symbolized – which is so poisonous in its charter to all kinds of posturing and conceited egotism'.[41]

Barfield illustrates how poets, by their metaphorical language, can restore conceptually a unity which in primitive times was experienced intuitively. The poetic imagination recreates something that has been lost from perception. This notion was taken up by Maud Bodkin (1875–1967) in her book *Archetypal Patterns in Poetry* (1934). Maud Bodkin had a psychological as well as a literary background and studied for a time under Carl Jung (1875–1961) in Zurich. She set herself to explore and explain the feelings and associations evoked by certain passages of poetry. She focuses especially on works such as Coleridge's 'The Ancient Mariner', Shakespeare's *Hamlet* and *Othello*, and Milton's *Paradise Lost*: for her concern is to demonstrate the part played by primordial images which recur in poetry that appeals by its expression of the inner life. These archetypal patterns involve recurring motifs such as that of the guilt-haunted wanderer – the figures of Cain, the Wandering Jew, the Flying Dutchman, and the like – which appear to be merged with that of Coleridge's Ancient Mariner. Exploration of the imagery of caverns and fountains, wind and calm, goes alongside examination of the opposition of God and Devil, Paradise and Hades, to illuminate the extent to which poets draw on universal symbols that touch deeply rooted centres of resonance in the reader's mind. Maud Bodkin is like Barfield in allowing for the growth of meaning in a poem independent of the poet's conscious intention.

Interest in the analysis of Shakespeare's imagery was stimulated when Caroline Spurgeon (1869–1942) published *Shakespeare's Imagery* (1935). Her schematic classification of recurring images was the first attempt at systematic documentation in this field. But the critic who made most fruitful use of this kind of tabulation was G. Wilson Knight (1897–1985), for he approached the exploration of imagery not with a scientific but with a metaphysical bent. It may be said that he took up where Walter Whiter left off at the end of the eighteenth century. His first critical works on Shakespeare, *The Wheel of Fire* (1930) and *The Imperial Theme* (1931), brought acute poetic sensitivity to bear on images and image-clusters, drawing out the symbolic content, examining the thematic relationships, and weaving patterns of thought therefrom which at least have the virtue of being well-grounded in alert reading of the texts. The books soon established themselves, and they exercised a crucial influence in redirecting attention away from study of characters as though they were actual beings to awareness of the function the poetry performs in constituting a patterned whole, rich in symbolic reverberations.

Wilson Knight explicitly protested against focus on characterisation which isolates one part only of the total fabric of a play, tearing it out 'ruthlessly for detailed analysis on the analogy of human life', and neglecting poetic symbolism. He regarded it as absurd for critics to dismiss the poetic content of a play with nothing more than a few vague expressions about the 'magic of poetry', whilst Hamlet is 'treated in Harley Street'.[42] It is one thing to work on the central core of a play as a visionary whole 'close-knit in personification, atmospheric suggestion, and direct poetic-symbolism'. It is another thing to digress into irrelevant real-life hypotheses.

There are plays which lend themselves better than others to Wilson Knight's imaginative exploration. Where there is a latent 'philosophical' content, as in the representation of conflicting ideologies in the Greek and Trojan camps in *Troilus and Cressida*, Wilson Knight exploits his method to extrapolate schematic dichotomies such as the rational and the emotional, the intellectual and the intuitive, the cynical and the romantic. The method encourages the reader to see Hector and Thersites, Ulysses and Pandarus, Archilles and Troilus, not as so many idiosyncratic individuals oddly brought into conjunction by an explorer of human nature who is fascinated by their juxtaposition in the interaction of person with person, but rather as essential pieces in a colourful poetic mosaic representing the coherent vision of a philosophically-minded poet.

In a similar analysis of the imagery of *Antony and Cleopatra*, Wilson Knight schematises the metaphorical pattern in terms of a contrast between the West and the East, the value of Empire and the value of Love, the world of efficiency and the world of sentiment. These are masculine and feminine worlds respectively. Cleopatra is enthroned on the water; Antony's proper footing is with Caesar on the firm-set earth. Against a background of imagery of oscillation, Antony wavers between his allegiance to love and Cleopatra, and his allegiance to war and Rome. It is highly symbolic that he is victorious by land and then defeated in the battle at sea. But perhaps Wilson Knight is most illuminating when he analyses the imagery of plays such as *Macbeth*, where the thematic strands develop powerful contrasts between what is of life and what is of death. The imagery of sleep and feasting, two major restoratives of the healthy life, is particularly far-reaching; the banquet is interrupted by the ghost of Banquo, and Lady Macbeth's sleep is interrupted by consciousness of bloody guilt: these are parallel movements in the total imaginative configuration. Moreover, the death-banquet, the hell-broth concocted by the weird sisters from absurd fragments torn from bodies in a way which desecrates the order of healthy natural life, symbolises the evil let loose by the villainy of Macbeth. And as the phantom of the dead Banquo interrupted the life-banquet, so this death-banquet produces phantoms suggestive of life and regality. Wilson Knight's work heralded an outburst of interest in symbolism which soon became familiar not only to students of Shakespeare and other poetic dramatists, but also to readers of novels by Dickens, Hardy, and other novelists whose minds worked poetically. So far as Shakespeare is concerned, it may be argued that symbolical criticism became more persuasive and less arbitrary when it was disciplined by understanding of Elizabethan presuppositions about the world and its inhabitants, such as was explicated by E. M. W. Tillyard (1889–1962) in his study *The Elizabethan World Picture* (1943).

11
The Twentieth Century: Post-war Developments

We have seen English critics strongly influenced by European thinkers at certain points in our literary history. Three of the major critics considered in the last chapter, Henry James, T. S. Eliot and Ezra Pound, were American-born. As the later decades of the century pass, the course of literary criticism in Britain is increasingly influenced, indeed often seemingly determined, by intellectual trends emanating from abroad. With the vastly improved facility of communication, philosophical and cultural innovation is readily projected on to the international scene. The closer involvement of critical developments in Britain with movements initiated abroad, and often fostered especially in the USA, inevitably gives a more cosmopolitan character to studies in this field.

It is always hazardous to try to survey recent developments in thinking. Since the Second World War we have seen an escalation in the way fashions succeed each other in the field of academic literary criticism. It is for the philosopher to say whether this shows literary men and women reflecting in their own sphere the ethos of a consumerist society, which relies on perpetual novelty to keep the wheels of industry turning. It is the literary historian's duty to record the passing fashions with as little prejudice as possible, avoiding on the one hand the temptation to write off every new 'ism' as one more brand of packaged trendiness, and on the other hand the easy assumption that when a clever person writes a clever book, then there must be wisdom to be derived from it, and the degree of wisdom is likely to be co-relative with the novelty of the thesis.

One or two general points need to be made about the drift of critical thinking as revealed in the review of successive theories made in this chapter. They concern the relationship between criticism and creation. There seems to be no clear connection between the particular kind of literature the last forty years have produced and the output of academic critical thinking that has accompanied it. We found a decisive connection earlier in the century between what the great modernist writers were doing and what the critics were arguing about. The critical thinking was securely earthed in the field of contemporary literature. This cannot be said of some of the more recent critical thinking exemplified here. Sometimes it seems to exist in isolation from the sphere of living literary productivity. It derives its impetus from philosophy, linguistics or social theory rather than from contemporary or past literature. When we considered the criticism of previous ages, the names of great past and contemporary writers were continually cropping up. Our last chapter dealt with many great writers who were themselves the propounders of critical theory. This invigorating relationship with living literature is much less in evidence in some recent critical theorising. Instead of sweeping us into contact with living literature, it so often takes us under the shadow of philosophers and political radicals.

The critical theories that have been fashionable in recent decades did not spring into existence without ancestry. To do justice to critical movements such as the 'Marxist' school or the 'Structuralist' school, it is necessary to look back to their origins in thinkers who worked earlier in the century or even late last century. When Eliot and his contemporaries were at work here, there were movements of thought in Europe which have burgeoned into fashionable schools of criticism in this country only since the Second World War. For this reason it would be undesirable to try to work through the history of critical thinking chronologically from decade to decade. Instead, the various schools will be looked at in turn.

Before turning to these categories, however, attention is given to two major critics who resist classification among them.

I C. S. Lewis and Northrop Frye

The critical output of C. S. Lewis (1898–1963) was distinctive in many ways. He revived the genre of historical criticism by his work on Mediaeval and Renaissance literature in *The Allegory of Love* (1936) and *English Literature in the Sixteenth Century* (1954). It is not just the scholarship in these books that stands out as distinctive; it is also the quality of presentation in which deft logic, aptly imaginative exemplification, and felicitous phrasing make study a delight. There are those, as we shall see, who want to judge a work of literature by its 'literariness' alone. If the work of literary critics themselves were to be evaluated by its 'literariness', then it would be Lewis's output, and not the output of critics fluent in the new jargons, that would shine amid dross. Whatever is said in praise of the Marxists, the structuralists, and for that matter many of the Leavisites, mastery of style has never been their forte. If major literary criticism has to be itself literature – in the sense that much of the work of Dryden and Johnson, Hazlitt and De Quincey was – then Lewis is one of a handful of writers who produced it in our age.

Quite apart from his literary history, from the jolt he gave to misunderstanding of Milton in his *Preface to Paradise Lost* (1942), and from his reply to T. S. Eliot's exaltation of Dryden over Shelley in the opening essay of *Rehabilitations* (1939), Lewis plunged into critical theory in three crucial publications. The first was a joint publication with E. M. W. Tillyard, *The Personal Heresy: A Controversy* (1939). It consists of alternate contributions from the combatants in a dispute which began in 1934 when Lewis wrote an essay in the English Association's journal *Essays and Studies*, and cited Tillyard's book on Milton as an instance in which poetry was treated as an expression of the poet's personality. The 'great poet', Lewis argued, may be merely the man who possesses the poet's skill in a high degree, not necessarily a man great in wisdom or virtue who happens to write poetry. It is not difficult to prove that major poets may be quite unfit as models of virtue. Poetry is 'an art or skill', but it differs from music because 'you cannot write or read one word of a poem by thinking only about poetry'.[1] The first word of a poem takes you outside poetry.

It may be argued that Lewis's literary criticism takes you outside literary criticism. He was deeply conscious of being at loggerheads with the spirit of his age. This was a matter both of religious faith and of cultural orientation. He ruminated on the significance of this in the inaugural lecture he gave at Cambridge when he was appointed to the chair of Mediaeval and Renaissance English Literature. Here he argued that the assumed Great Divide between the Middle Ages and the Renaissance is not so significant as the Great Divide between the Christian and the post-Christian ages which lies 'somewhere between us and the Waverley Novels, somewhere between us and *Persuasion*'. Christian and pre-Christian pagans had 'more in common with each other than either has with the post-Christian'. Lewis cites changes in political, social and artistic attitudes, in religion and technology, as evidence that we have cut ourselves off from the 'Old Western' culture and he wryly proposes himself as a rare surviving specimen of 'Old Western Man' who ought to be valued as a dinosaur would be valued if it had miraculously survived into our age.[2]

It is in his book *An Experiment in Criticism* (1961) that Lewis probes most deeply into literary theory. He sets himself the task of enquiring whether it might be plausible to 'define a good book as a book which is read in one way, and a bad book as a book which is read in another'. He argues that if people have an appetite for the swift recording of events, accompanied by insensitivity to aural effect and dislike for real vitality of description or dialogue, they may find good writing unpalatable and be cut off from real literary experience. He formulates a crucial distinction between those who 'use' literature, whether as pastime or puzzle or wish-fulfilment, treating words as mere 'pointers or signposts', and those who 'receive' it. Terms like 'magic' or 'evocation' are quite apt in trying to define 'the exquisitely detailed compulsions' which words exercise over the mind willing to receive. Lewis argues that the academic study of English literature has directed to the study of literature 'a great many talented, ingenious, and diligent people whose

real interests are not specifically literary at all'.[3] He is critical
of the readiness to foist 'philosophies of life' on to great poets.
He makes great play in mockery of what he calls 'the Vigilant
school of critics' to whom 'criticism is a form of social and
ethical hygiene'. For 'their conception of what is good in
literature makes a seamless whole with their total conception
of the good life'.[4] The Leavisites seem to be in Lewis's mind
as he castigates those for whom there is 'no specifically
literary good', for whom a passage of literature can be good
only if 'it reveals attitudes which are essential elements in the
good life'. He will have no truck with those whom you can
admire as critics 'only if you also revere them as sages'.[5]

There are numerous illuminating judgments thrown off in
this book. Many of them challenge fashionable assumptions
in the world of Eng. Lit. For instance, Lewis questions
whether evaluation is really an important function of
criticism and whether training the young in evaluative
techniques is really fruitfully educative. He quotes Arnold,
'The great art of criticism is to get oneself out of the way and
to let humanity decide', in contradistinction to the educational fashion for persistently pressing students for their
judgment on what they have read. Lewis insists that the
critics who have really helped him personally to understand
and appreciate literature are the 'Dryasdust' editors and
textual critics, the literary historians, and the emotive critics
who have infected him with their enthusiasm. The impulse to
go out of the self, to enter into other men's beliefs, and to be
admitted to experience other than our own is what is satisfied
by good literature.

Lewis was at work while the 'New Criticism' movement, as
we shall shortly see, was busily reducing the status of
biographical and historical study and laying primary emphasis on the autonomy of the work under scrutiny. A Canadian
critic came to prominence in the 1950s for whom close study
of a text involved a totally different concept of what the
critic must be about. This was Northrop Frye (b.1912), who
broke new ground with his book *Anatomy of Criticism* (1957),
the first of a series of critical works which are distinctive in
thought and, unlike so much modern criticism, lively in
presentation.

Frye believes that criticism should be a systematic and organised study. In *Fables of Identity* (1963) he claims that much supposed criticism is 'sonorous nonsense' that contributes nothing to a systematic structure of knowledge.[6] The business of up-grading and down-grading poets on a kind of stock exchange of literary reputations renders so-called evaluation absurd. As for those who primarily practise structural analysis, they stop short of recognising that literary criticism needs a 'co-ordinating principle' by which what is seen in an individual work can be grasped as part of a vast whole. In short, an immense source of critical enlightenment awaits us if we recognise that there may be much more in a poem than even the poet himself may have been aware of: for the poet delivers his offspring, the poem, and must allow it to be cut loose from the navel string of his private associations and ambitions. The key to understanding lies in recognition of archetypes which represent a 'unifying category' of criticism. Frye observes how 'random and peripheral' is the critical experience which is produced by mediocre works of art; while 'the profound masterpiece seems to draw us to a point at which we can see an enormous number of converging patterns of significance'. We may consider the 'intricate verbal texture' of the grave-digger scene in *Hamlet*. We may attend to the flow of imagery of corruption such as Wilson Knight attended to. We may dwell on the psychological complexities investigated by Bradley. We may examine the scene in terms of the theatrical conventions utilised. But the thing that would pull all these strands of scholarly organisation together would be 'to glimpse the archetype of the scene, as the hero's *Liebestod*'; the declaration of love, the fatal fight with Laertes, the leap into the grave, and the return from it.

Frye is one of those critics whose illustrations are more persuasive than his overall generalisations. When he traces limited patterns of significance by correlating the phase of dawn, spring, and birth with myths of revival, resurrection, and creation, and finding therein the archetype of romance, or by correlating the phase of zenith, summer, and marriage with myths of entry into Paradise, and finding therein the archetype of comedy, pastoral, and idyll, the reader cannot but feel that an elaborate schedule of the obvious is being manufactured. But when he fastens on a text, he can be fascinating; and anyone sceptical of his abstractions and universals should study a paper he delivered in 1958, 'Literature as Context: Milton's Lycidas'. It is a thorough-going demolition of the traditional estimate of 'Lycidas' as an elegy in which personal sincerity is sacrificed to artifice and redundant display of knowledge. Frye shows how the tradition of pastoral elegy is exploited, in which 'the subject of the elegy is not treated as an individual but as a representative of a dying spirit of nature'. The pastoral name 'Lycidas' is the equivalent of 'Adonis', and Milton exploits the imagery of the cycle of the sun, the cycle of the seasons, and the cycle of water. Orpheus is invoked as the archetypal poet who died young and was thrown into the water. St Peter is invoked as the archetypal priest ('the Pilot of the Galilean Lake'). There is no need to pursue Frye's examples further. They prove substantial in corroborating his demand that 'Lycidas' must be studied in relation to literature as a whole. It is packed with echoes from past literature. And the structural principle which informs it is myth. Poems cannot be properly examined in isolation. They are inherently connected with other poems of the same kind. Value judgments can be made only in dependence upon scholarship, which itself is dependent on 'a coordinated view of literature'.

II The 'new criticism'

Frye's way of digging into the text, like Wilson Knight's focus on poetic imagery, had the effect of encouraging close reading. So too, for that matter, had the influence of I. A. Richards and William Empson. It was in the USA, however, that concentration on the text-as-text had become a central plank in what became known as the 'New Criticism'. The poet John Crowe Ransom (1888–1974) became Professor of Poetry at Kenyon College, Ohio in 1937 and established the *Kenyon Review*. His book *The New Criticism*, which surveys some modern critics, including T. S. Eliot and I. A. Richards, came out in 1941, but Ransom had already nailed his colours to the mast in an essay 'Criticism Inc' in the *Virginia Quarterly Review* in 1937.[7]

Ransom's case is that University schools of English ought to concentrate precisely and systematically on their proper business, which is 'criticism'. And criticism is 'the attempt to define and enjoy the aesthetic or characteristic values of literature'. Professors of English should not be diverted into humanistic or leftist advocacy of a moral system, for their proper concern is with literature as an art with its own constitution and structure. They should not be content with historical scholarship for, indispensable as it may be, it is, like linguistic studies, only a buttress for the private act of appreciation and the public business of criticism. While granting the need for the student to learn how to enter into the mind of the past and shake off the mind of the present in order to appreciate the literature of other ages, Ransom insists that this admirable discipline does not constitute an adequate programme of English studies.

Ransom formulates an exhaustive schedule of the various routes of escape from true criticism which academics take. It is a list of the activities which are not criticism. There is 'personal registration', recording the subjective effects of a work. There is 'synopsis and paraphrase', the easiest of all escape routes. There are 'historical studies' and 'linguistic studies', 'moral studies' and any other concern with 'some abstract or prose content taken out of the work'. What remains from this bonfire? Ransom allows for 'studies in the technique of art', which in the case of poetry would concentrate on those devices which distinguish it from prose.

This distinction was crucial for Ransom. The poet wants to preserve in his celebration of the poetic object something which prose would destroy. He grasps it within a connotational 'tissue' which will keep it secure. There is thus a 'prose core', by literal concentration on which the critic can do violence to the object, and there is the 'residuary tissue' in which it is involved. This 'tissue' is in terms of the logic of prose superfluous, even 'irrelevant'.

Later Ransom developed this distinction as one between 'texture' and 'structure'. The 'structure' is the story, the object, the situation, or whatever, which gives us the 'argument' of the poem. The 'texture' is the 'thingness' of the things by which it is particularised.

Ransom taught at Vanderbilt University before going to Kenyon College, and one of his pupils at Vanderbilt was the poet and novelist Robert Penn Warren (1905–89). He and Cleanth Brooks (*b*.1906) together edited a series of books for students including *Understanding Poetry* (1938) and *Understanding Fiction* (1943). They ruled out the study of poetry for the purpose of gaining anything in the way of historical understanding or moral value. Cleanth Brooks thereafter wrote *Modern Poetry and the Tradition* (1939) and *The Well-Wrought Urn* (1947).[8] The sub-title of the latter is *Studies in the Structure of Poetry*, and Brooks seeks to pin down the characteristics which go to make poetic utterance what it is. The first chapter focuses on 'Paradox' and illustrates from examples as diverse as Wordsworth's 'Sonnet Composed on Westminster Bridge' and Donne's 'The Canonization' how the device enables the poet to say what direct statement could never convey, freeing the terms he uses from the stabilising influence of scientific thinking, and allowing them to escape into unexpected connotational novelties.

In an article contributed to the *Kenyon Review* in 1951 and headed 'The Formalist Critic',[9] Brooks reiterates his critical credo. 'Literary criticism is a description and evaluation of its object.' It concerns itself with the work itself. In reply to those who argue that this isolation of the work cuts it loose from its author and his life, and from its readers and their response, Brooks insists that what belongs to biography and psychology may be interesting but is not to be confused 'with an account of the work'. Such matters as the intensity of the author's feelings as he wrote or of the reader's responses when he reads are to be discounted. It is clear of course that Brooks is here defining the true scope of criticism rather than necessarily depreciating the value of historical, biographical, or other studies which may sustain it.

Perhaps the most thoroughgoing exponents of the New Criticism's exclusive emphasis on the text are W. K. Wimsatt (1907–75) and M. C. Beardsley (*b*.1915) whose book *The Verbal Icon: Studies in the Meaning of Poetry* (1954) includes essays first published in 1946 and 1949 on 'The Intentional

Fallacy' and 'The Affective Fallacy'.[10] Wimsatt and Beardsley insist that no poem can be judged by reference to the poet's intention. It is what is 'internal', what can be discovered from the text of a poem, that is public, while everything that is 'external' and 'not a part of the work as a linguistic fact' is private and idiosyncratic. For critical purposes it is better to study Coleridge's 'Kubla Khan' with a dictionary in your hands than with the elaborate investigation into Coleridge's reading made by Professor Lowes in *The Road to Xanadu*. Wimsatt and Beardsley are at pains to decry glib judgments of poetry in terms of 'sincerity', 'spontaneity', 'authenticity', 'genuineness' and other such concepts evasive of objectivity and precision. Their attack on the attempt to judge poetry as expression of feeling is matched in logical force by their attack on the attempt to judge it by its emotive effect on the reader. The poem must be confused neither with its cause nor with its results. The school of semantic criticism that arose from the work of I. A. Richards was over-simplistic in its distinction between the symbolic and emotive use of language. What is emotively received is limitlessly variable, and measurement by it can lead only to limitless relativism.

Of the various writers over whom the 'New Criticism' umbrella was loosely raised was the American poet Yvor Winters (1900–68). He is perhaps unique in that, as a poet, he began as an impressive practitioner in free verse and then rejected both free verse and imagism as deviations from the healthy poetic tradition. In criticism his reaction against modernism was spelt out in three books, *Primitivism and Decadence* (1937), *Maule's Curse* (1938) and *The Anatomy of Nonsense* (1943), whose contents were gathered together in *In Defence of Reason* (1947). There is in Winters's critical manifesto the swashbuckling air of the man who is going to get down to brass tacks without wasting time. A poem is a statement in words with a special concern to express feeling. Words, however, have an inescapable rational content. There must be a precise and genuine relationship between the feeling expressed and the understanding of the experience which motivates it. Winters defines as 'Pseudo-Reference' the kind of statement which merely masquerades as 'rational

coherence' by its vocabulary and syntax. Such is Wordsworth's pretence that the sight of the daffodils charmed away
his passions: the motive tendered by the poet is inadequate.
When this practice is intensified by abandonment of any
pretence of rational progression, and image succeeds to
image simply on the basis of mood, so that what coherence
remains is purely emotional, then Winters labels this practice
'Qualitative Progression'. It is something which may have its
proper subordinate function – for instance in Shakespeare
where what is rationally irrelevant may reveal the psychology of the hero with his logical place in the whole scheme.
But to give the practice centrality as the basic method,
extinguishing the rational from the language, while exploiting its associative potency, is not permissible. And here are
the grounds on which Winters attacks the French symbolists
and turns his guns on T. S. Eliot and Ezra Pound. *The Waste
Land* is 'broken blank verse interspersed with bad free verse
and rimed doggerel'. In eliminating any paraphrasable plot
and relying on the random flow of images, Eliot sacrifices
lucidity and precision. Any suggestion that a poem may have
a life of its own and that the poet can escape from full
responsibility for direct control of his medium is naturally
antithetical to Winters's insistence on the character of poetry
as statement.

III Formalism and linguistic criticism

The New Criticism had something in common with an
approach to literature which was developed earlier in the
century in Russia and was called 'Formalism'. For the
formalists the proper province of criticism is the 'literariness'
of a text. The critic is not concerned with the content of a
work of literature as such – with what it represents of human
life and so-called reality. He is concerned with the literary
devices employed in the work, and should seek a scientific
account of their character and function. In 'Formalism' we
can see foreshadowed the kind of critical approaches later
developed by the 'Structuralists'. It is concerned with the
technical devices which differentiate literary language from
ordinary utterance. For instance, there is the process of

'defamiliarisation' by which art can refresh perceptions 'automatised' by daily habituation. Whenever an object or act is described in such a way that our habitual notion of it is transformed, the process of defamiliarisation is at work. It is operative too when the literary presentation is punctured by intrusions which destroy the illusion of reality. Sterne's *Tristram Shandy* made a useful specimen for formalist critics in that it broke totally with the principle that art should conceal its artistries. We tend to demand of literature an approximation to what we know as external reality. It is aspects of literature which resist this demand that are especially valued by the formalists. We readers are too quick to try mentally to 'naturalise' anything in a text which seems alien to our familiar criteria of what is 'natural' and plausible, instead of accepting it as an aspect of its literariness.

Raman Selden, in his book *Contemporary Literary Theory* (1985), shows how formalist thinking gradually became dissatisfied with the 'notion of the text as a heap of devices'. As the mechanical concept 'device' was abandoned in favour of 'function', the isolation of literary development from other historical developments was ended, and attention to the content of literature was again allowed for. An influential scholar in this connection was Roman Jakobson (1896–1982) who worked in Prague in the 1920s before emigrating to the USA, to become eventually a key figure in what came to be called 'Linguistic Criticism'. The label is appropriate for a movement which saw 'the poetic' as something distinguishable in purely linguistic terms. Jakobson derived impetus from the work of the Swiss scholar, Ferdinand de Saussure (1857–1913) who changed the emphasis from what he called the 'diachronic' study of a language, which surveys its historical development, to the 'synchronic' study, which looks at it rather as a whole at a given cross-section of time. This represented a shift in interest from philology, in which language is studied historically, to what came to be called 'linguistics', in which it is studied 'synchronically'. Saussure rejected theories of meaning based primarily on the relationship between words and extra-linguistic objects and concepts. Language is a system of arbitrarily allotted signs which operate only in relation to each other in the total system. This view of language as a 'structure', propounded in a book compiled from notes made on Saussure's lectures, *Cours de linguistique générale* (1915), was to exercise a key influence on many thinkers, and on literary critics especially. It was Saussure who made the distinction between 'langue', the basic system of a given language, and 'parole', the language in practical use.

Jakobson developed a cunning theory of 'the poetic'. The 'vertical' relationship of linguistic elements exists between words of the same type that could be substituted for each other in a given sentence. This is the relationship between 'house', 'mansion', 'palace' and 'cottage'. The 'horizontal' relationship of linguistic elements exists between words which can be combined in a sentence such as 'The cottage caught fire'. These two relationships, of similarity and of contiguity, enable us to *select* linguistic elements and to *combine* them. Jakobson formulated the proposition: 'The poetic function projects the principle of equivalence from the axis of selection into the axis of combination.' The relationships between linguistic elements on the horizontal plane are treated by the poet as though they were relationships on the vertical plane.

Jakobson listed six component factors in verbal communication: An *Addresser*, a *Message*, and an *Addressee*; a *Context* (or 'referent') that is referred to, a *Code* common to addresser and addressee, and a *Contact* keeping them in communication. Language has corresponding functions, the *Cognitive* (or 'denotative') function oriented to the *Context*; the *Emotive* (or 'expressive') function expressing the attitude of the *Addresser*; and the *Conative* function oriented towards the *Addressee*. There are also functions directed to establishing or breaking *Contact* (the 'phatic' function) and towards checking up on the *Code* (the 'metalingual' function). Lastly there is the *Poetic* function which would focus on the *Message* for its own sake. Jakobson makes clear, of course, that generally it is not a question of one linguistic function monopolising communication but rather of exerting a predominance there:

> Poetic function is not the sole function of verbal art but only its dominant, determining function, whereas in all other verbal activities it acts as a subsidiary, accessory constituent.[11]

There are those sympathetic to the linguistic approach to literature who have argued that formalist theories insulate works of literature from social realities. Roger Fowler takes this line in *Literature as Social Discourse* (1981). When literature is seen in relation to social process, it is clear that language performs more functions than is presupposed in Jakobson's formulations. Literature is language, and the interpersonal function of language has to be reckoned with. Ignoring this fact and concentrating on formal structure is itself the product of a particular socio-historical situation, and operates to perpetuate values in detachment from living experience. It thus serves as a brake on change and 'open-ness'. The interaction involved in living utterance is not something from which literary language can escape, and three acts are combined in any utterance: the phonic enunciation; the extra-linguistic reference; and the act of stating, arguing, asking, testifying, or whatever. (These have been called the 'locutionary', 'propositional', and 'illocu-tionary' acts.) Fowler calls for attention to the overt or covert illocutionary aspects in literary criticism. Texts should be regarded 'as a *Process*', and full recognition given to the communicative interaction implicit in the utterance. Thus, for instance, a 'battery of infelicitous illocutions' disorients us towards the inscrutable in Blake's poem 'The Tyger', where a series of questions are addressed to an animal to which no reply could reasonably be expected.[12]

IV Structuralism and deconstruction

Traditional humanist criticism focused on works of art with the intention of discovering some truth in what they revealed or expressed. Formalism's concentration of attention on what is internal to the linguistic constructs prepared the ground for the full-blown 'structuralist' criticism exemplified by the French scholar Roland Barthes (1915–80) who denies that it is the business of criticism to make 'correct statements' in the light of ' "true" principles'. A poem cannot be regarded as 'an object independent of the psyche and the personal history of the person studying it'. Critics postulate a 'profound relationship' between the author they are dealing with and his works, and then have the absurdity to ignore any such relationship between themselves and what they are writing. Criticism is not concerned with 'the world' but with certain 'linguistic formulations'. It is a secondary language talking about a primary language. The question of 'truth' does not arise: only the question of 'validity'. The critic is not occupied in 'discovering' hidden things in an author's work, but in fitting together in one piece of furniture the language of his day and that of the author. Literature is susceptible of infinite reinterpretation because it conveys no message but a 'system of signs'.

So Barthes wrote in 'Criticism as Language'[13] contributed to *The Times Literary Supplement* in 1963. In a later article 'Science versus Literature'[14] (*TLS* 1967) he derided the notion that language is simply the 'medium of thought'. There is no such thing as a 'neutral state of language' from which the specialised languages of literature derive. We blind ourselves to the fundamental problems of utterance if we postulate a truth of content and reasoning in language such as science claims. Barthes's logic leads him to conclusions for which 'post-structuralist' is a fitter label than 'structuralist'. For he seems to carry to a point of absurdity that down-grading of the significance of the author which concentration on linguistic formulations required. In an essay, 'The Death of the Author' (1968),[15] he declares that 'writing is the destruction of every voice, of every point of origin'. Writing begins as the author dies. The author is a modern invention, 'the epitome and culmination of capitalist ideology'. All he can do anyway is to imitate, re-mix, and fabricate 'a tissue of quotations drawn from the innumerable centres of culture'. The idea of self-expression is meaningless when the 'self' in question is itself only 'a ready-formed dictionary'. Barthes replaces the author by a 'scriptor' who is not a bundle of passions and impressions but the owner of an immense dictionary. The scriptor has no anterior existence; he is 'born simultaneously with the text'. The unity of a text 'lies not in its origin but in its destination'. Author and Critic have reigned long enough. It is time to give the reader the primacy.

Structuralist thought finds in the relationships between the constituents of a sign-system, or code, the source of so-called 'meaning' not only in language but also in culture generally. There is a close connection between radical linguistic theories which have obtruded uncomfortably into the world of literary criticism in recent decades and much wider movements expressing dissatisfaction with traditional philosophical assumptions. Clearly the question whether a given text has any representative significance in relation to the extra-linguistic world (the real world) is not a limited technical question of interest only to literary scholars. Clearly too the question whether an author conveys something to a reader by laying upon his work the impress of an individual mind and his individual experience is a question striking at the roots of what has hitherto been regarded as 'commonsense'. The development of critical thinking in its seemingly more outrageous forms merely reflects wider movements of thought which fiercely resist notions of a transcendent or of any basis, metaphysical or religious, conferring the status of absolutes on any objective values. The itch to relativise is plainly evident in the structuralist's detachment of the text from the extra-linguistic world. It is equally evident in the post-structuralist's detachment of the word, the sign, from any anchorage in stability of significance.

Structuralism reached out to take control of all things as a science of signs. Post-structuralism – or 'Deconstruction', as it has come to be called – punctures this ambition. It does so by displaying the instability of signification. If you look up the word 'chair' in the dictionary, you will soon find yourself wandering from a 'movable four-legged seat' to talk of professorial posts, positions, chairmanship, sedans on poles, and the like. And if you try again with 'seat', you will follow a longer trail to parlimentary membership, to a country estate, to the human posterior, and to the section of the garment that covers it. In short, the *signifier* does not lead us here to a single *signified* but to a batch of *signifieds*, any one of which might lead us to another batch. Chains of meaning, interwoven chains of meaning, emerge whenever we try to pin down the relation between *signifier* and *signified*.

The French philosopher Jacques Derrida (b.1930) attacked the 'logocentrism' which, by giving primacy to speech over writing, presupposes a fusion between the signifier and the signified. Derrida gives primacy to writing, where the realisation of the meaning is always postponed by the very fact that it will always be read and re-interpreted in the future. This fact separates the signified from the signifier temporally. The meaning is 'deferred', and Derrida coined the word 'différance' to express the dual spatial 'difference' and temporal 'deferment' detaching the sign from the full presence of its meaning. He denies that writing is secondary to speech or doubles the gap between *signifier* and *signified*. Where Rousseau regarded writing as a supplement to speech, Derrida sees it as both taking the place of speech and adding to it. His general position as a philosopher, however, is to discard 'hierarchical' formulations of relationship by firstly reversing them (speech/writing; nature/civilisation; even good/evil) and then disposing of the reversal. In literature this process of 'deconstruction' enables us to identify when and where a text breaks the framework it seems to make for itself, and thus disintegrates.

In his essay 'Structure, Sign, and Play in the Discourse of the Human Sciences',[16] Derrida applies to the structuralist case the familiar philosophical trick of measuring it by its own measuring rods. He points to the 'structurality' of structure itself. It is impossible to think of a structure except as governed by a centre, within it or outside it. There is an inner contradiction here:

> The concept of centered structure is in fact the concept of a freeplay based on a fundamental ground, a freeplay which is constituted upon a fundamental immobility and a reassuring certitude, which is itself beyond the reach of the freeplay.

Derrida's use of terms such as 'freeplay', 'immobility', and 'certitude' reveal the extent of his relativism. The human search for a truth, a foundation, a 'full presence', is contrasted with the affirmation of 'freeplay' as an ultimate. He sees 'the history of metaphysics and the destruction of the history of metaphysics' as fit material for final deconstruction. We have no language with which to attack metaphysics that is not derivative from and infected by what it attacks. With devastating logic, Derrida argues that we are locked up even by our use of the word 'signifier' and the concept sign in complicity with the metaphysics we are opposing.

Reasoning of this kind takes us out of the sphere of literary criticism. Structuralist thinking which sticks more closely to matters relevant to us here has exploited what is called 'semiotics' or the science of signs. In its wider usage, semiotics has reference to any accepted conventions of dress, etiquette, gesture, and the various non-verbal means of communication. More limitedly, semiotics would study the general codes applicable to all linguistic utterance and the more specialised codes brought into play in literature. In England Jonathan Culler (*b*.1944), the author of *Struct-uralist Poetics* (1975) and *The Pursuit of Signs* (1981), has attempted to examine the intelligibility of literary works, that is to say 'the ways in which they make sense, the ways in which readers have made sense of them'.[17] Literary studies cannot have as their prime aim an understanding of the meaning of individual works. Interpretations proliferate. The concern of criticism is to discover *how* this happens. Divergence of interpretation presents a useful challenge. For the function of criticism is to 'analyse the interpretive operations that produce these disagreements'. Thus Culler's application of structuralist thinking is not to the text directly, but to the reader and the act of reading. He seeks to formulate the system of conventions and rules which is brought into play when a reader interprets a text.

Literary theory, of the kind articulated by structuralists and their deconstructionalist successors, is not necessarily proposed as a substitute for literary history or conventional 'lit crit'. But the insistence on regarding language as a system of signs and not a vehicle of meanings gives to the various attempts to define literariness an air of arid alienation from human realities. It also, of course, produces an abundance of technical jargon whose very tastelessness advertises to the sensitive reader an unfitness for what he knows as 'literary judgment'. The American scholar Paul de Man (1919–83) locates 'literariness' in the exercise of the 'autonomous potential of language' rooted in the fact that the relationship between word and thing is 'not phenomenal but conventional'.

> Literature is fiction not because it somehow refuses to acknowledge 'reality', but because it is not *a priori* certain that language functions according to principles which are those, or which are *like* those, of the phenomenal world. It is therefore not *a priori* certain that literature is a reliable source of information about anything but its own language.[18]

Paul de Man argues that 'resistance to theory is a resistance to the use of language about language'. He locates literariness in use of language which gives primacy to the rhetorical over the grammatical and logical function. This means that the text will contain elements insusceptible to being decoded grammatically. Indeed the interplay of the rhetorical with the grammatical leaves a residue that resists rendering of its significance. Reading involves unsettling confidence in the adequacy of grammatical and logical analysis by pursuing the questions thrown up in examination of the rhetorical dimensions. That these questions are ultimately unanswerable is illustrated by De Man in his essay 'The Resistance to Theory', where fanciful readings are suggested of the word 'Fall' in the title of Keats's 'The Fall of Hyperion': suppose the 'Fall of Hyperion' is read as the 'Fall' (Failure) of the earlier version of the poem, 'Hyperion', and so on.

V Marxist criticism

'Christopher Caudwell' was the pseudonym adopted by Christopher St John Sprigg (1907–37), a self-educated rebel from his own class who turned communist, joined the International Brigade, and was killed in Spain. His book *Illusion and Reality* (1937) was the first thorough-going work of Marxist criticism in Britain. It includes a historical survey of the development of poetry. The Romantic poets are seen against the background of the Industrial Revolution in which the proletariat were deprived of lands and tools, and driven into factories where industrial capital devalued their labour. The poets, for all their supposed radicalism, represent a bourgeois revolution, essentially self-contradictory. The self-centred Byronic cynicism represents demoralisation in the aristocratic class rather than rebellion against it. Shelley expresses 'a far more genuinely dynamic force' in making a demand for suffering humanity as a whole, but his call for a restoration of shattered human relations stops short of recognising what class alone has the strength to restore them. Wordsworth lives on the products of industralism while he enjoys a world of Nature 'unspoilt' by industralism – but indeed a Nature which ages of human toil have rendered safe from danger and wild beasts. Keats, on whom financial limitations pressed hardest, felt so trapped by bourgeois reality that he recommended a total flight from reality.

Thus Keats was the poet who provided the 'dominating vocabulary of future poetry'. With the Victorians the bourgeois illusion enters an even more tragic stage. Like Darwin, Tennyson 'projects the conditions of capitalist production into nature (individual struggle for existence)'. Tennyson's ruthless Nature is capitalism transmogrified. Browning flees from the present 'to the glories of the virile Italian springtime of the bourgeoisie', and his 'foggy verbalism' reflects the intellectual dishonesty of this evasion. Arnold pushes forward the separation of the poet from society by the battle against the Philistine in which he fights his 'mirror reflection'. Then the 'art for art's sake' movement seals the separation of the world of art from the world of reality. It introduces 'commodity-fetishism' into poetry: the bourgeois poet is the producer serving as market the remote, passive Public. Caudwell, by the way, showed no sympathy for the radicalism of the English left-wing poets of the thirties. They were bourgeois artists whose claim to alliance with the proletariat stopped short of forsaking bourgeois art. They contented themselves with 'crude and grotesque scraps of Marxist phraseology' while flaunting in life their bourgeois 'independence' and indiscipline.

Caudwell used a Marxist dialectic which makes no concessions. The Marxist analysis inevitably coloured the critical work of some scholars who shared the Leavisite attitude to contemporary society. The Leavisite critique presupposed the existence once of a pre-industrialised England in which life was healthily lived in conscious community by men who made tools for men who used them to produce goods and nourishment for men who needed them. It was a small step to move from the critique of a self-seeking academic establishment with its network of influences and of corrupt media to political condemnation of the capitalist system which supported them. A fellow editor of *Scrutiny*, L. C. Knights (*b*.1906) attracted attention in 1933 with his essay 'How many children had Lady Macbeth?', which reduced to absurdity the application to Shakespeare of the detective methods employed by such critics as A. C. Bradley. He entered the fray, not only in thus mocking conventional criticism, but also in analysing critical developments in their social context. For instance, in an essay published in *Scrutiny* in 1937, and later included in his volume *Explorations* (1946), he attacked the received view of Restoration Comedy.[19]

Knights's argument is that Elizabethan drama drew on a rich common language, but that in the decades that followed the Restoration, English literature and culture were consciously 'upper-class' as never before or since. Vigour and power vanished from the literary idiom as the 'old cultural unity' disintegrated. The prose of the comedies is 'poor and inexpressive'. Congreve's style is 'nerveless'. It seems to preen itself while employing empty antitheses and saying nothing. There is neither subtlety nor fresh 'wit'. The Restoration comic writers regurgitate 'a miserably limited set of attitudes'. Thee are no real 'values', just a set of trivial conventions. Constancy in love and marriage 'is a bore'. The sexual appetite 'needs perpetually fresh stimulus'. These attitudes are for ever re-manipulated like the jokes on comic postcards. It is impossible to regard any of the dramatists as having 'a coherent attitude of his own'. In short, the comedies are 'trivial, gross, and dull'. And back of it all is a thoroughly bored society desperately demanding to be entertained.

There is something altogether too heavy-handed about Knight's demolition job. When we reach the complaint that

Millamant in *The Way of the World* never enlivens her social round for a moment 'by the play of genuine intelligence', we are apt to wonder whether the time has not come for someone to write an essay on 'How many good books has Millamant read?'. For the solemnity seems misplaced.

It will be evident that many of the theories which have influenced the more radical British literary critics since the Second World War are European in origin. Among the formative Marxist influences was that of the German playwright Berthold Brecht (1898–1956), who settled in East Germany in 1949. He had early propounded his theory of 'epic' theatre, rejecting the traditional Aristotelian doctrine, with its cultivation of illusion. The business of the dramatist is to shock his audience into awareness of social injustice. This cannot be done by devising shapely plots and involving the audience's emotions with those of the characters in an inevitable movement towards catastrophe. Brecht applied a principle of 'alienation' whereby the audience, instead of being lulled into empathy with the characters, are reminded that they are but watching actors. Thus technical devices were employed to 'distance' the action from the spectators and enable them to pass judgment with some detachment on corruptions portrayed. The so-called 'method acting' which emanated from the practice of the Russian producer Konstantin Stanislavsky (1863–1938) encouraged the actor to lose himself in his role and to become emotionally absorbed in it, improvising with supposed 'spontaneity'. By contrast, the Brechtian practice encouraged stylised gesture and bold cartoonery in character-projection of a kind which vigorously externalised its social significance.

Brecht's exploitation of the Formalist principle of 'defamiliarisation' was scarcely in accord with the official Soviet call for 'social realism'. But his thinking was certainly in line with the basic Marxist premise that it is social and economic conditions which produce our ideologies and not vice-versa. One of the difficulties of dealing with East European critics is that for several decades the expression of intellectual positions had to be moderated so as not to offend tyrannical authorities. The distinguished Hungarian critic Georg Lukácz (1885–1971) experienced some official displeasure, and his work is to be read in awareness of pressures that played upon him. His knowledge of French and English literature may have made him suspect, but it has given his work a wider European appeal than it might have had. There is a celebrated essay 'The Ideology of Modernism',[20] which formed a lecture delivered in 1955. It criticises 'modernist' literature for its excessive concern with style and technique. Lukácz sees the stream-of-consciousness technique in Joyce's *Ulysses* as something more than mere technique. It is a 'formative principle governing the narrative pattern and presentation of character', and the 'perpetually oscillating patterns of sense- and memory-data' create an 'epic structure which is *static*' rather than dynamic.

Lukácz's basic objection to 'modernism' lies in its loss of the 'Aristotelian' view of man as a social animal. Modernist writers present man in a solitariness seemingly basic to the human condition. Man is seen as incapable of relationships with others, always at a loss in the world. Joyce's Dublin, however lovingly depicted, is 'little more than a back-cloth'. Identifying solitary man, incapable of significant relationships, with reality itself nullifies all concrete potentiality. The surrender to subjectivity and inwardness leads to the disintegration of human personality. Lukácz's protest against the negation of outward reality, the 'attenuation of actuality', and the consequent 'dissolution of personality' is illustrated by reference to Joyce, Beckett, T. S. Eliot, and Kafka. It is accompanied by an attack on the decadent concern with 'neurotic aberration', with stylistic distortion, and with 'recourse to the pathological'. Perspective is of vital importance in art, and modernism would deprive literature of any sense of it, leaving us, for example, with Kafka's vision of man at the end of *The Trial*, trapped by incomprehensible circumstances in a state of total impotence and paralysis.

Both Brecht and Lukácz were crucial influences on the British critic Raymond Williams (1921–88) in his movement towards a Marxist viewpoint. Williams, the son of a railway signalman in Wales, came under Leavis's influence at Cambridge. The peculiar Leavisite blend of austere moralism and commitment to the idea of common culture with secularist insensitivity to the Christian tradition not unnaturally drove disciples leftwards. Williams's own personal experience as a young scholar from a working-class home made him acutely anxious to relate literature to the lives of the kind of people with whom he had been brought up. In his books, *Culture and Society 1780–1850* (1958) and *The Long Revolution* (1961), he wrestled with the broader cultural problem in historical and then in theoretical analysis. His literary criticism proper is always coloured by this concern. There is a section in *The Long Revolution* on 'Realism and the Contemporary Novel'.[21] It analyses the various usages of the word 'realism' in literary criticism: as a technical description of accuracy and liveliness in presentation, as a concept 'opposed to idealisation or caricature', as the commonplace in contradistinction to the heroic or romantic, and then as granting recognition to the unpleasant and the sordid. In this last usage it can assume a revolutionary function. In the present century the word often implies 'fidelity to psychological reality' in the West, while in the Soviet Union the concept 'socialist realism' maintains an older connotation. Williams's own view is that the realist tradition in fiction is best represented by 'the kind of novel which creates and judges the quality of a whole way of life in terms of the qualities of persons'. In this respect the highest marks are given to Tolstoy's *War and Peace*, George Eliot's *Middlemarch*, and Lawrence's *The Rainbow*, because in these novels the true balance is achieved. The general life is fully represented as affecting the individuals, yet the individuals remain ends in themselves in whose personal lives the quality of the general life is seen at its most significant. Neither the society nor the individual is given priority.

In illustration Williams observes how literal 'realism' was discredited for some by 'detailed stocktaking descriptions of shops or back-parlours or station waiting-rooms' in the manner of Arnold Bennett, and its disrepute drove Virginia Woolf to an opposite extreme in *The Waves*, 'where all the furniture, and even the physical bodies, have gone out of the window' to leave mere 'voices in the air'. This represents an imbalance just as damaging. Williams regrets the twentieth-century polarisation of the realist novel into the 'social' novel and the 'personal' novel, representing accurate observation of the aggregate or of the units respectively. He then subdivides the 'social' novel into the social 'documentary' novel and the social 'formula' novel. The former tells you what it is like to live 'in a mining town, or in a university, or in a merchant ship', and the characters are miners, or dons, or sailors before they are human persons, for the 'social-descriptive function' of the novel is its 'shaping priority'. The 'formula' novel (such as Aldous Huxley's *Brave New World* or George Orwell's *1984*) explores the relationship between individuals and society, but lacks the dimensions of a substantial society and substantial persons.

Williams then categorises the 'personal' novel in the same terms, 'documentary' and 'formula'. The documentary personal novel deals in detail with personal relationships, but the society is a 'highly personalised landscape' specially adapted to frame the individual portraits rather than 'a country within which the individuals are actually contained'. E. M. Forster and Graham Greene are cited in exemplification. The other kind of personal novel in the 'personal formula' category takes only one person seriously. Such is Joyce's *Portrait of the Artist as a Young Man*. 'A world is actualised on one man's senses; not narrated or held at arm's length' and powerful intensity is achieved. Williams traces the falling-off of this technique in Joyce Cary and Kingsley Amis, where the 'final version of reality is parodic and farcical'. Williams labels this genre the novel of 'special pleading'. As it has developed, it tends towards a form from which 'the reality of society is excluded'. Williams urges a renewal of the great tradition of realism, exploring the vital interpenetration of person with community, and representing society in personal terms and persons in social terms.

There was a notable development in Williams's thinking towards a thoroughgoing Marxist position in the decade succeeding the publication of *Culture and Society*, and he summed it up in the Introduction to his *Marxism and Literature* (1977). Here he analyses the basic concepts, 'Culture', 'Language', 'Literature', and 'Ideology', then examines the basic principles of Marxist cultural theory, and finally tackles questions of literary theory. There is much in recent critical writing which gives the impression of substance attenuated by a kind of conceptual profligacy into arid verbalism. Marxist thinkers are not guiltless in this respect. In chapter 8 of section II, headed 'Dominant, Residual, and Emergent', Williams weaves a web of verbal abstractions to embroider the trite notion that at any given time elements from the past and elements foreshadowing the future will exist under the shelter of what is culturally dominant. The mode of reasoning confirms the impression given when he categorised twentieth-century novels as 'social' and 'personal', 'documentary' and 'formula' of a mind too quick to apply verbal docketing to the stuff of life.

Marxist thinking in this field has shifted from the crude notion that socio-economic conditions directly determine the character of works of art. The Marxist position is that the ruling class is able to preserve its dominance because they can impose on the popular consciousness an ideology which justifies that dominance. For instance, the idea of 'freedom' for all embraces labourers as well as entrepreneurs and allows concealment of the true relationship of exploitation. Ideology, whether political, social, or religious, represents a relationship between individuals and real life which is imaginary. The concept of ideology is crucial in much recent Marxist literary criticism. Terry Eagleton (b.1943) argues in *Criticism and Ideology: A Study in Marxist Theory* (1976)[22] that a literary text is not the 'expression' of ideology. It is a 'production' of ideology rather as the performance of a play is the production of the text. Literary texts do not represent historical reality, but they operate on ideology, and ideology relates individuals to history in various ways, allowing 'multiple kinds and degrees of access to that history'. In so far as history is present in a text, it is present as an ideology. For Eagleton what is signified *'within the text'*, the imaginary or 'pseudo'-real, is not to be 'directly correlated with the historically real'. The signification of a text is located at two removes from historical reality. But the ideology of the text is not something that antedates the text; it is 'identical with the text'. Scientific criticism needs 'the science of ideological formations' but its concern is specifically with 'the laws of the production of ideological discourses as literature'. Eagleton sees the process of that production in structural terms. In constituting itself as a structure, the text destructures and

reconstitutes ideology and is itself partially destructured by
the effect of ideology upon it. Text and ideology operate on
each other in a process of 'mutual structuring and destructur-
ing in which the text constantly overdetermines its own
determinations'.

VI Feminist criticism

Activists in the Feminist movement in the present century
have naturally turned their attention to the world of
imaginative literature, anxious to see how far it has misrepresented women through the ages or contributed to
imposing on them a falsely limited notion of their role. In
this respect, like the Marxists and the Leavisites, the feminists
are dissatisfied with the wider social and cultural situation.
Neither the Marxist nor the Leavisite critique can be isolated
from the accompanying view of historic development, and it
is impossible to isolate feminist literary criticism from the
feminist reading of history and the radical social posture it
encourages. In fact, of course, writing is not an area of
activity from which women have been excluded or in which
they have failed to gain equality with men. As novelists the
great contemporaries, Scott and Jane Austen, share a
supremacy. 'Edgeworth, Ferrier, Austen have all given
portraits of real society far superior to anything man, vain
man, has produced of the like nature', Scott wrote in his
Diary. When the present writer surveyed the English Novel
in the Romantic Period he found himself having to deal with
twelve women and nine men. The women included, as well
as the three named by Scott, Mary Brunton, Lady Morgan,
Mary Shelley, Elizabeth Inchbald, Mary Hays, and Amelia
Opie. Not all are what would be called 'feminist' in ideology.
One of the difficulties of handling some of the recent feminist
criticism is that we are invited to suppress the inclination to
regard as genuinely 'feminine' much of the output of women
writers of the past.

Simone de Beauvoir (1908–86), partner of the French
Existentialist philosopher, Jean Paul Sartre (1905–80),
wrote *Le deuxième sexe* (1949), translated as *The Second Sex*
(1960), in which she found the origin of female subservience

to men not in any natural inferiority but in the age-old dominance of men. She argues that whereas a man 'never begins by presenting himself as an individual of a certain sex', a woman has to define herself as a woman from the start. The masculine is regarded as the very type of humanity and woman is seen as relative to man. Women as a body lack the cohesion to assert themselves against this categorisation. While art, literature, and philosophy are essentially 'attempts to found the world anew on a human liberty; that of the individual creator',[23] women are so moulded and indoctrinated by tradition that they are prevented from assuming the status of beings with liberty. Meanwhile a conspiracy is kept alive which implies that women by nature lack creative genius.

In England Virginia Woolf (1882–1941) in *A Room of One's Own* (1929) tussled with some of the problems specific to the woman writer. She insisted that the lack of a 'room of one's own' and the kind of financial and social independence it represented put a brake on women's ambitions in literature. She felt that literary forms had been hardened by centuries of masculine writing into something unsuitable for women, indeed that the sentence structure which writers such as Charlotte Brontë and George Eliot grappled with was essentially masculine in character and not natural in feminine hands. Virginia Woolf shared personally in Bloomsbury's rebellion against Victorian ideals of pure, unselfish womanhood, against the image of the ministering angel, and against conventional inhibitions of female delicacy on the subject of sexuality and passion. And in rebelling too against the shopkeeping naturalism of popular male novelists such as Arnold Bennett, she sought a form and style which would do justice to the way in which women think and feel. The novelist Dorothy Richardson (1873–1957) had already experimented with a stream-of-consciousness technique which was intended to represent a feminine counterbalance to masculine realism; but the work of both Virigina Woolf and Dorothy Richardson would seem to some extreme later feminists to represent a withdrawal from the fray into an enclosure of femininity. In any case, the assumption that there is such a thing as a feminine style of writing which avoids the decisiveness and authoritativeness characteristic of the masculine mind is arguable. Virginia Woolf cites Jane Austen's style by contrast with that of Gibbon or Johnson; but the shapeliness and pithiness of Jane Austen's sentences could be said to derive from Sheridan. The style of Ivy Compton-Burnett has also been cited as characteristically feminine; and it could be argued that her presentation by-passes the masculine demand for rational clarity and attention in due proportion to what is 'important' and what is not. On the other hand, her intense ironic fatalism seems to derive from the Greek tragedians, and her dissection of humbugs and psychological blackmailers smacks more of Meredith than of Jane Austen.

Two questions have been at issue in feminist criticism. There is firstly the question of how women have been represented in literature. This, in feminist eyes, has been crucial in sustaining an ideal that has strait-jacketed women. The stereotyping of female roles in male-produced literature has had a malign influence on women readers in imposing traditional roles upon them. This is the problem of 'woman as reader'. And secondly there is the problem of 'woman as writer', the special questions arising for her in an area where established theory of form and practice is the product of long male predominance. On the first question, Josephine Dono-van (b.1941) an American academic, born in the Philippines, protests that most literature written by men presents women only in relation to male protagonists rather than as 'seats of consciousness' in themselves. A true 'Self', who is not 'an Other', will have a 'reflective, critical consciousness', will be a 'moral agent, capable of self-determined action'. But 'sexist ideology necessarily promotes the concept of woman-as-object or woman-as-other'.[24] Josephine Donovan insists that this is a moral, not just an aesthetic, issue. She formulates the stereotypes of woman in western literature, good and evil, virgin ideal and sex object, inspirer and seductress, as vehicles of salvation or destruction for the male hero. Any female who reads as a woman will find such representations alien, for they tell us little of women's 'own personal responses to events'. In this way Homer, Dante and Goethe come under judgment.

For Josephine Donovan the crucial question is not whether woman can identify with the male self, but whether she ought to. This becomes a social and political issue, for the substance and criteria of established literary studies serve as propaganda for a sexist ideology. Ignoring questions of content in this way dehumanises criticism.

Elaine Showalter (*b*.1941) born in Cambridge, Massachusetts, shifted the focus of attention from 'woman as reader' to 'woman as writer' in her book *A Literature of their Own: British Women Novelists* (1977). Here, and later in an essay 'Towards A Feminist Poetics'[25] contributed to Mary Jacobus (ed.), *Women Writing and Writing About Women* (1979) she defined succeeding generations of British women novelists. They represent three stages, Feminine, Feminist, and Female. In the 'feminine' phase women tried to match the 'intellectual achievements of male culture', representing woman in what was assumed to be her proper womanly role. Elaine Showalter dates this phase from 1840 to 1880. It is the age of the Brontës and George Eliot. The assumption of male pseudonyms is characteristic of an attitude which buried the strictly 'feminine' substance 'between the lines'. The succeeding 'feminist' phase (roughly 1880 to 1920) was the age in which women asserted themselves in determined efforts for political and social equality, and women's literature was able to protest against unjust treatment of women. In this phase, however, women's literature remained dependent upon the predominant masculine aesthetic in that protest, like imitation, is parasitical. It was only with the coming of Dorothy Richardson, Katherine Mansfield, and Virginia Woolf that a deliberate 'female' aesthetic appeared. It 'transformed the feminine code of self-sacrifice into an annihilation of the narrative self'. It counterbalanced the male materialism of Bennett and Wells, and, like the work of D. H. Lawrence, it accepted a world 'totally polarized by sex'. But however female in form, however erotic in its symbolism, it failed to explore the actual physical experience of women. It was only with the coming of post-war novelists such as Iris Murdoch, Muriel Spark, Doris Lessing, Margaret Drabble and Beryl Bainbridge that we find an authentically female literature representing woman's experience and her view of life. They have broken the taboos in their use of vocabulary formerly restricted to men and in focusing on all areas of female experience.

Elaine Showalter has the honesty to refer frankly to the core of incertitude at the heart of much feminist theory about literature. Do women writers achieve equality by producing a literature clearly distinguishable in its own right, or do they achieve it by merging their work indistinguishably in the literary mainstream? In the former case they accept a sexist differentation. In the latter case they yield to assimilation. But she is fiercely critical of the way in which recent movements in literary criticism have exploited specifically 'male' responses, while claiming to speak universally.

> The new sciences of the text based on linguistics, computers, genetic structuralism, deconstruction, neo-formalism and deformalism, affective stylistics and psychoaesthetics, have offered literary critics the opportunity to demonstrate that the work they do is as manly and aggressive as nuclear physics – not intuitive, expressive, and feminine, but strenuous, rigorous, impersonal, and virile ...[26]

She sees the 'manic generation of difficult terminology' in literary science creating 'an élite corps of specialists who spend more and more time mastering literary theory, less and less time reading the books'. When she argues that 'the experience of women can easily disappear' under the diagrams of the structuralists, many who agree with her will surely want to add 'and the experience of men too'. She fears the development of a 'two-tiered system of "higher" and "lower" criticism', scientific and humanistic, which will subtly assume gender identities, masculine and feminine, and reassert a sexual polarity.

Elaine Showalter's reasoning is a far cry from the near-hysteria of extreme feminists who demand in literature an expression of female sexuality which will burst through the bonds of male logic with a poetic power that defies the tyranny of logocentric meaning. Hélène Cixous (b.1937) contributed an essay 'The Laugh of the Medusa'[27] to *New French Feminisms* (1976), edited by Elaine Marks and Isabelle de Courtivron. She speaks as woman locked in struggle against 'conventional man', but she rejects the concept of the 'typical woman' because of the inexhaustible richness of individual variations. Women have an empire to proclaim – the raptures and visions of erotic experimentation 'in particular as concerns masturbation'. There is a vast amount to be said by women about feminine sexuality, but it cannot be said by adopting the system of discourse which governs phallocentric thinking, built as it is on a philosophico-theoretical basis. It appears that for Hélène Cixous reason and syntax stand in the way, preventing women from writing 'through their bodies'. Plainly it is difficult to reason with a writer for whom the whole tradition of reason is to be rejected as an aspect of phallocentric domination. All we can do is to draw attention to the ardour which informs her protest.

A more politically-oriented feminist voice is that of Elizabeth A. Meese (b.1943) born in Norfolk, Virginia, who contributed an essay 'Sexual Politics and Critical Judgment'[28] to *After Strange Texts: The Role of Theory in the Study of Literature* (1985), edited by Gregory S. Jay and David L. Miller. Elizabeth Meese takes her starting-point from the work of Stanley Fish (b.1938) who wrote *Is there a Text in This Class?* (1980). Fish belongs to the school of critics who consider a text in relation to its effect upon a reader. This school allows for the distinction between the 'implied reader', whose response to the text would accord with the invitations it issues, and the 'actual reader' who responds on the basis of his own established predilections. Thus, for instance, in reading Defoe's *Moll Flanders*, a reader might adjust his responses to Moll's outbursts of penitence according to complex calculations of how far each one consorts or fails to consort with the norms of valuation seemingly represented in the book. The reader makes successive adjustments of this kind in his progress through a book. Fish applies this theory of reader-adjustment to the smallest unit of the sentence in an approach which he calls 'affective stylistics'. Sentences involving complex syntactical structure are examined to illustrate how the sequence of words, in which one suggestion may be interrupted by another, compels a moment-by-moment readjustment of response by the reader. He quotes a sentence of Pater's:

This at best of flamelike, our life has, that it is but the concurrence, renewed from moment to moment, of forces parting sooner or later on their ways.

Fish became aware of the fact that his own experience of reading had been the basis of his theorising. He therefore developed the notion of the 'interpretive community', thus transferring the experiential validation of his case from himself to the literary establishment.

At least that is how Elizabeth Meese sees it. She regards 'interpretive community' as a cover label for 'authoritative community' and smells the rat of 'gender-based literary tribalism'. She projects as the arch-enemy a privileged body holding in its hands the power to legislate in the sphere of literary evaluation. The rulers can feign that persuasion is operative in dialogue because they argue under the umbrella of extra-literary presuppositions, social and political, which determine the nature of truth. This concept of truth as dependent upon power systems which themselves obstruct knowledge is one that gives impetus to various so-called 'minorities' in their rejection of what they see as established hierarchies of authority. Elizabeth Meese uses it to assert a feminist challenge to the 'methods and techniques of the inherited critical tradition'. Since the determination of what constitutes reason rests where the centre of power is – in 'the community of élite white men', the task of feminist criticism is to revise 'the politics of "truth"'. And this is not just a question of formulating contraries and opposing the male to the female, the outsider to the insider; for such a process fosters the very oppositional logic by which privilege is sustained. That too has to be rejected for any 'sameness' of dialogue involves complicity with the phallocentric tradition. The word 'phallogocentric' is coined to indicate how the 'phallocentric' tradition has taken over the 'logos'. The attitude of defiance is basically a socio-political one. In so far as it affects the world of literary criticism, its implications are yet to be worked out.

Must a new and grave incertitude intrude upon the writer whose lot it is to close a history of literary criticism on so problematic a note? Is the writer called upon to ask himself just how much of what he has written is invalidated by his inescapable phallogocentricism? He is loth to believe that his half of the world's readers must remain uncertain whether what they say can ever have full currency in the region of discourse occupied by the other half. There is comfort, however, in knowing that, if it is possible to offend without intention to do so, the converse is also the case. We have Harriet Martineau's word for it in the climax of her paean of praise for Scott the novelist:

and finally he has advocated the rights of woman with a force all the greater for his being unaware of the import of what he was saying.

Notes

Chapter 1: The Classical Age

1. Quotations from the *Poetics* are taken from *Aristotle: On the Art of Poetry*, translated by Ingram Bywater (Oxford: Clarendon Press, 1920).
2. Quotations from Horace are taken from Allen H. Gilbert, *Literary Criticism, Plato to Dryden* (Detroit: Wayne State University Press, 1962), pp. 136–9
3. Allen H. Gilbert, p. 155
4. D. A. Russell & M. Winterbottom (eds), *Ancient Literary Criticism, The Principal Texts in New Translations* (Oxford: Clarendon Press, 1972), p. 243.
5. Russell & Winterbottom, p. 145.
6. Russell & Winterbottom, p. 298.
7. Russell & Winterbottom, p. 380.
8. Russell & Winterbottom, p. 299.
9. Russell & Winterbottom, p. 372.
10. Russell & Winterbottom, p. 361.
11. Quoted by William K. Wimsatt Jr & Cleanth Brooks in *Literary Criticism, A Short History, vol I Classical Criticism* (London: Routledge & Kegan Paul, 1970), p. 143. Translation taken from G. Saintsbury, *A History of Criticism and Literary Taste in Europe*, vol I, pp. 351–2.

Chapter 2: The Middle Ages

1. Quoted by Wimsatt & Brooks, vol I, p. 122.
2. St. Augustine, *The City of God (De Civitate Dei)*, translated by John Healey (1610) (London: Dent, Everyman, 1945), p. 49.
3. Quotations from St. Augustine, *Confessions*, are taken drom the translation by E. B. Pusey (1838) (London: Dent, Everyman, 1907).

4. Frederick Coplestone, *History of Philosophy*, vol II, *Mediaeval Philosophy Augustine to Scotus* (London: Burns, Oates & Washbourne Ltd, 1950), p. 71, from Sermon 241.
5. St Thomas Aquinas, *Summa Theologica* (London: Dominican Latin text and English translation, 1964), part I, question 5, article 4.
6. Aquinas, part I, question 39, article 8.
7. J. W. H. Atkins, *English Literary Criticism, The Mediaeval Phase* (Cambridge University Press, 1943), p. 67.
8. Russell & Winterbottom, p. 510.
9. Allen H. Gilbert, p. 202.
10. Allen H. Gilbert, p. 211.

Chapter 7: The Eighteenth Century II

1. T. S. Eliot, *The Use of Poetry and the Use of Criticism* (London: Faber & Faber, 1933), p. 64.

Chapter 8: The Romantic Age

1. Peter Morgan, *Literary Critics and Reviewers in Early Nineteenth-Century Britain* (Beckenham: Croom Helm, 1983, p.78).

Chapter 9: The Victorian Age

1. T. S. Eliot, *The Sacred Wood* (1920), (London: Methuen & Co Ltd, 1960) p. 17.
2. T. S. Eliot, *The Sacred Wood*, p. 21.
3. Quoted by R. V. Holdsworth (ed), *Arthur Symons, Poetry and Prose*, (Cheadle: Fyfield Books, Carcanet Press, 1974), p. 11.
4. Quoted by R. V. Holdsworth, op. cit., p. 16.
5. James Joyce, *Ulysses, The Corrected Text*, edited by H. W. Gabler (Harmondsworth, Middlesex: Penguin Books), p. 168.

Chapter 10: The Twentieth Century I

1. Leon Edel & Gordon N. Ray (ed), *Henry James and H. G. Wells* (Westport, Connecticut: Greenwood Press, 1979), pp. 103–5.
2. Quoted by Edel & Ray, p. 247
3. Quoted by David Lodge (ed), *20th Century Literary Criticism* (London: Longman, 1972), p. 60 from T. S. Eliot (ed), *Literary Essays of Ezra Pound* (1954).
4. Quoted by David Lodge, p. 65.

5. Quoted by John Press, *A Map of Modern English Verse* (London: Oxford University Press, 1969), p. 61.
6. Quoted by John Press, p. 41.
7. Quoted by David Lodge, p. 59, from 'A Retrospect'.
8. Quoted by John Press, p. 38, from D. D. Paige (ed), *The Letters of Ezra Pound 1907–1941* (1951), pp.388–9.
9. Foreword to Sondra J. Stang (ed), *The Ford Madox Ford Reader* (London: Collins, 1987), p. viii.
10. Virginia Woolf, *Contemporary Writers*, with a Preface by Jean Guiguet (London: The Hogarth Press, 1965), p. 120.
11. 'Modern Fiction' is reprinted in David Lodge, pp. 86–91.
12. Woolf, *Contemporary Writers*, p. 158.
13. Woolf, p. 91.
14. Woolf, p. 147.
15. Bernard Blackstone, *Virginia Woolf* (*Writers and their Work*), (Harlow: Longmans, Green, 1962), p. 22.
16. E. M. Forster, *Two Cheers for Democracy* (London: Edward Arnold, 1951), pp.232–2.
17. Quoted by John Press, p. 146, from *The Athenaeum*, 5 Dec. 1919.
18. Richard Rees (ed), *John Middleton Murry, Selected Criticism 1916–1957* (London: Oxford University Press, 1960), p. 4.
19. *John Middleton Murry, Selected Criticism 1916–1957*, p. 11.
20. T. S. Eliot, *For Lancelot Andrewes, Essays on Style and Order* (London: Faber & Faber, 1970), p. 7 (Preface).
21. T. S. Eliot, *The Sacred Wood* (London: Methuen & Co Ltd, 1920), p. 53.
22. *The Sacred Wood*, p. 58.
23. *Elizabethan Essays* (London: Faber & Faber, 1934), p. 50.
24. *Points of View* (London: Faber & Faber, 1941), p. 14.
25. *The Use of Poetry and the Use of Criticism* (London: Faber & Faber, 1933), p. 151.
26. *Points of View*, p. 71.
27. *Points of View*, p. 74.
28. I. A. Richards, *Principles of Literary Criticism* (London: Kegan Paul, Trench, Trubner & Co Ltd, 1934), pp. 32–3.
29. *Principles of Literary Criticism*, p. 47.
30. *Principles of Literary Criticism*, p. 246.
31. *Principles of Literary Criticism*, pp. 267–8.
32. I. A. Richards, *Practical Criticism* (London: Routledge & Kegan Paul, 1929), pp. 14–17.
33. *Principles of Literary Criticism*, p. 291.
34. Quoted by John Press, p. 119.

35. William Empsom, *Seven Types of Ambiguity* (London: Chatto & Windus, revised 1953), p. 25.
36. Empsom, p. 48
37. Empsom, p. 133
38. R. P. Bilan, *The Literary Criticism of F. R. Leavis* (Cambridge: Cambridge University Press, 1979), p. 95.
39. Denys Thompson, *What to Read in English Literature* (London: Heinemann, 1975), p. 115.
40. Quoted by R. P. Bilan, p. 109.
41. Owen Barfield, *Poetic Diction* (London: Faber & Gwyer, 1928), p. 148
42. G. Wilson Knight, *The Wheel of Fire* (London: Oxford University Press, 1930), p. 14

Chapter 11: The Twentieth Century II

1. E. M. W. Tillyard & C. S. Lewis, *The Personal Heresy, A Controversy* (London: Oxford University Press, 1939), p. 113.
2. The lecture *De Descriptione Temporum* is reprinted in David Lodge (ed), *20th Century Literary Criticism*, pp. 443–52.
3. *An Experiment in Criticism* (Cambridge, 1961), p. 86.
4. *An Experiment in Criticism*, p. 125.
5. *An Experiment in Criticism*, p. 127.
6. *Fables of Identity: Studies in Poetic Mythology* (New York: Harcourt Brace Jovanovich Inc, 1963). The relevant sections, 'The Archetypes of Literature' and 'Literature as Context: Milton's *Lycidas*' are reprinted in David Lodge, pp. 443–52.
7. The essay was published in Ransom, *The World's Body* (New York: Charles Scribner's Sons, 1938). It is reprinted in David Lodge, pp. 228–39.
8. Published by Methuen, London, and Harcourt Brace Jovanovich, New York.
9. The article is reprinted in K. M. Newton (ed), *Twentieth-Century Literary Theory, A Reader* (Basingstoke and London: Macmillan Education, 1988), pp. 45–8.
10. The two essays are reprinted in David Lodge, pp. 334–58.
11. Roman Jakobson, 'Linguistics and Poetics', reprinted by K. M. Newton (ed) in *Twentieth-Century Literary Theory*, pp. 119–25. The passage derives from Jakobson's 'Closing Statement: Linguistics and Poetics' in Thomas Sebeok (ed), *Style in Language* (Cambridge, Mass., 1960), pp. 350–9.
12. The section referred to here, 'Literature as Discourse' is reprinted in K. M. Newton, pp. 125–9, from Roger Fowler, *Literature as*

Social Discourse: The Practice of Linguistic Criticism (London: Batsford, 1981), pp. 80–94.

13. 'Criticism as Language' is reprinted in David Lodge, pp. 647–51.

14. 'Science versus Literature' is reprinted in K. M. Newton, pp. 141–4.

15. 'The Death of the Author' is reprinted in K. M. Newton, pp. 154–7 from *Image–Music–Text*, trans. Stephen Heath (London: Collins, 1977), pp. 142–8.

16. Reprinted in K. M. Newton, pp. 149–54, from *The Structuralist Controversy: The Languages of Criticism and the Sciences of Man*, eds. Richard Macksey and Eugenio Donato (Baltimore: Johns Hopkins University Press, 1972), pp. 147–65.

17. See 'Semiotics as a Theory of Reading', reprinted in K. M. Newton, pp. 172–6, from Jonathan Culler, *The Pursuit of Signs: Semiotics, Literature, Deconstruction* (London: Routledge & Kegan Paul, 1981), pp. 47–51

18. K. M. Newton, p. 160. 'The Resistance to Theory' is reprinted in Newton from *Yale French Studies*, 63 (1982), pp. 7–17.

19. 'Restoration Comedy: the reality and the myth'. The essay is reprinted in David Lodge, pp. 212–26.

20. The essay is reprinted (in part) in David Lodge, pp. 474–87, from *The Meaning of Contemporary Realism*, trans John & Necke Mander (London: Merlin Press Ltd, 1963).

21. Reprinted in David Lodge, pp. 581–91, chapter 7 of *The Long Revolution* (Harmondsworth: Pelican, 1965).

22. The passage in question, 'Towards a Science of the Text', is reprinted in K. M. Newton, pp. 247–51, from *Criticism and Ideology* (London: Verso, 1976).

23. Quoted by Raman Selden (ed.), *The Theory of Criticism from Plato to the Present* (London: Longman, 1988), pp. 533 & 534.

24. Josephine Donovan, 'Beyond the Net: Feminist Criticism as a Moral Criticism', reprinted in K. M. Newton, pp. 264–8, from *Denver Quarterly*, 17 (1983), pp. 40–53.

25. Reprinted in K. M. Newton, pp. 268–72, from Mary Jacobus (ed.), *Women Writing and Writing about Women* (London: Croom Helm, 1979), pp. 25–40.

26. N. M. Newton, pp. 270–1.

27. Reprinted in Raman Selden. See pp. 541–3.

28. Reprinted in K. M. Newton, 272–7, from *After Strange Texts* (Alabama: University of Alabama Press, 1985), pp. 86–100.

Further Reading

History of criticism

ATKINS, J.W.H.: *English Literary Criticism*, 3 vols, I *The Mediaeval Phase* (London: Methuen, 1952), II *The Renascence* (London: Methuen, 1947), III *Seventeenth and Eighteenth Centuries* (London: Methuen, 1951)

FOAKES, R.A.: *Romantic Criticism 1800–1850* (London: Edward Arnold, 1968)

MORGAN, PETER F.: *Literary Critics and Reviewers in Early Nineteenth Century Britain* (Beckenham, Kent: Croom Helm, 1983)

PRESS, JOHN: *A Map of Modern English Verse* (London: Oxford University Press, 1969).

SELDEN, RAMAN: *A Reader's Guide to Contemporary Literary Theory* (Brighton: The Harvester Press, 1985)

SPINGARN, J.E.: *Literary Criticism in the Renaissance* (London: Macmillan, 1989)

WATSON, GEORGE: *The Literary Critics, A Study of English Descriptive Criticism* (London: Chatto & Windus, 1964)

WELLEK, R.: *A History of Modern Criticis 1750–1950*, 4 vols (London: Cape, 1955–66)

WIMSATT, WILLIAM K. Jr & CLEANTH BROOKS: *Literary Criticism; A Short History*, 4 vols, I *Classical Criticism*, II *Neo Classical Criticism*, III *Romantic Criticism*, IV *Modern Criticism* (London: Routledge & Kegan Paul, 1970)

Critical Texts: Anthologies

ELLEDGE, SCOTT (ed.): *Eighteenth Century Critical Essays*, 2 vols (Ithaca, NY: Cornell University Press, 1961)

GILBERT, ALLEN H.: *Literary Criticism Plato–Dryden* (Detroit: Wayne State University Press, 1962), A Guide with full selections

GREGORY SMITH, C. (ed.): *Elizabethan Critical Essays*, 2 vols (Oxford: Clarendon Press, 1904)

HODGART, PATRICIA & THEODORE REDPATH (ed.): *Romantic Perspectives, The Work of Crabbe, Blake, Wordsworth, and Coleridge as seen by their Contemporaries* (London: George Harrap, 1964)

HOFFMAN, DANIEL C. & SAMUEL HYNES (ed.): *English Literary Criticism, Romantic and Victorian* (London: Peter Owen, 1966)

HYNES, SAMUEL (ed.): *English Literary Criticism, Restoration and Eighteenth Century* (London: Peter Owen, 1964)

JONES, EDMUND D. (ed.): *English Critical Essays (Sixteenth, Seventeenth, and Eighteenth Centuries* (London: Oxford University Press, 1947)

LODGE, DAVID (ed.): *Twentieth-Century Literary Criticism, A Reader* (London & New York: Longman, 1972)

NEWTON, K.M. (ed.): *Twentieth-Century Literary Theory, A Reader* (Basingstoke & London: Macmillan, 1988)

RUSSELL, D.A. & M. WINTERBOTTOM (ed.): *Ancient Literary Criticism, The Principal Texts in New Translations* (Oxford: Clarendon Press, 1972)

SELDEN, RAMAN (ed.): *The Theory of Criticism from Plato to the Present, A Reader* (London: Longman, 1988)

SPINGARN, J.E. (ed.): *Critical Essays of the Seventeenth-Century*, 3 vols, *I 1605–1650, II 1650–1685, III 1685–1700* (Oxford: Clarendon Press, 1908–9)

Individual Critics

ARNOLD, MATTHEW: *Essays Literary and Critical*, ed. G.K. Chesterton (London: Dent, Everyman's Library, 1906)

ASCHAM, R.: *The Scholemaster*, ed. Edward Arber (English Reprints) (Westminster: Constable, 1897)

BARFIELD, OWEN: *Poetic Diction, A Study in Meaning* (London: Faber & Gwyer, 1928)

BODKIN, MAUD: *Archetypal Patterns in Poetry, Psychological Studies of Imagination* (London: Oxford University Press, 1934)

BRETT-SMITH, H.F.B. (ed.): *Peacock's Four Ages of Poetry, Shelley's Defence of Poetry, Browning's Essay on Shelley* (Oxford: Basic Blackwell, 1923)

COLERIDGE, S.T.: *Biographia Literartia* (London: Dent, Everyman's Library, 1975)

DRYDEN, JOHN: *Dramatic Poesy and Other Essays*, intro. W.H. Hudson (London: Dent, Everyman's Library, 1912)

EDEL, LEON & GORDON N. RAY (ed.): *Henry James and H.G. Wells, A Record of their Friendship, their Debate on the Art of Fiction, and their Quarrel* (Westport, Connecticut: Greenwood Press, 1979)

ELIOT, T.S.: *The Sacred Wood* (London: Methuen)

ELIOT, T.S.: *Selected Essays* (London: Faber, 1973)

ELYOT, SIR THOMAS: *The Governour* (London: Dent, Everyman's Library, 1937)

EMPSOM, WILLIAM: *Seven Types of Ambiguity, A Study of its Effects in English Verse* (London: Chatto & Windus, 1977)

FRYE, NORTHROP: *Anatomy of Criticism* (Princeton University Press, 1957)

HAZLITT, WILLIAM: *Lectures on the English Poets and The Spirit of the Age* (London: Dent, Everyman's Library, 1910)

HOLDSWORTH, R.V. (ed.): *Arthur Symons, Poetry and Prose* (Cheadle: Carcanet Press, Fyfield Books, 1974)

HOUTCHENS, L.H. & C.W. HOUTCHENS (ed.): *Leigh Hunt's Literary Criticism* (London: Oxford University Press, 1956)

HYDER, CLYDE K. (ed.): *Swinburne as Critic* (London & Boston: Routledge & Kegan Paul, 1972)

JOHNSON, DR SAMUEL: *Lives of the Poets, Selections* (London: Dent, Everyman's Library, 1980)

JONES, VIVIEN: *James The Critic* (London: Macmillan, 1985)

JORDAN, JOHN E. (ed.): *De Quincey as Critic* (London & Boston: Routledge & Kegan Paul, 1973)

KNIGHT, G. WILSON: *The Wheel of Fire, Esssays in Interpretation of Shakespeare's Sombre Tragedies* (London: Oxford University Press, 1930)

KNIGHT, G. WILSON: *The Imperial Theme, Further Interpretations of Shakespeare's Tragedies* (London: Oxford University Press, 1931)

KNIGHTS, L.C.: *Explorations* (Reprint, Greenwood Press, 1976)

LEAVIS, F.R. (ed.): *Selections from 'Scrutiny'* (Cambridge: Cambridge University Press, 1968)

LEWIS, C.S. & E.M.W.TILLYARD: *The Personal Heresy, A Controversy* (London: Oxford University Press, 1939)

LEWIS, C.S.: *An Emperiment in Criticism* (Cambridge: Cambridge University Press, 1961)

MOORE, HARRY T. (ed.): *Sex, Literature and Censorship, Essays by D.H. Lawrence* (London: Heineman, 1955)

MORGAN, PETER F. (ed.): *Jeffrey's Literary Criticism, A Selection* (Edinburgh: Scottish Academic Press, 1983)

PUTTENHAM, GEORGE: *The Arte of English Poesie*, ed, G.D. Willcock & A. Walker (Cambridge: Cambridge University Press, 1936)

REES, RICHARD (ed.): *John Middleton Murry, Selected Criticism 1916–1957* (London: Oxford University Press, 1960)

RICHARDS, I.A.: *Principles of Literary Criticism* (London: Kegan Paul, Trench, Trubner, 1934)

SCOTT, SIR WALTER: *The Lives of the Novelists* (London: Dent, Everyman's Library, 1910)

STANG, SONDRA J. (ed.): *The Ford Madox Ford Reader* (London: Paladin, Collins, 1987)

SWIFT, JONATHAN: *A Tale of a Tub and Other Satires* (London: Dent, Everyman's Library, 1909)

UGLOW, JENNIFER (ed.): *Walter Pater, Essays on Literature and Art* (London: Dent, 1973)

WAIN, JOHN (ed.): *Johnson as Critic* (London and Boston, Routledge & Kegan Paul, 1973)

WOOLF, VIRGINIA: *Contemporary Writers*, with a Preface by Jean Guignet (London: The Hogarth Press, 1965)

Volumes in the 'CRITICAL HERITAGE' series contain (often contemporary) reviews of the respective authors which together give an overview of nineteenth-century critical reviewing. The following volumes have been found especially useful:

BARENS, JAMES E. (ed.): *Shelley* (London & Boston: Routledge & Kegan Paul, 1975).

CARROLL, DAVID (ed.): *George Eliot* (London: Routledge & Kegan Paul, 1971).

COLLINS, PHILIP (ed.): *Dickens* (London: Routledge & Kegan Paul, 1971).

HAYDEN, JOHN O. (ed.) *Scott* (London: Routledge & Kegan Paul, 1970).

JUMP, JOHN D. (ed.): *Tennyson* (London: Routledge & Kegan Paul, 1967).

MADDEN, LIONEL (ed.): *Robert Southey* (London & Boston: Routledge & Kegan Paul, 1972.

RUTHERFORD, ANDREW (ed.): *Byron* (London: Routledge & Kegan Paul, 1970).

TILLOTSON, GEOFFREY & DONALD HAWES (ed.): *Thackeray* (London: Routledge & Kegan Paul, 1968).

WILLIAMS, JOAN (ed.): *Meredith* (London: Routledge & Kegan Paul, 1971).

Chronological Table

DATE BC	CRITIC AND TITLE	EVENT
c. 570		Xenophanes (b.)
	Xenophanes: *Satires*	
c. 525		Theagenes of Rhegium (b.)
490		Battle of Marathon
480		Battle of Salamis
440		High point of Pericles's power
c. 427		Plato (b.)
404		Athens defeated by Sparta
	Plato: *Ion*	
c. 384		Aristotle (b.)
	Plato: *Republic*	
	Aristotle: *Poetics*	
338		Philip of Macedon master of Greece
336–23		Alexander the Great's conquests
276		Rome defeats Pyrrhus
264–146		Roman struggle with Carthage
70		Virgil (b.)
65		Horace (b.)
63		Cicero Consul
55	Cicero: *De Oratore*	Seneca the Elder (b.?)
46	Cicero: *Orator*	
c. 45	Cicero: *De Claribus Oratoribus*	
44		Death of Caesar
42		Battle of Philippi
27–14		Augustus in power
c. 15	Horace: *Ars Poetica*	
AD		
14–17		Tiberius Emperor
c. 20–25	Seneca: *Controversiae and Suasoriae*	
c. 35		Quintilian (b.)

DATE	CRITIC AND TITLE	EVENT
c. 45		Plutarch (b.)
54–68		Nero Emperor
c. 60	Petronius: *Satyricon*	
	Plutarch: *Moralia*	
c. 90	Quintilian: *Institutio Oratoria*	
c. 100	Longinus: 'On the Sublime'	
117–138		Hadrian Emperor
c. 205		Plotinus (b.)
c. 232		Porphyry (b.)
251		Barbarians begin invasion of the Empire
300		Constantine becomes Emperor
c. 300–305	Plotinus: *Enneads* (published by Porphyry)	
320		Constantinople becomes capital of Roman Empire
	Donatus: *Ars Minor* and *Ars Major* (4th cent.)	
354		Augustine (b.)
c. 400	Macrobius: *Saturnalia*	Augustine, *Confessions*
410		Rome sacked by Alaric
c. 420	Martianus Capella: *De Nuptiis Mercuriae et Philologiae*	Gradual withdrawal of Roman legions from Britain Anglo-Saxon invasions
597		Coming of Christianity to Britain
c. 628		Benedict Biscop (b.) Monasteries founded at
674, 682		Wearmouth and Jarrow
c. 673		Bede (b.)
c. 700		*Beowulf*
	Bede: *De Arte Metrica*	
c. 735		Alcuin (b.)
	Alcuin: *De Orthographia* and *De Rhetorica*	
787		First Danish invasions
c. 849		Alfred the Great (b.)
894		Alfred translates Pope Gregory's *Cura Pastoralis*
1066		Norman Conquest
1100–35		Henry I King
c. 1115		John of Salisbury (b.)
	John of Salisbury: *Policraticus* and *Metalogicon*	
1170		Thomas à Becket murdered

DATE	CRITIC AND TITLE	EVENT
c. 1200	Geoffrey de Vinsauf: *Poetria Nova*	
1215		Magna Carta
c. 1224		Thomas Aquinas (b.)
1265		Dante (b.)
	Dante: *Convivio, De Vulgari Eloquentia*	
1313		Boccaccio (b.)
1346		Battle of Crécy
c. 1360–70	Boccaccio: *Il commento alla Divina Commedia*	
1362		Langland: *Piers Plowman*
1384–98		Chaucer: *Canterbury Tales*
1458–86		Wars of the Roses
c. 1490		Sir Thos. Elyot (b.)
1509–47		Henry VIII King
c. 1529		Puttenham (b.)
1530	Elyot: *The Governour*	
1549	du Bellay: *Défense et illustration de la langue française*	
1554		Sidney (b.), Gosson (b.)
1558–1603		Elizabeth Queen
1559	Minturno: *De Poeta*	Chapman (b.?)
1561		Bacon (b.)
1564		Shakespeare (b.)
1570	Ascham, *The Scholemaster*	Scaliger: *Poetics*
1574		Jonson (b.)
1575	Gascoigne: *The Posies of George Gascoigne*	
1577		Drake sails round the world
1578	Chapman: *Achilles Shield* (Preliminary Address)	Peacham (b.?)
1579	Gosson: *The School of Abuse*, Lodge: *Defence of Poetry*	Spenser: *Shepheardes Calender*
1580	Harvey: *Three Proper and Witty familiar letters*	
1586	Webbe: *Discourse of English Poetry*	
1587		Mary Queen of Scots executed
1588		Spanish Armada, Hobbes (b.)
1589	Puttenham: *The Arte of English Poesie*	
1591	Harington: 'A Brief Apology for Poetry' (*Orlando Furioso*)	
1595	Sidney: *Defence of Poesie*	

DATE	CRITIC AND TITLE	EVENT
1597		Bacon's *Essays*
1600	Jonson: *Everyman out of his humour*	
1602	Campion: *Observations in the Art of English Poesie*	
1603	Daniel: *Defence of Rhyme*	James I King (−1625)
	Bacon: *The Advancement of Learning*	
1605		Davenant (*b.*)
1608		Milton (*b.*)
1613		Butler (*b.*)
1618		Cowley (*b.*)
1620	Jonson: *Timber, or Discoveries*	Mayflower sets sail for
1622	Peacham: *The Compleat Gentleman*	America
1625–49		Charles I King
1627	Drayton: *Epistle to Henry Reynolds*	
1631		Dryden (*b.*)
1632	Reynolds: *Mythomystes*	
1635		Sprat (*b.*)
1641		Rymer (*b.*)
1642–51		Civil War
1642		Milton: *Apology for Smectymnuus*
1649		Execution of Charles I
1650	Davenant: *Gondibert* (Preface and Hobbes's 'Answer')	
1656	Cowley: *Poems* (Preface)	
1657		Dennis (*b.*)
1660		Restoration of Charles II
1664	Dryden: *The Rival Ladies* (Dedicatory Epistle)	Vanbrugh (*b.*)
	Flecknoe: 'A Short Discourse of the English Stage'	
1665	Howard: *Four New Plays* (Preface)	Great Plague of London
1666		Great Fire of London
1667	Sprat: *History of the Royal Society*	Milton: *Paradise Lost*, Swift (*b.*)
1668	Dryden: *Essay of Dramatic Poesy*	
	Dryden: *A Defence of an Essay of Dramatic Poesy*	
	Howard: *The Great Favourite* (Preface)	
	Shadwell: *The Sullen Lovers* (Preface)	

DATE	CRITIC AND TITLE	EVENT
1671	Shadwell: *The Humorists* (Preface) Dryden: *The Mock Astrologer* (Preface)	
1672	Dryden: *The Conquest of Granada* (Prefatory Essay)	Buckingham: *The Rehearsal*, Addison (*b.*), Rapin: *Réflexions sur l'usage d'eloquence*
1674	Boileau: *L'art poétique*	
1675	Hobbes: 'The Vertues of an Heroick Poem' (*Odyssey*), Philips, *Theatra Poetarum*	Wren began to build St Paul's Le Bossu: *Traité de Poème épique*
1677	Dryden: *The State of Innocence* (Preface)	Purcell appointed to Chapel Royal
1678	Butler: *Upon Critics Who Judge of Modern Plays*, Dryden: *All for Love* (Preface) Rymer: *The Tragedies of the Last Age*	Titus Oates Plot Bunyan: *Pilgrim's Progress*
1679	Dryden: *Troilus and Cressida* (Preface)	
1681	Dryden: *The Spanish Friar* (Preface)	
1683		Young (*b.*)
1684	Roscommon: *Essay on Translated Verse*	
1685	Wolseley: Rochester's *Valentinian* (Preface)	Monmouth Rebellion
1686	Mulgrave: *An Essay Upon Poetry*	Newton: *Principia*
1688	Fontenelle: *Digression sur les Anciens et les Modernes*	Pope (*b.*)
1689–1702		William and Mary
1690	Temple: 'An Essay upon the Ancient and Modern Learning'	Battle of the Boyne; Locke: *Essay concerning Human Understanding*
1691	Langbaine: *An Account of the English Dramatic Poets*	
1693	Dryden: *Examen Poeticum* Dennis: *The Impartial Critic* Rymer: *A Short View of Tragedy*	
1694	Wotton: *Reflections Upon Ancient and Modern Learning*	Death of Queen Mary
1695	Blackmore: *Prince Arthur* (Preface)	
1696	Dennis: *Remarks on a Book entitled Prince Arthur*	Kames (*b.*)
1697	Blackmore: *King Arthur* (Preface)	

DATE	CEITIC AND TITLE	EVENT
1698	Collier: *Short View of the Immorality and Profaneness of the English Stage* Vanbrugh: *A Short Vindication*	
1700	Blackmore: *Satyr Against Wit* Dryden: *Fables Ancient and Modern* (Preface)	Thomson (*b.*)
1701	Dennis: *The Advancement and Reformation of Modern Poetry*	Act of Settlement
1702	Farquhar: 'A Discourse upon Comedy'	Anne Queen (–1714)
1704	Dennis: *The Grounds of Criticism in Poetry* Swift: *The Battle of the Books*	Battle of Blenheim
1706	Watts: *Horae Lyricae*, 2nd edit. (Preface)	
1707		Union of Parliaments, England and Scotland; Fielding (*b.*)
1709	Pope: 'Discourse on Pastoral Poetry'	The *Tatler* founded; Johnson (*b.*)
1711	Pope: *An Essay on Criticism* Shaftesbury: *Characteristics of Men, Manners, Opinions, Times*	The *Spectator* founded Hume (*b.*)
1712	Addison: Papers on *Paradise Lost* and 'The Pleasures of Imagination'	
1713	Pope's Critique of Philips's *Pastorals*	The *Guardian* founded
1714–27		George I King
1715	Hughes: edition of Spenser's works Pope: Homer's *Iliad* (Preface)	Rebellion of Old Pretender
1722		J. Warton (*b.*)
1724	Welsted: *A Dissertation Concerning the Perfection of the English Tongue*	Defoe: *Tour through the Whole Island of Great Britain* (1724–6)
1725	Hutcheson: *An Inquiry into the Original of our Ideas of Beauty and Virtue* Pope (ed.), *The Works of Shakespeare*	
1726	Pope: 'Postscript' to the *Odyssey* Spence: *Essay on Pope's Odyssey*	Swift: *Gulliver's Travels*

DATE	CRITIC AND TITLE	EVENT
	Thomson: *Winter* (Preface)	
1728	Pope: 'The Art of Sinking in Poetry'	T. Warton (*b.*)
1729		Burke (*b.*)
1731		Fielding: *Tom Thumb the Great*
1733–4	Theobald: edition of Shakespeare	
1742	Fielding: *Joseph Andrews* (Preface)	Handel: *Messiah*
	Trapp: *Lectures on Poetry*	Jacobite Rebellion;
1745		Mackenzie (*b.*)
1748		Richardson: *Clarissa*
1749	Fielding: *Tom Jones* (Introductory chapters)	
1750–2	Johnson: *The Rambler*	
1751	Johnson: Papers on Criticism (*Rambler*)	
1754	T. Warton: *Observations on the Faerie Queene*	
1756	J. Warton: *Essay on the Genius and Writings of Pope*	
1757	Burke: *A Philosophical Enquiry into the Sublime and the Beautiful*	
	Hume: *Four Dissertations*	
1758–60	Johnson: the *Idler* papers	
1759	Johnson: *Rasselas*	Wolfe died at Quebec;
	Young: *Conjectures on Original Composition*	Voltaire: *Candide*; Sterne: *Tristram Shandy*
1761		Rousseau: *Julie*
1762	Hurd: *Letters on Chivalry and Romance*	
	Kames: *Elements of Criticism*	
1763	Blair: *A Critical Dissertation on the Poems of Ossian*	
1765	Johnson (ed.): *The Plays of Shakespeare*	
1766	Hurd: *A Dissertation on the Idea of Universal Poetry*	Wordsworth (*b.*); Rousseau: *Confession*
1770		Watt's steam engine
1771		Scott (*b.*)
1772	Jones: 'On the Arts commonly Called Imitative'	Coleridge (*b.*)
1773	Goldsmith: 'Essay on the Theatre'	Jeffrey (*b.*)
		Goethe: *Werther* (1774)
1774–81	T. Warton: *The History of English Poetry*	

DATE	CRITIC AND TITLE	EVENT
1776	Beattie: *Essays on Poetry and Music*	American Declaration of Independence; Smith: *Wealth of Nations*;
1775–88		Gibbon: *Decline and Fall*
1778		Hazlitt (*b.*)
1781	Johnson: *Lives of the English Poets*	
1783	Beattie: *Dissertations Moral and Critical*	
1784		Hunt (*b.*)
1785	Cumberland: *The Observer* started	End of War of American Independence; De Quincey (*b.*)
1786	Mackenzie: Papers on Falstaff (*Lounger*)	Mozart: *Marriage of Figaro*
1787	Lowth: *Lectures on the Sacred Poetry of the Hebrews* (Latin version, 1753)	
1789		Bastille stormed, French Revolution
1790	T. Warton (ed.): *Milton's Minor Poems*	Burke: *Reflections on the Revolution*
1793		Reign of Terror in France
1794	Whiter: *Specimen of a Commentary on Shakespeare*	Godwin: *Political Justice*; Lockhart (*b.*)
1798	Wordsworth and Coleridge: *Lyrical Ballads*	Irish Rebellion; Haydn: *Creation*
1799		Napoleon First Consul
1800	Wordsworth: *Lyrical Ballads* 2nd edition (Preface)	Union of Great Britain and Ireland
1802	Jeffrey: 'Lake School of Poetry' identified in review of Southey's *Thalaba* (*Edinburgh*)	*Edinburgh Review* founded
1804		Napoleon crowned Emperor
1805		Battle of Trafalgar
1807	Jeffrey: Review of Wordsworth's *Poems in two volumes* (*Edinburgh*)	
1808	Lamb (ed.): *Specimens of English Dramatic Poets*	The *Examiner* founded
1809	Byron: *English Bards and Scotch Reviewers*	The *Quarterly Review* founded
1810		The *Reflector* founded
1812	Scott: Review of Byron's *Childe Harold* i–ii (*Quarterly*)	Napoleon's Russian campaign

DATE	CRITIC AND TITLE	EVENT
1814	Jeffrey ridicules Wordsworth's *Excursion*	Scott, *Waverley*
1815		Battle of Waterloo
1817	Coleridge: *Biographia Literaria* Hazlitt: *Characters of Shakespeare's Plays*	*Blackwood's Magazine* founded
1818	Croker: Review of Keats's *Endymion* (*Edinburgh*) Hunt: Shelley's *Revolt of Islam*, review and selections (*Examiner*)	Austen: *Persuasion* M. Shelley: *Frankenstein*
1819	Hazlitt: *Lectures on the English Poets* Lockhart: Review of Shelley's *Revolt of Islam* (*Blackwood's*)	'Peterloo' massacre Ruskin (*b.*)
1819–24		Byron, *Don Juan*
1820	Jeffrey: Review of Keats's *Poems* (*Edinburgh*) Peacock: *The Four Ages of Poetry*	George IV King (–1830)
1821	Hunt: Piece on Byron (*Examiner*) Lockhart: *Letter to the Right Hon. Lord Byron by John Bull* Scott: *Lives of the Novelists*	
1822		Arnold (*b.*)
1822–35	Wilson and Hogg: 'Noctes Ambrosianae'	
1825		Stockton and Darlington
1825–53	Lockhart, editor of the *Quarterly*	Railway
1826		Bagehot (*b.*); Hutton (*b.*)
1831	Carlyle: 'Characteristics'	
1832	Keble's Oxford Lectures on Poetry began	Reform Bill; Stephen (*b.*) Tractarian movement
1833	Mill: 'What is Poetry?' and 'Two Kinds of Poetry' (*Monthly Repository*)	
1835	Smith: 'The Philosophy of Poetry' (*Blackwood's*)	
1837		Victoria Queen; Swinburne (*b.*)
1838	Carlyle: Review of Lockhart's *Life of Scott* (*London and Westminster*)	
1840	Shelley: *Defence of Poetry* (written 1821)	Victoria married to Albert
1847		Factory Act ('Ten Hours Bill')

DATE	CRITIC AND TITLE	EVENT
1848	Lewes: Article on Thackeray after publication of *The Book of Snobs* (*Morning Chronicle*)	
1850		Pre-Raphaelite movement
1853	Arnold: *Poems* (Preface)	Tennyson: *In Memoriam*
1853–6		Crimean War
1855		Bagehot and Hutton become editors of the *National Review*
1856	Ruskin: *Modern Painters* vols iii and iv	
1857		Saussure (*b.*)
1857–8		Indian Mutiny
1858	Bagehot: 'Charles Dickens' (*National Review*)	
1859	Bagehot: Review of Tennyson's *Idylls of the King* (*National Review*)	Darwin: *On the Origin of Species*
1861		American Civil war begins
1863	Arnold: *Literature and Dogma*	
1864	Arnold: 'The Function of Criticism at the Present Time' (*National Review*) Bagehot: 'Wordsworth, Tennyson, and Browning' (*National Review*)	
1865	Arnold: *Essays in Criticism* (i)	Symons (*b.*); Yeats (*b.*)
1867	Swinburne: 'Matthew Arnold's New Poems' (*Fortnightly Review*)	Marx: *Das Kapital*
1869	Arnold: *Culture and Anarchy* Hutton: 'Mr Dickens's Services to Literature' (*Spectator*)	Browning: *The Ring and the Book*
1871	Stephen: 'Some Words about Walter Scott' (*Cornhill*)	Verdi: *Aida*
1871–2	Hutton: Reviews of Eliot's *Middlemarch* as it came out	
1872	Lewes: Review of Forster's *Life of Dickens* (*Fortnightly Review*)	
1873	Pater: *Studies in the History of the Renaissance* (Preface)	Ford (*b.*)
1874	Stephen: *Hours in a Library* (further volumes, 1876, 1879)	
1875	Swinburne: *Essays and Studies*	
1876		Wagner's *Ring* at Bayreuth
1877	Swinburne: *A Note on Charlotte Brontë*	Martineau: *Autobiography*

DATE	CRITIC AND TITLE	EVENT
1879	Bagehot: *Literary Studies* Hutton: Review of Meredith's *The Egoist* (*Spectator*)	
1880	Arnold: *The Study of Poetry*	
1883	Pattison: Review of Meredith's *Poems and Lyrics of the Joy of Earth* (*Academy*)	Hulme (*b.*)
1885		Pound (*b.*); Lawrence (*b.*)
1888	Arnold: *Essays in Criticism* (ii) Hutton: *Literary Essays*	Eliot (*b.*); Ransom (*b.*)
1889	Pater: *Appreciations*	Murry (*b.*)
1891	Wilde: *Intentions*	Death of Parnell
1893	Symons: 'The Decadent Movement in Literature'	Richards (*b.*)
1895		Leavis (*b.*)
1897	Meredith: *An Essay on Comedy*	Queen Victoria's Diamond Jubilee
1898		Brecht (*b.*); C. S. Lewis (*b.*)
1899	Symons: *The Symbolist Movement in Literature*	Gosse (ed.): *The Life and Letters of John Donne*
1900	Yeats: 'The Symbolism of Poetry'	Elgar: *The Dream of Gerontius*
1900–04	Saintsbury: *The History of Criticism and Literary Taste in Europe*	
1901–10		Edward VII King
1904	Bradley: *Shakespearean Tragedy* Yeats: 'Ireland and the Arts' (*United Irishman*)	Puccini: *Madam Butterfly*
1906		Brooks (*b.*); Empsom (*b.*)
1907–10	James: Prefaces to Collected Edition of Novels	1907 Wimsatt (*b.*); Caudwell (*b.*)
1908		The *English Review* started
1910	Pound: *The Spirit of Romance*	George V King (–1936)
1911	Ford: *The Critical Attitude*	National Health Insurance
1911–13	Murry edits *Rhythm*	Act
1912		Frye (*b.*)
1914	James: 'The Younger Generation' (*Times Literary Supplement*)	First World War begins
1915	Aldington (ed.): *Some Imagist Poets* (Preface)	Allied landings at Gallipoli
1916	Saintsbury: *The Peace of the Augustans*	Battle of the Somme
1918	Pound: *A Retrospect*	Armistice ends the War

DATE	CRITIC AND TITLE	EVENT
1919	Woolf: 'Modern Fiction' Woolf: Review of Richardson's *The Tunnel* (*Times Literary* *Supplement*)	Murry becomes editor of the *Athenaeum*
1920	Eliot: *The Sacred Wood*	Anglo-Ireland War
1922	Murry: *The Problem of Style*	Eliot: *The Waste Land*; Joyce: *Ulysses*
1923	Ogden and Richards, *The* *Meaning of Meaning*	
1924	Eliot: *Homage to John Dryden* Ford: *Joseph Conrad* Hulme: *Speculations* Richards: *Principles of Literary* *Criticism*	First (brief) Labour Government
1925	Lawrence: 'The Novel' and 'Morality and the Novel'	
1927	Forster: *Aspects of the Novel* Graves and Riding: *A Survey of* *Modernist Poetry*	BBC established
1927–47	Granville Barker: *Prefaces to* *Shakespeare*	
1928	Barfield: *Poetic Diction* Eliot: *For Lancelot Andrews*	Votes given to women
1929	Richards: *Practical Criticism*	New York Stock Exchange collapses
1930	Empsom: *Seven Types of* *Ambiguity* Knight: *The Wheel of Fire* Lawrence: *A propos of Lady* *Chatterley's Lover*	107 Nazis elected to the Reichstag Derrida (*b.*)
1931	Knight: *The Imperial Theme* Murry: *Son of Woman*	Walton: *Belshazzar's Feast*
1932	Eliot: *Selected Essays* Leavis: *New Bearings in English* *Poetry*	Hunger march of unemployed to London
1933	Eliot: *The Use of Poetry and the* *Use of Criticism* Housman: 'The Name and Nature of Poetry' Knights: 'How Many Children had Lady Macbeth?'	Hitler becomes German Chancellor
1934	Bodkin: *Archetypal Patterns in* *Poetry* Eliot: *Elizabethan Essays*	Elgar, Delius and Holst (*d.*)
1935	Spurgeon: *Shakespeare's Imagery*	Eliot: *Murder in the Cathedral*

DATE	CRITIC AND TITLE	EVENT
1936	Lawrence: *Phoenix I* (Posthumous Papers)	Spanish Civil War begins Accession and abdication of
	Leavis: *Revaluations*	Edward VIII; George VI
	Lewis: *The Allegory of Love*	King
1937	Caudwell: *Illusion and Reality*	Tolkien: *The Hobbit*
	Ransom: 'Criticism Inc.'	
	Winters: *Primitivism and Decadence*	
1938	Ford: *The March of Literature*	Munich Agreement signed
	Ransom and Brooks: *Understanding Poetry*	
1939	Lewis and Tillyard, *The Personal Heresy*	Second World War begins Yeats and Ford (*d.*)
	Lewis: *Rehabilitations*	
1940	Woolf: 'The Leaning Tower'	Battle of Britain
1941	Eliot: *Points of View*	Hitler invades Russia
	Ransom: *The New Criticism*	Joyce and Woolf (*d.*)
1942	Lewis: *A Preface to Paradise Lost*	Siege of Stalingrad
1943	Ransom and Brooks: *Understanding Fiction*	Eagleton (*b.*)
1946	Knights: *Explorations*	Nuremburg War Trials
1947	Brooks: *The Well-Wrought Urn*	India Independence Act
	Winters: *In Defence of Reason*	Britten: *Peter Grimes*
1948	Eliot: *Notes towards the Definition of Culture*	Russians blockade West Berlin
	Leavis: *The Great Tradition*	
1951	Brooks: 'The Formalist Critic'	
1952	Leavis: *The Common Pursuit*	Elizabeth II Queen
1954	Lewis: *English Literature in the Sixteenth Century*	Tolkien: *The Fellowship of the Ring*
	Wimsatt and Beardsley: *The Verbal Icon*	
1955	Lukácz: 'The Ideology of Modernism'	Beckett: *Waiting for Godot*
1957	Frye; *Anatomy of Criticism*	
	Eliot: *On Poetry and Poets*	
1958	Williams: *Culture and Society*	European Common Market
1960	Jakobson: 'Linguistics and Poetics'	formed
1961	Williams: *The Long Revolution*	
	Lewis: *An Experiment in Criticism*	
1963	Barthes: 'Criticism as Language'	President Kennedy assassinated
1965	Eliot: *To Criticize the Critic*	Eliot (*d.*)
	Woolf: *Contemporary Writers* (ed. Guiguet)	

DATE	CRITIC AND TITLE	EVENT
1966	Derrida: 'Structure, Sign and Play in the Discourse of the Human Sciences'	Homosexual acts between consenting adults legalised
1968	Derrida: 'The Death of the Author' Lawrence: *Phoenix II*	
1969	Press: *A Map of Modern English Verse*	USA Moon Landing
1972	Lodge (ed.): *Twentieth-Century Literary Criticism, A Reader*	Pound (*d.*)
1975	Culler: *Structuralist Poetics*	
1976	Cixous: 'The Laugh of the Medusa' Eagleton: *Criticism and Ideology*	Britten (*d.*)
1977	Showalter: *A Literature of their Own* Williams: *Marxism and Literature*	Queen Elizabeth II's Silver Jubilee
1979	Jacobus: *Women Writing and Writing About Women*	Margaret Thatcher becomes P.M.
1980	Fish: *Is there a Text in this Class?*	
1982	de Man: 'The Resistance to Theory'	Falklands War
1983	Donovan: 'Beyond the Net: Feminist Criticism as a Moral Criticism'	
1985	Meese: 'Sexual Politics and Critical Judgment' Selden: *A Reader's Guide to Contemporary Literary Theory*	End of year-long miners' strike
1986–8	Woolf: *The Essays of Virginia Woolf* (ed. McNeillie), vols I– III	
1988	Newton (ed.): *Twentieth-Century Literary Theory, A Reader*	

Index

Note: Figures in **bold** type indicate where a given writer's critical work is directly under survey.